Rethinking Psychology

Can subliminal messages motivate behaviour? Can you train your brain to increase your intelligence? Does parenting style affect personality?

Psychologists and non-psychologists looking to understand human behaviour and cognition are forced to contend with a number of complexities unique to the field. Not least amongst these is the fact that psychology lacks the superficially attractive precision of theories in the hard sciences. It is inevitable, then, that non-psychologists are susceptible to numerous psychological myths.

In this thought-provoking exploration of 43 of the most common psychological myths, Michael W. Eysenck examines the complexity of psychological science as well as the distortion of data, not only through the media but also by researchers, textbook writers, and individuals themselves. He challenges the notion that the substantial progress made by psychology has provided enough convincing experimental evidence to successfully demolish these inaccuracies and explores the ways in which psychological research should be systematically improved so that psychology can take its place as a robust scientific discipline. Highly engaging, this is an informative read for psychologists at all levels, as well as members of the general public interested in challenging their own psychological understanding.

Michael W. Eysenck graduated from University College London. He then moved immediately to Birkbeck University of London as a lecturer where he did his PhD on the von Restorff and 'release' memory effects. His research for several years focused on various aspects in memory (e.g., levels of processing; distinctiveness). Since then, his main focus has been on anxiety and cognition (including memory) in healthy populations and patients with anxiety disorders. Some of this research has focused on cognitive biases especially those affecting attentional and memory processes. Theoretically, he proposed his influential attentional control theory of anxiety in 2007 based on the assumption that anxious individuals' problems with cognitive processing often revolve around impaired attentional control. Most of this research and theorising was carried out at Royal Holloway University of London where he was Professor of Psychology between 1987 and 2009 (Head of Department, 1987–2005) and where since 2013 he has been a fellow. He continued this research during the period 2010–2020 at the University of Roehampton. He has published 67 books in psychology (many relating to human memory) including two research monographs on anxiety and cognition. He has been in *Who's Who* since 1989.

Rethinking Psychology
Finding Meaning in Misconceptions

Michael W. Eysenck

Routledge
Taylor & Francis Group

LONDON AND NEW YORK

Designed cover image: Getty Images © thanaphiphat

First published 2025
by Routledge
4 Park Square, Milton Park, Abingdon, Oxon OX14 4RN

and by Routledge
605 Third Avenue, New York, NY 10158

Routledge is an imprint of the Taylor & Francis Group, an informa business

© 2025 Michael W. Eysenck

The right of Michael W. Eysenck to be identified as author of this work has been asserted in accordance with sections 77 and 78 of the Copyright, Designs and Patents Act 1988.

British Library Cataloguing-in-Publication Data
A catalogue record for this book is available from the British Library

Library of Congress Cataloging-in-Publication Data
Names: Eysenck, Michael W., author.
Title: Rethinking psychology : finding meaning in misconceptions / Michael W. Eysenck.
Description: Abingdon, Oxon ; New York, NY : Routledge, 2025. | Includes bibliographical references and index.
Identifiers: LCCN 2024053902 | ISBN 9781032980119 (hardback) | ISBN 9781032978185 (paperback) | ISBN 9781003596677 (ebook)
Subjects: LCSH: Psychology—Social aspects. | Psychology. | Human behavior. | Common fallacies.
Classification: LCC BF57 .E97 2025 | DDC 150—dc23/eng/20250111
LC record available at https://lccn.loc.gov/2024053902

ISBN: 978-1-032-98011-9 (hbk)
ISBN: 978-1-032-97818-5 (pbk)
ISBN: 978-1-003-59667-7 (ebk)

DOI: 10.4324/9781003596677

Typeset in Sabon
by Apex CoVantage, LLC

To Lola and Tiu

Contents

"There are more things in heaven and earth, Horatio, than are dreamt of in your philosophy".

[Hamlet speaking to his friend Horatio in Shakespeare's play *Hamlet*.]

Preface

The origins of this book lie in Lilienfeld et al.'s (2010) highly influential book, *50 Great Myths of Popular Psychology.* Its central messages were that most people (including undergraduate students of psychology) have numerous mistaken beliefs about psychology and we know this because of scientific research carried out by psychologists. Both messages seemed approximately correct to me but raised various questions in my mind. In the following paragraph I list some of them.

First, can psychological research produce definitive answers to complex issues about human behaviour? Second, is psychology a science comparable to physics or chemistry, or is it inferior to those sciences, or is it a different kind of science? Third, have psychologists assessed people with sufficient thoroughness that we can be confident they actually subscribe to the numerous myths they allegedly possess? Fourth, if these myths are genuinely believed even by psychology students, why is that the case? Is it due to distorted media coverage, inaccurate textbook coverage, wishful thinking, slipshod thinking and some combination of these factors? Fifth, what can be done to stop people believing in myths? Sixth, how can we accelerate progress in scientific psychology so it produces ever-clearer accounts of psychological phenomena?

Those are the questions to which I have sought answers in this book. You, the reader, must judge of the validity of those answers. More generally, I believe passionately that psychology can become the most important of all the sciences in contributing to the well-being of society. A two-stage process is required to allow psychology to achieve its potential. First, we need to be brutally honest about its current limitations and the negative impact of the enormous amount of 'fake news' about psychology. Second, the fragmentary nature of findings in psychology must be replaced by a more integrative approach designed to make psychology a cumulative science. My optimism that this is achievable explains why the title of the last chapter in this book is 'Brave new world'.

I would like to thank Leah Burton for her support and expertise in connection with this book and everyone else at Taylor & Francis involved in it.

Their contributions included finding a better title for this book than the one I had thought of originally!

This book is appropriately dedicated to our beloved cat (Lola) and dog (Tiu), both of whom have added considerably to the enjoyment of my life and that of my wife Christine. Mercifully, Lola and Tiu have stopped 'fighting like cats and dogs' and have (hopefully!) achieved a genuine respect and liking for each other.

Finally, my greatest hope is that this book leads its readers to think more deeply and sceptically about research in psychology. Ponder what the great psychologist and philosopher William James said, "A great many people think they are thinking when they are merely rearranging their prejudices".

Michael W. Eysenck

1 Is psychology a science?

Psychologists have published hundreds of thousands of research articles at an exponentially increasing rate on all aspects of human cognition and behaviour. As a result, most psychologists strongly believe psychology has established itself as a scientific discipline. They also believe psychology has contributed substantially to society, most notably through the development of increasingly effective forms of therapy for mental disorders and interventions to facilitate people's adoption of healthier lifestyles.

How can psychology establish its scientific credentials? According to the philosopher of science, Sir Karl Popper (1957), "Science must begin with myths and with the criticism of myths". As this book will show, numerous non-psychologists believe dozens (perhaps hundreds) of myths about human behaviour and psychology's ability to debunk these myths can be taken as evidence that it is a scientific discipline. Lilienfeld et al.'s (2010) book, entitled *50 great myths of popular psychology*, was a landmark here. Its emphasis was on the notion that members of the public believe numerous myths about human behaviour that have been convincingly disproved by psychologists. While the title refers to 50 myths, the book actually demolishes 250 additional myths (or mythlets) giving us a grand total of 300 myths and mythlets.

Since the publication of Lilienfeld et al.'s book, several other authors have joined in the hunt for myths in psychology. Examples include *In the know: Debunking 35 myths about human intelligence* by Warne (2020), *Great myths of personality* by Donnellan and Lucas (2021), *Great myths of the brain* by Jarrett (2014) and *Great myths of intimate relationships: Dating, sex, and marriage* by Johnson (2016). The overarching message conveyed by these books is that psychologists have discovered numerous 'truths' about human behaviour and that their understanding of human behaviour far exceeds that of non-psychologists (members of the public). There is the implicit assumption that psychologists' superior understanding has been achieved because the scientific method has been applied successfully to unravel the mysteries of human behaviour.

In my opinion (spoiler alert!), most books on myths in psychology have oversimplified (and often exaggerated) psychologists' achievements and have also minimised non-psychologists' understanding of human behaviour. To

DOI: 10.4324/9781003596677-1

explore the first issue, I will discuss whether psychology is a scientific discipline. Even if it qualifies as a science, there is the related issue of whether psychology is as scientific as other sciences (e.g., physics; chemistry).

Throughout this book, I consider whether it is really true that most members of the public are easily duped and gullible and have woefully mistaken beliefs about human cognition and behaviour. We will see that most attempts to assess the myths held by members of the public are inadequate and provide weaker evidence of the widespread acceptance of mythical views about human behaviour than generally believed. Some of the relevant issues are discussed briefly towards the end of this chapter.

"Psychology is an inferior kind of science"

How do most people regard psychology? At one time there was widespread scepticism that psychology was a science. However, it is now generally accepted that psychology is, indeed, a science. In a recent study (Richardson & Lacroix, 2021), 91% of people responded "Yes" to the question, "Is psychology a science?" However, it is still perceived as less scientific than most other sciences. On a 5-point scale, psychology averaged 3.63, significantly lower than chemistry (4.78), physics (4.70), biology (4.70), medicine (4.67) and astronomy (4.00). The only glimmer of hope was that psychology was rated more scientific than geography (2.80) and sociology (2.47).

In 2012, the microbiologist Alex Berezow identified what he regarded as psychology's greatest limitations:

> Psychology isn't science. Why can we definitively say that? Because psychology often does not meet the five basic requirements for a field to be considered scientifically rigorous: clearly defined terminology, quantifiability, highly controlled experimental conditions, reproducibility and, finally, predictability and testability. . . . To claim it [psychology] is "science" is inaccurate. Actually, it's worse than that. It's an attempt to redefine science. Science, redefined, is no longer the empirical analysis of the natural world; instead, it is any topic that sprinkles a few numbers around. This is dangerous because, under such a loose definition, anything can qualify as science.

Berezow's (2012) inflammatory ideas incensed and infuriated most psychologists (probably deliberately!). Rather than apologising, Berezow (2015) added insult to injury:

> I would bet my house on the discovery of the Higgs boson, the accuracy of the periodic table, or the efficacy of vaccines. Yet, there is not a single fact in psychology upon which I would be willing to make a similar wager.

Berezow's attacks on psychology were greatly exaggerated in various ways. First, as Berezow (2012) admitted, "To be fair, not all psychology research is equally wishy-washy. Some research is far more scientifically rigorous. And the field often yields interesting and important insights". Second, his criticisms focused exclusively on psychology but are equally applicable (or inapplicable) to all the social sciences (including economics, anthropology and sociology). Third, even the so-called 'hard' sciences do not fulfil all Berezow's criteria. For example, string theory is one of the most prominent theories in physics but there have been serious concerns about its testability.

In all honesty, however, the main reason psychologists were angered by Berezow's remarks was because they contained a grain of truth. Consider the distinction between scientific laws (well-established phenomena) and theories (explanations typically subject to modification and change). Arguably, there should be more laws and a lower ratio of theories to laws relative to theories in the 'hard' sciences than the 'soft' ones such as psychology. Roeckelein (1997) analysed science textbooks published between 1980 and 1996. Here are the average figures across several disciplines (number of laws and ratio of theories to laws are in parentheses): physics (29.0; 0.4:1), chemistry (19.6; 0.5:1), biology (8.3; 2.6:1), psychology (5.9; 3.8:1), anthropology (4.0; 2.8:1) and sociology (1.0; 7.3:1).

In the following section I discuss Berezow's (2012) major criticisms. As we will see, psychologists increasingly accept that psychology is beset by numerous problems and 'crises'. However, effective solutions to many of these problems have been proposed.

Reproducibility and the 'replication crisis'

Berezow (2012) argued that psychology often lacks reproducibility (the ability to repeat a previous experiment and obtain similar findings). Reproducibility is often considered the lifeblood of science because comprehensive theories in a given scientific area cannot be developed if many findings fail to replicate. Berezow must have felt vindicated when psychologists had a rude awakening in 2015 on this very issue. Numerous psychologists from several countries collaborated to discover whether 100 empirical studies published in leading psychological journals could be replicated (or reproduced). To the immense chagrin (or even despair) of psychologists, only 36% of the original findings were replicated (Open Science Collaboration, 2015)! These findings were promptly dubbed a 'replication crisis'. However, the term 'crisis' is too emotive. It would be more accurate to argue that any individual study provides a somewhat unreliable estimate of the 'true' state of affairs.

We need to consider *why* it is so difficult to replicate research findings in psychology. My starting point is that psychologists often exhibit self-flagellation by assuming psychology is the *only* science facing major problems. Reassurance that self-flagellation is not required was provided by Baker (2016). She asked over 1,500 researchers (mostly from sciences such as biology, physics and engineering, medicine and chemistry) to consider whether there was a reproducibility crisis in their subject. Overall, 52% admitted there was a significant crisis and a further 38% indicated there was a slight crisis. When asked whether they had ever failed to replicate someone else's research findings, nearly 90% of scientists working in chemistry said they had experienced such a failure, and the corresponding figures for other sciences were 78% (biology), 68% (physics and engineering) and 67% (medicine).

The scientists also indicated how much of the published work in their field was reproducible (could be replicated). Chemists and physicists claimed the figure was 75% in their subject area but this figure fell to 65% among biologists and to just over 50% for researchers in medicine. Thus, most sciences have a replication or reproducibility crisis although its magnitude is greater in psychology. Note, however, that replication success in the 100 studies considered by the Open Science Collaboration (2015) varied across different areas within psychology. While only 25% of effects in social psychology replicated, the comparable figure for cognitive psychology was 50%. The higher figure for cognitive psychology probably reflects greater control over the experimental situation in most cognitive research.

There are various possible reasons for the 'replication crisis' in psychology. In the following sections we consider some of these reasons together with suggestions for minimising replication problems.

Questionable research practices

John et al. (2012) discovered much evidence of questionable research practices among researchers in psychology who responded anonymously to a questionnaire. The most extreme questionable research practice is making up or falsifying data, and mercifully only 1% admitted having done that. However, many other questionable practices also reduce the chances of replicating findings. Examples include the following (percentages admitting to each practice are in parentheses): failing to report all the data (65%), selectively reporting only those experiments that "worked" (45%) and pretending unpredicted findings had actually been predicted (30%).

John et al.'s (2012) findings paint a very unflattering (but grossly distorted) picture. They assessed the proportion of researchers who had *ever* engaged in a given questionable research procedure (the *admission* rate). However, they then misinterpreted it as indicating the prevalence or commonness of that questionable procedure. In fact, the *prevalence* rates are only about 20% of the *admission* rates (Fiedler & Schwarz, 2016). Thus, questionable research practices are a minor contributor to replication failures.

Inadequate statistical power

The chances of replicating a previous finding depend heavily on statistical power: this is the probability you will obtain a statistically significant effect assuming the effect actually exists. Several factors jointly determine statistical power. However, the sample size (number of participants) is of special importance. Adequate statistical power is often (somewhat arbitrarily) defined as 80% (i.e., there is an 80% chance of replicating a previous genuine finding).

Stanley et al. (2018) found across nearly 8,000 research publications that the average statistical power was only 36%. The reassuring take-home message is that the replication rate in psychology would probably increase substantially if most research studies had adequate statistical power.

Meta-analysis

How should we respond to the 'replication crisis'? One common answer is to use meta-analysis: findings from numerous studies are combined and integrated using various statistical techniques. This approach has increased dramatically in popularity. According to *Web of Science,* there were 536 articles in psychology with 'meta-analysis' in the title published between 2007 and 2012. There was a *nine-fold* increase in such articles over the time period 2017 to 2022!

Meta-analysis may superficially appear to be the answer to all our prayers. In principle, meta-analyses should provide more robust and reliable findings than *single* studies with their idiosyncratic flaws and limitations. However, the meta-analytic approach is often flawed. The most serious problems arise because those conducting meta-analyses make several subjective decisions. As Watt and Kennedy (2017) pointed out, "Decisions about studies to be included [in a meta-analysis], statistical analyses, and moderating factors are made after the analysts know the outcomes of the studies. These retrospective decisions provide high potential for bias" (p. 1). The relevant issues are discussed at length in Chapter 11.

Clear-cut evidence of bias by meta-analysts was reported by Yank et al. (2007) in an investigation of 124 meta-analyses of the effectiveness of anti-hypertensive drugs. Meta-analysts having financial links to drug companies were *five* times more likely to claim positive findings than those without such links.

Deciding which studies should be included in a meta-analysis is especially problematical. Since research studies in psychology vary hugely in quality, it makes sense to include only studies satisfying appropriate quality criteria. However, there are hundreds of different quality rating schemes (Sharpe & Poets, 2020).

There is also the file-drawer problem which Ferguson and Heene (2012, p. 556) described in over-the-top terms as an "800-lb gorilla in psychology's living room". This problem (also called 'publication bias') refers to the strong tendency for researchers to publish only significant or positive findings. This happens because most journals are reluctant to publish non-significant findings, and the exclusion of unpublished studies from meta-analyses artificially increases the effect sizes of reported findings.

We can gain some insight into the likely extent of publication bias by seeing what happens when we try to eliminate it. In principle, this can be achieved by using registered reports: researchers submit to their chosen journal a detailed account of a proposed study including the hypotheses, research methods to be used and how the data will be analysed. If their submission is successful, the journal commits itself to publishing the research study when completed *regardless of whether the hypotheses are supported.*

Scheel et al. (2021) discovered that the first hypothesis contained within registered reports produced positive findings only 44% of the time. This is dramatically lower than the corresponding figure of 96% for the first hypothesis in standard or traditional articles where the findings are included in the initial journal submission. Some of this very large difference is due to the presence of publication bias with traditional articles but its absence from registered reports. In addition, however, researchers may be less inclined to test risky hypotheses (i.e., those unlikely to be correct) with standard reports because they are unlikely to be able to publish their research if their findings are non-significant.

Solving the replication crisis

Psychologists have responded constructively to the so-called replication crisis (Shrout & Rodgers, 2018). One approach is to improve the use of meta-analysis. Most meta-analyses are based on very rich and potentially informative databases. However, there is often substantial variation in reported findings across different meta-analyses focusing on the same topic. Ironically, meta-analyses are often used to address the replication crisis but often fail to replicate!

What is required are systematic attempts to minimise the probability that researchers' biases will distort the findings. One useful approach is pre-registration, i.e., researchers indicate explicitly their decisions on all the main issues involved in a meta-analysis *before* carrying out their meta-analytic study. Of especial importance is *transparency*: the researchers should be totally explicit about issues such as the criteria determining whether any given study is included or excluded.

The greatest bugbear of meta-analyses is that different meta-analyses in a given area of research often produce conflicting findings. A fruitful approach is to carry out an *umbrella* review where disagreements among different meta-analyses are highlighted and attempts made to resolve those disagreements (Papatheodorou, 2019).

As discussed earlier, another major reason for replication failures is inadequate statistical power mostly stemming from an insufficient sample size. However, inadequate statistical power is remediable (e.g., by using larger sample sizes). Fraley and Vazire (2014) found that relatively recent studies in social psychology and personality had statistical power of almost 50%

(i.e., there was nearly a 50% chance of replicating previous genuine findings) compared with only 15% in earlier research.

Three final points need to be made. First, It is much easier for studies and meta-analyses to have adequate statistical power if their focus is on genuine effects of moderate or large size. Second, in research on almost any topic in psychology there is a strong consensus with respect to many central findings. When writing this book, I have (almost) invariably discovered that there is a bedrock of well-established findings.

Third, an important recent approach involves the use of 'Big Data': the same study is carried out at several different laboratories (multiple-laboratory replications) and all the studies are pre-registered. In principle, this approach ensures there is adequate statistical power and that the findings are not subject to publication bias. Reassuringly, the pattern of findings is similar across the two approaches (Lewis et al., 2022).

Highly controlled experimental conditions

As mentioned earlier, Berezow (2012) correctly identified the use of "highly controlled conditions" as a key criterion for a field of research to be regarded as a proper science. Use of the experimental method is very important to the entire scientific approach within psychology. Indeed, it is often regarded as the 'gold standard', and it forms the basis for hundreds of thousands of experimental studies in psychology every year. In essence, use of the experimental method involves a high level of *control* over the experimental situation (e.g., the nature of the current task; presence vs. absence of distraction). Researchers can then observe the consequences for participants' cognition and behaviour of an experimentally controlled environment.

The basic use of the experimental method involves an independent variable (some aspect of the situation manipulated by the experimenter) and a dependent variable (some aspect of the participants' behaviour). Suppose participants attempt to learn and remember 20 random words. The independent variable might relate to the level of noise (high vs. low) in the experimental situation during learning and the dependent variable might be the number of words recalled accurately.

If the number of words recalled is significantly lower in the high-noise condition than in the low-noise condition, we could conclude that a high level of noise causes reduced learning and memory. However, claims about causality often need to be made cautiously. Consider a thought experiment on malaria carried out in a hot country. Half the participants sleep in bedrooms with the windows open and the other half sleep in bedrooms with the windows closed. Those sleeping in rooms with the window open are more likely to catch malaria. The independent variable (i.e., windows open vs. closed) is relevant to catching malaria. However, our findings tell us nothing about the major causal factor in malaria (i.e., infected mosquitoes).

Use of the experimental method does *not* ensure that valid and replicable findings will be obtained. A major issue in psychology (but very few other sciences) relates to the artificiality of laboratory research. The aim of most psychological research conducted in the laboratory is *generalisability* (i.e., the findings should generalise to the real world outside the laboratory). This emphasis on the applicability of laboratory findings to real life is often described as 'ecological validity'. A factor influencing ecological validity is *representativeness* (i.e., the naturalness of the experimental situation, stimuli and task) (Kvavilashvili & Ellis, 2004). A high level of representativeness (otherwise known as mundane realism) can increase the generalisability of experimental findings but does not necessarily do so.

Researchers on topics such as eyewitness testimony and prospective memory (remembering to carry out some action) have sometimes argued that representativeness is so important that these topics should be studied under naturalistic conditions. In fact, generalisability is much more important. Use of the experimental method is often the best way of producing generalisability and so well-controlled research conducted in the laboratory can be preferable to less controlled naturalistic research (Kvavilashvili & Ellis, 2004).

Another factor limits the conclusions that can be drawn from research using the experimental method. The overwhelming majority of research involving use of the experimental method has been on people from Western, Educated, Industrialised, Rich and Democratic (WEIRD) societies (Henrich et al., 2010). WEIRD societies account for only 12% of the world's population. However, 96% of the participants in research published in leading psychology journals are from these societies (Arnett, 2008).

Relatively little research has directly compared findings from WEIRD and non-WEIRD societies. Am exception is a large-scale study by Klein et al. (2018), who assessed the replicability of 28 classic and contemporary findings in research in social and cognitive psychology originally carried out on WEIRD samples. The extent to which findings were replicated was broadly comparable for WEIRD and non-WEIRD samples. However, there are various important cultural differences (discussed later in the chapter).

In sum, most psychological research is conducted under highly controlled conditions. However, that is often insufficient to ensure that the findings obtained are applicable to situations and cultures other than those studied in the research. Other limitations of the experimental method are discussed later and at greater length in Chapter 11.

Demand characteristics

The very fact that participants in most experiments know they are being observed by the experimenter can influence their behaviour. For example, they may try to work out the experimenter's hypothesis. As a result, participants can be influenced by demand characteristics which can be defined as cues within an experimental situation that influence or distort participants' behaviour. The crucial underlying assumption is that participants actively think about their experiences in the laboratory, try to guess the experimenter's expectations of them and then plan how they will behave (Sharpe & Whelton, 2016).

Young et al. (2007) provided an amusing example of demand characteristics. They used a questionnaire to assess motion sickness in a virtual environment designed to create motion sickness. Participants completing the questionnaire before as well as after the virtual environment reported much more motion sickness (e.g., nausea) than those only given it afterwards. The former participants were alerted to the demand characteristic that the study concerned motion sickness – it was almost as if taking the questionnaire beforehand made them sick!

The existence of demand characteristics in the sentient beings studied within psychology (but not in the objects and substances studied within physics or chemistry) is a major reason why psychology is more complex than those sciences. However, there are various ways researchers can reduce the impact of demand characteristics (Corneille & Lush, 2023). For example, participants can be given a post-experimental interview to ascertain how they perceived the experimental situation. Only the data from participants whose behaviour appeared unaffected by demand characteristics are then analysed. Note, however, that what participants say during such interviews may also be influenced by demand characteristics (e.g., saying what they think the researcher wants to hear).

Experimenter bias

Experimenters can influence the outcomes of experiments via 'experimenter bias', which can be defined as systematic distortions in research findings due to the experimenter's beliefs, expectations or behaviour. Experimenter bias is related to demand characteristics but the emphasis is more on the experimenter's role in producing biased findings.

A notorious example of experimenter bias involved a horse called Clever Hans. He showed an amazing ability to count by tapping his hoof the correct number of times when asked mathematical questions (e.g., "If the eighth day of the month comes on a Tuesday, what is the date of the following Friday?") by his owner and teacher Wilhelm von Osten.

The psychologist Oskar Pfungst harboured strong doubts that Hans was as clever as he appeared to be. He discovered Clever Hans was responding to von Osten's subtle movements when the horse had tapped out the correct answer. All Clever Hans was doing was using these movements as the cue to stop tapping (Samhita & Gross, 2013)!

There is plentiful evidence of experimenter bias (see Rosenthal, 1994, for a review). Such bias is often relatively subtle and hard to detect. Here is an example from research on the effects of brain training on intelligence (see Chapter 4). Most of this research has been based on the assumption that enhancing working memory (involved in attentional control and correlated with intelligence) through training will increase IQ. Several studies (e.g., Jaeggi et al., 2008, 2010) have involved assessing intelligence at two points in time. Participants in the experimental condition receive training on a task requiring extensive use of working memory between those two assessments whereas those in the control condition receive nothing during that time period. Intelligence scores typically increase more in the experimental than the control condition.

Do the aforementioned findings indicate that brain training increases intelligence? Superficially, the answer is "Yes". However, the answer is actually "Probably not", because the previous findings can be explained in other ways. Admittedly, one possibility is that training working memory genuinely enhances intelligence. Alternatively, spending several hours performing a demanding cognitive task (typically having been told they were being given 'brain training') leads participants to *expect* their performance on an intelligence test to improve and these expectations provided the requisite motivation. Foroughi et al. (2016) found that the mere expectation that brain training would enhance intelligence produced an increase of between 5 and 10 points of IQ.

Moving targets

There is another way in which the fact that psychologists study sentient beings poses problems absent from the so-called 'hard' sciences. Unlike physical phenomena, human activity is directly impacted by the communication of scientific findings. As Gergen (1973, p. 313) stated,

> Herein lies a fundamental difference between the natural and social sciences. In the former, the scientist cannot typically communicate his knowledge to the subjects of his study such that their behavioural dispositions are modified. In the social sciences such communications can have a vital impact on behaviour.

Suppose you are walking alone inside a building when you come upon a man slumped against a wall. Would you go to his assistance? Beaman et al. (1978) discovered only 25% of participants helped the man, thus confirming the common assumption that most bystanders are reluctant to provide help. However, Beaman et al. exposed other participants to information about bystander intervention (including the frequent reluctance of bystanders to help victims) two weeks before the staged incident of the slumped man. In this condition, 43% of participants assisted him. This study shows that many phenomena in psychology are *moving targets*: people's increasing awareness of phenomena in psychology can create changes in those phenomena.

Distal vs. proximal factors

We have discussed limitations with the experimental method most commonly identified by textbook writers. However, the single most important limitation is rarely discussed. Suppose we want to establish the factors causally influencing a given form of behaviour. Most behaviour is influenced by a lengthy chain of events (Sanbonmatsu & Johnston, 2019). Causes occurring a long time prior to the behaviour in question (e.g., childhood experiences; genetic factors; personality) exert *indirect* influences on current behaviour: these are *distal* causes. Causes occurring much more recently (e.g., the current situation) exert more immediate and *direct* influences on behaviour: they are *proximal* causes.

Consider the factors causing road rage (drivers' angry or aggressive behaviour). Distal factors influencing whether road rage occurs include the following: personality (low in agreeableness; low in conscientiousness); violence within the family during childhood; clinical history (e.g., psychopathic or antisocial behaviour) (Britt & Garrity, 2006). Proximal factors include the following: heavy traffic; being tail-gated; another driver making obscene gestures; slow driver ahead; another driver cutting in; driver feeling stressed (Wu et al., 2018).

Why is the distinction between distal and proximal factors very important? Proximal factors can generally be *manipulated* as independent variables whereas distal factors cannot. Refer back to the road rage example. We could set up a simulation experiment where drivers were exposed to manipulated proximal factors: heavy vs. light traffic; being vs. not being tail-gated; having a slow driver ahead present or absent; and so on. However, we cannot manipulate distal factors such as personality and clinical history. This is a major limitation because such manipulation is of the essence when using the experimental method.

Distal factors: correlational evidence

Many major findings in psychology involve distal factors that cannot be manipulated. Such findings are frequently correlational (e.g., divorce is associated with negative outcomes in the children whose parents have divorced; life events are associated with many mental disorders). Correlational evidence does not allow us to work out the direction of causality. However, that does not mean psychologists are powerless to investigate causal issues. Consider the finding that 25% of children with divorced parents (but only 10% of children whose parents had not divorced) have serious long-term social, emotional and psychological problems (Hetherington & Kelly, 2002).

The previous finding describes a correlational relationship between experiencing parental divorce and having psychological problems. It has seemed obvious to numerous psychologists that experiencing divorce causes psychological problems. However, the correct interpretation is more complex because divorce is not a *random* event. Jockin et al. (1996) found the probability that if one twin has been divorced so has the other is higher in identical or monozygotic twins than fraternal or dizygotic twins. Thus, whether parents divorce depends partly on genetic factors. More specifically, Jockin et al. found parents high in negative emotionality (a personality trait resembling neuroticism) were more likely to divorce than those low in negative emotionality.

O'Connor et al. (2003) studied children adopted at a young age, some of whom were at genetic risk because their biological parents were high in negative emotionality. Those children at high genetic risk had greater emotional problems and worse social adjustment than those at low genetic risk if there was a divorce in the adoptive home. However, genetic risk had no effect on children's adjustment in the absence of divorce. Thus, genetic factors influence the impact of divorce on children.

In sum, it is typically difficult (or impossible) to provide a definitive interpretation of correlational findings within psychology. However, psychologists can sometimes obtain additional information greatly clarifying interpretive issues.

What happens when the experimental method is not used?

We have seen that there are several limits to the applicability of the experimental method and you may doubt its value. However, consider what happens when psychologists fail to use the experimental method. Here I will consider the consequences when two of the most famous psychologists (Sigmund Freud and Noam Chomsky) proposed extremely influential theoretical ideas in the absence of scientific evidence based on the experimental method or other scientific approaches.

Freud had many brilliant theoretical ideas (e.g., mental illness can be cured by psychological methods; there is a reasonably close relationship between an individual's personality and their susceptibility to mental illness; we can enhance our understanding of adults' behaviour by considering their childhood experiences). However, he failed to carry out any scientific research. He did report case studies of individual patients he had treated using psychoanalysis. However, these case studies strongly reflected Freud's personal biases and it is notoriously difficult to generalise from the treatment of specific individuals.

One of the most enduring of Freud's theoretical ideas is that successful therapy for adult mental disorders requires insight into childhood problems. However, modern forms of therapy such as cognitive behavioural therapy have proved more effective than psychoanalysis even though they largely (or totally) ignore childhood problems (see Chapter 8). Another of Freud's ideas that remains very popular relates to repression: he assumed most patients had repressed or unconscious memories of traumatic childhood experiences and making patients consciously aware of those repressed memories was vital to the therapeutic process (see Chapter 3). In fact, there is vanishingly little support for either of these ideas.

In sum, most of Freud's numerous theoretical ideas were expressed so vaguely that they could not be tested by experimental research. Those Freudian ideas that could be tested experimentally have nearly all been shown to be wrong.

Noam Chomsky is rightfully hailed as the 'father of linguistics' (the scientific study of language and its structure). Even though he is not a psychologist, Chomsky has played a major role in the development of the psychology of language with his extremely influential books such as, *Knowledge of language: Its nature, origin, and use* (1957), and *Aspects of the theory of syntax* (1965).

Chomsky's enormous contributions make it all the more revealing to consider what happened when he proposed far-reaching theoretical ideas about the psychology of language in the absence of systematic experimental research. He started with several assumptions. First, only the human species has a fully developed language. Second, all the world's languages are broadly similar. Third, young children acquire language very rapidly and this cannot be explained on the basis of the impoverished language they receive. Fourth, Chomsky (1986, p. 18) claimed that variation across children in language development, "is marginal and can be safely ignored across a broad range of linguistic investigation". Fifth, Chomsky argued that humans possess an innate universal grammar (a set of grammatical principles found in all languages). This universal grammar explains why nearly all children learn language so rapidly.

Unfortunately, *all* the previous assumptions (except for the first one) are wrong! With respect to the second assumption, it is true that most European languages are very similar. However, large differences appear when *all* the world's 6,000 to 8,000 languages are considered. Evans and Levinson (2009, p. 429) did precisely that and concluded "There are vanishingly few universals of language in the direct sense that all languages exhibit them". With respect to the third assumption, most children are exposed to child-directed speech (i.e., short, simple, slowly spoken sentences used by parents and other caregivers). Children's rate of language acquisition is fastest when the speech input they experience is tailored to their current knowledge of language (Kidd & Donnelly, 2020). In spite of experiencing rich speech input, children's speech for the first 2 years after they start to speak does *not* progress rapidly: they use a small set of familiar verbs and often repeat back what they have just heard (Bannard et al., 2009).

With respect to the fourth assumption, there are actually very large individual differences in children's language acquisition (see Kidd & Donnelly, 2020). For example, Bavin et al. (2008) found 12-month olds' receptive or comprehension vocabulary ranged from 0 to 397 words and their production of spoken vocabulary ranged from 0 to 57 words.

With respect to the fifth assumption, no compelling evidence for the existence of an innate universal grammar has ever been produced. Instead of Chomsky's assumption that language is special and depends on language-specific processes, there is increasing evidence that language acquisition depends on general cognitive processes also involved in attention, learning, problem solving, memory, decision making and so on. As Tomasello (2008, p. 150) argued, language is "cognition packaged for purposes of interpersonal communication" (Tomasello, 2008, p. 150). Chomsky assumed correctly that only humans have a fully developed language, and he claimed this was because we are the only species having an innate universal grammar. However, it is much more plausible to argue we are the only species to have proper language because we possess greatly superior cognitive processes and structures.

Clearly defined terminology

Berezow (2012) argued that one of the main criteria for a science is that it uses a clearly defined or precise terminology. Ironically, much of the terminology used in psychology was more clearly defined 60 years ago than it is now! Nearly all theories in psychology use constructs or concepts referring to internal processes or structures. MacCorquodale and Meehl (1948) distinguished between two types of internal construct: intervening variables and hypothetical constructs. Intervening variables link stimuli and responses. The behaviourists attached great importance to intervening variables. For example, Hull (1943) emphasised intervening variables such as 'habit strength' (stimulus-response relationships which become stronger with repeated learning trials) and 'drive' (a motivational construct that could, for example, refer to the number of hours of food deprivation). Intervening variables are anchored to observable stimuli and responses and so are relatively precise. However, they merely *re-describe* experimental findings and so lack explanatory power.

Hypothetical constructs are less precise than intervening variables but possess more explanatory power (Greenwood, 1999). Recently, David Groome and I (Eysenck & Groome, 2023) identified 14 classic studies in cognitive psychology post-dating the behaviourist era. These studies used numerous hypothetical constructs but practically no intervening variables. Here is a more-or-less random selection of such hypothetical constructs: attention; episodic memory; semantic memory; loss aversion; cognitive heuristics or rules of thumb; short-term memory; long-term memory; retrieval; ventral visual pathway; and dorsal visual pathway. The complexity of all of these hypothetical constructs is such that we cannot at present provide precise definitions of them.

Have psychologists done the right thing by moving away from well-defined intervening variables to somewhat vague hypothetical constructs? The answer is an unqualified "Yes". Hypothetical constructs are imprecisely defined but serve to enhance our theoretical understanding and promote important new original research. Of key importance, the definitions of hypothetical constructs often become progressively more precise and imbued with meaning following advances in empirical knowledge. Consider the hypothetical construct of 'episodic memory' (see Chapter 3). Initially (Tulving, 1972), this referred exclusively to memory for past personal events or episodes containing information about what, where and when (Nairne, 2015). More recently, its meaning has broadened: "A critical function of episodic memory is to support the construction of imagined future events by allowing the retrieval of information about past experiences, and the flexible recombination of elements of past experiences, into simulations of possible future scenarios" (Schacter & Madore, 2016, p. 246). Note that the original definition of 'episodic memory' was limited in extent rather than wrong.

The progressive refinement of hypothetical constructs over time is common to most sciences. In physics, the construct of 'temperature' was initially assessed by individuals' subjective sensations of warm and cold (Chang, 2004). This was followed by the development of thermometers, and then theoretical developments by physicists led to an increasingly thorough understanding of temperature. Another example from physics is the term 'electron', which was initially defined as an elementary unit of electric charge. However, it is now defined as an elementary particle that is a fermion, having features such as a charge of –1 and spin of 1/2 (Eronen & Bringmann, 2021).

Predictability and testability: the 'theory crisis'

Berezow (2012) identified predictability and testability as two criteria for theories in psychology to be considered scientific and argued that psychology falls short with respect to both of them. Many psychologists accept that most psychological theories have poor testability and predictability. Eronen and Bringmann (2021) coined the term 'theory crisis' to refer to these limitations.

The criterion of testability resembles Popper's (1968) criterion of falsifiability: a theory's predictions must be sufficiently explicit that it is possible in principle to disprove it. According to Popper, we cannot confirm a theory is correct: the first 100 tests of a given theory may all produce supporting evidence. However, the 101st test may not. Popper's answer was that theorists should focus on falsifiability. However, Uchino et al. (2010) found that 77% of research articles in social psychology emphasised confirmation via testing the hypothesis favoured by the researcher(s).

Sanbonmatsu et al. (2015) shed light on the conflict between Popper's (1968) views on science and the actual behaviour of researchers in psychology. They distinguished between absolute or universal and non-absolute hypotheses. Absolute hypotheses claim a given phenomenon *always* occurs. In contrast, non-absolute hypotheses make the more modest claim that a phenomenon occurs only under certain conditions (e.g., in some cultures but not others; only in some groups within society). Popper focused on absolute hypotheses: with such hypotheses, falsification or disconfirmation is possible in principle. In contrast, a confirmatory approach is typically more informative than a disconfirmatory one with non-absolute hypotheses.

Sanbonmatsu et al. (2015) found 96% of researchers in psychology mostly tested non-absolute hypotheses and 91% of them used a confirmatory approach when testing such hypotheses. However, 81% of researchers would focus on disconfirmation or falsification when testing absolute hypotheses.

It is generally believed that Popper (1968) attached excessive importance to falsification and that falsifying hypotheses is less clear-cut than he assumed. For example, Fugelsang et al. (2004) studied molecular biologists working on how genes control and promote replication in bacteria. Over half of their experimental findings were inconsistent with their expectations. The scientists typically responded by changing their experimental methods rather than abandoning their theories. In 45% of cases, this produced findings consistent with the scientists' original theory, thus demonstrating the value of not abandoning theories immediately when confronted by inconsistent findings.

What lies behind the 'theory crisis' identified by Eronen and Bringmann (2021)? Many concepts or constructs used within psychology lack precise definition (discussed earlier). Consider the apparently unambiguous notion of 'impaired concentration'. Wilshire et al. (2021) obtained evidence to the contrary when they asked clinical patients about their experience of impaired concentration. Some described it as 'blanking', others described it as their mind drifting away from the current topic and yet others described it as their concentration being interrupted by intrusive thoughts.

Resolving the 'theory crisis'

The alleged 'theory crisis' is due to the fact that most theories are vaguely expressed and consequently hard to test. As Murphy (2011) pointed out, such theories provide theorists with considerable (and arguably undesirable) 'wriggle room'. What is the solution? An increasingly popular answer is that theories in psychology should be expressed much more precisely. Murphy (2011, p. 300) advocated the use of computer models that "require the researchers to be explicit about a theory in a way that a verbal theory does not". In similar fashion, Oberauer and Lewandowsky (2019) favoured formal modelling: "a theory that is formalised, so that hypotheses can be derived from it through automatic derivation (e.g., logical proof, mathematical proof, computer simulation)" (p. 1597).

This proposed focus on more explicit and formal theories is only superficially attractive. Suppose someone uses computational modelling to construct a very precise and detailed theory within some area of psychology. Such a theory would probably be proved wrong almost immediately because its very precision and specificity would greatly increase the chances of falsification. Emphasising the development of very precise theories is analogous to attempting to run before you can walk. In the following sections I consider the relevant issues.

Theories: generality vs. precision?

It is arguable that the 'theory crisis' can be resolved by accepting that most theories in psychology are appropriately expressed in somewhat imprecise terms. Sanbonmatsu and Johnston (2019) advocated this point of view. They pointed out that every theorist in psychology confronts a fundamental problem: "There is an extreme trade-off between generality and precision in which basic theories [possessing generality] do not make the precise predictions needed for the development of applications and in which applied models are lacking in generality" (p. 672). Thus, theorists confront an apparently intractable dilemma. Theories in psychology can be placed along a continuum. At one end are theories having the advantage that they make relatively precise predictions but the disadvantage of being very limited in scope. At the other end are theories having the advantage of generality but the disadvantage that they don't make precise predictions and so are very hard to test.

How can we resolve the aforementioned dilemma? One approach would be to create narrow theories making testable predictions (e.g., by focusing on a specific experimental paradigm or task). Consider research on visual search where a specified target presented among various distracting stimuli must be detected. Treisman and Gelade (1980) instructed observers to decide rapidly whether a given target was present in an array of items. Theoretically, they claimed that search for complex targets involved a *random* search process where items were processed serially (one by one) via focal attention.

Treisman and Gelade's (1980) experimental paradigm and theories based on it (e.g., Humphreys, 2016) are very limited because they ignore the most important factor determining speed of visual search in everyday life. Ehinger et al. (2009) asked observers to search for a person in 900 photographs of real-world outdoor scenes. Most initial eye fixations were on plausible locations (e.g., pavements) rather than implausible ones (e.g., the sky). Thus, observers' knowledge of where objects are likely to be located strongly influences their search process and disproves theories emphasising the *randomness* of visual search.

The other major approach to theory creation is to produce theories of general applicability even though their testability and falsifiability may be fairly low. Among the classic studies in cognitive psychology identified by Eysenck and Groome (2023), eight contained highly influential theories. All were general in nature and none was based on findings from a single paradigm or experimental task.

You may be surprised to learn that most theories contained within these classic studies were known to be false when first proposed! For example, Marr (1982) produced a complex computational theory based on the assumption that visual perception relies almost exclusively on bottom-up processes directly influenced by environmental stimuli. In fact, the information contained within the two-dimensional retinal image is highly *ambiguous* (Born & Bencomo, 2021) and so top-down processes (e.g., expectations based on previous knowledge) are necessarily involved. Marr (1982, p. 101) admitted that "top-down processing is sometimes used and necessary". However, this vague statement was far short of acknowledging fully the role of top-processes in visual perception.

Eysenck and Groome (2023) also discussed Tulving and Thomson's (1973) encoding specificity principle. According to this principle, retrieving an event from episodic memory involves a relatively *passive* process where the information available in the retrieval environment is compared directly with the information stored in the relevant memory trace. The probability of successful retrieval depends on the amount of *overlap* between the retrieval-cue information and the memory-trace information. The encoding specificity principle has been extremely influential. However, a simple thought experiment disproves it: if you tried to recall what you did 10 days ago, you would almost certainly use some fairly complex strategy going far beyond simply matching retrieval-cue and memory-trace information.

You may have been amazed to discover that leading theories in psychology were clearly false from the outset. However, this state of affairs is not limited to psychology. Lakatos argued that, "all theories are born refuted and die refuted" (cited in Musgrave & Pigden, 2021). A famous example is Newton's theory of gravity which could not fully explain the moon's motion. In addition, it was discovered in 1859 that Mercury's orbit shifted faster than predicted on Newton's theory. Attempts to explain away this anomaly centred on the notion that some undetected sizeable body other than the sun was influencing Mercury's orbit, but no evidence to support this notion was provided. Nevertheless, Newton's theory remained dominant until superseded by Einstein's theory of relativity several decades later in 1915.

How did the various theorists in psychology discussed earlier cope with the imprecision and limited testability and falsifiability of their theories? Most explicitly admitted they were not proposing a fully fledged theory making numerous testable predictions. For example, Tulving (1972) proposed a theoretical approach based on a distinction between episodic memory (memory for personal events and experiences) and semantic memory (general knowledge and factual information). However, he accepted that "The point of view of the two [i.e., episodic and semantic memory] as separate systems represents an orienting attitude or a pre-theoretical position whose major usefulness may turn out to lie in facilitating theory construction".

Another classic study was Baddeley and Hitch's (1974) working memory model which accounts for performance on numerous memory and non-memory tasks (e.g., chess playing; solving problems in mathematics). It originally had three components: a central executive (an attention-like system of limited capacity); a phonological loop (for the processing and brief storage of speech-based information); and a visuo-spatial sketchpad (for the processing and brief storage of visual and spatial information). As Repovš and Baddeley (2006, p. 12) admitted,

> Initially, it [the central executive] was conceived in rather vague terms as a limited capacity pool of general processing resources. As such, it

functioned as a homunculus [a tiny man] and served as a convenient ragbag for unanswered questions related to the control of working memory and its two slave subsystems.

As discussed earlier, Popper (1968) exaggerated the importance of falsification and falsifiability as important criteria for a theory to be regarded as scientific. However, falsification and falsifiability are both desirable features of scientific theories (although less important than claimed by Popper). Since the most important theories in cognitive psychology possess strictly limited falsifiability, it is important to consider more closely why these theories are important. Two key reasons follow from the views of Lakatos (1976). First, successful theories are 'progressive': they are modified periodically with each modification predicting some unexpected novel facts.

Second, Lakatos (1976) argued that successful theories are *productive*: they generate fruitful questions guiding subsequent lines of research. In other words, successful theories provide the impetus for future research as well as providing accurate accounts of current knowledge.

Conclusions

There are various reasons why psychologists should not hang their heads in shame because psychology has proved less successful than sciences such as physics and chemistry. First, making progress in *any* science is much harder than most non-scientists imagine. Scientists are often peering into the unknown with little to guide them. As a consequence, their efforts are more likely to lead to dead ends rather than significant progress. Psychology may have progressed less than several other sciences. However, it has made massive progress over the past hundred years or so and its future prospects are bright. The most promising way to enhance our understanding of human behaviour and cognition is by the rigorous application of the experimental method and other experimental techniques (see Chapter 11).

Second, it is reassuring to discover that most of the problems besetting psychology are shared by other sciences. For example, it is often difficult to replicate findings in all sciences including physics and chemistry. While the percentage of replicated findings is lower in psychology than many other sciences, successful replications are much more common in some areas of psychology (e.g., cognitive psychology) than other areas (e.g., social psychology). Note also that psychologists are systematically addressing the replication crisis by increasing the statistical power of studies and carrying out many more increasingly sophisticated meta-analyses.

What should psychologists do?

There are basically two main ways psychologists could respond to the challenge of 'catching up' with the so-called hard sciences. First, they could slavishly emulate the scientific approach taken by researchers in sciences such as physics and chemistry. Second, they could assume that psychology is a different kind of science and so the optimal approach for psychologists to adopt starts from that assumption. In the following sections we consider these two approaches.

Psychology should copy the 'hard' sciences

We have seen that psychology is less successful than 'hard' sciences such as physics and chemistry and so can be regarded as a 'pale imitation' of those sciences. There is also an unflattering and unfavourable stereotypical view of psychologists (Sanbonmatsu et al., 2023). Kirby et al. (2019) found that earth scientists perceive social scientists (including psychologists) to be less competent than natural scientists in three ways (lower perceived respect; less methodological rigour in their research; and lower intelligence).

An unpalatable response to the previous state of affairs was provided in an editorial of the journal *Nature* entitled ironically 'In praise of soft science': " 'Hard' scientists should stop looking down their noses at social scientists, and instead share methods that could help them address pressing societal problems" (Nature, 2005, p. 1003). I don't know whether this condescending suggestion was genuine or whether it was deliberately designed to inflame and antagonise psychologists and other social scientists. Either way, the suggestion is both insulting and totally ill-conceived.

Psychology is often regarded as a second-rate (or even third-rate) science lagging well behind the well-established 'hard' sciences. Sometimes its apparent relative 'failure' compared to other sciences is attributed to the fact that it evolved as a scientific discipline much later than most other sciences. While it is notoriously difficult (or even impossible) to date the start of any science, scientific experimentation in psychology undoubtedly developed much later than in physics and chemistry. Isaac Newton (1642–1727) played a prominent role in establishing physics as a scientific discipline during the seventeenth and eighteenth centuries. Antoine-Laurent de Lavoisier (1743–1794), the 'father of chemistry', was actively experimenting towards the end of the eighteenth century.

In contrast, Gustav Fechner (1801–1887) was a leading pioneer in developing psychology as a scientific discipline. He was almost the first psychologist to show that psychological issues could be investigated using a purely scientific approach based on the experimental method. Fechner established a clear-cut relationship between the physical intensity of a stimulus and its subjective or psychological magnitude, an area of research known as psychophysics. He discussed this research at length in his 1860 book called *Elemente der Psychophysik* [Elements of Psychophysics].

However, the difference between psychology and other sciences is much less if we focus on the development of theoretical ideas. Aristotle (384-322 BC) made numerous theoretical contributions to psychology over 2,000 years ago (see Shields, 2020). For example, he argued that some important individual differences in humans are due to heredity whereas others stem from habitual patterns of responding established early in life. He also developed a theoretical account of human emotions having many similarities with contemporary theories. It has commonly been assumed that most emotions are irrational and serve no useful function. In contrast, Aristotle argued that emotions are generally both rational and functional. For example, anger serves the function of satisfying our desire for revenge if someone treats us badly.

Ibn al-Haytham (965–1039), generally known as Alhazen, discovered numerous phenomena of visual perception one thousand years ago. For example, he argued that perception involves unconscious inferences and observers need to take account of eye motion when deciding whether motion of the retinal image is due to an object or to eye movement (Howard, 1996). Alhazen also discovered the laws of reflection and refraction of light and played a major role in the development of the pinhole camera.

Earlier we discussed a clear-cut example of the folly of slavishly copying the practices adopted in the hard sciences. The most successful theories in physics and chemistry are expressed in very precise mathematical form whereas successful theories in psychology are typically expressed in somewhat imprecise verbal terms. As argued previously, theories in psychology expressed in precise and formal terms are typically very narrow in scope; if precisely formulated theories are more general, they are very rapidly shown to be wrong.

In sum, it is unlikely that psychology's comparatively recent adoption of the experimental method plays more than a minor role in its apparent 'inferiority' to other sciences. A reasonable implication is that psychology's salvation does not lie in pretending to be a 'hard' science.

Psychology is a different kind of science

An alternative approach has as its starting point an acceptance that psychology is a different kind of science to most other sciences. Psychology is intrinsically much more complex than any other science because of its subject matter (i.e., human beings). Sanbonmatsu et al. (2021, p. 13) provided a succinct summary of the situation:

> If human behaviour were simpler, phenomena characterised by greater uniformity in causal relations across time and context, psychological science would be a very different enterprise. The rigour of research in the field undoubtedly would be an order of magnitude higher. Unfortunately, the failure to recognise the inherent limitations imposed by the complexity of behavioural phenomena and the continual pressure to achieve unrealistic scientific standards has been a continual source of criticism, self-doubt, and turmoil in psychology.

Thus, psychology can reasonably be regarded as a different kind of science. Below we discuss three major ways psychology's complexity make it unique.

First, there are enormous differences between (and within) cultures among the almost eight billion people in the world. For example, Westerners have a more analytic cognitive style (narrowly focused and de-emphasising context) whereas East Asians have a more holistic cognitive style (broadly focused and emphasising context) (Nisbett et al., 2001). According to the social orientation hypothesis, these cultural differences are found because Westerners mostly have an independent social orientation (emphasising self-direction and autonomy) whereas East Asians have an interdependent social orientation (emphasising harmony and relatedness). Varnum et al. (2010) reviewed the relevant research and concluded there is reasonably strong support for the social orientation hypothesis.

There are also striking individual differences *within* cultures. Much research has indicated that there are large individual differences in intelligence (see Chapter 5) and in personality (see Chapter 6). These within-culture differences combined within cross-cultural differences reduce the likelihood of discovering many (or even any) universal laws of behaviour applicable to the whole of humankind and greatly restrict the generalisation of findings in psychology. The heterogeneity found within the world's population provides a challenge faced by other social sciences such as sociology and anthropology but not by the physical sciences.

Second, another major complexity associated with psychology is that the experimental method can only be used with respect to factors that can be manipulated or controlled by the researcher. As we have seen, human behaviour is influenced indirectly by numerous important distal (remote) factors such as intelligence, personality, childhood experiences, life stressors and social and intimate relationships. However, this is often not an insuperable obstacle to obtaining a reasonable understanding of these factors' actual influence.

Third, experiments in psychology differ radically from those in physical sciences such as chemistry and physics. Human beings form the subject matter of experiments in psychology and they actively form expectations concerning the experiment and the experimenter's hypotheses. In addition, their participation in an experiment is a learning experience where their expectations and understanding of the experimental situation often change over time. None of these complicating factors is involved in experimentation within the physical sciences.

We can regard psychological experiments as resembling a social situation involving interaction between researcher and participant. For example, participants often experience evaluation apprehension (motivation to be positively evaluated by the experimenter). Orne (1962) exploited this motivation to the full. He presented participants with approximately 2,000 sheets on each of which they had to do 224 additions. When they had completed each sheet, they had to tear it up into at least 32 pieces and then proceed to the next sheet. Almost unbelievably, most participants were willing to perform this meaningless task for several hours!

The aforementioned experiment illustrates the artificiality of many experimental situations – it is unlikely you could persuade someone to spend hours on a meaningless task in everyday life. Claxton (1980) provided an amusing example of this artificiality. Several experimental studies have involved asking participants to decide as rapidly as possible whether sentences such as "Can canaries fly?" are true or false. In the laboratory, participants perform this task uncomplainingly. However, as Claxton pointed out, "If someone asks me, 'Can canaries fly', in the pub, I will suspect either that he is an idiot or that he is about to tell me a joke".

In sum, people's behaviour often differs depending upon whether or not they are in an experimental situation and this raises the issue of ecological validity (the extent to which laboratory findings generalise to everyday settings). Such complexities are generally not found in experimental research in the physical sciences.

Summary and conclusions

Psychology's status as a scientific discipline rests primarily (but not exclusively) on its use of the experimental method to identify and quantify the roles of numerous factors in influencing behaviour. The fact that use of the experimental method is central to nearly all sciences (including physics and chemistry) confirms its fundamental importance to scientific progress.

Theorists in psychology have to contend with the unique complexities of psychology. Their optimal approach is to produce theories that are progressively refined as research evidence accumulates and that are productive in the sense of guiding the research enterprise. A key aspect of this approach is that it avoids the superficially attractive precision of theories in the hard sciences.

Myths in psychology

As mentioned earlier, the substantial progress made by psychology as a scientific discipline can be demonstrated by focusing on the public's alleged gullibility and willingness to endorse numerous myths about psychology. Many psychologists have written books on myths in psychology claiming to have discovered dozens (or even hundreds) of myths believed by substantial numbers of non-psychologists. However, two assumptions are required to substantiate this claim. First, psychological research must have established the existence of numerous well-established general phenomena. Second, the assessment of myths needs to be reliable and valid so we can have confidence that the actual beliefs of non-psychologists have been determined. As we will see, some scepticism is warranted with respect to both assumptions.

Have psychologists successfully identified numerous general phenomena?

This chapter has shown that the subject matter of psychology is very complex. Findings in psychology are often specific to a given situation or context and so fail to *generalise* to other situations or contexts. However, most questionnaire studies use extremely general or absolute statements that ignore the possibility the statement might be true in some contexts but false in others.

Here is an example of psychologists exaggerating the generality of a phenomenon. Meinz et al. (2024) used the following statement: "During an emergency, having more people present increases the chance that someone will help". They found 63% of introductory psychology students endorsed this statement as true. Meinz et al. considered the previous statement mythical based on much research showing a victim is less likely to be helped if an incident is seen by many people rather than only a few: this is known as the bystander effect. This effect is thought to occur because the presence of several other bystanders means each bystander experiences little sense of personal responsibility: there is 'diffusion of responsibility' (Darley & Latané, 1968).

Most research supporting the bystander effect involved staged laboratory conditions. In real-life situations, victims are *not* always more likely to be helped when there are very few bystanders. Philpot et al. (2020) analysed CCTV footage of 219 public conflicts and found a strong *positive* relationship between the number of bystanders and the probability of intervention. When predicting whether bystanders will intervene, we also need to consider social factors. If the bystanders know each other beforehand, victims are *more* likely to be helped when there are more bystanders (Fischer et al., 2011).

Here is another example of psychologists claiming a finding is more general than is actually the case. Another example of a non-mythical myth based on a very general statement comes from Furnham and Robinson (2022). They discovered that 51% of people (58% if those saying 'Don't know' were eliminated) agreed with this statement: "Personality measures can be faked so they are not valid". Furnham and Robinson argued that personality measures cannot be faked and so over half of people believe a myth.

This is a controversial topic. However, faking good is prevalent on personality questionnaires when individuals are motivated to do so (e.g., when applying for a job). Salgado (2016) compared the scores of job applicants and job incumbents on the 'Big Five' personality factors. Job applicants had higher scores on extraversion, openness, agreeableness and conscientiousness and lower scores on neuroticism meaning their scores on all factors moved in the socially desirable direction.

Does this widespread faking invalidate personality questionnaires? According to Ones et al. (1996), the answer is a resounding "No". They argued that much faking consists of providing socially desirable but inaccurate responses on personality questionnaires. They then carried out various meta-analyses. Their key finding was that the ability of the Big Five personality factors to predict job performance was *unaffected* when they removed the effects of social desirability from these factors. They concluded that social desirability (faking good) did not reduce the validity of personality questionnaires.

However, other evidence indicates faking can impair the validity of personality questionnaires. Wood et al. (2022) asked participants to complete a Big Five questionnaire in a control and a simulated job applicant context. Responses were more socially desirable in the latter condition (e.g., reduced neuroticism but increased conscientiousness and agreeableness). Of most importance, participants' personality scores were less predictive of the ratings of their personality made by other people in the job applicant condition. As Wood et al. concluded, "There was a decrease in validity overall, with the applicant context reducing the accuracy of personality measurement" (p. 386).

Anglim et al. (2018) obtained evidence of faking good when they compared the personality scores of individuals completing a personality questionnaire as part of an actual job application and under confidential research conditions. The predictive validity of the personality scores was significantly lower in the actual job application (faking good) condition.

Psychologists can also be guilty of misinterpreting their own findings. Consider the statement used by Furnham (1992): "Dangerous riots are most likely to occur when temperatures reach extremely high levels (e.g., around 95–100 degrees Fahrenheit)" [35° to 38° centigrade]. He discovered 46% of people believe it is true. However, Furnham argued that this statement is false. Baron and Ransberger (1978) reported evidence apparently indicating the previous statement is false. They analysed civil disorders in the United States between 1967 and 1971. The probability of such disorders increased up to a temperature of about 84° Fahrenheit (29° centigrade) and then decreased sharply.

Carlsmith and Anderson (1979) argued that there was a flaw in Baron and Ransberger's (1978) interpretations of their findings. There may be far more civil disorders when the temperature is close to 84° Fahrenheit rather than between 95° and 100° simply because there are far more days when the temperature is close to 84° than when it is between 95° and 100°. When Carlsmith and Anderson re-analysed Baron and Ransberger's data controlling for the number of days with various temperatures, they discovered the probability of rioting increased progressively with temperature up to the mid-90° s.

Throughout the rest of the book we will see further examples of 'myths' that are actually not myths at all. Other myths that are only partially true because they apply only in certain contexts will also be discussed.

Have myths in psychology been accurately assessed?

Myths in psychology have typically been assessed by presenting lay people with numerous statements relating to issues in psychology and inviting them to decide whether each statement is true or false. Psychologists typically assess myths in psychology by presenting people with a questionnaire containing various statements and asking them to indicate whether each statement is true or false. Such questionnaires often provide a superficial assessment of people's beliefs about each issue. There are two main reasons why this is the case. First, there are often limitations in the statements used and/or the response options available to respondents. Second, people may spend very little time thinking about the statements, as a result of which their answers do not necessarily reflect their actual beliefs. We will consider each of these reasons in turn.

Poorly designed questionnaires

One limitation of many such questionnaires (e.g., the Abnormal Psychology Misconceptions Questionnaire: Basterfield et al., 2023) is that participants cannot respond "I don't know" to any item. Gardner and Dalsing (1986) found students given that option were 8% less likely to endorse various myths than those forced to choose between true and false. Since students (and members of the public) often lack relevant knowledge about most myths, it is hard to decide whether their true-false judgements reflect mythical beliefs rather than simply quasi-random responding.

A preferable approach is to provide respondents with five options with respect to each statement (definitely true; probably true; probably false; definitely false; don't know). Furnham and Hughes (2014) adopted this approach and identified several myths claimed to be true by more than 50% of respondents. For example, one of the mythical statements was: "The rates of depression in women increase dramatically during the post-partum [after birth] period". A total of 57% of people indicated the statement was true versus only 13% who said it was false. However, the strength of support for this myth seems relatively weak if we examine the responses in more detail: only 16% responded "definitely true", 3% responded "definitely false" and 30% responded "don't know". Thus, this myth was only strongly believed by one-sixth of the respondents.

Another limitation of many questionnaires is that there has been excessive reliance on assessing people's beliefs about each issue by using a *single* item. This can produce seriously misleading findings. Here is an example (see Chapter 3). Simons and Chabris (2011) presented members of the public with the following statement: "Human memory works like a video camera, accurately recording the events we see and hear so that we can review and inspect them later" (p. 3). They discovered 63% of members of the public agreed with that statement.

Brewin et al. (2019) argued that findings from the single statement earlier did *not* prove that most people have profoundly mistaken views about the nature of human memory. Agreeing to the video-camera metaphor merely indicates that people believe there are some similarities between a video camera and human memory. For example, many people might agree that "Lawyers are like sharks". However, that would not imply they think lawyers have fins or that they eat fish, seals and birds! Brewin et al. found that public support for the video-camera metaphor did not differ significantly from support for several other metaphors to describe human memory including diary entries, a library, rooms in a house and a storehouse.

Superficial responding

It is hard to know other people's beliefs with precision. However, respondents to questionnaires about psychological myths often seem to provide superficial answers that don't accurately reflect their beliefs. For example, Basterfield et al. (2023) found 95.5% of students claimed that the following statement is true: "All people who confess to crimes are guilty of them". The incredible inference that can be drawn from this finding is that only 4.5% of university students have ever heard of cases where the police extracted false confessions from innocent individuals by applying massive psychological pressure!

In fact, there are hundreds of cases where innocent individuals made false confessions to crimes. Compliant confessions occur as a result of psychologically aggressive police interrogation techniques (e.g., isolation; provision of manufactured evidence). There are also voluntary confessions. For example, when the baby of the famous aviator Charles Lindbergh was kidnapped, 200 people seeking notoriety confessed to the crime. In another case, an innocent man confessed to murder to impress his girlfriend (Radelet et al., 1992)!

Basterfield et al. (2023) also found that 95.4% of students accepted this statement as true: "Children never lie about whether they were abused". In fact, many children (especially younger ones) will say they have suffered sexual abuse if they are repeatedly asking leading questions by an authority figure (Hughes-Scholes & Powell, 2008). In many cases, children claim to have been sexually abused because they have been pressurised by a parent who is determined to win a child custody battle during divorce proceedings. It seems improbable that very few students have ever heard of such cases.

Let's return to the previous issue of whether most people really believe that human memory is like a video camera. Brewin et al. (2019) initially found 56% of members of the public agreed with the video-camera metaphor. After that, they presented them with other statements. For example, they found that 70% of their participants agreed that "Human memory is not like a video camera because we cannot play back events exactly as they happened", so at least 26% of them provided a response *inconsistent* with their earlier endorsement of human memory as like a video camera! When the participants were subsequently re-presented with the statement about human memory being like a video camera, only 32% of them agreed with it. Thus, many participants lacked a deep-held belief in the video-camera metaphor.

A major reason why respondents' answers often fail to reflect their actual beliefs is because of acquiescence response set (the tendency to answer "Yes" to questionnaire items). This is shown clearly in the study by Brewin et al. (2019) discussed earlier. Many respondents subscribed to the video-camera metaphor for memory but also subscribed to various other very different metaphors.

Here is another example of acquiescence response set (discussed further in Chapter 8). Basterfield et al. (2023) found that 85% of students agreed that "Mental illnesses are due almost entirely to people's life experiences". That strongly implies the great majority of people believe genetic factors play a minimal role in mental illness. However, the picture looks very different in a study by Willoughby et al. (2019). They investigated people's beliefs in the roles of environmental and genetic factors with respect to several psychological characteristics following the following instructions:

> Both genetic factors and environmental factors contribute to differences among people. Environmental factors can for example include culture, upbringing, eating habits and exposure to pollution. For each of the characteristics below, indicate to what extent you think genetic and environmental factors contribute to differences among people.
>
> (p. 141)

Willoughby et al. (2019) considered four mental disorders (schizophrenia; bipolar disorder; attention deficit/hyperactivity disorder; depression). On average, genetic factors were thought to account for 60% of individual differences with respect to these mental disorders. These findings seem totally inconsistent with the belief that mental illnesses are due "almost entirely" to an individual's life experiences!

There are two plausible reasons for the huge apparent discrepancy between people's beliefs about the causes of mental illness in the two studies. First, in contrast to those used by Willoughby et al. (2019), the item used by Basterfield et al. (2023) does not explicitly mention genetic factors. This may have made respondents less likely to consider the possibility that genetic factors are important. Second, the item used by Basterfield et al. is somewhat ambiguous. That item may lead respondents to think as follows: *when* someone develops a mental disorder, it is typically preceded by one or more very negative life experiences; therefore, the occurrence of a mental disorder is almost entirely due to those negative experiences. In contrast, Willoughby et al.'s (2019) approach focuses on individual differences and the factors determining *whether* someone develops a mental disorder. Adverse life experiences are important in determining when someone develops a mental disorder whereas genetic factors are important in determining whether any given individual will develop a disorder.

Lassonde et al. (2016) reported findings suggesting that individuals' endorsement of any given psychological myth is often not based on a deep-seated and dogmatic belief. Lassonde et al. (2016) presented students with refutation texts providing correct information about common psychological myths. This reduced students' endorsement of myths by 40%.

Why is there so much superficial responding by members of the public completing questionnaires relating to psychological myths? One key reason is that they have strictly limited knowledge of research relating to most topics in psychology. Another reason is that most people believe that if you are unsure of your answer on a multiple-choice test, you should stick with your initial answer. For example, Benjamin et al. (1984) found that 75% of students and 55% of academics have this belief even though most students who changed their answers improved their scores. This disconnect between beliefs and reality has been termed the 'first-instinct fallacy'. This fallacy is one of the reasons why many individuals provide superficial responses on questionnaires containing mythical statements because it dissuades people from thinking more deeply about statements and contemplating changing their answers.

Why do so many people subscribe to the first-instinct fallacy? Occasions on which we changed a correct answer into an incorrect one tend to be especially memorable because they cause us to engage in self-recrimination (Kruger et al., 2005). Such memories lead us to avoid self-recrimination subsequently by accepting our first answer.

Summary and conclusions

We must reject the assumptions that research has established the correctness of numerous statements about research findings in psychology whereas members of the public often have profoundly mistaken beliefs concerning those statements. Reality is considerably more nuanced than that. It has proved difficult to identify findings in psychology that are relatively unaffected by changes in context, cultural background, individual differences and so on. As a consequence, some alleged myths are either not myths at all (non-mythical myths) or are only partially true. More examples of non-mythical myths are discussed later in this book.

Attempts to assess psychological myths believed by a majority of members of the public have mostly been inadequate and superficial for several reasons. First, when people are not allowed to respond "don't know" to a statement, they may be forced to express a definite opinion in the absence of any relevant knowledge. Second, most myths have been assessed by a single statement and responses to this statement may well fail to indicate what respondents really believe. Third, respondents often have to indicate whether numerous statements are true or false, and this may lead them to respond rapidly and without considering each statement in detail. Fourth, if respondents are unsure of an answer, they may provide it anyway because of their belief in the first-instinct fallacy. Fifth, respondents may be susceptible to acquiescence response set (tendency to agree with statements).

In sum, we have discussed several reasons why we should not simply take all so-called myths at face value. We must consider the strength of the relevant experimental evidence and decide whether it is reasonable to assume that the questionnaire responses provided by members of the public actually reflect their beliefs. This sceptical approach will be of value when evaluating the 40(+) 'myths' discussed in Chapters 2–9.

2   Visual perception

Throughout our waking hours we perceive the visual world around us, and so it would seem likely that we have become experts in understanding the basic workings of the visual system. It is true that visual perception typically seems simple and effortless as a result of evolutionary processes over the millennia. In fact, however, visual processing is incredibly complicated, as attested by the fact that approximately 50% of the human cortex is devoted to it. Only recently have psychologists begun to understand its full complexity.

Our ignorance of the workings of visual perception goes beyond our very limited knowledge of its complexity. In spite of our huge familiarity with visual perception, we often believe its powers are even greater than they are. These exaggerated beliefs manifest themselves in several myths discussed shortly.

Myth: subliminal messages can motivate people's behaviour without their awareness

It seems natural to assume that visual perception is a processing activity involving conscious awareness. However, it is possible in principle that someone could process a visual stimulus to some extent without having any conscious awareness of it and that such processing could influence that person's behaviour. What is involved here is generally referred to as 'subliminal perception'. The 'limen' refers to the sensory threshold (the weakest stimulus detectable at the conscious level). Thus, 'subliminal perception' refers to perception occurring in spite of the presented stimulus being below the threshold of conscious awareness. In contrast, subliminal persuasion involves motivating and changing behaviour as well as subliminal perception.

The notion of subliminal persuasion first attracted widespread interest in 1957. In that year, James Vicary, a struggling market researcher, claimed to have flashed the phrases DRINK COCA-COLA and EAT POPCORN for 1/3000th of a second numerous times during the showing of a film called *Picnic*. Even though the phrases were presented well below the threshold of conscious awareness, Vicary reported that these subliminal stimuli caused cinema sales of Coca-Cola to increase by 58% and those of popcorn by 18%. Subsequently, Vicary admitted he had fabricated the entire study.

DOI: 10.4324/9781003596677-2

Other publicity seekers subsequently claimed subliminal perception had powerful effects. Wilson Bryan Key claimed subliminal messages inducing sexual arousal were contained in numerous adverts. For example, Key (1973) discussed a dubious experiment where hundreds of people viewed a Gilbey Gin advert allegedly containing the subliminal word 'sex' embedded in ice cubes. Nearly two-thirds reported feeling 'aroused', 'sensuous' and 'romantic'. There was no control group in this study and so we do not know what percentage of individuals would have reported feeling sexy without the subliminally presented word.

Most members of the general public believe in the reality of subliminal perception (perception without awareness). Taylor and Kowalski (2003) found 83% of introductory psychology students agreed that "Subliminal messages can motivate people's behaviour without their awareness". More recently, Meinz et al. (2024) discovered that 75% of introductory psychology students and 84% of advanced psychology students agreed with this statement: "Subliminal messages can persuade us to purchase products".

Research evidence

In order to accept the reality of subliminal persuasion, we would have to show that subliminal perception exists and that it can motivate people's behaviour (e.g., to buy products). There has been far more (and higher-quality) research on subliminal perception than subliminal persuasion. Accordingly, I will focus on subliminal perception. If subliminal perception cannot be shown to exist, it follows logically that subliminal persuasion does not exist either.

The most popular approach to investigating subliminal perception involves obtaining two measures from each observer on each trial. First, there is a *performance* measure (some assessment of perception or memory). Second, there is an *awareness* measure (e.g., verbal report). Subliminal perception is inferred when above-chance performance is accompanied by a total lack of awareness. Numerous studies adopting this approach have reported evidence of subliminal perception (Shanks, 2017).

Can we simply conclude that subliminal perception is a genuine phenomenon? Unfortunately not. The crucial problem relates to measures of awareness. The most-used such measure involves the observer providing a "yes" or "no" response to indicate whether they had conscious awareness of a stimulus. This approach seems reasonable because we want to establish the observer's subjective experience. However, we have no sure-fire way of assessing the validity of the observer's reports, which may not accurately reflect the observer's experience.

Another problem is that the yes-no measure involves the dubious assumption that conscious experience is an all-or-none phenomenon that is either present or not. Alternatively, we could assume that conscious experience is *graded*. This led Ramsøy and Overgaard (2004) to develop the 4-point

Perceptual Awareness Scale (PAS). The four points were as follows (Overgaard & Sandberg, 2021, p. 2):

(1) 'No experience' (NS): No subjective experience of the stimulus, not even the 'faintest sensation' that anything was presented. Not even a feeling that something might have been presented.
(2) 'Brief glimpse': A variation in subjective experience that is 'stimulus related'. One does not have any clue what the stimulus was (e.g., a geometric shape, a natural scene and a red dot), just an experience of 'something being there'.
(3) Almost clear experience: A somewhat blurry and not very clear experience of a stimulus, however with some idea about its nature. One is typically less confident about the stimulus than if one has had a clear experience.
(4) Clear experience: An experience of seeing the entire stimulus without problems.

Ramsøy and Overgaard (2004) discovered that observers found it hard to distinguish between the categories of 'no experience' and 'brief glimpse'. More specifically, they often dismissed brief meaningless glimpses as unconscious or lacking in experience. Several subsequent studies have compared the findings using the PAS and the dichotomous (yes-no) measure (Overgaard & Sandberg, 2021). Typically, there was little or no evidence of subliminal perception when observers gave the 'no experience' rating on the PAS but apparently strong evidence of subliminal perception when they responded "No" on the dichotomous scale. These findings suggest that the true extent of subliminal perception is greatly exaggerated in studies relying on the yes-no measure of conscious awareness.

There are other reasons for arguing that subliminal perception is much less common than generally assumed. Consider research by Koivisto and Grassini (2016). They presented stimuli very briefly to one of four locations. Observers correctly identified the location on 38% of trials (chance = 25%) even when they indicated no stimulus awareness on a modified version of the PAS. This finding might indicate genuine subliminal perception. Alternatively, however, it might be due to observers' conservative response bias (i.e., claiming not to have seen stimuli of which they were vaguely aware).

How can we decide between the two interpretations? Koivisto and Grassini (2016) adopted the following line of argument. Correct performance (i.e., identification of stimulus location) on no-awareness trials could be due to weak awareness or to simple guesswork. Those observers showing the greatest response bias should have been more likely than those showing the least bias to have had weak awareness on no-awareness trials. As predicted, correct performance on no-awareness trials was much more likely to be accompanied by conscious awareness (assessed by brain-wave activity) for high response-bias observers. As Koivisto and Grassini concluded, apparent evidence for subliminal perception occurred mainly when "observers were very weakly aware of the stimulus, but behaved conservatively and claimed not to have seen it" (p. 241).

Another approach to subliminal perception involves studying patients with damage to parts of the brain centrally involved in visual perception. The history of such research dates back to the First World War and to research conducted by George Riddoch (a captain in the Royal Army Medical Corps). He was known as "Wee Georgie" and achieved fame by regularly performing the Highland Fling on a billiard table during pre-Christmas celebrations. He remains famous for his studies on soldiers partially blinded by gunshot wounds. These wounds destroyed their primary visual cortex (an area at the back of the brain involved in early visual processing) on one side of their brain. These soldiers responded to motion in those parts of the visual field where they claimed to be blind. The apparently paradoxical nature of their condition was neatly captured by Weiskrantz et al. (1974), who coined the term 'blindsight'.

Two major explanations of blindsight have been offered. First, it may exemplify perception without awareness (i.e. subliminal perception). Second, it may indicate degraded conscious perception (termed the "qualitatively degraded conscious vision hypothesis" by Phillips, 2021, p. 558). Those advocating this explanation typically argue that accurate perceptual performance by blindsight patients is due to conscious perception unacknowledged because of conservative response biases.

Much research supports the degraded conscious vision hypothesis. First, many blindsight patients typically adopt conservative response biases (Phillips, 2021). Second, blindsight patients should acknowledge conscious perception of visual stimuli if their response criterion is manipulated appropriately. Stoerig and Barth (2001) presented a bright white stimulus to a blindsight patient, GY, and asked him to "press when you see something". In this condition, GY produced practically no responses. When this condition was repeated with the instruction to "press when you are aware of something", GY acknowledged conscious awareness in many allegedly 'blind' regions. These findings are easily explained by assuming that GY's response criterion for acknowledging awareness was much lower with the latter instructions.

In similar fashion, Overgaard et al. (2008) asked a blindsight patient, GR, to decide whether a triangle, circle or square had been presented. When they used a yes-no measure of conscious awareness, GR indicated she had not seen the stimulus on 79% of trials but nevertheless identified its shape correctly 46% of the time (chance = 33%). These findings apparently indicate subliminal perception. However, when Overgaard et al. used the 4-point Perceptual Awareness Scale (PAS) to assess conscious awareness, GR admitted some conscious awareness of the stimulus on 90% of the trials but her identification of the shape was correct only 25% of the time when she reported seeing a weak glimpse of the stimulus. Thus, GR's subliminal perception disappeared when her response criterion was lowered with the PAS.

In sum, the qualitatively degraded conscious vision hypothesis provides a plausible account of many findings. However, we must consider an issue raised by Phillips (2021, p. 597): "If blindsight is conscious, why do subjects routinely deny it?" Since their experience is so impoverished, (lacking information about objects, colours and shapes) it is perhaps natural they are somewhat reluctant to acknowledge that experience as conscious. Of relevance, neurotypical individuals presented with stimuli close to the threshold of vision often exhibit a conservative response criterion (Phillips, 2021).

In view of the weak evidence for subliminal perception, it is unsurprising that there is even less evidence for subliminal persuasion (Pratkanis, 1992). For example, in 1958, the Canadian Broadcasting Corporation flashed the subliminal message "phone now" 352 times during one of its programmes. However, this failed to trigger any increase in the number of telephone calls.

Conclusions

The existence of subliminal perception remains controversial. However, much recent evidence suggests that evidence of what on the surface appears to be subliminal perception actually involves individuals being excessively cautious about indicating that they have had a conscious visual experience.

Why do most people still believe in the myth of subliminal persuasion? First, it has attracted considerable media publicity over the decades. If you google the term 'subliminal persuasion', you will produce 760,000 hits as of July 2023. Second, the notion that our behaviour can be controlled in a sinister fashion by stimuli of which we have no conscious knowledge is sensational and exciting.

Third, there is accumulating evidence that consciously perceived stimuli can influence individuals' behaviour without their awareness or intention (Bargh & Ransberger, 2016). For example, in a study by Cohn et al. (2014), bankers at home tossed a coin several heads having been told they would receive $20 each time the coin came up heads. Cheating was more common among those bankers whose workplace identity had been made salient by answering questions about their work than those who were not presumably because that increased their tendency to focus on money. Thus, unconscious processes can be involved in persuasion even though the triggering stimuli are consciously perceived.

Myth: we generally detect changes in objects

You watch a video of two people in a restaurant where the plates suddenly change from red to white or a scarf worn by one person disappears having been forewarned a sudden change would occur. Then you estimate what percentage of people would detect these changes if not forewarned. Levin et al. (2002) found 46% claimed they would have detected the changed colour of the plates and 78% would have detected the disappearing scarf. In fact, however, previous research carried out by Levin and Simons (1997) had revealed that the actual figure was 0% for both changes!

We will shortly be discussing several examples of 'change blindness', which is an inability to detect changes in visual objects. The phenomenon demonstrated by Levin et al. (2002) is 'change blindness blindness', which is the amazing discrepancy between people's ability to detect unexpected changes and our drastic overestimates of that ability.

Before discussing possible explanations for change blindness (and our failure to recognise how widespread it is), I will consider some everyday examples. Change blindness is of great usefulness to film directors because we typically fail to detect unintended continuity mistakes when a scene in a film has been re-shot. Here are a few examples from James Bond films. In *Skyfall* (2012), James Bond is followed by a white car. Mysteriously, this car suddenly becomes black and then reverts to being white! In *Spectre* (2015), a plane is chasing a car. During the chase, one of the wheels falls off the plane when it hits the car. In the next scene, however, the plane's landing gear is intact. In *No Time to Die* (2021), James Bond, Logan and Felix walk down a market with the passers-by changing between front and back shots of them.

Why are most of us so susceptible to change blindness? Beck et al. (2007) identified the single most important factor. Observers were presented with an array of objects, one of which then changed. When the observers were *forewarned* one object would change (intentional condition), 83% of them detected the changed object. In contrast, only 38% detected it when not forewarned (incidental condition). However, the findings were very different when other people were asked whether they personally would have detected the change: 71% predicted they would have noticed the change in the intentional condition and this dropped only slightly to 68% in the incidental condition. Thus, we are largely unaware that our ability to detect changes is much worse when we are not forewarned.

Beck et al. (2007) identified another reason for change blindness. In the incidental condition, change detection was greatly affected by the number of objects presented: it was 65% when there were only four objects but plummeted to 8% with 10 objects. In contrast, 84% of participants predicted they would have detected the change with four objects and the corresponding figure dropped only to 52% with 10 objects. Thus, predicted change detection with many objects present was more than six times the actual figure.

What causes change blindness? The most obvious theoretical approach is to assume that focused attention is the key to change blindness. We typically attend to regions of a visual scene most likely to contain interesting or important information. Change blindness typically occurs when the situation minimises the probability that observers will focus their attention on the object that changes. In other words, change detection occurs when the changed object is the central focus of attention in foveal vision (the fovea is a small area within the retina in the centre of the field of vision where visual acuity is greatest).

No one denies the importance of focal attention and foveal vision to change blindness. However, there are two key reasons to adopt a broader theoretical approach. One reason is that the aforementioned approach incorrectly implies that very little useful information is extracted from visual areas outside the focus of attention. More specifically, it de-emphasises the potential role of peripheral vision (the area outside foveal or central vision).

The other reason is that change detection is relatively complex because it depends on the successful completion of five separate processes (Jensen et al., 2011). First, attention must be directed to the change location. Second, the pre-change visual stimulus at the change location must be encoded into memory. Third the post-change visual stimulus at the change location must be encoded into memory. Fourth, the pre- and post-representations must be compared. Fifth, there needs to be conscious recognition of the difference between the two representations.

Research evidence

Hollingworth and Henderson (2002) investigated the role of focal attention in change blindness and change detection. They recorded observers' eye movements while they viewed visual scenes (e.g., kitchen; living room). Objects within each scene could change in two different ways: (1) *type* change: the object was replaced by an object from a different category (e.g., a plate replaced by a bowl); (2) *token* change: the object was replaced by another object from the same category (e.g., a small plate replaced by a large plate).

There was much greater change detection when the changed object was fixated prior to the change than when it was not. Unsurprisingly, change detection was greater following type change than form change (50% vs. 30%) because type changes are more dramatic and obvious. From the perspective of the focused attention approach, what is surprising is that form changes were mostly undetected even when the changed object had been directly fixated.

More convincing evidence that focused attention is not the sole determinant of whether observers detect changed objects was reported by Levin et al. (2018). Observers were presented with instructional videos and told they would be asked whether they had detected a visual change at some point in each video. Gaze duration in the area around the visual change did not differ between observers detecting the change and those who did not. However, observers detecting the change had better recognition memory for the pre- and post-change objects than those who exhibited change blindness.

The aforementioned findings indicate that focused attention on the changed object is often insufficient to produce change detection. What is important for change detection is that the changed object is processed thoroughly before and after the change occurs. Focused attention on that object does not guarantee that its processing will be thorough.

It is perhaps natural to think that detecting changes in objects depends almost entirely on focal rather than peripheral vision. As Rosenholtz (2016, p. 439) pointed out, it is often assumed that, "peripheral vision is impoverished and all but useless". That is the case when there is visual crowding (several objects close to each other in peripheral vision). However, peripheral vision can promote change detection with minimal visual crowding. Sharan et al. (2016) found that change detection occurred 85% of the time when the changed object was in peripheral vision without visual crowding. However, the percentage was much lower with considerable visual crowding.

In sum, there are several reasons we are excessively optimistic that we would detect an unexpected changed object. We fail to realise that it is considerably harder to detect a changed object if we have not been forewarned that an object will change. We also have only a very partial awareness that detection of an unexpected changed object rapidly becomes much more difficult as the number of objects in vision increases. Our mistaken beliefs about change detection are perhaps forgivable since we rarely (if ever) come upon an object that suddenly changes into a different object in our everyday lives.

Inattentional blindness

We turn now to a phenomenon known as 'inattentional blindness', which is the failure to detect an unexpected object appearing in the visual environment. Simons and Chabris (2011) presented people with the following statement: "People generally notice when something unexpected enters their field of view, even when they're paying attention to something else". Over three-quarters (77%) agreed with that statement. In contrast, only 19% of memory experts agreed with it, suggesting it may be a myth.

The best-known study on inattentional blindness was carried out by Simons and Chabris (1999). Observers watched a video where they saw two teams of students (one team dressed in white and the other in black) pass a ball to their team mates. At some point, a woman in a black gorilla suit walks into camera shot, looks at the camera, thumps her chest and then walks off. Altogether, the gorilla is on screen for 9 seconds (see the video at www. simonslab.com/videos.html).

Before seeing the video, some observers were instructed to count the number of passes made by the team in white. After the video, they gave their answer and were then unexpectedly asked whether they had noticed anything unusual while watching the video. Amazingly, only 42% of the observers had spotted the gorilla! In contrast, Levin and Angelone (2008) found 88% of people thought they would have detected the gorilla in that condition of Simons and Chabris (1999) study.

You may be wondering whether inattentional blindness is also found in everyday life. Evidence that it is was reported by Hyman et al. (2009).

Students were walking across a large square in the grounds of their university when a unicycling clown cycled close to them wearing a vivid purple and yellow outfit, large shoes and a bright red nose. You would think it would be difficult to avoid spotting such a surprising sight. In fact, however, only 49% of students walking on their own noticed the clown.

Inattentional blindness is a potential hazard for pilots. White and O'Hare (2022) found novice pilots were much less likely to detect various objects (e.g., aircraft; airport vehicles) when engaged in a mobile-phone conversation. Inattentional blindness is also a key reason why it is so dangerous for drivers to use a mobile phone while driving. Strayer and Drews (2007) found drivers using a mobile phone remembered seeing only 50% as many clearly visible objects (e.g., pedestrians; advertising hoardings) as those not using a phone.

Explaining inattentional blindness

How can we explain inattentional blindness? As its name strongly implies, a crucial reason many observers fail to notice an unexpected object is because they are attending to the assigned task and so fail to attend to the unexpected target object. Attention-set theory is based on that assumption. According to this theory, top-down attentional control is used to process stimuli categorised as relevant while not processing those categorised as irrelevant (see Hutchinson et al., 2022).

Strong support for the attention-set account comes from research manipulating the similarity between task stimuli and the unexpected target. Inattentional blindness typically occurs much more often when features of the unexpected target are dissimilar to those of task stimuli and so the target seems irrelevant. Let's return to the study by Simons and Chabris (1999). As we saw earlier, inattentional blindness was shown by 58% of the observers when the gorilla was black and they counted passes by the team in white. In another condition, observers counted the number of passes made by the team in black (i.e., the colour matched that of the gorilla). In this condition, only 17% of the observers showed inattentional blindness.

Rosenholtz et al. (2016) showed the importance of attentional processes in explaining the previous findings. They repeated the Simons and Chabris (1999) study, finding that observers counting black team passes had eye fixations closer to the gorilla than those counting white team passes.

Some of the strongest evidence that inattentional blindness is very often due to top-down attentional control was reported by Hirschhorn et al. (2024). Observers were on a bus in a virtual reality city environment and were given the difficult task of focusing on a given bee in a group of three bees. Inattentional blindness was assessed by a failure to detect a target stimulus presented on several bus stops en route. Even though the target stimulus was viewed in foveal vision for prolonged periods of time, observers reported no conscious awareness of it on 91.5% of trials. Inattentional blindness rates remained extremely high across the 40 trials of the experiment in spite of the fact that the observers expected a target stimulus to be presented. This finding indicates that the attentional demands of the bee-tracking task largely prevented conscious detection of the target stimulus.

Attentional processes are also important in another way. As Wolfe et al. (2022, p. 815) pointed out, "Observers experience their best guess about the state of the world". For example, Kaya et al. (2021) argued that drivers who are also cyclists would have higher *expectations* that vulnerable road users (e.g., cyclists and pedestrians) might be present. As predicted, drivers who cycle regularly were less likely to commit visual scanning failures by failing to check thoroughly for the presence of vulnerable road users.

Summary and conclusions

It is perhaps natural to assume that change blindness reflects an unfortunate defect in our visual system. However, that assumption is only partially correct. As Fischer and Whitney (2014) pointed out, our visual world is typically relatively stable over short periods of time. Accordingly, it is generally worthwhile for us to sacrifice perceptual accuracy from time to time to ensure we have a continuous, stable perception of our visual environment.

Inattentional blindness may also seem like an unfortunate defect. However, it is typically desirable for us to attend closely to a current task because that maximises the probability of performing it successfully. On occasion, however, it means we fail to detect a task-irrelevant object appearing in vision.

Why do most people minimise the tendency to exhibit change blindness and inattentional blindness? With respect to change blindness, there is a general failure to realise it is much easier to detect changed objects when you have been told to expect change than when you have not been forewarned. With respect to inattentional blindness, there is a dearth of research evidence as to why it is generally assumed that inattentional blindness is a relatively rare phenomenon. However, most people are probably unaware that a demanding task can greatly inhibit the ability to have conscious experience of non-task stimuli.

Myth: visual perception provides us with very rich and accurate information about the environment at a glance

Consider what you can see right now as you look around. I am fairly certain that you have the impression that almost everything in your field of vision can be seen clearly and precisely. I am also fairly certain that you would agree with the following statement: "The moment we open our eyes, we experience a vast, richly detailed visual world extending well into the periphery" (Cohen et al., 2016). In other words, we can see the environment with great accuracy from a single glance.

This belief in the richness and precision of our visual perception is widely accepted. However, the phenomena of change blindness and inattentional blindness apparently indicate that we often greatly exaggerate the power of visual perception. As discussed earlier, Levin et al. (2002) found that 46% of people said they would notice plates changing colour and 78% said they would notice the disappearance of a scarf. In contrast, Levin and Simons (1997) found that 0% of those watching short videos detected the changed colour of plates or the disappearance of a scarf when actually presented with these events.

There are four reasons why the aforementioned findings may be less impressive than they appear. First, the participants in Levin and Simons' (1997) study were not expecting to see changes to any of the objects. In contrast, those in the Levin et al. (2002) study had the pre- and post-change objects identified for them by the experimenter using a laser pointer. Thus, the experiences of the participants in the two studies were radically different.

Second, you have never seen (or will ever see!) a scarf suddenly disappear or plates on a table suddenly change colour. Thus, what was seen by the participants in the Levin and Simons' (1997) was so *unrepresentative* of real life that we need to be very careful before drawing any sweeping conclusions.

Third, the objects that are changed in research on change blindness are typically ones that are unfamiliar to the observers. It seems likely that changes are easier to detect with familiar objects than with unfamiliar ones and Cohen et al. (2024) recently found observers more likely to detect changes in the periphery of vision with familiar rather than unfamiliar stimuli.

Fourth, most research on change blindness has shown that observers can be surprisingly oblivious to changes in some fairly simple object within a visual scene. Nevertheless, it seems highly probable that observers were consciously aware of the gist or meaning of the visual scene. Indeed, it has often been suggested that observers can perceive the gist of a scene extremely rapidly and without attention (e.g., Koch & Tsuchiya, 2007). As Cohen et al. (2021, p. 1695) pointed out, "While it is easy to imagine a person failing to notice the keys on the dining room table, it is difficult to imagine how they could fail to notice that their dining room has been changed into a glacier".

Perceiving the gist of a scene

Can observers perceive the gist of a scene with great speed in the absence of attention? Supporting evidence was reported by Mack and Rock (1998): observers accurately reported the gist of a scene shown in a photograph flashed unexpectedly onto a screen for only 30 ms. Cohen et al. (2021) investigated this issue further. Observers were given an object-detection task (i.e., "Is a human face present or absent?") when presented with large images of scenes. On the final trial, there was a total mismatch between the central 7% of the image and the 93% forming the periphery (e.g., a table surrounded by a glacier; part of a coffee shop surrounded by a desert scene). Amazingly, 73% of observers did not notice anything unusual about this bizarre image, indicating they had failed to perceive the gist of the scene.

The previous findings are remarkable. Why did most observers fail to notice the complete mismatch between the visual scene shown in the periphery and the object shown in central vision? One reason relates to attention: the observers focused their attention predominantly on the object presented centrally rather than the peripheral scene.

Another reason is that the crucial image was presented for only 288 ms. Visual perception consists of eye fixations lasting approximately 250 ms followed by saccades (rapid eye movements). Thus, the image was accessible to vision for only a *single* fixation. In contrast, visual perception depends on transsaccadic integration (the integration of information from successive fixations). Unsurprisingly, complex processes are required to produce such integration very rapidly and as yet these processes are not fully understood. However, we do know that the visual system anticipates the retinal consequences of the next eye movement (Wilmott & Michel, 2021).

As a result of transaccadic integration of visual information, our visual perception is typically relatively rich and detailed. However, we lack conscious awareness of such integration which helps to explain why we are surprised by the very limited information available from a single eye fixation.

Peripheral vision

Earlier we discussed the distinction between central or foveal vision and peripheral vision. The fovea covers approximately the central 1.7° of the visual field; it has high acuity and provides clear evidence concerning the colours of objects. In contrast, peripheral vision covers the considerably larger surrounding area; it has increasingly low acuity and sensitivity to colour in areas furthest from the fovea.

In spite of its limitations, peripheral vision plays a vital role in our everyday perception. For example, actions such as steering a car or walking up stairs can be performed using only peripheral vision (Vater et al., 2022). Patients whose peripheral vision is severely impaired find it very difficult to navigate their way through the environment. One reason why peripheral vision is so useful is that foveal and peripheral vision are closely interconnected; indeed, processing in foveal vision can enhance peripheral vision (Stewart et al., 2020).

Peripheral vision is useful, but we mustn't exaggerate its role in perception. Cohen et al. (2016) provided two simple demonstrations you can carry out yourself. Ask a friend to hold their arm up to the side to indicate how close to the centre of their field of vision a playing card would need to be for them to identify it (e.g., as a jack of clubs). Then put a card in their hand held at arm's length far into the periphery of vision and ask them to move it slowly towards the centre of their field of view stopping as soon as they can identify the card correctly. Most people wildly underestimate how close the card needs to be to the fixation point to identify it.

Here is the second demonstration. Ask a friend to fixate an object in front of them. Place a small coloured object in your hand and move it slowly from the extreme periphery of your friend's visual field towards the centre of their field of view. Tell your friend to say "Stop" when they detect any motion of the object. Then ask them to tell you the object's colour. Your friend will be very surprised that they cannot identify the object's colour at better than chance level.

The study by Cohen et al. (2021; discussed earlier) indicated that observers often fail to process the gist of a scene presented briefly to the periphery. Cohen and Rubenstein (2020) carried out a similar study to see whether we can process colour presented to peripheral vision for 288 ms. In one condition, observers were presented with a series of brightly coloured photographs and indicated whether the last photograph contained a face in foveal vision. On the final, critical trial, the photograph had been altered so its entire peripheral region totally lacked colour.

Intuitively, it seems as if colour processing occurs 'automatically' and effortlessly. Accordingly, the observers should all have noticed the absence of colour. In fact, Cohen and Rubenstein (2020) found 70% of observers failed to notice the absence of colour. As Cohen and Rubinstein concluded, "The immediate percept of a single fixation is shockingly impoverished and lacks a surprising amount of colour" (p. 5).

The above phenomenon where observers claim to perceive non-existent colours in peripheral vision is known as the 'pan-field colour illusion'. Okubo and Yokosawa (2023) presented natural images briefly. Only the central area of each stimulus was in colour. However, observers often exhibited the pan-field colour illusion by perceiving the entire image as being in full colour. An important factor in this illusion is observers' tendency to adopt a liberal response criterion (i.e., having a bias towards indicating that the image was full colour). This bias was greater when a relatively large area in the centre of the image was in colour because this increased the expectation that the entire image was in colour.

Theoretical considerations

There is much controversy about the appropriate interpretation of the findings discussed earlier. We start with an apparently simple explanation for the puzzling discrepancy between the apparent richness of our perceptual experience and the numerous findings suggesting strongly it is not actually very rich. According to advocates of this explanation, there is no real puzzle: we genuinely have a rich experience of the world about us but this richness is typically not captured by the measures (e.g., self-report) used to assess that perceptual experience.

Block (e.g., 2011) is a prominent theorist who endorses the views expressed in the previous paragraph. He argued there are two types of perceptual consciousness: (1) phenomenal consciousness (our initial raw private experience); and (2) access consciousness, the contents of which are available for use by other cognitive processes (e.g., attention; memory). Of crucial importance, our immediate perceptual experience (phenomenal consciousness) is much richer than the information about that experience we can communicate to others (access consciousness). This is because the limited capacity of processes such as attention and memory prevents us from being able to think about or report the full richness of our perceptual experience. The take-home message is that our immediate perceptual experience is as rich as we believe it to be but it "overflows" our capacity to report it.

Research apparently supporting Block's (2011) overflow argument was reported by Sperling (1960). Observers saw a spatial array consisting of three rows of four letters each for 50 ms. They typically reported only four or five items but claimed to have seen many more. He tested this claim by presenting an auditory cue very shortly after the offset of the array instructing observers to recall the letters from only one row. Performance on this partial-recall task suggested that the observers had accurately perceived nine letters. That finding implies that observers in the full-report condition were right to claim they had seen more than four or five items.

Subsequent research by de Gardelle et al. (2009) using the Sperling paradigm indicates that matters are more complicated. Unknown to the participants, they occasionally introduced a pseudo-letter (produced by rotating and flipping a real letter) into one of the non-cued rows. These pseudo-letters were typically perceived as real letters. Thus, the participants' perceptual experience was less accurate and detailed than they thought it was, and it was strongly influenced by their expectation that the stimulus array would consist only of real letters.

It is not clear that the overflow argument sheds light on phenomena such as change blindness and inattentional blindness. There are also issues relating to the notion of phenomenal consciousness – it appears to be a will-o'-the-wisp lasting a very short time before disappearing. A central problem is that it has no obvious special value or function: since it does not connect to cognitive processes such as attention and memory, it would seem to have negligible impact on our thinking or behaviour.

The major alternative to the overflow argument is based on the assumption that we often exaggerate the richness of our perceptual experience. The challenge is to explain *how* and *why* this happens given that one might imagine that mistaken views about our own perceptual experience would have been corrected through a lifetime of perceiving the world around us.

Odegaard et al. (2018) argued that the apparent richness of visual perception is illusory rather than genuine. They identified two plausible reasons why this happens: (1) filling-in; and (2) subjective inflation. As we have seen, the information available in peripheral vision is relatively weak and limited. However, filling-in involves combining foveal and peripheral information to produce a coherent gist-like representation based on plausible *assumptions* about what is likely to be present in the periphery.

Since the filling-in process is often inaccurate (e.g., objects are assumed to be present in spite of their absence), it might be imagined we would become aware of many of these inaccuracies. According to Odegaard et al. (2018), this happens relatively rarely because we typically *overestimate* the quality of the visual representations we have formed. This overestimation is what Odegaard et al. term 'subjective inflation'. Subjective inflation occurs because our perceptual experience when presented with ambiguous or weak visual information is typically influenced by our prior expectations based on past experience.

Myth: everyone agrees on the colour of a dress (or #theDress)

Suppose you showed a colour photograph of a dress to several friends and discovered to your great surprise that there were vehement disagreements among them concerning its colour. This surprise would probably occur because of the common belief that the colours we perceive are determined wholly by the wavelengths of light reflected from any given object. In fact, that belief is a myth.

On the 7 February 2015, Cecilia Bleasdale took a photograph of the dress she had decided to wear to her daughter's imminent wedding and posted it on the internet (you can see it by googling 'the dress Wikipedia'). It immediately became known as "#theDress" and went viral, attracting nine million tweets within two days of being posted. Celebrities disagreed vociferously about the colour of the dress. Taylor Swift saw it as blue and black but the controversy left her "confused and scared" (eh?). There was disagreement between Kim Kardashian and Kanye West, who were married to each other at the time. Kim Kardashian thought the dress was white and gold whereas Kanye West thought it was blue and black.

Such disagreements perplexed many vision experts as well as celebrities and other members of the public. As Bosten (2022, p. 102) pointed out, "When a stimulus such as #theDress . . . comes along that reveals a huge difference in colour perception across individuals, it is nearly as surprising to colour scientists as it is to the general public".

What colour do *you* think the dress is? Wallisch (2017) found in a sample of over 13,000 observers around the world that 57% claimed the dress was white and gold but 28% said it was black and blue! Kawasaki et al. (2021) obtained rather different findings in a study across three countries in different parts of the world (Sweden, India and China). Overall, 62% of observers perceived the dress as black and blue and only 29% saw it as white and gold. These changes may reflect people's greater familiarity with #theDress and more people now knowing it is actually black and blue.

Before discussing how different observers could have such different colour perception of the same dress, note that the intense interest in #theDress led researchers to produce photographs of other objects provoking major differences in colour perception. For example, there is The Jacket. Across three different countries (Sweden, China and India), 50% perceived it as green and gold, 23% as white and blue and 8% as black and brown (see Kawasaki et al., 2021). It is actually white and blue so under one-quarter of the respondents identified The Jacket's colours accurately!

Witzel and Toscani (2020) also found there is nothing special about #theDress. They started by creating visual stimuli of a tie, an egg, a fish, a peephole and a jacket having similar two-colour properties to #theDress. There were strong individual differences in how the colours were perceived for all these stimuli. Of importance, how observers perceived the colours of these stimuli predicted to some extent how they perceived the colours of #theDress. Thus, the findings with #theDress can also be found with many other realistic-looking images having a similar colour distribution.

It might be argued that all the aforementioned research involved the use of somewhat artificial or carefully contrived conditions. However, there are also real-life cases where there were large individual differences in perceived colour. For example, consider the mystery concerning the colour of the Czech writer Franz Kafka's eyes. They were variously described as 'dark', 'grey', 'blue' and 'brown' (Taylor et al., 2024). To add to the confusion, Kafka's eyes are described as 'dark blue-grey' on his passport and his girlfriend Dora said they were 'shy, brown'!

Individual differences in the colours perceived in a dress (or Kafka's eyes) may seem trivial. In fact, they are important because they show that visual perception is far more complex than might be imagined. Psychologists discovered well over 100 years ago that artificial ambiguous drawings are seen in different ways by different people. One such drawing can be seen as two faces or a goblet and another one can be seen as a young girl or an old lady. Research on #theDress has shown that people can see very different things even with naturalistic, real-life stimuli.

How can we explain pronounced individual differences in the perceived colour of #theDress (and many other objects)? Before answering that question directly, consider the nature of visual perception. Of key importance, our subjective impression that visual perception is very simple and automatic is totally wrong. As Born and Bencomo (2021, p. 272) pointed out, "For any given 2-dimensional (2D) projection on the retina, there is an infinitude of possible 3D objects that could have produced that projection". Since visual perception is *under-determined* by the visual information available to us, we have to make *inferences* (mostly unconscious) based on our knowledge and expectations.

The starting point is to appreciate that our colour judgements are complex. Suppose you look at a lab coat illuminated by sunlight and then the same object illuminated by artificial light. If you used only the information about the wavelengths reflecting from the object, you would decide the colour of the object was more orangey when viewed by artificial light. In fact, however, you would probably perceive the lab coat as white in both conditions.

There are various reasons why observers find it hard to assess the colours of #theDress. Jeong and Jeong (2021) pointed out that the colours within #theDress are low in saturation, meaning that they appear pale and washed out. As we would expect, it is harder to assess an object's colour accurately when it is low rather than high in saturation.

Another reason why it is harder to assess the colour of #theDress than many other stimuli is because dresses can be almost any colour. As a result, we cannot use knowledge of familiar colour to assist us in assessing the colour of a dress. In contrast, most everyday objects have a familiar colour (e.g., bananas are yellow and tomatoes are red). Vandenbroucke et al. (2016) presented typically red objects (e.g., *tomato*) and typically green objects (e.g., *pine tree*) in an ambiguous colour intermediate between red and green. Familiar colour influenced the perceived colour (i.e., typically red objects were perceived as redder than typically green objects) and also influenced the early processing of colour in the brain.

The factors identified mentioned earlier (i.e., low saturation of colour; unfamiliar colour) make it hard to judge the colour of #theDress accurately. However, they don't explain why observers have such differing opinions concerning its colours. Wallisch (2017) argued that the ambiguity of the illumination of #theDress provides the key. According to him, the upper part of #theDress implies illumination by daylight (but with #theDress in shadow) whereas the lower part implies artificial illumination. More specifically, observers' assumptions about the illumination drive differences in the perceived colours of #theDress.

Suppose some observers assume #theDress is in shadow. Shadows over-represent blue light, and so if these observers attribute any blueness in #theDress to the illumination, they would perceive it as white and gold. That would also be the case if observers thought #theDress was illuminated by natural light (this is because the sky is blue). Suppose other observers assume #theDress is illuminated by artificial light. This would make the image yellowish, and so factoring out the influence of the apparent illumination would cause the image to look blueish, leading these observers to perceive #theDress as black and blue.

Wallisch (2017) obtained support for his hypotheses. Of those observers assuming #theDress was illuminated by natural light (even if it was in shadow), 72% perceived #theDress as white and gold compared to only 48% who perceived it as illuminated by artificial light.

The aforementioned findings suggest that the perceived colours of #theDress are strongly influenced by the assumed nature of the illuminant. However, they are limited because all Wallisch (2017) found was that the perceived colour of #theDress *correlated* with the perceived nature of the illuminant. More compelling evidence might be obtained by *manipulating* the illuminant to discover whether that had the predicted effect on perceived colour. Precisely that was done by Lafer-Sousa et al. (2015). Observers saw #theDress presented in an obviously warm environment with direct illumination or in a cool environment with a shadow over it and the context. Of those observers who originally perceived #theDress as black and blue, 80% decided it was actually gold and white when seeing it in shadow. Of those originally perceiving #theDress as gold and white, 64% changed their minds and judged it to be black and blue when seeing it in direct illumination. Thus, the perceived illumination has a direct impact on #theDress's perceived colour.

Other factors also determine individual differences in how #theDress is perceived. For example, those with prior knowledge of its actual colour are more likely to perceive it as black and blue than those lacking such knowledge (Wallisch, 2017). Another factor is whether observers are Larks (i.e., go to bed and get up early) or Owls (i.e., go to bed and get up late). Owls are less likely than Larks to perceive #theDress as gold and white. This probably occurs because they have a greater tendency to perceive the illumination as artificial light (which they are exposed to during more of their waking hours than are Larks) (Wallisch, 2017).

Nearly all the research on #theDress has involved the use of two-dimensional photographs, and it is arguable that observers would perceive its colours more accurately if they viewed it under more realistic (and informative) three-dimensional conditions. Ashton et al. (2020) showed observers #theDress under three-dimensional conditions while simulating the apparent lighting conditions found in the famous photograph. Observers were as likely to perceive the colours of #theDress as inaccurately under those conditions as was the case with the photograph.

There is a final point about the illumination of #theDress. As Ashton et al. (2020) pointed out, observers trying to assess the illumination of an object often make the single-source assumption (i.e., there is a *single* illuminant). This assumption is violated in #theDress photograph where there is shadow in the foreground but direct light behind. Ashton et al. found colour perception of #theDress in three-dimensional conditions was systematically distorted when there were two different light sources.

Why is colour perception mostly accurate?

It would make no evolutionary sense if our ability to perceive the colours of all objects were as flawed as most people's perception of the colours of #theDress. Of key importance here is colour constancy, which is the tendency for any given object to be perceived as having the same colour under varying viewing conditions. As Gegenfurtner et al. (2024, p. 17) pointed out, we have an intriguing puzzle here: "In everyday life, we take colour constancy for granted, whereas in the lab constancy turns out to be between mediocre and incomplete". Indeed, I suspect you would find it hard to think of occasions (apart from looking at #theDress) when you were aware of significant deficiencies in your colour constancy.

The answer to the puzzle is that most laboratory research has involved very artificial tasks that seriously underestimate the extent of colour constancy in everyday life. For example, Foster and Reeves (2022) calculated colour constancy on a scale from 0 = no constancy to 1 = perfect constancy from numerous laboratory experiments most of which were less artificial than much early research. Mean colour constancy was 0.74. They wondered whether colour constancy for natural outdoor scenes (e.g., buildings; flowers; trees) would be reduced under changes in the light (e.g., clouds passing over the sun). Accordingly, they simulated daylight changes on images of outdoor scenes and found impaired colour constancy was found only for parts of them.

More strikingly, Gegenfurtner et al. (2024) carried out a relatively naturalistic study where participants identified the colour of an absent personal object under five different illuminations. They discovered colour constancy was "close-to-perfect" (p. 1).

What is important is that the light reflected from a given surface (e.g., a dress) combines information from the surface itself (i.e., its reflectance) and from the illumination source (i.e., the illuminant). As a consequence, observers have to draw accurate inferences about the illuminant to perceive the actual colour of the surface accurately. This was confirmed by Bannert and Bartels (2017). The accuracy with which the illuminant of a scene was processed predicted the extent of colour constancy.

Conclusions

There are various unusual features of the famous photograph of #theDress which explain why observers find it so difficult to assess accurately its colours. Easily the most important feature is that the nature of the illumination sources is *ambiguous* whereas in everyday life we generally have accurate information about the illuminant (e.g., the sun; artificial light). Other features are that dresses (unlike most objects) do not have a familiar colour and #theDress has relatively pale colours.

In sum, the colours we perceive when viewing an object or photograph are "mental constructions" (Shevell, 2019, p. 194) based on using several types of information. Observers typically have access to accurate information about the illuminant of an object and so exhibit high colour constancy. However, the famous case of #theDress shows that accurate colour perception can be seriously disrupted if the information available to observers is both complex and ambiguous.

Myth: most people are 'face experts'

In spite of the fallibilities of human memory, most of us often exhibit very good face recognition and memory; indeed, many psychologists have described humans as 'face experts' (Young & Burton, 2018). There are several reasons for claiming that we have expertise (at least with respect to familiar faces). First, the average person can recognise approximately 5,000 familiar and famous faces (Jenkins et al., 2018). Second, nearly all faces are broadly similar to each other (e.g., nose in the middle; mouth underneath two eyes on opposite sides of the face; eyebrows; and so on). These similarities make it an achievement to be able to recognise thousands of familiar faces with ease. Third, recognition memory for degraded familiar faces (e.g., viewed in poor lighting; faces with some features omitted) is generally good (Young & Burton, 2018).

The above findings make sense, because it is very important to our social lives to be good at face recognition. We can see this by considering individuals with prosopagnosia ('face blindness'). JK, a woman in her early thirties, described an acutely embarrassing incident caused by her prosopagnosia: "I went to the wrong baby at my son's daycare and only realised that he was not my son when the entire daycare staff looked at me in horrified disbelief" (Duchaine & Nakayama, 2006, p. 166).

There was a rude awakening from the complacent view that we are nearly all face experts when Jenkins et al. (2011) reported the findings from their epoch-making research. Dutch people were shown 40 photographs and sorted them into piles with a separate pile for each individual shown in the array. There were 20 photographs of each of two Dutch celebrities and participants' sorting performance was almost perfect.

There was a clever twist to Jenkins et al.'s (2011) study. *British* people (who didn't know anything about the two Dutch celebrities) were shown the same 40 photos and sorted them into piles. They produced an average of 7.5 piles indicating they believed that seven or eight different individuals were represented in the array! This finding is remarkable given that the task imposed no demands on memory because all the photos were visible throughout. The take-home message is very clear: face recognition can be dramatically harder with unfamiliar faces than with familiar ones.

Why are we surprised by the above findings? Part of the answer lies in the Dunning-Kroeger effect: individuals incompetent at a given task are often blissfully unaware of their own incompetence. This effect was found with face recognition by Zhou and Jenkins (2020). Participants decided whether pairs of unfamiliar faces matched. Those whose performance was in the bottom 25% did not differ from those in the top 25% in terms of how well they thought their performance compared to that of other participants.

Further striking evidence that most people lack insight into the limitations of their own face-recognition abilities was reported by Sauerland et al. (2016). Participants were misinformed that they had previously decided that some pairs of unfamiliar photos showed the same face (they had actually decided they showed different faces) and vice versa. Participants rarely detected the deception and typically provided specific reasons why they had made the decision they hadn't made.

The evidence discussed so far seems totally consistent with Young and Burton's (2018, p. 100) conclusion: "Although we are usually good at recognising familiar faces, most of us experience substantial problems in recognising the identities of unfamiliar faces. . . . In effect, we are familiar face experts [but not unfamiliar face experts]". Note that rather different processes are involved in the recognition of familiar and unfamiliar faces. There is much evidence that familiar face recognition depends heavily on *internal* facial features (i.e., eyes, nose and mouth), whereas unfamiliar face recognition relies more on *external* facial features (i.e., hair, ears and contour) (see Latif & Moulson, 2022). In their study, Latif and Moulson (2022) found that the usually large face recognition advantage for familiar over unfamiliar faces disappeared when participants had access only to internal face features.

White et al. (2022) argued that two somewhat separate perceptual abilities can be required with respect to face recognition when observers are presented with two faces. First, there is the ability to discriminate between two photos of different faces (telling people apart). Second, there is the ability to realise that two photos of the same face portray the same individual (telling people together).

White et al. (2022) compared performance on the two abilities when both faces were familiar or unfamiliar. The prediction that performance would be better in the telling people apart and telling people together conditions when both faces were familiar was strongly supported. However, the impact of familiarity was massively greater in the telling people together condition (i.e., recognising that two photos are of the same person) than the telling people apart condition (i.e., recognising that two photos are of different individuals). Supporting evidence comes from the study by Jenkins et al. (2011; discussed earlier). Participants often failed to recognise that two photos showed the same individual. However, they very rarely (under 1% of trials) made the mistake of believing that photos of two different individuals actually showed the same person.

Why is recognition of unfamiliar faces so poor?

Why are most of us relatively oblivious to our poor ability to recognise that two different photos are of the same unfamiliar person or to match a live unfamiliar person to a photo? How can we explain these limitations on our face-recognition ability?

With respect to the first question, some blame attaches to psychologists carrying out research on face recognition (Young & Burton, 2017). Until relatively recently, participants in research on face recognition would typically study photos of unfamiliar faces. This would be followed by a recognition-memory test where the original photos would be mixed in with further photos of unfamiliar faces and participants would endeavour to pick out those previously studied.

Performance was typically good, suggesting we have no real problem with recognising unfamiliar faces. Crucially, however, the memory test involved photos *identical* to those previously studied. Such research has limited relevance to the real world and produced very misleading findings. This historical context helps to explain why most psychologists working on face recognition were surprised we often find it very difficult to recognise two different photos are of the same person.

Our unawareness of our mediocre ability to recognise unfamiliar faces occurs in part because most of us spend very little of time asking ourselves whether an unfamiliar person is the same unfamiliar person we saw some time ago. As a consequence, we lack personal experience of how difficult that task can be. For me personally, a rare exception is watching a film and wondering whether someone who appears on screen is the same as someone who was in the previous scene.

Why do we often mistakenly believe that two photos of the same person actually show two different individuals? Of central importance, different photos of any given individual typically exhibit considerably more *variability* than one might imagine. Jenkins et al. (2011) presented observers with 20 photos of each of 20 unfamiliar individuals and had them rate each face's attractiveness. Surprisingly, there was more variability in attractiveness ratings *within* rather than *between* individuals indicating that different photos of an individual often differ considerably in attractiveness. As you may have noticed, beautiful celebrities often look surprisingly unattractive when photographed unexpectedly in everyday life.

One might think a lifetime of experience would have allowed us to cope with within-individual variability. However, that does not appear to be the case. A key reason we find it hard to cope with within-individual variability was discovered by Burton et al. (2016): how one face varies across different photos differs from how other faces vary. In other words, each face has its own *idiosyncratic* variability across different photos. One source of variability is of the angle of the face to the camera, and others include facial expression, presence vs. absence of make-up, presence vs. absence of facial hair and style of haircut.

Real-world face recognition: expertise

You may be thinking all this research on unfamiliar faces is of limited real-world relevance. If so, you could hardly be more wrong! There are numerous situations in which you have to prove your identity by producing documentation such as a passport, driving licence including a photograph of yourself and some other form of photographic identification.

In addition, there are literally millions of CCTV cameras in the UK, and evidence obtained from them is used to identify individuals responsible for crimes. Bruce et al. (1999) investigated the extent to which suspects could be identified from a CCTV video. Observers saw a target face taken from a

CCTV video together with an array of 10 high-quality photographs. When the target was present in the array, observers selected that person only 65% of the time. When the target was not present, 35% of observers nevertheless claimed one face in the array was the target person!

Most of us have strictly limited expertise in identifying unfamiliar faces. Perhaps individuals with extensive experience in identifying unfamiliar faces might perform dramatically better. For example, we would expect experienced passport officers (8 years of service on average) to decide with great accuracy whether a photograph is that of a person physically present. In fact, White et al. (2014) found 14% of fraudulent photos (i.e., photos of the wrong person) were wrongly accepted and 6% of valid photos were rejected! Part of the reason why invalid photos were accepted as valid was because of *document bias*: photos embedded in documents are more likely than those in isolation to trigger incorrect "same person" responses (Feng & Burton, 2021).

It can be argued that the study was unrealistic because 50% of the photos were invalid or non-matching. We must certainly hope that the prevalence of travellers clutching invalid passports is nothing like 50%. Weatherford et al. (2021) addressed this issue with security professionals and non-professionals. Performance by both groups of participants on matching trials was considerably *worse* when the match rate was low (10%) than when it was high (90%): approximately 30% in the former condition and 47% in the latter. This is the low prevalence effect. It occurs because the infrequency of matches in the 10% condition led the participants to have a low expectation there would be a match on any given trial.

It is clear that considerable experience in jobs requiring matching unfamiliar faces produces only modest increases in performance at best. Alternatively, we could simply identify individuals especially good at face matching. This approach has proved more successful in that large numbers of so-called super-recognisers have been discovered. Robertson et al. (2016) asked metropolitan police officers to decide whether face pairs depicted the same person. Police trainees had a mean accuracy of 81% compared to 96% for super-recognisers.

Why are super-recognisers so much better than the rest of us at recognising unfamiliar faces? It is due mostly to genetic factors. Wilmer et al. (2010) found the face-recognition performance of monozygotic (identical) twins was much more similar than that of dizygotic (fraternal) twins. This finding is consistent with those discussed earlier in which even extensive practice at identifying unfamiliar faces produced little or no improvement in face-recognition performance. The ability to identify unfamiliar faces is surprisingly specific: it correlates very modestly with IQ and is only weakly associated with other forms of visual object recognition (Wilmer, 2017).

White et al. (2022) in a study referred to earlier considered the superiority of super-recognisers to typical observers in more detail. Super-recognisers were better than typical observers with respect to telling people apart. However, their superiority was markedly greater with respect to perceiving two photos of the same individual as showing the same face (precisely the skill most of us lack).

Conclusions

Our ability to recognise familiar faces is massively superior to our ability to recognise unfamiliar ones. Since we spend most of our time successfully recognising familiar faces, we are mostly unaware that we have limited ability to recognise that the same unfamiliar face is shown in two photographs.

The key problem is that any given individual's face shows considerable variability across different photographs. It follows that we should be able to improve recognition of unfamiliar faces if we *combined* information from multiple photographs of the same unfamiliar individual to create an average. Jones et al. (2017) obtained evidence supporting this prediction. Observers had significantly better recognition memory for an unfamiliar face when they had previously seen seven computer-generated synthesised images of that individual than when they had seen a single photograph of the same individual. This finding has important real-world applicability: the police can use computer-based systems to generate synthesised images from a single photograph which could enhance the ability of eyewitnesses to identify the culprit of a crime.

Finally, note that observers must decide how similar two photos need to be for them to make the judgement they are of the same person. They may adopt a conservative response criterion (i.e., there must be substantial similarity for them to respond "same") or a liberal criterion (i.e., relatively modest similarity suffices for them to respond "same"). The percentage of correct "same" responses is significantly increased by persuading observers to adopt a relatively liberal response criterion (Stabile et al., 2024). That can be an advantage if it is very important to detect that two photos show the same person. However, the disadvantage is that there are more false alarms (i.e., falsely claiming that two photos are of the same person) which will often be problematical.

Why do we believe so many myths about visual perception?

A key reason why many people believe several myths about visual perception is because it is so complex. However, as mentioned earlier, visual perception typically seems remarkably simple and effortless and so it is hard to accept that the underlying processes are actually stupendously complicated.

If visual perception is as straightforward as we like to believe, researchers in artificial intelligence (AI) should have found it easy to produce AI systems accurately mimicking human perception. In contrast, they should have found it hard to develop AI systems mimicking high-level complex human cognition (e.g., chess; the Chinese game Go). However, Moravec (1988, p. 15) argued the opposite in his famous paradox: "It is comparatively easy to make computers exhibit adult level performance on intelligence tests or playing checkers [draughts], and difficult or impossible to give them the skills of a one-year old when it comes to perception and mobility".

How can we make sense of Moravec's paradox? According to Moravec (1988), visual perception has become increasingly sophisticated over billions of years of evolution. Our visual perception is now so efficient that we are unaware of its underlying processes. In contrast, high-level cognition developed much later in evolutionary history and so we are all too aware of its limitations.

Moravec's paradox is only partially correct. AI systems perform outstandingly well on relatively specific cognitive tasks (e.g., outperforming the world champions at chess and Go), but they are substantially below human levels of performance on general cognitive tasks (e.g., intelligence tests) (Eysenck & Eysenck, 2022).

Everyday perception vs. perception in the laboratory

Our susceptibility to various myths about visual perception depends very much on the contrast between visual perception in everyday life and in the laboratory.

Accordingly, I will discuss the similarities and differences between perception in those two situations. Visual perception always involves a visual task. In everyday life, the task may consist of avoiding obstacles as we walk down the street, assessing the trajectory of a tennis ball when playing tennis and monitoring the road in front as we drive a car. Note that we are often not consciously aware of the visual task we are performing at any given point in time. In the laboratory, in contrast, the visual task is typically determined by the experimenter.

In either case, performance on visual tasks is limited by two key limiting factors: (1) decision complexity and (2) involvement of peripheral vision (Rosenholtz, 2020). Performance suffers when decision complexity is high (e.g., when observers perform two tasks at the same time) and/or observers are reliant on the relatively impoverished information available in peripheral vision compared to central or foveal vision.

The visual tasks we perform in everyday life typically involve low decision complexity because we mostly perform only a single task at any given time (e.g., walking to the station to catch a train). Observers performing even relatively complex visual tasks are rarely reliant on the limited information provided by peripheral vision. The reason is that we typically make 3 or 4 saccades (rapid eye movements) per second. As discussed earlier, there is a process of transsaccadic integration in which information obtained from successive saccades is integrated and combined. Note that we are not aware that our conscious visual perception is based on integrated information from several different saccades.

Of particular importance, there are direct interactions between foveal or central vision and peripheral vision. This has important consequences. For example, if crucial visual information is in peripheral vision on an initial saccade, it will often be in foveal vision on the subsequent saccade. Transsaccadic integration also explains why we are unaware of any clear differences between foveal and peripheral vision.

We turn now to the research evidence disproving some of the myths of visual perception discussed in this chapter:

(1) Change blindness occurs in part because of decision complexity: observers are presented with a visual scene containing many objects and the visual task they perform is not identical to the one of interest to the researchers because they are not forewarned that one object will change.

(2) Inattentional blindness also involves decision complexity. Observers are unwittingly in a dual-task situation in which they are given a task to perform that is very different from the task of detecting the introduction of an unexpected object. In addition, the unexpected object is typically in peripheral vision because observers are fixating on task-relevant stimuli.

(3) Research indicating that we are sometimes oblivious to apparently obvious aspects of peripheral vision (e.g., gist; colour) is easily explained. Observers see each visual image so briefly they have only a single fixation. Unlike everyday perception, there is no opportunity to change the fixation point to place initially peripheral information in foveal vision or to engage in trans-saccadic integration. In addition, there is decision complexity because the observers have to perform an additional visual task based on information in foveal vision.

(4) Most of the time, it is relatively easy to assess the colour of any given object. In everyday life, objects often have intense colours, they have a familiar colour (e.g., grass is green; the sky is blue) and we can see the source of the illumination on the object. In contrast, decision making with respect to the colour of #theDress is very difficult. Its colours are pale and washed out, dresses do not have a familiar colour, and the source of the illumination is ambiguous and complex. In everyday life, it is typically very easy to judge the colours of objects and colour constancy is high. The fact that #the Dress is very unrepresentative of the objects we typically encounter in everyday life explains our surprise that there is so much disagreement about its colour.

(5) In everyday life, face recognition typically involves recognising the faces of family members, our friends and our acquaintances. Decision complexity is low because we have so much stored information about all these familiar faces that we can effortlessly recognise them. In contrast, we rarely find ourselves trying to decide whether two photographs are

of the same unfamiliar face. Our lack of stored information about unfamiliar faces means that decision complexity is high. We greatly underestimate the complexity of unfamiliar face recognition because we fail to appreciate how much easier it is to recognise familiar than unfamiliar faces.

3   Mysteries of memory

Everyone has massive personal experience of the workings of their memory. For example, you can probably remember telling a friend what you did on your most recent holiday, trying to remember the meaning of a word you encounter in a book and trying to recall the best way to travel somewhere by bus.

In fact, we make extensive use of our memory all the time. As I look out of the window of my study, I know I am seeing trees, grass, garden chairs and a table because I am accessing the relevant information stored in long-term memory. In similar fashion, I am only able to engage in a conversation with a friend because my stored knowledge of the English language allows me to understand what my friend is saying and respond to it. I also rely on my long-term memory when I ride my bicycle or play tennis.

In view of our non-stop use of our own memory system, it might be imagined we would all be experts in understanding how human memory works. In fact, that is not the case. As I hope to demonstrate, most people believe various myths about human memory in spite of their copious daily experience of how it actually works.

Myth: "Memory is like a video camera"

What is the nature of human memory? This issue was addressed by Simons and Chabris (2011) and discussed briefly in Chapter 1. They found 63% of the public agreed with the statement "Human memory works like a video camera, accurately recording the events we see and hear so that we can review and inspect them later" (p. 3). As Simons and Chabris pointed out, this finding implies that most people think memories provide complete representations of what they have seen or heard, that memory is a passive process and that memory is unchanging over time. In similar fashion, Alvarez and Brown (2002) discovered that 36% of their respondents believed we retain essentially perfect records of our experiences.

Lilienfeld et al. (2010) identified the notion that memory is like a video camera as one of the 50 great myths of popular psychology. We will consider the relevant evidence shortly. Before doing so, however, note that the

DOI: 10.4324/9781003596677-3

views of memory experts differ massively from those of lay persons. Simons and Chabris (2011) found that 0% of experts on human memory accepted the notion that human memory is like a video camera. Akhtar et al. (2018) confirmed the existence of large discrepancies in views about the nature of human memory between lay persons and memory experts. Most members of the public (and police officers) believed that memories are like videos whereas the great majority of memory experts believed memories are typically fragmentary rather than video-like.

Is memory error-prone? Yes

There is compelling evidence that human memory is typically fragmentary and prone to error and so differs radically from a video camera and/ or tape recorder. Consider a simple demonstration based on research by Johnson-Laird and Stevenson (1970). Read the following passage:

> The duchess invited John to tea. She was an artist and had produced many paintings. After tea, she showed him one of her favourite paintings. John liked the painting and bought it from the duchess. When John returned home, the painting had pride of place on his wall. He derived great pleasure from looking at it.

Now that you have read the passage, decide whether it contained the following sentence: *John liked the painting and the duchess sold it to him.* Johnson-Laird and Stevenson (1970) found most of their participants thought they had heard that sentence before. That indicates they had no memory for the syntax of the fourth sentence in the passage even though they had heard it only approximately 50 seconds earlier. Thus, unlike the functioning of a tape recorder, we typically forget the precise wording of sentences almost immediately.

Ikier et al. (2024) reviewed numerous factors producing memory errors and distortions. For example, consider the misinformation effect (discussed further in Chapter 9). In essence, an eyewitness observes a crime or other event and is subsequently presented with misleading information relating to that event. This misleading information typically causes eyewitnesses to make errors in their recall of the event: Blank and Launay (2014) found evidence of a strong misinformation effect in a meta-analysis.

Ikier et al. (2024) also discussed how memory errors are created based on Bartlett's (1932) theoretical ideas. Bartlett argued that what we remember (including our errors when remembering) depends on the schemas we possess. Schemas are packets of information about the world, sequences of events and objects. For example, we have a schema about actions typically occurring during a restaurant meal (Bower et al., 1979): these actions include *being given a menu*; *ordering*; *eating* and *paying the bill*.

Schematic information causes us to form *expectations* of what we will see and encounter in various situations. This leads to a crucial prediction of schema theory: we often 'remember' schema-consistent objects and actions corresponding to our expectations even when they were not present.

Brewer and Treyens (1981) tested the previous prediction. They asked participants to spend 35 seconds in a room resembling a graduate student's office. The room contained a mixture of schema-consistent objects you would expect to find in such an office (e.g., *desk*; *calendar*; *pencils*) and schema-inconsistent objects you would not expect to find (e.g., *skull*; *toy*; *top*). Brewer and Treyens focused on objects that had *not* been present in the office but were 'recognised' with high confidence. As predicted, nearly all these recognition-memory errors related to schema-consistent objects (e.g., books; filing cabinet). Similar findings were reported for participants who recalled the objects in the office: 'recall' of objects not present was greater for schema-consistent than schema-inconsistent objects.

Another way memory fails to resemble a video camera is that it is highly *selective* whereas a video camera does not distinguish at all between important and trivial information. Clear-cut evidence of the selectivity of human memory was reported by Gomulicki (1956). Some participants wrote a précis (summary) of a story visible in front of them whereas others recalled the same story from memory. Still other participants were provided with each précis and recall and had great difficulty in telling them apart. Thus, story recall closely resembles a précis in focusing primarily on the most important information.

Is memory error-prone? Not necessarily

The research discussed so far has been laboratory-based, and much of it (e.g., studies on the misinformation effect) was explicitly designed to produce memory errors and distortions. As a consequence, the findings stemming from such research may exaggerate the susceptibility to error of human memory.

Clear-cut evidence that memory experts are in danger of exaggerating the fallibility of human memory was reported by Diamond et al. (2020). Some participants (mean age = 27 years) were exposed to a respiratory-mask-fitting procedure whereas others (ranging in age from 19 to 75) were exposed to an audio-guide tour of a hospital. They subsequently recalled as many details as possible of the event they had experienced. The time between the event and recall was two days for the audio-guide tour and an average of 267 days (nearly 9 months) for the mask-fitting procedure.

Memory experts estimated the percentage of accurately recalled details for the various conditions. They estimated recall would be best in 30-year olds recalling the audio-guide tour after a retention interval (mean estimate = 40% accuracy) compared to under 30% for 70-year olds. For recall of the mask-fitting procedure after 2 years, estimated accuracy was 20%. The actual findings were very different from any of these estimates. Diamond et al. (2020) found participants' recall of details was highly accurate (between 93% and 95%) regardless of their age or length of the retention interval.

Findings resembling those of Diamond et al. (2020) have been reported by other researchers. Wynn and Logie (1998) investigated the accuracy of students' recall of an event early in their first term at university (e.g., a course-advising session; introduction to university talk). Their key finding was that event recall was consistently accurate at periods of time up to 6 months afterwards.

Why was memory performance so accurate in the studies by Diamond et al. (2020) and Wynn and Logie (1998)? One key reason is that the events being remembered were relatively *distinctive*. For example, exposure to a respiratory-mask-fitting procedure differs considerably from anything that most of us experience on a day-to-day basis. Memory for such distinctive events is less likely than memory for more familiar events to be subject to interference and confusion with other events (Eysenck, 1979).

Let us now return to the two examples of error-prone memory performance under laboratory conditions discussed earlier. First, we consider the strong misinformation effect obtained by Blank and Launay in a meta-analysis. They also carried out a meta-analysis on misinformation studies where participants were warned of the presence of misinformation after viewing an event. This warning reduced the misinformation effect to between one-third and one-half its size when no warning was provided. Thus, many memory errors can be reversed if appropriate information is provided.

Second, we saw in the study by Brewer and Treyens (1981) that people sometimes falsely recognise and recall schema-consistent objects they have not seen. Steyvers and Hemmer (2012) pointed out that this study exaggerated the fallibility of human memory because the contents of the graduate student's office were manipulated. Many participants showed schema-consistent 'recall' by claiming there were books in the office, but in nearly any typical office there would have been numerous books. Steyvers and Hemmer showed participants naturalistic photographs of various scenes (e.g., *office*; *kitchen*). With these more realistic scenes, there were very few false recalls of schema-consistent objects.

Do we want our long-term memory to be accurate?

The notion that memory is like a video camera seems consistent with the assumption that the main function of memory is to provide us with accurate information about the past (especially events of personal significance). Historically, laboratory research primarily focused on experiments where participants learned information (e.g., lists of words; pairs of words) and the measure of success was the number of items correctly recalled or recognised subsequently.

There is sometimes a comparably strong emphasis on memory accuracy in everyday life (e.g., sitting an examination; remembering a friend's address).

However, it is debatable whether accuracy is of primary importance in most everyday life situations. In fact, what we remember in our everyday lives is often determined by our personal goals.

Suppose you tell a friend about your experiences at a recent party. I would hazard a guess that the goals of entertaining and impressing your friend might triumph over the goal of describing with great accuracy exactly what happened (I may be maligning you!). Supporting evidence was reported by Brown et al. (2015). They found 58% of students admitted they had 'borrowed' other people's memories when describing their personal experiences to someone else.

When your account of an event is deliberately exaggerated, does that distort your subsequent memory of it? That question was answered affirmatively by Dudukovic et al. (2004). They asked some people to recall a story entertainingly whereas others recalled it accurately. When both groups were subsequently instructed to recall the story accurately, those previously instructed to recall the story entertainingly were less accurate and recalled fewer details. This is the 'saying-is-believing' effect: deliberating distorting what one says about a past event to suit a given audience causes subsequent misremembering of that event.

Higgins et al. (2021) went beyond the 'saying-is-believing' effect to argue that our social motives have strong effects on how we remember. We are motivated to create a sense of shared reality with other people where our feelings and beliefs about another person or event are the same as those of others with whom we seek interpersonal closeness. This striving for shared reality leads to a 'sharing-is-believing' effect where memory is distorted because the goal of belonging trumps the goal of accurate remembering.

In sum, our long-term memory is influenced by various goals. In the past, cognitive psychologists exaggerated the role played by the goal of accuracy in determining what we remember and how we remember it. It has been known for a long time that what we say about the past to other people is often influenced by our attempts at being polite, being friendly and impressing our listener(s). However, it has only recently become clear that these attempts produce changes in our long-term memory for the past.

Summary and conclusions

In spite of evidence (e.g., Diamond et al., 2020) indicating that long-term memory can be surprisingly accurate, there is strong evidence that our memory is typically far less accurate than a video camera. As we have also seen, our memory also differs from a video camera in being very selective in terms of the precise information that can be recalled. Our recall of the past is also inaccurate because we often focus on impressing or entertaining other people when describing past events rather than on being accurate.

Why do so many people believe that human memory is like a video camera given the massive evidence that it is very different in its functioning?

The answer is perhaps surprising: very few people actually believe that our memory is like a video camera! In Simons and Chabris's (2011) article, only 24% strongly agreed that human memory works like a video camera, with a further 39% only "mostly agreeing" that it is like a video camera. More evidence that most people don't believe that our memory is anything like as accurate as a video camera comes from research using memory questionnaires. For example, the Multifactorial Memory Questionnaire assesses individuals' assessment of their own memory ability and their satisfaction with their own memory. Most people have many doubts about their memory ability and limited satisfaction with it (Troyer & Rich, 2018).

The strongest evidence that most people don't actually believe that our memory works like a video camera was reported by Brewin et al. (2019; see Chapter 1). They discovered that the findings depend heavily on the precise statement used. For example, 93% of people agreed with the statement that "When we witness an event, what we see can be shaped by our personal beliefs or biases". This is, of course, totally inconsistent with the notion that memory is like a video camera!

In sum, most members of the public have reasonably correct and coherent views concerning the nature of memory when those views are explored in depth. In contrast, memory experts are vividly aware of hundreds of artificial laboratory experiments indicating that human memory can be highly error-prone. As a result, they are in danger of exaggerating memory's deficiencies. If our memory system worked as poorly as some memory experts claim, it is very improbable that the human species would have evolved as successfully as it has done.

Myth: memories do not change over time: they are permanent

Many people believe in the permanence of human memory. When presented with the statement, "Once you have experienced an event and formed a memory of it, that memory does not change" (p. 3), 48% of people agreed with it (Simons & Chabris, 2011). In contrast, 0% of memory experts agreed with it. More strikingly, Patihis et al. (2014) found 67% of undergraduate students endorsed the statement, "Memory of everything experienced is stored permanently in the brain, even if we can't access all of it". Brewin et al. (2019) found with a more representative sample of members of the public that 62% agreed with that statement.

Research findings: electrical brain stimulation

Penfield (1958) produced what at the time was regarded as dramatic support for the permanent memory hypothesis. He applied low-intensity electrical brain stimulation to the neocortex of epileptic patients who were awake during neurosurgery to identify the source of the epilepsy. These patients sometimes produced apparently amazingly detailed personal or autobiographical memories. Accordingly, Penfield and Perot (1963, p. 689) concluded,

> Past experience, when it is recalled electrically, seems to be complete including all the things of which an individual was aware at the time . . . since the events were often unimportant, it seems likely that the whole stream of consciousness must be so recorded somewhere.

Penfield (1969, p. 165) discussed all his research findings and came to the following conclusion:

> It is clear that the neuronal action that accompanies each succeeding state of consciousness leaves its permanent imprint on the brain. The imprint, or record, is a trail of facilitation of neuronal connections that can be followed again by an electric current many years later with no loss of detail, as though a tape recorder had been receiving it all.

He had previously claimed that the impact of the electrical stimulation was "as though a wire recorder, or a strip of cinematographic film with sound-track, had been set in motion within the brain" (Penfield, 1959, p. 1720) thereby producing a very detailed experience of an event from the patient's past.

Penfield's research has had an enormous impact on psychologists. Loftus and Loftus (1980) found that 84% of psychologists agreed with the following statement: "Everything we learn is permanently stored in the mind, although sometimes particular details are not accessible". When questioned, many of them said their agreement was firmly based on the research of Wilder Penfield.

Curot et al. (2017) reviewed the entire 80-year research literature on the effects of low-intensity electrical brain stimulation on memory retrieval. Such stimulation produced involuntary recall of personal memories on only about 0.5% of occasions, and very few of those memories were vivid. The precise reasons why Penfield's findings have not been replicated in recent decades are unclear. However, changes in operative procedures (e.g., greater use of anaesthetic drugs; time constraints) and alterations in the details of electrical brain stimulation are probably both partly responsible (Curot et al., 2020).

Sjöberg (2023) argued that there are two main ways of interpreting the effects of electrical brain stimulation. First, there is Penfield's view that this stimulation augments normal memory function leading patients to relive a previous experience completely, as if "the sights and sounds and thoughts of a former day" were retrieved (Penfield, 1959, p. 1719). Second, an alternative viewpoint is that electrical stimulation causes "'synthetic constructions' in the form of mental events, falsely interpreted as memories" (Sjöberg, 2023, p. 2737).

There are four main reasons for arguing that the research evidence is more consistent with the notion of 'synthetic constructions' than augmented memory function. First, there is practically no evidence indicating that electrical stimulation causes complete memories to be recalled. Penfield found recovered memories in only 3.5% of the patients who received electrical stimulation of the brain (Loftus & Loftus, 1980). Some memories produced by electrical stimulation were vague rather than vivid (e.g., one patient said "that reminded me of something" and another simply reported "a memory"). Overall, most of the memories were fragmentary rather than complete.

Second, many other 'memories' reported by Penfield seem much more like imaginative reconstructions than true memories (Loftus & Loftus, 1980). For example, one patient referred to sounds in a lumberyard although she said she had never been in a lumberyard! Another patient said she saw herself as she had appeared in childbirth which was clearly not reliving an earlier experience.

Third, several laboratory studies have suggested that electrical brain stimulation can cause false rather than accurate memories. For example, Fried et al. (1982) presented a stimulus to their participants and then instructed them to select it from several stimuli following a distraction task. When electrical brain stimulation was administered during retrieval, this increased the tendency for participants to claim they remembered stimuli that had not actually been presented.

Fourth, the percentage of patients receiving electrical brain stimulation who report recalling personal memories has dropped dramatically in recent decades (Curot et al., 2017). As discussed earlier, there are various potential explanations for this change. However, it seems likely that Penfield's expectation that patients would produce personal memories in response to electrical stimulation may have caused some of them to produce imaginary memories.

Research: other findings

In very general terms, there are two possible reasons why an individual cannot remember something they learned previously. First, the memory may be *inaccessible* (i.e., it is still stored in long-term memory but cannot be retrieved). Second, the memory may be *unavailable* (i.e., it has been lost from the memory system). Advocates of the notion of permanent memory must assume that memories that cannot be retrieved are available in long-term memory even though they are demonstrably inaccessible.

Convincing evidence that inaccessible memories can nevertheless be available was provided by Tulving and Pearlstone (1966). In one of their conditions, participants were presented with 48 words. Each word belonged to a different category and was preceded by its category name (e.g., *Weapons – Cannon*). Those participants given a test of free recall produced an average of 15 words, meaning that 33 list words were inaccessible. Other participants were provided with the category names at the time of recall.

These participants recalled an average of 35 words. Thus, approximately 60% of words inaccessible on the free recall test were actually available in memory.

Findings such as those of Tulving and Pearlstone (1966) by no means demonstrate that *all* long-term memories are permanent. Providing the effective retrieval cues in the form of category names increased memory performance but 27% of the items were not recalled even in this condition. Note also that recall was assessed very shortly after the material had been presented.

Brown and Kulik (1977) argued that dramatic events perceived as surprising and having real consequences for the individual activate a special neural mechanism that "prints" the details permanently in memory. Examples of such dramatic events are the assassination of President Kennedy in 1963 and the terrorist attacks on the United States on 11 September 2001. They introduced the term 'flashbulb memories' to describe such memories and claimed they are exceptionally accurate (e.g., they possess "an almost perceptual clarity" (p. 73) and permanent.

Several memory experts (e.g., Conway et al., 1994) subsequently expressed their agreement with Brown and Kulik's (1977) views concerning the characteristics of flashbulb memories as did most members of the general public. For example, a study conducted by the Pew Research Center for the People and the Press (2002) found 97% of those questioned said they could "remember EXACTLY where [they] were or what [they] were doing the MOMENT [they] heard the news about the 11th September terrorist attacks".

In spite of the popular support for the notion that flashbulb memories are permanent, it definitely should be regarded as a myth (Eysenck & Keane, 2020).

For example, Pezdek (2003) asked people a few weeks after 9/11 whether they had seen the videotape of the first plane striking the first tower on 9/11 on the day it happened. They found that 73% responded "Yes", in spite of the fact that only videotape of the second tower being hit was available on the day itself.

Talarico and Rubin (2003) compared the consistency of memory over time for flashbulb memories for 9/11 and everyday memories. Flashbulb memories showed no more consistency than everyday memories over a 32-week period of time. In contrast, however, the reported vividness of flashbulb memories was much greater than that of everyday memories.

Hirst et al. (2015) found a similar disconnect between memory consistency or accuracy and subjective reports in a 10-year study of flashbulb memories for 9/11. There was rapid forgetting for the details of flashbulb memories of 9/11 within the first year afterwards but very little thereafter. In spite of the strong evidence of forgetting, Hirst et al. found that "A delay of 10 years did not diminish participants' extraordinarily high level of confidence in their flashbulb memories" (p. 618). In sum, flashbulb memories are unremarkable in their accuracy and permanence but are remarkable with respect to subjective vividness and confidence in the accuracy of those memories.

Research: brain mechanisms

Convincing evidence that many memories are not permanent comes from research focusing on relevant brain processes. Hardt et al. (2013) argued that much forgetting is caused by decay, which is "forgetting due to a gradual loss of the substrate of memory" (p. 111). More specifically, there is a decay process (operating mostly during sleep) that removes numerous trivial memories from the memory system.

Moreno (2021) reviewed research on molecular brain mechanisms associated with forgetting. There is much evidence that such mechanisms are involved in the removal of specific memories of marginal usefulness and the protection of more useful ones.

Finally, another important brain process is hippocampal neurogenesis. This involves generating new neurons in the hippocampus (especially during early development but continuing into adult life). It is unsurprising that changes within the hippocampus should affect memory and forgetting given that it is of crucial importance in the formation of new memories. Madsen and Kim (2016) reported that long-term retrieval in mice was impaired by drugs increasing hippocampal neurogenesis but enhanced by drugs that decreased it. Subsequently, Tran et al. (2019) showed that even modest rates of hippocampal neurogenesis can cause substantial long-term forgetting.

Summary and conclusions

The major problem when investigating the issue of whether memories are permanent is that absence of evidence is not evidence of absence. In other words, it is remarkably difficult to obtain compelling evidence that memories have been irrevocably lost from the memory system. However, the overall picture that emerges from research on this topic strongly suggests that memories are not permanent.

When we considered the public's apparently misguided support for the notion that human memory is like a video camera in some detail, we discovered that most members of the public have a more sophisticated and nuanced view of human memory than that. Precisely the same is true with respect to the myth that memories are permanent. As mentioned earlier, Simons and Chabris (2011) found that 48% of members of public agreed that memories are permanent and unchanging. However, only 16.5% agreed strongly that memories are permanent and twice as many (31.1%) agreed mostly with that statement. In addition, 49% did not agree that memories are permanent. Thus, there was hardly massive support for the assumption that all memories are permanent and unchanging!

Brewin et al. (2019) explored people's views on memory permanence further. They discovered that 76.5% agreed with this statement: "A memory can decay over time until that memory no longer exists". Since Brewin et al. also found that 66.7% of participants believed that all memories are stored permanently in the brain, that means that at least 43% of them agreed that all memories are stored permanently and that memories can decay and cease to exist!

As we saw earlier, Simons and Chabris (2011) found that 48% of the public agreed that memories are unchanged over time and Brewin et al. (2019) found that 62.5% agreed that memories are stored permanently. In apparent contrast to these beliefs, Brewin et al. also found that 73% of people agreed that "Memory is constantly being reconstructed and changed every time we remember something".

Myth: repression and 'return of the repressed' are very common

Virtually everyone has heard of Sigmund Freud's notion of repression. According to Freud (1915/1963, p. 86), "The essence of repression lies simply in the function of rejecting and keeping something out of consciousness". Repression was of central importance to Freud's entire psychoanalytical approach to understanding and treating mental disorders. He believed many patients had repressed memories of traumatic or incredibly unpleasant childhood events (especially physical or sexual abuse). The emphasis of psychoanalytic therapy was to allow patients to retrieve these repressed memories as a major part of recovery from mental disorder: this is known as 'return of the repressed'.

Hundreds of millions of people around the world believe firmly in the existence of repression. Patihis et al. (2014) found 77% of the public in the United States and the United Kingdom believe that traumatic experiences are often repressed, and 64% believe these traumatic experiences can be recalled accurately in therapy. There is even evidence that the percentage of people believing in repressed traumatic memories has recently increased from a high baseline (McNally, 2024).

Strikingly, Magnussen et al. (2006) found 40% of Norwegians believe that people who have committed a murder can repress the memory of that event. Personally, I would be exceptionally sceptical if I found myself talking to someone known to have committed a murder who denied all knowledge of having done so.

Otgaar et al. (2019) reviewed research on belief in the existence of repressed memories by clinical psychologists, other professionals for whom it is important to assess others' memory accurately (e.g., judges; child-protection workers) and members of the public. Overall, 58% expressed belief in repressed memories. For example, Merckelbach and Wessel (1998) found 94% of students had this belief. Of note, 70% of clinical psychologists (the group that should be the most knowledgeable) recognised the existence of repressed memories and the percentage has increased over recent years.

It is often assumed that Freud believed that repression is invariably an unconscious process. That assumption is incorrect. Freud mostly referred to unconscious repression but he also believed there could be deliberate suppression of traumatic memories. For example, Freud sometimes used repression to refer to the inhibition of the capacity for emotional experience (Madison, 1956). According to this definition, repression can occur even when there is conscious awareness of traumatic thoughts provided those thoughts lack emotional content.

When members of the public express a belief in repression, do they do so because they believe in unconscious or deliberate suppression of unpleasant thoughts? Dodier et al. (2021) found 71% of their participants accepted the concept of repression, 74% accepted unconscious repression, and 54% accepted deliberate memory suppression. Thus, most lay people who believe in the existence of repression do so because they believe in unconscious repression.

Research evidence

The picture presented so far has been one-sided. We have seen that a majority of clinical psychologists and members of the public believe in the existence of repression (especially unconscious repression). In order to correct the balance, we must also consider the views of memory experts. They are significantly more sceptical of the existence of repressed memories than practising therapists, students and members of the public (Patihis et al., 2021).

Huge numbers of individuals claim to have had recovered memories. Patihis and Pendergrast (2019) discovered that 4% of adult Americans reported recovered memories of abuse in therapy for which they had no previous memory. The implication is that an amazing 9 million Americans have experienced recovered memories! However, their key finding (casting serious doubt on the genuineness of these reported recovered memories) is that they were 20 times more prevalent among patients whose therapists had discussed the possibility of repressed memories than those whose therapists had not done so.

McNally (2024) discussed experimental evidence that also raises questions about the genuineness of many recovered memories. Individuals reporting recovered memories of childhood sexual abuse have greater difficulty than controls in distinguishing between memories of things perceived from things imagined than controls under laboratory conditions.

One of the most important studies in this area was carried out by Geraerts et al. (2007). They identified three groups of adults who had experienced childhood sexual abuse: (1) suggestive therapy group: individuals whose original recovered memories occurred *inside* therapy; (2) spontaneous recovery group: individuals whose original recovered memories occurred *outside* therapy; and (3) continuous memory group: individuals who had continuously accessible memories of sexual abuse from childhood onwards.

Geraerts et al. (2007) assessed the genuineness of the alleged recovered memories of these three groups of patents by taking account of corroborating evidence (e.g., the abuser had confessed; someone else had also claimed to have been abused by the same person). They discovered corroborating evidence for 45% of the continuous memory group, for 37% of the spontaneous memory group, but for 0% of the suggestive therapy group. Thus, recovered memories initially recalled inside therapy are probably much less likely to be genuine than those initially recalled outside therapy.

Findings consistent with those of Geraerts et al. (2007) had been reported earlier by Lief and Fetkewicz (1995). They studied patients who admitted they had previously reported false recovered memories. Approximately 80% of those patients had had a therapist who strongly suggested they had been sexually abused in childhood. However, it is not easy to establish the truth of such retracted allegations: social support and social influence were often important determinants of the decisions to report and then repudiate alleged childhood abuse (Ost, 2017).

How can we best explain repressed memories?

We have seen that Freud's theoretical approach to repression is more complex than is typically assumed. However, one of Freud's key assumptions was that the central reason why repression occurs is to reduce the intolerable anxiety associated with traumatic memories. It follows that the likelihood of repression occurring for memories of childhood physical and/or sexual abuse should increase progressively as the distress and trauma associated with such memories increase.

Contrary to the previous prediction, however, memory is generally *better* for strongly negative emotional events than for less emotional events (Bowen et al., 2018). Goodman et al. (2019) also obtained findings inconsistent with the Freudian account. They carried out a longitudinal study on childhood maltreatment (including sexual abuse). Greater traumatic impact of the abuse and greater distress associated with it were both associated with more accurate subsequent memory for the abuse. In similar fashion, war veterans traumatised by gruesome acts they have committed or witnesses typically remember these acts very vividly for several decades thereafter (McNally, 2003).

Pope and Hudson (1995) argued that Freud's repression theory would receive support if research fulfilled two criteria. There should be confirmatory evidence that the alleged childhood abuse actually happened and that the individuals concerned developed amnesia for that abuse. Pope and Hudson searched through the relevant literature but discovered no studies satisfying both criteria.

Otgaar et al. (2021) pointed out that unconscious repression is highly similar (or identical) to dissociative amnesia (see Chapter 8). According to the fifth edition of the *Diagnostic and Statistical Manual of Mental Disorders* (DSM-5; American Psychiatric Association, 2013) dissociative amnesia "involves a period of time when there is an inability to recall important biographical information . . .[it is] always potentially reversible because the memory has been successfully stored" (p. 298).

Suppose that dissociative amnesia (or unconscious repression) is a genuine phenomenon. According to Pope et al. (2007), we would expect to find numerous accounts of repressed memory or dissociative amnesia in the world's literature in the era before Sigmund Freud and other psychologists popularised it. They tested this expectation by offering $1,000 to the first person providing an example of a repressed memory or dissociative amnesia for a traumatic event in any work of fiction or non-fiction prior to 1800. They received over 100 replies referring to works in many different languages. However, none of the works cited contained a clear account of a repressed memory.

We saw earlier that patients are far more likely to claim to have recovered repressed memories of childhood abuse when the possibility of such memories was emphasised by their therapist than when it was not. It also needs to be borne in mind that patients (especially in the United States) can sometimes receive huge sums of money by suing the perpetrator of the alleged abuse. In a case in Akron, Ohio, Julie Herald sued her uncle (Dennis Hood) for having sexually abused her between the ages of 3 and 15. She was awarded $5 million in punitive damages plus a further $150,000 in compensatory damages (Fields, 1992), which is the equivalent of £10 million today.

Many memory experts (e.g., Ceci & Loftus, 1994) subscribe to the false-memory perspective, according to which numerous recovered memories of childhood abuse are false (especially those originally recalled during recovered-memory therapy). This perspective is often contrasted with the approach of Freud, who allegedly believed recovered memories are genuine. Ironically, there is a substantial overlap (although generally ignored!) between the two approaches.

Freud expressed various views concerning the nature of repressed memories of childhood abuse at different times (Ahbel-Rappe, 2006). Freud (1896) argued for the genuineness of such memories even though the patients he treated were very reluctant to accept his interpretation that they had been sexually abused. Freud bizarrely regarded this reluctance as evidence that his interpretation was correct!

Ten years later, Freud (1906) pointed out that his earlier views implied that there were far more cases of childhood sexual abuse than seemed plausible, one of the main points made 100 years later by advocates of the false-memory perspective. This realisation led Freud to change his mind: "I have learned to explain a number of fantasies of seduction as attempts at fending off memories of the subject's own sexual activity (infantile masturbation)" (p. 274). Thus, Freud had become a believer in false memories!

According to false-memory theorists, it should be relatively easy to create false childhood memories under controlled laboratory conditions. The most popular way of testing this prediction is by using the 'lost-in-the-mall' technique (Loftus & Pickrell, 1995). Adults are given descriptions of child-hood events allegedly provided by their parents or other family members. One event is made up by the researchers but all the others are genuine. After that, the participants recall these childhood events on two or three occasions using techniques resembling those used in therapy to produce recovered memories. Finally, there is an interview designed to assess whether or not the participants have formed a false memory.

Scoboria et al. (2017) reviewed eight studies where the 'lost-in-the-mall' technique had been used. They discovered that 30% of participants developed a false memory and a further 23% accepted the false memory as genuine to some extent. These findings demonstrate that false memories can easily be formed. What is trickier is to decide whether these findings have much relevance when it comes to explaining recovered memories of childhood abuse. It would surely be much harder to produce false memories for traumatic events than for relatively trivial events (e.g., putting a toy in a teacher's desk). For example, I am confident it would be extraordinarily difficult or impossible to persuade you that you murdered someone when you were a child.

Engelhard et al. (2019) argued there are numerous cases of allegedly recovered memories that had not previously been repressed (as claimed by Freud) and that are accurate (in contrast to the prediction from the false-memory perspective). A crucial insight was that children experiencing sexual abuse often fail to interpret it as being traumatic at the time the relevant events occurred.

Support for the previous viewpoint was reported by Clancy and McNally (2005/2006). They discovered only 8% of women with recovered memories of childhood sexual abuse perceived it as traumatic when it occurred. The great majority described their childhood memories as confusing or uncomfortable. In other words, they did not fully understand their experiences as sexually abusive at the time. It may seem incredible that young children could fail to appreciate the appalling nature of the abuse to which they were subjected. However, it perhaps becomes more understandable (but still inexcusable) given that the sexual abuse often consisted of fondling by someone close to them who did not harm or threaten them (McNally, 2012).

Such findings led Engelhard et al. (2019) to provide a theoretical account that was significantly different from previous accounts. In essence, they argued that non-traumatic memories of childhood sexual abuse are *not* repressed but rather are not accessed over a period of years because of "ordinary forgetfulness" (p. 92). These memories are often recalled in adulthood when those who had been abused are presented with relevant triggers or reminders. This often leads them to *reinterpret* their childhood experiences as having been sexually abusive and traumatic. McNally (2012) found that one-third of these adults met diagnostic criteria for post-traumatic stress disorder when they recalled their childhood abuse and reinterpreted it correctly as morally reprehensible behaviour by the adult concerned.

Summary and conclusions

It is hard to establish the truth about the recovery of repressed memories of childhood abuse. The alleged events typically occurred many years previously and there is often no direct corroborating evidence that they actually happened. In addition, patients may have various motives (e.g., financial gain) for claiming to have been sexually abused. Another major reason for scepticism about the genuineness of many allegedly recovered memories is that such memories are predominantly reported by patients whose therapists had explicitly emphasised the possibility that they had been sexually and/or physically abused.

In sum, there is very little evidence to support the notions of repression or return of the repressed. As Otgaar et al. (2022) argued, it is much more plausible to explain these alleged phenomena in terms of ordinary and well-established memory mechanisms (e.g., ordinary forgetfulness).

Myth: amnesic patients have forgotten their pasts

Amnesia (which involves severely impaired memory) is most often caused by closed head injury. However, amnesia has several other potential causes including alcohol abuse (known as Korsakoff's syndrome), brain tumours and the effects of medications (e.g., anti-anxiety drugs such as the benzodiazepines).

Most people have definite views about amnesia and what amnesic patients can and cannot do. For example, 83% of the general public believe the following statement: "People suffering from amnesia typically cannot recall their own name or Identity". In addition, 91% of British people believe amnesic patients who have forgotten who they are and who fail to recognise others can nevertheless be normal in every other way (Chapman & Hudson, 2010) and the comparable figure is 93% for American respondents (Hux et al., 2006). When the same individuals were given the following statement: "After head injury, it is usually harder to learn new things than to remember things from the past", 33% of British people and 52% of Americans agreed with it.

There is a bizarre view that patients becoming amnesic because of a bump on the head can have their memory restored by another bump on the head. Approximately 40% of North Americans subscribe to this viewpoint (Guilmette & Paglia, 2004) as well as 26% of British individuals (Chapman & Hudson, 2010).

Where do the aforementioned beliefs come from? It is perhaps natural to assume that they come from films. Over the years, more than 200 films have focused on amnesia, nearly all making use of these beliefs. For example, in the film *Overboard* (1987), Goldie Hawn falls from her yacht and this shock causes amnesia and a profound change in her personality. She immediately switches from being a rich and spoilt socialite into a loving mother. Subsequently, she remembers her previous identity when she sees her husband again.

As Baxendale (2004) pointed out, profound amnesia in films made in Hollywood "is something of an occupational hazard for professional assassins" (p. 1481). One of the most famous examples is to be found in the Bourne trilogy. Jason Bourne (played by Matt Damon) is a CIA assassin who wakes up with two bullets in his head having been rescued unconscious from the Mediterranean. He has no memory of who he is or what has happened to him. Over time, he gradually recovers his identity. The probable inspiration for Jason Bourne is a real-life American, Ansel Bourne (1826–1910), who had two totally separate identities, each having no knowledge of the other. His condition resembled that found in multiple personality disorder or dissociative identity disorder (see Chapter 8).

Most people's views of amnesia are formed from films they have seen. However, the origins of one prominent misconception about amnesia precedes the start of the movie era. Francois Xavier Bichat was an anatomist and physiologist. In 1805, he proposed Bichat's law of symmetry: the brain's hemispheres are symmetrical and need to operate in synchrony if we are to function effectively. A possible implication of this law is that if your memory is damaged by a blow to one side of the head it might be restored by a blow to the other side of the head restoring symmetry and synchrony.

In the twentieth century, numerous films made use of these ideas (Baxendale, 2004). Consider the film *Tarzan the Tiger* (1929). Tarzan receives a blow to the head which causes amnesia and prevents him from going in pursuit of the villain who has sold Jane (who becomes his wife) into slavery. Mercifully, he receives another blow to the head which removes the amnesia, after which he defeats the villain and rescues Jane.

Research evidence

We turn now to the relevant experimental evidence to see whether there is any validity in most people's beliefs about amnesia. Before doing so, I need to provide some context. Psychologists have identified two main types of amnesia: retrograde and anterograde amnesia. Retrograde amnesia refers to problems in remembering events and information from the time period *prior* to onset of amnesia. In contrast, anterograde amnesia refers to reduced capacity for learning and remembering information encountered *after* the onset of amnesia. In those terms, as discussed earlier, two-thirds of British members of the public and half of Americans believe that retrograde amnesia is typically more severe than anterograde amnesia.

I mentioned earlier that closed head injury is the commonest cause of amnesia. However, most psychological research with amnesic patients has focused on Korsakoff's syndrome (amnesia caused by chronic alcoholism). Why is this? Patients with closed head injury are unsurprisingly very diverse with the extent of the brain damage dependent on the precise nature of the injury. In addition, such patients often have several different cognitive impairments making it hard to interpret their memory deficits. In contrast, patients with Korsakoff's syndrome typically have similar brain damage in the hippocampus and surrounding areas within the medial temporal lobes. More generally, the great majority of amnesic patients have damage to these brain areas.

Retrograde amnesia

Much research on retrograde amnesia has focused on the impact of brain damage on episodic memory (a form of long-term memory concerned with personal experiences). Nairne (2015) identified the three "Ws" of episodic memory: remembering a specific event (*what*) at a given time (*when*) in a given place (*where*). Bayley et al. (2006) found that amnesic patients with damage limited to the hippocampus had essentially intact episodic or auto-biographical memories for events spanning the entire time period from childhood through to the recent past. Patients with more widespread brain damage within the medial temporal lobes had retrograde amnesia for recent events but intact memory for events from childhood and early adulthood.

It is often assumed that episodic memory in amnesic patients has a temporal gradient with the adverse effects of amnesia being greatest for recent memories and least for distant memories. That assumption is approximately correct, and most amnesic patients have reasonably good episodic memories for events occurring well before the onset of amnesia. However, that assumption exaggerates the consistency in the data. Spiers et al. (2001) reviewed 147 cases of amnesia and found some patients had practically no retrograde amnesia whereas others had severe retrograde amnesia for events occurring throughout their pre-amnesia lives.

We will consider two amnesic patients with especially severe retrograde amnesia. First, there is Kent Cochrane (K.C.), an amnesic patient who suffered widespread brain damage (including within the hippocampus) when he rode his motorcycle off an exit ramp of a highway. Before the accident, Kent Cochrane had been a thrill-seeking and adventurous individual but afterwards he became tranquil and soft-spoken (Gao et al., 2020). When his memory was tested, it emerged that, "He cannot recollect any personally experienced events" (Tulving, 2002, p. 13).

The most famous amnesic was Henry Molaison (H.M.). He underwent brain surgery to reduce his severe epileptic symptoms. This surgery involved the removal of the medial temporal lobes (including the hippocampus). It was initially believed that Henry Molaison had preserved episodic memories for personal events going back to childhood. However, thorough investigation revealed that these memories were very impoverished (Steinvorth et al., 2005) and his memories for childhood events was as bad as his memory for events occurring closer in time to the onset of amnesia.

Why have views concerning the extent of Henry Molaison's retrograde amnesia for personal events changed over the years? Of central importance is the distinction between episodic memory (which involves re-experiencing previous events) and semantic memory (a form of long-term memory consisting of general knowledge about the world, language and so on). An individual's memory for personal events in their lives can be based on episodic or semantic memory. For example, you may remember your first day at secondary school as being a mixture of exciting and frightening (episodic memory) or as an event that took place on 4 September (personal semantic memory).

It is thus possible that the pre-amnesia personal events remembered by some amnesic patients may depend heavily on semantic memory and so not be 'genuine' episodic memories involving re-experiencing. That was the case with Henry Molaison. As we have seen, Steinvorth et al. (2005) found he had practically no episodic memories for his past. However, when his personal semantic memories were assessed by asking him to supply facts about his personal past, his recall of such facts was in the normal range for events of childhood and early adulthood.

Kent Cochrane also had preserved general semantic memory for the time period before amnesia onset. When shown family photographs from different periods of his life, Kent Cochrane named everyone in all the photographs, thus indicating relevant semantic memories. However, he had minimal (or non-existent) episodic memories of the events shown in the photographs.

In sum, retrograde amnesia is sometimes greater than most memory researchers believe but more in line with the beliefs of numerous members of the public. However, the great majority of amnesic patients exhibit substantially less retrograde amnesia than is generally believed to be the case.

Anterograde amnesia

What about anterograde amnesia (i.e., the inability to learn and remember events occurring following the onset of amnesia)? It was almost total in Kent Cochrane and Henry Molaison. For example, Kent Cochrane continued to react with horror and disbelief every time he was told about 9/11. He repeatedly said he had never met Shayna Rosenbaum before even though she was a researcher he had seen approximately eight times a year over a 5-year period. In similar fashion, Henry Molaison failed to recognise doctors and other people he had met numerous times, he had no idea where he lived, and he could not remember where he had eaten his last meal (Eichenbaum & Cohen, 2023).

Over a week of testing, H.M. made fewer and fewer mistakes on a mirror-tracing task (drawing objects seen only in reflection), even though he never remembered ever having done the task before and had to have the goal explained to him each day. In other words, his declarative memory for the rules of the game and for experiencing it in the past was impaired, but his memory for how to perform the task (procedural memory) was spared.

You may be wondering whether findings from a single amnesic patient are sufficient to overthrow most people's beliefs about amnesia. In fact, H.M.'s memory problems were significantly greater than those of the great majority of amnesic patients with hippocampal damage (Aly & Ranganath, 2018). Reassuringly, in the years since the original research on H.M., numerous other amnesic patients have exhibited a similar (although less dramatic) pattern (Eichenbaum & Cohen, 2023).

Summary and conclusions

On the face of it, the accumulating empirical evidence has demonstrated that several beliefs about amnesia are myths. First, it is a myth that most amnesic patients have completely lost their memories of past events. Second, it is a myth that amnesic patients find it easier to remember new experiences after the onset of amnesia than to remember experiences pre-dating the amnesia. Third, it is a myth that patients becoming amnesic because of a blow to the head can recover as a result of a second blow to the head.

Coverage of these myths by psychologists (e.g., Lilienfeld et al., 2010) usually concludes that people are totally misguided in believing any of these myths. In contrast, I would argue that the true situation is more nuanced (at least so far as the first two myths are concerned). Some amnesic patients (e.g., Henry Molaison; Kent Cochrane) have essentially no personal memories of events occurring before they became amnesic, with the memories they do recall being based on semantic rather than episodic memory. However, these amnesic patients are very unrepresentative of amnesic patients in general, the great majority of whom have reasonable good memory for their pre-amnesia personal experiences (especially those dating from some time prior to the onset of amnesia).

With respect to anterograde amnesia, it is certainly true that most amnesic patients have a very poor ability to remember consciously their experiences that occur following the onset of amnesia. However, they have *not* lost the ability to engage in new learning. Consider procedural memory, which is memory concerned with knowing how to perform skilled actions in the absence of conscious awareness of what has been learned. Spiers et al. (2001) reviewed 147 cases of amnesia and discovered that all showed intact skill learning following the onset of amnesia.

Finally, it would be totally unethical to test the assumption that patients who have become amnesic through a blow to the head would have their memory restored by another blow to the head. However, all our understanding of how the brain works would indicate that this approach would probably increase amnesic patients' memory problems and definitely would not reduce them.

Myth: the only function of (episodic) memory is to provide access to our past experiences

We all have numerous memories about the past which we typically access by using episodic memory (although autobiographical memory can also be involved). According to Tulving (2002, p. 5), episodic memory, "makes possible mental time travel through subjective time from the present to the past, thus allowing one to re-experience . . . one's own previous experiences". As discussed earlier, it involves remembering the what, when and where of personal events (Nairne, 2015).

So far, so obvious. We have seen that our personal memories (recalled using episodic memory) are exclusively concerned with the past, which seems naturally to lead to the conclusion that episodic memory is all about the past. However, that poses a problem for two reasons. First, it is not immediately clear that episodic memory is of much use to us in our everyday lives. It may be fun to use episodic memory (or autobiographical memory) to think back over memorable life experiences, but that does not make it of much value as we cope with the day-to-day pressures of life.

Second, as Schacter and Addis (2007, p. 773) pointed out, "Episodic memory is . . . a fundamentally constructive rather than reproductive process that is prone to various kinds of errors and illusions". Thus, the puzzle is to explain why we have a memory system (i.e., episodic memory) that appears to have limited usefulness and is not reliably accurate. It seems doubtful that evolutionary processes would have provided us with a memory system that only allows us to indulge in nostalgia for our past experiences.

Past vs. future

While it seems natural to assume that the episodic-memory system's sole function is to allow us to access our stored memories of past experiences, it is increasingly recognised that is not the whole story. Towards the end of the nineteenth century, Bradley (1887) wrote an article entitled, "Why do we remember forwards and not backwards?" According to him, "The answer . . . is practical necessity. Life being a process of decay and of continual repair and a struggle throughout against dangers, our thoughts, if we are to live, must mainly go the way of anticipation" (p. 581).

Over a century later, Schacter and colleagues (e.g., Schacter & Addis, 2007) proposed their constructive episodic simulation hypothesis providing a more detailed account of how memory can be used to anticipate the future. The key assumption was that episodic memory is used to imagine what might happen in the future and to plan that future as well as simply providing access to past events. In other words, there are important similarities between episodic memory retrieval of past events and episodic simulation of hypothetical future events. However, episodic simulation is more demanding because it involves the use of control processes to combine details from several past episodic memories.

Schacter and Addis's (2007) constructive episodic simulation hypothesis helps to explain why episodic memory is constructive (information from various sources is combined) and so does not provide a literal reproduction of the past. Its constructive nature makes episodic memory fallible but also gives it the substantial advantage of flexibility. This flexibility allows us to imagine future possibilities in novel and creative ways that would simply not be possible if episodic memory were accurate but rigid and inflexible.

Research evidence

The main claim of the constructive episodic simulation hypothesis is that a central core of cognitive processes associated with episodic simulation is common to remembering past episodic events and imagining future events. This hypothesis can be tested in several ways, all of which have provided supportive evidence.

Benoit and Schacter (2015) reviewed research where brain activity during episodic retrieval and episodic simulation was assessed. As predicted by the previous hypothesis, several brain areas were activated during both tasks. Of particular importance, the hippocampus (of central importance in episodic memory and retrieval) was also activated during episodic simulation. As predicted, brain areas (e.g., dorsolateral prefrontal cortex) associated with cognitive control were activated more during episodic simulation than episodic retrieval.

Benoit and Schacter (2015) showed that imagining future events is generally *associated* with hippocampal activation. However, such evidence does not show that the hippocampus is *causally* involved in imagining future events. We could obtain stronger and more direct evidence by studying amnesic patients with hippocampal damage. All amnesic patients with damage to the hippocampus have great difficulty in acquiring new episodic memories following the onset of amnesia (Spiers et al., 2001). Accordingly, we can predict that amnesic patients should have an impaired ability to imagine future events. Hassabis et al. (2007) found that amnesics' imaginary experiences consisted of isolated fragments lacking the richness and spatial coherence of healthy individuals' experiences.

Schacter and Madore (2016) studied an amnesic patient, K.C. (discussed earlier), with extensive damage to various brain areas including the hippocampus. K.C. could not recall any episodic memories from the past. As predicted, he was also unable to imagine any hypothetical future events.

We have just seen that humans having very poor ability to recall past episodic memories are also very deficient at imagining potential future events. Another prediction is that humans with good episodic memory for past events should perform well when imagining hypothetical future events. Of relevance here is research on developmental changes (Clayton & Wilkins, 2018). Three-year-old children perform badly on tests of episodic memory and episodic future thinking, performance on both tests is transitional in four-year olds, and five-year olds pass tests of episodic memory and episodic future thinking. Thus, there is a tight linkage between episodic memory ability and future thinking ability.

We can apply a similar logic to cross-species comparisons: species with good episodic memory should also exhibit good future thinking and planning. Several non-human species demonstrate elements of episodic memory. There is clear behavioural evidence that great apes, rodents and corvids (crows) can remember the main features of past events (e.g., what food they have hidden away; where that food is; and when they hid it) (Clayton, 2017). As predicted, these species are also good at executing plans for future events (Clayton, 2017).

The accumulating evidence that there are great similarities between the processes involved in episodic memory and those involved in imagining the future raises an important issue: how do we distinguish between remembered and imagined episodic representations? According to Mahr et al. (2023), cultural learning is important. For example, parents may gently indicate that their child's claimed memories of various events are actually imaginary, as a result of which the child gradually learns to interpret their episodic representations accurately as memories or imaginations.

Creativity

We have seen that the processes underlying episodic memory can be used to imagine the future. It is also becoming clear that these same processes are involved in creative thinking. Of particular interest has been divergent creative thinking, which involves generating multiple possible solutions to a given problem. It is typically assessed using the Alternate Uses Task (AUT). On this task, participants produce as many alternate uses of a common object (e.g., a brick) as they can. The number of uses produced provides a measure of divergent creative thinking.

Two lines of research indicate that episodic retrieval plays an important role in creative thinking. First, since amnesic patients have severe problems with episodic memory, such patients should have impaired divergent creative thinking on the AUT. As predicted, amnesic patients perform much worse than healthy controls on various tests of creative thinking including the AUT (Duff et al., 2013).

Second, if episodic retrieval is involved in divergent creative thinking, we would predict that similar brain regions are activated during episodic memory, imagining the future and divergent thinking. Beaty et al. (2018) discovered that several core regions (e.g., the hippocampus) were activated during the performance of all three tasks.

Beaty et al. (2018) obtained only correlational evidence which does not demonstrate these brain areas are directly involved in performing the various tasks. Thakral et al. (2020) addressed this issue by using transcranial magnetic stimulation (TMS) to disrupt the functioning of the hippocampus (of key importance to episodic memory). TMS led to reduced hippocampal activity. Of most importance, it caused participants to generate fewer episodic details when they imagined the future and to produce fewer creative ideas on the Alternative Uses Task (AUT). Such evidence suggests episodic retrieval is causally involved in divergent creative thinking.

Thakral et al. (2021) investigated the assumption that the same flexible and constructive episodic memory system that enhances divergent creative thinking can also make memory error-prone. Accordingly, they made the counterintuitive prediction that individuals making the most use of episodic memory would have the best performance on a creative thinking task but would also make the most errors. As predicted, there was a correlation of 0.49 between divergent thinking and memory errors.

Evidence that episodic retrieval plays a role in divergent creative thinking does exclude the possibility that other memory systems are also involved. Gerver et al. (2023) discovered there was a modest relationship between episodic memory and divergent creative thinking on the AUT. However, there was a stronger relationship between semantic memory (general knowledge about concepts and the world) and divergent creative thinking. Individuals with high semantic memory have formed more associations among the concepts they know than those with low semantic memory and so can think more creatively.

Conclusions

Until comparatively recently, most research on episodic memory focused solely on individuals' ability to remember past personal events accurately. However, what is actually most important is to use episodic memory to anticipate and plan for possible future events. There is compelling evidence that episodic memory processes are involved both in our recall of the past and our imagining of the future. There is also accumulating evidence that creative thinking also depends in part on episodic memory processes.

What is required is to develop an enhanced understanding of precisely *how* episodic memory allows us to anticipate and imagine the future. Most episodic memories relate to highly specific events occurring at a given time and such specific memories are typically of limited value when predicting the future. However, what actually happens is that an initially detail-rich episodic representation is transformed into a gist-like representation involving semantic memory (general knowledge) (Robin & Moscovitch, 2017). Such gist-like representations capture the essence of what we have experienced in the past and provide a much better basis for anticipating the future than is provided by specific episodic memories.

Myth: forgetting is a bad thing

It is generally believed that forgetting is a bad thing. This is perhaps especially the case among middle-aged people who may be worried that any increase in forgetting is potentially an indication they are in the early stages of Alzheimer's disease. What is indisputable is that we have all had embarrassing experiences due to forgetting. For example, when introducing people to each other, you have probably occasionally realised with a sinking feeling that you have forgotten someone's name. As Graf (2012) pointed out, people who frequently forget events from the past are regarded as having a "faulty brain".

In spite of the bad publicity forgetting has received, it is often desirable and useful. Suppose you were in the apparently enviable position of remembering everything perfectly. The human being who probably represented the closest approximation to that was the famous Russian mnemonist Solomon Shereshevskii (often referred to as S.). His extraordinary memory ability was discovered when he worked as a journalist. The editor of the paper he was working on noticed that S. could repeat back verbatim everything that was said to him without making any notes. The psychologist Alexander Luria (1968) found S. could remember lists of over 100 digits perfectly over several years. According to Luria, "There was no limit either to the *capacity* of S.'s memory or to the *durability* of the traces he retained".

An important part of S.'s secret was that he had exceptional imagery powers and synaesthesia (the tendency for processing in one modality to evoke other sense modalities). For example, when hearing a tone, he said, "It looks like fireworks tinged with a pink-red hue". Ironically, however, his memory was so fantastic that it had a hugely disruptive effect on his everyday life. For example, when he was listening to a prose passage, this was his experience: "Each word calls up images, they collide with one another, and the result is chaos" (Luria, 1968, p. 65). Sadly, S. eventually ended up in an asylum.

The potentially destructive power of having an excellent memory is also shown by the case of Jill Price. She is an American woman with highly superior autobiographical memory due to her obsessional interest in the events of her life, which she describes as follows: "This is OCD [obsessive-compulsive disorder]. I have OCD of my memories". You may envy her ability to recall phenomenal amounts of information about her past. However, she regards it as a major problem: "I call it a burden. I run my entire life through my head every day and it drives me crazy!!!" (Parker et al., 2006).

Jill Price is not unique. Indeed, many other individuals with highly superior autobiographical memory have as many obsessional symptoms as clinical patients with obsessive-compulsive disorder (Santangelo et al., 2018).

The notion that forgetting can be very useful was first proposed long before research was conducted on remarkable individuals such as Solomon Shereshevskii and Jill Price. For example, according to the great psychologist William James (1890, p. 680), "If we remembered everything, we should on most occasions be as ill off as if we remembered nothing". However, proving there is nothing new under the sun, advocacy of the virtues of forgetting go back at least as far as the Roman orator, lawyer and politician Marcus Tullius Cicero (106–43 BC). In his *De Oratore*, Themistoclesis offers him the secret of perfect memory. Cicero replied that it would, "oblige him much more if [the speaker] could instruct him how to forget . . . what he chose" (Cicero, 2009).

If august figures such as Cicero and William James are correct, then forgetting must serve various useful functions. Nørby (2015) identified three such functions. First, deliberate forgetting can enhance our psychological well-being. Stramaccia et al. (2021) found that healthy individuals can suppress memories whereas those with clinical or sub-clinical disorders (e.g., anxiety; depression) cannot. Similarly, most people remember considerably more positive than negative personal or autobiographical events from their past but depressed individuals do not (Groome et al., 2020).

Second, it is useful to forget outdated information causing interference with currently relevant information. For example, you know where most of your friends live. When they move, it is advantageous to forget where they used to live because that it may make it harder to remember where they now live.

Third, it is usually counterproductive to remember all the specific details of information you have heard or read. In general, it is much better to remember the *gist* of what we have seen or heard while discarding or forgetting the details. Here is a trivial example. Suppose you have recently read an exciting novel and a friend asks you to describe it. They confidently expect you to provide an overview of the central themes of the novel rather than producing random sentences verbatim!

Decision making

Richards and Frankland (2017) focused on the crucial issue of the primary functions or purposes of remembering and forgetting. They argued as follows: "The goal of memory is to not the transmission of information through time, *per se*. Rather, the goal of memory is to optimise decision making. As such, transience [forgetting] is as important as persistence [remembering]" (p. 1071).

How does forgetting play a positive role in enhancing decision making? If our decision making is to be effective, it is important we are not bombarded by numerous conflicting memories (Richards & Frankland, 2017). However, we would be highly susceptible to conflicting memories in the absence of forgetting. For most of us, our life changes rapidly. As a consequence, it is valuable to forget outdated information when trying to make decisions about our current environment. The environment is also 'noisy' in the sense that it is very variable over time. Optimal decision making occurs if we forget unusual rare events and instead focus on the overall gist or essence of many events so that we focus on what is the case on average.

Three major roles of forgetting

The advantages of forgetting can be summarised by identifying three major roles that it supports (Fawcett & Hulbert, 2020). First, the role of Guardian (facilitating an individual's ability to possess a positive, stable and coherent self-image) is assisted by forgetting some negative self-relevant information. Second, the role of Librarian (promoting efficient cognitive functioning) is supported by forgetting that reduces mental clutter, updates our memories and eliminates specific details to permit the acquisition of a general knowledge base. Third, the role of Inventor (encouraging the development of flexible exploration and creativity) is supported by forgetting that assists us in escaping from outdated ideas and strategies from the past.

In sum, while forgetting elements of the past can often have negative consequences, it is also important to consider the positive consequences of forgetting. As Fawcett and Hulbert (2020, p. 12) pointed out,

> If the need to accurately predict the future has fundamentally shaped our ability to draw upon the past, then much of the transience, distortions, and biases associated with memory can be viewed as a part of a larger plan for the world's inhabitants to survive and thrive.

Prospective forgetting

So far I have focused exclusively on forgetting of events and knowledge from the past (known as retrospective forgetting). However, it is also important to consider prospective memory failures (i.e., forgetting to carry out some intended action). For example, you may have had the experience of totally forgetting to meet up with a good friend of yours. Someone with deficient prospective memory is regarded as a "flaky person" (Graf, 2012). It would seem reasonable to assume that failures of prospective memory would be exceptionally rare if it is very important to carry out the intended action. However, this assumption is dubious.

Failures of prospective memory can be fatal. Dismukes and Nowinski (2006) studied 75 cases where pilot memory failures caused an incident or accident. In 74 of those cases, the failure involved prospective memory. For example, on 31 August 1988, a Boeing 727 was in a long queue awaiting departure from Dallas-Fort Worth airport. The crew members forgot to set the wing flaps and leading edge slat to 15 degrees in anticipation of take-off (a failure of prospective memory) because they were unexpectedly instructed to move up past the other planes on the runway. As a consequence, the plane crashed beyond the end of the runway causing 14 deaths and 76 injuries.

The key reason pilots exhibit failures of prospective memory is because their usual routine is interrupted by some unexpected event. Latorella (1998) found that commercial pilots interrupted while flying in a simulator made 53% more errors than those not interrupted.

Failures of prospective memory are also of central importance in "hot car deaths" (deaths of children from heatstroke due to their parents failing to take them out of a car). Tragically, almost 40 children a year die of heatstroke in cars in the United States. For example, consider the case of one-year-old Ray Ray Reeves-Cavaliero who died on 25 May 2011. Her father (Brett) should have turned left to the daycare centre at a T-junction but mistakenly turned right and drove straight to work.

Diamond (2019) reviewed several cases of hot car deaths. Such deaths often occur because there are very few environmental cues to remind the parent that their infant is in the car. In the previous case, nearly all of Brett Reeves-Cavaliero's drive to work on that fateful morning was the one he would have taken if his infant daughter had not been in the car. In addition, a parent may forget their child is in the car if he/she is unusually quiet.

Mercifully, fatal failures of prospective memory by pilots or parents are exceptionally rare. However, other much more common prospective-memory failures are also potentially dangerous. For example, Avci et al. (2018) reviewed research on the relationship between prospective-memory performance and adherence to medication by patients with HIV/AIDS. Patients with poor prospective memory were much less adherent to their medication than those with good prospective memory, a form of forgetting that can have serious health consequences.

In sum, forgetting in the form of failures of prospective memory can have catastrophic consequences. Thus, while forgetting often conveys benefits with respect to retrospective memory, it is less desirable with respect to prospective memory. It is noteworthy that those emphasising the advantages of forgetting (e.g., Nørby, 2015; Fawcett & Hulbert, 2020) have ignored prospective-memory failures.

Conclusions and summary

There is compelling evidence that retrospective forgetting of the past can often prove beneficial. Among other advantages, it allows us to maintain or enhance psychological well-being and one's self-image, to forget outdated information, to eliminate the trivial details of what we have experienced, and it can also promote effective decision making and creativity. However, the advantages of prospective forgetting are less obvious, and it can lead to tragic consequences such as plane crashes or 'hot car deaths'.

If retrospective forgetting is so useful, why do most of us believe that forgetting is a weakness and a problem? Consider what happens when you are engaged in decision making. The quality of your decision making may be enhanced by forgetting of trivial or irrelevant information. However, you are very unlikely to have any conscious awareness of the success of your forgetting mechanisms. Alternatively, your decision making may be impaired by failures of forgetting leading to retrieval of information that interferes with the decision-making process. You would probably be unaware that forgetting failures are having a disruptive effect. In sum, we de-emphasise the usefulness of retrospective forgetting because we are typically unaware of the useful role it plays in our everyday lives.

4 Thinking and cognition

There are an estimated 8.7 million species of animals (mostly invertebrates) and plants on our planet. It has also been estimated that approximated 99% of all the species that have ever lived are extinct. In this tough Darwinian world, the dominance of the human species can rightly be regarded as an extraordinary achievement.

How did we achieve this dominance? It clearly doesn't depend on physical attributes: many other species are larger and stronger than we are, and numerous other species can move faster than we can or have superior eyesight and hearing. The obvious answer is that we possess superior cognitive abilities and intelligence. In principle, this superiority could take two forms. First, humans may possess cognitive abilities totally lacking in other species: human exceptionalism. For example, human intelligence is unique because we are conscious, possess language and can think rationally. Second, other species may possess the same (or similar) cognitive abilities to us but to a much lesser extent.

Laland and Seed (2021) reviewed research on five cognitive abilities that are arguably unique to humans: mental time travel (e.g., imagining the future); tool use; problem solving; social cognition and communication. They discovered that none of these abilities is unique to humans, leading them to the following conclusion: "Other animals possess specialist competencies that can rival our own, but no other species consistently outperforms humans across multiple cognitive domains" (p. 705).

One might imagine that humans would be intensely relaxed about their superiority to all other species and metaphorically pat themselves on the back. In fact, however, millions of people are optimistic they can become even more intelligent if they set our minds to it. They believe they could achieve outstanding performance in any given domain if they devote thousands of hours to practice, that they could become significantly more intelligent by engaging in brain training and that they could use their brains much more effectively if they could find a way to use more than 10% of their brains.

Interestingly, millions of people hold beliefs that seem much more pessimistic about the excellence of human thinking and intelligence. We consider two examples in this chapter. First, it is widely believed that people's decision

DOI: 10.4324/9781003596677-4

making would be improved if they relied less on rational thinking and more on intuition. Second, most people think that human intelligence is in imminent danger of being dwarfed by artificial intelligence (AI). Indeed, some AI experts believe that the time will come when humans effectively become the slaves of AI systems rather than their master.

Myth: 10,000 hours of practice produce outstanding performance

You have probably heard of the '10,000-hour rule'. This is the notion that outstanding expertise in any given domain requires 10,000 hours (or 10 years) of intensive practice or training. This notion originated in the research and theorising of Anders Ericsson, a Swedish psychologist who lived for several decades in the United States. In a very influential article, Ericsson et al. (1993, p. 392) made the following claim:

> [H]igh levels of deliberate practice are necessary to attain expert level performance. Our theoretical framework can also provide a sufficient account of the major facts about the nature and scarcity of exceptional performance. Our account does not depend on scarcity of innate ability (talent).

What did Ericsson et al. (1993) mean by 'deliberate practice'? It is characterised by four key features. First, the practice task is neither too easy nor too hard. Second, the learner receives informative feedback about their performance. Third, the learner has the opportunity to repeat the task. Fourth, the learner is able to correct their errors.

Ericsson made two key assumptions. First, deliberate practice is *necessary* for the development of high levels of expertise. Second, such practice is also *sufficient* (implying that other factors such as talent are not required).

Several writers of popular books have endorsed Ericsson's theory. Notably, Malcolm Gladwell (2008), in his best-selling book entitled *Outliers: The story of success*, wrote that "10,000 h is the magic number of true expertise" (p. 11). In fairness, he mentioned the role of talent in passing but he attached far more importance to prolonged practice.

Research evidence

As predicted by Ericsson's theoretical approach, level of expertise in any domain is typically correlated or associated with the amount of practice. For example, Campitelli and Gobet (2011) found in a review that total practice hours correlated approximately 0.50 with chess-playing expertise, indicating a relatively close relationship between the two variables. Discovering that two variables are correlated does not demonstrate that one causes the other. However, it seems plausible that number of hours spent practising would have a causal impact on expertise.

Ericsson's theory is attractive. It implies that anyone could become out-standingly successful in any domain if they were willing to devote huge amounts of time to deliberate practice. In other words, you could become the next Mozart, Shakespeare and Serena Williams. If only!

Can you see any potential problems with Ericsson's theory? One key issue Ericsson (and Gladwell) ignored was the following: why do individu-als in any given domain of expertise (e.g., chess; golf; music) differ so much in the amount of time they devote to deliberate practice? Individuals with high levels of innate talent typically enjoy early success which is likely to motivate them to devote much extra time to practice. In contrast, someone totally lacking in talent would be very ill-advised to devote thousands of hours to the impossibly difficult task of becoming an expert. Thus, a major reason why amount of practice is moderately associated with performance is because early successful (or unsuccessful) performance strongly influences subsequent practice hours.

Support for the previous interpretation of the evidence was reported by Mosing et al. (2014) in a twin study on music practice and music ability. Genetic factors (ignored by Ericsson) accounted for between 40% and 70% of individual differences in the numbers of hours devoted to music prac-tice, a finding most easily explained by assuming that individuals with more innate talent practised more. Another finding inconsistent with Ericsson's theory was that there was no difference in music ability between monozy-gotic (identical) twins who differed in the hours they devoted to practice. Overall, the relationship between music practice and music ability depended mostly on genetic factors rather than the environmental factors emphasised by Ericsson.

The notion that the number of hours of deliberate practice is all-important is also disproved by the Norwegian chess player Magnus Carlsen. He became a chess grandmaster at the extraordinarily young age of 13 and the world champion at the age of 22 in November 2013. In 2014, he was rated the strongest player in the history of chess, and the gap between him and the second-best player (Levon Aronian) was nearly as large as that between the second and fourteenth best players.

Several facts about Carlsen's chess-playing achievements are inconsist-ent with the notion that hours of practice are crucially important (Gobet & Ereku, 2014). He became a grandmaster after only 5 years of deliberate prac-tice although Ericsson claimed that 10 years of such practice are required to attain outstanding expertise. Subsequently, when Carlsen became world champion, he had devoted 7 years fewer to deliberate practice than the aver-age of the next 10 best players in the world. Among the leading 11 players in the world, there was a small *negative* association between rating and the number of years of practice instead of the theoretically predicted strong posi-tive association.

The case of Magnus Carlsen is by no means unique. Consider the cases of Tiger Woods and Serena Williams. Woods became the golf's world number one at the age of 21 and Serena Williams became world number one in women's tennis when only 20. In both cases, the hours of deliberate practice they had accumulated were considerably fewer than those accumulated by most of their less-successful fellow competitors.

Earlier I mentioned a study by Campitelli and Gobet (2011) where total practice hours correlated 0.50 with chess-playing performance. This finding suggests that the amount of practice accounts for 25% of individual differences in performance. More recently, Hambrick et al. (2020) discussed the findings from five meta-analyses (reviews of research findings) addressing this issue. The percentage of individual differences in performance accounted for by hours of deliberate practice varied across meta-analyses from 14% to 37% (average = 24%).

The previous findings indicate that hours of deliberate practice are of importance in accounting for performance levels. However, Ericsson assumed that individual performance differences depend mostly on amount of deliberate practice. That assumption implies that practice hours should account for well over 50% of individual differences in performance. Thus, the findings from *all* five meta-analyses are inconsistent with predictions from Ericsson's theory.

An issue that has bedevilled much research in this area is the appropriate definition of 'deliberate practice'. Numerous definitions have been proposed, and Ericsson himself has changed his mind several times with respect to how best to define the term (Hambrick et al., 2020). There is the further complication that the assessment of practice in many studies consisted simply of the number of hours devoted to practice rather than ensuring that such practice was deliberate. However, it can safely be concluded that hours of deliberate practice account for much less than 50% of individual differences in performance on any reasonable definition of deliberate practice.

The findings become more complex when we delve into the details. Macnamara et al. (2016) reported that hours of practice accounted for 18% of individual differences in sports performance. However, practice hours accounted for only 1% of individual differences in sports performance among *elite* performers compared to 19% for *sub-elite* ones! Nearly all elite performers have benefited from excellent environmental conditions (e.g., top-class coaching; massive competitive experience; sustained deliberate practice) and so large performance differences among them cannot be due to differences in the quality of their environmental conditions. Instead, *differences* among elite performers are due predominantly to genetic factors (especially innate talent).

Ullén et al. (2016) proposed a much more realistic theoretical approach to expertise than the one advocated by Ericsson in their impressive-sounding multi-factorial gene-environment interaction model. The fundamental assumption of the model is that expertise is multiply determined: genetic factors influence an individual's motivation, interests, personality and intelligence and these factors also partly determine the amount of deliberate practice an individual is willing to undergo. Of great importance are *inter-actions* between genes and environment. We can see two examples of such interactions in a twin study by Hambrick and Tucker-Drob (2015). First, genetic influences on music accomplishment were greater among those individuals who engaged in music practice. Second, there were genetic effects on the amount of music practice, and these effects were even greater than genetic effects on music accomplishment.

Conclusions

The notion that the development of outstanding expertise in a specific domain depends solely on the number of hours devoted to practice is a myth that ignores the crucial role of genetic factors. How can we explain the origins of this myth? Several factors are involved. First, psychologists must bear an important part of the blame. Ericsson et al.'s (1993) article has been cited 11,000 times in the psychological literature, and his theoretical views had a transformative effect on expertise research. In fairness, however, many psychologists have criticised Ericsson's approach ever since it was proposed 30 years ago and the critics have recently become more numerous and vociferous.

Second, many people involved in providing coaching and training to individuals seeking to develop expertise are also culpable. The idea that anyone can become an outstanding tennis player, golfer or chess player if they receive huge amounts of well-directed coaching is an excellent recruiting officer for those who are young, ambitious and suggestible.

Third, nearly everyone has discovered that their performance in any given domain typically increases progressively (if slowly!) as they devote more and more time to practice. Thus, we have personal experience of the potentially very large benefits of prolonged practice. It is easy to assume that what is true at a *within*-person level is also true at a *between*-person level (Hambrick et al., 2020). In other words, since our personal acquisition of expertise develops very heavily on practice hours, we may assume that practice hours also determine which individuals have higher levels of expertise than others. In fact, this assumption is mistaken. Everyone's performance improves as a result of practice. However, some individuals learn much faster than others and also have considerably greater potential. For example, the outstanding golfers Tiger Woods and Jack Nicklaus both broke par when they were 11 or 12 years old. In contrast, only approximately 0.5% of golfers ever break par in a lifetime of playing golf.

Fourth, it is appealing for all of us to think we have the potential to achieve almost any ambitious goal if we devote 10 years of our lives to it. Indeed, there is a natural tendency to want to believe it is true even though our rational mind tells us that we lack the innate talent or ability to be outstandingly successful.

Myth: brain training improves your brain functioning and intelligence

Millions of people have spent literally billions of pounds on various brain-training apps such as *Lumosity, Peak* and *Elevate* in the hope or expectation that these apps would make their brains work more efficiently and intelligently. This expectation is very widespread. Furnham and Horne (2021) found 77% of people accepted the following statement as true: "Brain training programs can raise IQ". Ng et al. (2020) reported that 80% of people believe "brain-training" programs enhance thinking ability. Most people were also confident that several other cognitively and intellectually stimulating activities would also enhance brain function. For example, 85% believed that learning a new language or how to play a musical instrument would improve brain function and 80% thought brain function would be enhanced by solving crossword puzzles.

It is often thought that the belief that the brain or mind can be trained to work more effectively has relatively recent origins. Nothing could be further from the truth as can be seen in the following passage from the Dhammapada written in the third century BC (Buddhaghosa, 1996):

The mind is very hard to check.
And swift it falls on what it wants;
The training of the mind is good,
A mind so tamed brings happiness.

The aforementioned beliefs all relate to transfer of training. If training on an initial task facilitates the learning of (and performance on) a second task, we have positive transfer. Thus, all brain-training programs are designed to produce positive transfer to general brain function. It seems plausible that these programs would have general beneficial effects if we think of the brain as a muscle: if you exercise a muscle, it typically becomes stronger and works more effectively. In fact, however, the brain is *not* a muscle and its workings are hugely more complex than those of any muscle.

Psychologists distinguish between near transfer and far transfer (although there is no clear-cut dividing line between the two). "Near transfer" refers to beneficial effects of training when two tasks are *similar* to each other (e.g., mastering one mobile phone facilitates mastering another one). In contrast, "far transfer" describes beneficial effects when two tasks are *dissimilar*. Our focus will be primarily on far transfer: the claims made by those advocating brain-training programs relate to far transfer and there is overwhelming evidence for near transfer.

Research findings

How effective has brain training been in enhancing thinking and intelligence? Starkly different answers have been provided by expert psychologists.

In 2014, an international group of more than 70 scientists argued there is no good evidence that brain training is effective. This led another international group of 133 scientists to claim that "a substantial and growing body of evidence shows that certain cognitive-training regimens can significantly improve cognitive function, including in ways that generalise to everyday life" (see Simons et al., 2016, p. 104).

Transfer of training from brain-training programs to thinking ability or intelligence (if found) would exemplify far transfer. More specifically, many brain-training programs are designed to enhance the functioning of working memory. Working memory is involved in very general processes such as attentional control (e.g., minimising distractibility), shifting attention optimally to focus on the most relevant information within a current problem and the short-term storage of information. The great importance of working memory is indicated by the finding that individuals with high working memory capacity are generally more intelligent than those with low capacity (Kovacs & Conway, 2016). It seems plausible that brain-training programs enhancing working memory would exhibit far transfer to numerous cognitively demanding tasks.

Shipstead et al. (2012) carried out the first meta-analysis on the effects of working memory training. There were small and often non-significant effects on attention and long-term memory. Of most importance, any beneficial effects were typically found only on tasks very similar to those used in training. Thus, there was evidence of near transfer but not far transfer.

Gathercole et al. (2019) provided an updated meta-analytic review of research on the effects of working memory training. The positive effects of such training were nearly all only small or moderate and were greatest when the original task and the subsequent transfer task were the same or very similar.

Similar findings were reported by Kassai et al. (2019). They reviewed research in which a specific high-level skill (working memory; inhibitory control; or cognitive flexibility) was trained. There was moderate transfer when the transfer task required the same high-level skill as the one trained (near transfer). However, there was no transfer effect when the transfer task required a different high-level skill from the one that had been trained (far transfer).

Those believing firmly that brain training has beneficial effects on thinking and intelligence could plausibly argue there are two major limitations with the research studies included in the meta-analyses discussed earlier. First, relatively short periods of time were typically devoted to brain training: Watrin et al. (2022) found the average training time in recent studies was only 13 hours. Since we spend much of our everyday lives practising cognitive skills resembling those incorporated into brain-training programs, more prolonged training periods may be needed to enhance intelligence. Second, there are numerous forms of brain training but research has mostly focused on training designed to enhance working memory.

The first limitation was addressed by Watrin et al. (2022). Their participants received *three* times the typical amount of training over a 2-year period. However, the effects of all this training on fluid intelligence (ability to engage in novel reasoning) and crystallised intelligence (accumulated knowledge and expertise) were non-significant.

Stojanoski et al. (2020) addressed both limitations discussed earlier. They studied more than 1,000 people who had used various brain-training programs for up to 5 years and assessed the effects of these programs with tests of attention, working memory, planning and reasoning. There were no discernible beneficial effects of brain training on any of these tests even among those who had spent the most time engaged in brain training.

In spite of the numerous failures to find any beneficial effects of brain or mind training on intelligence, some researchers have reported significant findings. Au et al. (2015) performed a meta-analysis on 20 brain-training studies and concluded there was an average gain of three to four IQ points. Does the existence of such positive findings indicate that brain training can produce far transfer to intelligence? As discussed later, the answer is a resounding "No".

How can experimental research produce findings misleadingly indicating that brain training enhances intelligence? Consider an informative study by Foroughi et al. (2016). They used two different flyers to recruit participants. One was suggestive ("*Brain training & cognitive enhancement: Numerous studies have shown working memory training can enhance fluid intelligence*") whereas the other was non-suggestive ("*Email today & participate in a study: Need SONA credits? Sign up today and earn up to 5 credits*"). Those who agreed to participate received one hour of brain training before and after completing an intelligence test. It is highly improbable that such limited training could genuinely enhance intelligence.

What did Foroughi et al. (2016) find? As expected, those who had responded to the non-suggestive flyer showed no effect of the brain training. In contrast, responders to the suggestive flyer showed an improvement of between 5 and 10 IQ points. This is a placebo effect rather than a genuine effect of training: the *expectation* that brain training would enhance intelligence produced measurable benefits to tested IQ.

Foroughi et al. (2016) re-analysed findings from the studies included in Au et al.'s (2105) meta-analysis. Participants in most of those studies were explicitly informed they would receive cognitive or brain training and that this training had the potential to improve or enhance intelligence. There was much more evidence of IQ gains in these studies than in those using non-suggestive recruitment methods (see Chapter 10).

Other cognitive activities

Brain or cognitive training has received enormous publicity over the past 20 years. Long before that, however, it was widely believed that other cognitively and intellectually stimulating activities had widespread beneficial effects. For example, it was thought that learning Latin would enhance your reasoning power and intelligence. Such beliefs are still prevalent. As mentioned earlier, Ng et al. (2020) found the great majority of people believe that learning a new language, doing numerous crossword puzzles and learning to play a musical instrument would all increase brain function.

Sala et al. (2019) re-analysed previous meta-analyses of research on chess, video games and music. There was limited evidence that reasoning or intelligence was enhanced more following training in these activities compared to control groups not receiving such training. However, some studies used passive control groups where the participants were not actively engaged in any cognitive task, and so the training and control groups differed in several ways (e.g., expectations that intelligence would increase). As a consequence, it is very hard to interpret the findings from such studies. When these studies were removed from the meta-analyses, chess, video games and music training produced no far transfer at all (see Chapter 11).

Conclusions

The notion that brain training can produce large increases in intelligence or IQ is a myth (although some interesting developments are discussed shortly). Why do so many people subscribe to this myth? One key reason is that it is comforting to think that we could fairly easily increase our intelligence if we so chose. The other key reason is that numerous companies producing brain-training programs have a very strong vested interest in persuading members of the public that their intelligence can rapidly and fairly effortlessly be increased. These issues are discussed further in Chapter 10.

Future directions

Where do we go next? The highest priority is to develop a more theoretical understanding of "the curse of specificity" (i.e., the virtual non-existence of far transfer). Well over 100 years ago, Thorndike and Woodworth (1901) proposed their identical-elements theory. According to this theory, training on one task will only enhance performance on a second task provided the two tasks share identical or common elements. Near transfer occurs because two similar tasks share many elements whereas far transfer does not because two dissimilar tasks share very few common elements.

This theory accounts for most findings but provides a limited approach. The crucial notion of "identical elements" is imprecise and is hard to translate into specific cognitive processes. In addition, there is a real danger of circular reasoning: if there is positive transfer between two tasks, we infer they must share common elements; if there is no transfer, they don't share any identical elements. In other words, the central weakness with the identical-elements theory is that it does not readily generate falsifiable hypotheses.

Some progress has been made recently. von Bastian et al. (2022) argued that most brain-training approaches have attempted to increase cognitive *capacity*. However, it probably better to focus on increasing cognitive *efficiency* (using our existing cognitive capacity more efficiently). One promising route to increasing cognitive efficiency and far transfer is via training meta-cognition (knowledge and beliefs about one's own cognitive processes and performance). For example, Jones et al. (2020) provided meta-cognitive training in three strategies (planning; monitoring; and evaluating) which learners could apply across different tasks. In another study, Carpenter et al. (2019) trained the meta-cognitive ability of increasing the accuracy of learners' estimates of their own performance (Carpenter et al., 2019). In both cases, meta-cognitive training led to significant far transfer.

In sum, it is probably premature to abandon the notion that brain training can have general beneficial effects. One ground for optimism is that (very late in the day) researchers are starting to develop a theoretical understanding of the cognitive processes involved in transfer of training. A second ground for optimism is that very general meta-cognitive processes (e.g., ability to transfer strategies across tasks; ability to assess one's own performance) may permit at least modest increases in brain function and intelligence.

A third ground is that the many thousands of hours we have all spent using our cognitive processes such as working memory and attention appear to have increased our intelligence. This notion is supported by the Flynn effect, which consists of a surprisingly rapid rise in mean IQ in numerous Western countries over the past 50 years. Overall, there was a increase of 2.31 IQ points per decade across many countries (Trahan et al., 2014). However, if we adjust the score to take account of the progressively increasing difficulty of major intelligence tests, the 'true' Flynn effect becomes approximately five points per decade (Gonthier & Gregoire, 2022).

Myth: we only use 10% of our brains

We saw in the previous section that most people have excessively optimistic beliefs about the possibility of increasing their brain power and intelligence. Such beliefs strongly imply that most of us fail to use our brains effectively. It thus comes as no surprise to discover that many people also believe we use only a small fraction of our brains in everyday life. For example, Bensley and Lilienfeld (2015) presented two groups of students with the following statement: "Most people only use 10% of their brains". In one group, 51% agreed and in the other group 60% agreed.

This "ten-percent" myth is closely related to another myth, namely, that we are capable of using much more of our brain power than we typically use. Higbee and Clay (1998) found students believed on average that we use 22% of our potential brain power but that we are capable of using 57% of our brain power. The implication is that we make effective use of only 40% of the brain power we could use!

Where do these myths come from? One obvious reason for their popularity is that it is great news to discover that our brains have huge untapped power. It is flattering to imagine that we could think far more effectively if we could just harness some of the unused 90% of our brains.

These myths have helped to fuel self-help books claiming to provide the secret to unlocking our unused brain power. Some start by going way beyond what we might call the "ten-percent myth". Russell (1984) in *The Brain Book* makes the following startling statement:

> It is frequently stated that we use only 10 percent of our full mental potential. This, it now appears, is a substantial overestimate: We probably do not use even 1 percent–more likely 0.1 percent or less.
>
> (Russell, 1984, p. 7)

On this absurd and utterly incredible notion, we could increase our brain power a hundredfold by simply making use of 10% of our potential!

Another reason why it might seem possible that most of us are not using our brains very effectively is the fantastic complexity of the human brain. It has 100 billion neurons each having between 1,000 and 10,000 connections (synapses) to other neurons. It seems plausible that we find it hard or impossible to make maximal use of all this complexity.

There are several other sources for the 10% myth. One is the child prodigy, William Sidis. His intellectual development was accelerated by the efforts of his father Boris Sidis (a psychiatrist at Harvard University). William Sidis could read the *New York Times* at the age of 18 months and he became the youngest-ever student at Harvard University at the improbably young age of 11. William James, the famous American psychologist, used the case history of William Sidis to publicise his reserve energy theory, according to which most people achieve only a smallish fraction of their intellectual potential.

Another likely source for the 10% myth is a case study reported by a British doctor, John Lorber (1981). He studied a patient suffering from hydrocephalus (colloquially known as 'water on the brain'). This is a serious condition in which large quantities of cerebrospinal fluid accumulate within the brain ventricles (cavities). This creates considerable pressure causing the cerebral cortex to be forced outwards towards the skull. Lorber estimated that the patient's brain weighed only about 10% of that of healthy individuals. Nevertheless he had an IQ of 126 (in the top 5% of the population) and obtained a first-class honours degree in mathematics from Sheffield University.

The case of this extraordinary student attracted worldwide attention when Lewin (1980) published an article about him entitled 'Is your brain really necessary?' in the prestigious journal *Science*. Lorber (1983) also reported on other patients with hydrocephalus where more than 90% of the cranium was filled with cerebrospinal fluid. One woman had an IQ of 118, a girl aged five had an IQ of 123 and a 7-year-old boy one of 128.

A central problem with evaluating the evidence from these patients with extreme hydrocephalus is that it is very hard to assess their brain weight accurately. Lorber admitted: "I can't say whether the mathematics student has a brain weighing 50 grams or 150 grams, but it's clear that it is nowhere near the normal 1.5 kilograms" (cited by Lewin, 1980). An issue here is whether the brain has been destroyed or merely compacted. Subsequent calculations taking into account the fact that the heads of most hydrocephalics are larger than normal suggested that the brain volume of these patients was greater than initially supposed (Jackson & Lorber, 1984).

Hemispherectomy

Patients with severe epilepsy or other diseases causing recurrent brain seizures are sometimes subjected to hemispherectomy, a radical surgical procedure in which one of the cerebral hemispheres is removed. The obvious expectation is that hemispherectomy would have a devastating effect on most (or all) cognitive functions. It would also be expected that removal of the left hemisphere would generally lead to inferior language abilities compared to removal of the right hemisphere because language processing occurs predominantly in the left hemisphere.

In fact, the aforementioned expectations are not always fulfilled. Vanlancker-Sidtis (2004) studied BL, who had hemispherectomy of the left hemisphere at the age of five. He had above-average intelligence as an adult and obtained a university degree in business and sociology. After that, he worked as an accountant. His language and communication skills were assessed when he was 49 years old. These skills were generally of a high level except that he experienced some problems with complex language processing.

The case of BL is exceptional. More typical findings were reported by Pulsifer et al. (2004). They studied 31 children who had been subject to hemispherectomy because of encephalitis (brain inflammation) and epilepsy. Hemispherectomy reduced the children's IQ by only approximately five points regardless of whether it involved the left or the right hemisphere. However, the findings are very different from those for BL. The children's average IQ prior to surgery was only 80.5, which is in the bottom 10% within the population. Their IQs reduced only slightly following surgery because the adverse effects of hemispherectomy on intelligence were counteracted by a lessening of their pre-operative symptoms (e.g., frequent epileptic seizures). It would be an over-simplification to argue that the findings demonstrate that hemispherectomy has a very limited impact on intelligence.

Brain activity

One way of finding out how much of the brain is actively involved in information processing and cognition is to use techniques such as functional magnetic resonance imaging (fMRI) to record brain activity. For example,

Godwin et al. (2015) compared brain activity of hard-to-detect visual stimuli when they were (or were not) consciously perceived. Their key finding was that conscious perception was associated with integrated activity across most of the brain whereas the absence of conscious perception was associated with much more limited and non-integrated brain activity.

King et al. (2013) also found that conscious awareness in healthy individuals was associated with widespread integrated brain activity. However, brain activity was much less and poorly integrated in patients who were minimally conscious or in a vegetative state (total absence of conscious awareness).

We need to be somewhat careful in interpreting the aforementioned findings because they present essentially correlational findings indicating the existence of an *association* between conscious awareness and integrated brain activity. Thus, while it is possible that integrated brain activity triggers conscious awareness, it is also possible that conscious awareness triggers integrated brain activity. However, the common finding that there is integrated activity across most of the brain when someone is consciously aware of external stimuli is very hard to reconcile with the notion that we use only 10% of our brains.

The general issue of the brain's efficiency was addressed in an influential article by Bullmore and Sporns (2012). Their starting point was to identify two major principles relating to brain organisation:

(1) *Principle of efficiency*: the ability to integrate information across the brain. High efficiency can be achieved by having numerous connections within (and between) brain networks.
(2) *Principle of cost control*: costs (especially the use of energy and space) can be minimised if the brain is organised so there are limited, mostly short-distance, connections.

Of course, it would be ideal if our brains combined high efficiency with low costs. Alas, the two principles are in direct conflict: as efficiency increases so do the costs. Suppose that the human brain was constructed to maximise efficiency by having all 100 million of its neurons directly interconnected. It has been estimated that this would require a brain 12.5 miles wide!

Reassuringly, Bullmore and Sporns (2012) discovered that our brains display a near-optimal trade-off between cost and efficiency providing reasonably high efficiency with manageable costs. They are efficient because they possess a 'small world' structure in which only a few nodes or links are required to connect most small brain regions to each other. This is achieved at significant cost: our brains consume 20% of our body's energy in spite of accounting for only 2% of our body weight (Clark & Sokoloff, 1999).

We can understand the efficiency of the brain's organisation by considering an analogy between the brain and the world's airports. Passengers would prefer to fly directly from any airport to any other airport no matter how far away. However, that would be prohibitively expensive because it would need a huge number of planes to service all the flights required. Most of these flights (e.g., Southend to Belo Horizonte in Brazil) would have very few passengers and would make massive losses.

In fact, there are relatively few hub airports (e.g., Heathrow; Paris Orly; Schiphol in Amsterdam) and a much larger number of small, 'feeder' airports. This provides a very efficient system which mirrors the organisation of the human brain. There are several major hubs in the brain with strong connections among them. The term 'rich club' refers to these hubs (mostly based in the frontal and parietal lobes) and their inter-connections.

Summary and conclusions

There are plentiful sources of evidence indicating that we use far more than 10% of our brains in our everyday lives. The 10% myth does us all a huge disservice given the reasoning and thinking power of the human brain. If you remain unconvinced that the human brain is efficient and uses nearly all of its capacity, compare what it can accomplish against the achievements of supercomputers and other forms of AI. On the face of it, it is an unfair contest. The human brain weighs only 3 pounds and its size is a mere 1,200 cubic centimetres. In contrast, the USA's Frontier supercomputer (the most powerful supercomputer in the world in 2022) occupies 7,300 square feet of floor space and weighs a massive 300 tons. Thus, the human brain is less than 1/230,000th. the weight of Frontier!

What about energy consumption? The human brain uses a meagre 20 watts of power per hour, which is barely sufficient to power a very weak light bulb. Frontier uses one million times as much power making it necessary to pump 6,000 gallons of water per minute through its system to cool it down.

In spite of its small size and modest energy consumption, the human brain is demonstrably superior in many ways to supercomputers and other forms of AI (discussed thoroughly in the next section). Our ability to think and reason more effectively than AI systems seems incompatible with the notion that we use our three-pound human brain inefficiently.

In my opinion, the notion that we use only 10% of our brains is patently absurd. Evolution via natural selection is typically a very slow and laborious business. As Richerson and Boyd (2005, p. 135) put it, "All animals are under stringent selection pressure to be as stupid as they can get away with". More precisely,

> Natural selection chooses the better of present available. . . . The animal that results is not the most perfect design conceivable. . . . It is the product of a historical sequence of changes, each one of which represented. . . . the better of the alternatives that happened to be around.
>
> (Darwin cited by Richerson & Boyd, 2005, p. 46)

It is almost inconceivable that evolution could have provided humans with enormous brain power, 90% of which we fail to use.

Myth: Artificial Intelligence (AI) will soon be much more intelligent than humans

It is increasingly assumed by the media (and by millions of members of the public) that artificial intelligence (AI) will soon be considerably more intelligent than humans. More worryingly, numerous experts in AI agree. Grace et al. (2018, p. 731) provided experts at an AI conference in 2015 with the following definition: "High-level machine intelligence (HLMI) is achieved when unaided machines can accomplish every task better and more cheaply than human workers". On average, the experts predicted there was a 50% chance of HLMI occurring by 2060 and a 10% chance of that happening by 2024 (they got that wrong, didn't they?).

Gruetzemacher et al. (2020) provided an updated assessment of AI's likely impact on the labour market from attendees at AI conferences in 2018. On average, they believed 22% of jobs could already be done as well by existing AI and this figure would rise to 60% by 2028 and to 90% by 2043.

There is far too much research comparing intelligence in AI with that in humans to consider it all here (see M. Eysenck & C. Eysenck, 2022, for a comprehensive account). Accordingly, I will focus on AI's ability to use language effectively in all its major forms (speech perception; speaking; reading; and writing) for three reasons. First, language ability is of central importance to career success in most jobs within Western societies. Second, language ability correlates moderately highly with IQ and is thus an approximate measure of intelligence. Third, a huge amount of research effort has been devoted to enhancing language abilities in AI systems in recent years.

Chatbots

One of the best-known AI achievements is the development of chatbots (computer programs that can hold conversations with humans). You have probably had conversations with chatbots such as Alexa or Siri. As Adi-wardana et al. (2020, p. 1) pointed out, "The ability to converse freely in natural language is one of the hallmarks of human intelligence, and is likely a requirement for true artificial intelligence".

Turing (1950) argued that we can assess chatbots' language skills by using the Turing test. He argued that

> The idea of the test is that a machine has to try and pretend to be a man, by answering questions put to it, and it will only pass if the pretence is reasonably convincing. A considerable portion of a jury . . . must be taken in by the pretence.

> (cited in Copeland, 2004)

On 6 and 7 June 2014, a chatbot (Eugene Goostman) had a conversation with a human. This caused great excitement because 33% of human judges decided that Eugene Goostman was human on this Turing test! However, any excitement should be tempered by the fact that two-thirds of the judges did *not* think that the chatbot was a human. In addition, the test was rigged in that Eugene Goostman was allegedly a 13-year-old Ukrainian – this provided a plausible explanation for his ungrammatical or irrelevant contributions.

There has been progress since 2014. Adiwardana et al. (2020) trained a chatbot called Meena to hold a conversation with human judges. Meena's language skills were rated for (1) *sensibleness* (did its contributions make sense in the conversational context?) and (2) *specificity* (were its contributions specific or relevant?). Meena was close to human performance on specificity (70% vs. 75%) but further away on sensibleness (87% vs. 97%). Overall, Meena performed better than any previous chatbot.

Chatbots often exhibit surprisingly human-like language skills. However, their language performance is less impressive than it appears on the surface. First, the Turing test involves highly restricted conversations – the human typically produces only one or two sentences before the chatbot responds. The chatbot can identify one or two keywords and produce a sensible response based on its stored memory of related conversations. This would be much harder to do if the human spoke for 20 or 30 seconds before the chatbot responded (as often happens in everyday life).

Second, it is relatively easy to find questions to which chatbots produce ridiculous answers. Consider part of the conversation the computer scientist Scott Aaronson (2014) had with Eugene Goostman:

Scott: Which is bigger, a shoebox or Mount Everest?
Eugene: I can't make a choice right now. I should think it out later. And I forgot to ask you where you are from . . .
Scott: How many legs does a camel have?
Eugene: Something between 2 and 4. Maybe, three?:-))) By the way, I still don't know your speciality – or, possibly, I've missed it?
Scott: How many legs does a millipede have?
Eugene: Just two, but Chernobyl mutants may have them up to five. I know you are supposed to trick me.

It is not difficult to spot who is the human and who is the chatbot!

Accessing general knowledge

Jeopardy! is a very popular American game show. What is distinctive about it is that players are presented with answers and must indicate what question would produce that answer. For example, the clue might be, "Assembled from dead bodies, the monster in this Mary Shelley book turns against his creator". The correct answer is, "Who was Frankenstein?" Much of the time, whichever contestant presses their buzzer first after the clue has been read out has the first chance to provide the correct answer. Only if they provide an incorrect answer is another contestant allowed the opportunity to supply the answer.

In 2011, an IBM AI system named Watson (in honour of the company's founder Thomas Watson) battled against two of the most successful human contestants ever. One was Brad Rutter (who had 74 consecutive winning appearances on the show) and the other was Ken Jennings (who had won $3.5 million from the show).

The match took place on three successive evenings in mid-February 2011. Who is your money on? In fact, it was virtually no contest – Watson won $77,147 compared to Jennings' $24,000 and Rutter's $21,600. On the face of it, Watson's achievement indicates it had a huge amount of general knowledge and very impressive language skills. It is indisputably true that Watson is incredibly knowledgeable: it had access to 200 million pages of information including the whole of *Wikipedia*. Its processing speed was also phenomenal: it can allegedly process the equivalent of one million books per second which has be useful in a general-knowledge game.

In fact, there is less here than meets the eye. Most questions on *Jeopardy!* are sufficiently straightforward that all three contestants knew the correct answer. Watson won because it hit the buzzer in as little as 10 milliseconds, which is 30 or 40 times faster than any human. More worryingly, Watson was often very insensitive to question subtleties. For example, when the category was "Computer keys" and the clue was "A loose-fitting dress hanging from the shoulders to below the waist", Watson incorrectly responded, "What is a chemise?" In fact, the right answer is, "What is a shift?"

It is instructive to consider the search engine Google at this point because it is a form of AI used by billions of people to track down general knowledge. It has access to far more information than any human has stored in their long-term memory: it stores 10,000 Petabytes of information (1 Petabyte is equivalent to 500 billion pages of text). One might imagine that Google would incredibly rapidly and effortlessly produce the correct answer to almost any conceivable general-knowledge question. However, that is not the case. Try asking Google a slightly complex question such as, "Which Prime Minister's name is the same as that of an Army rank?" When I did this, Google produced 29 million results in 0.61 seconds. However, the correct answer (John Major) was nowhere to be seen on the first two pages. Instead, what appeared consisted mostly of the names of irrelevant Prime Ministers (especially Churchill) or a list of Army ranks.

When I googled "Which Prime Minister had the same name as part of Hampstead?" Google produced 1.8 million answers in 0.50 seconds. On the first page, I discovered that Charles Perceval was one of our Prime Ministers, that Harry Styles and Dominic Cumberbatch live in Hampstead and that Boris Johnson has the same surname as American Presidents Lyndon B. Johnson and Andrew Johnson. Alas, there was no answer to my question.

In sum, chatbots and search engines possess many strengths and can often provide very rapid answers to questions. However, they are limited because it is relatively easy to fool them when they are asked unexpected questions or questions framed in an unusual way. More specifically, Google often produces information that is strongly associated with only part of the query. For example, the question "Which Prime Minister's name is the same as that of an Army rank?" produces information related only to Prime Ministers (e.g., a list of Prime Ministers) or to Army ranks (e.g., a list of Army ranks). There is no attempt to link the two different parts of the question. There was also a failure to link Prime Ministers and parts of Hampstead when Google was asked "Which Prime Minister had the same name as part of Hampstead?" (the answer is Heath).

Text generation

Most AI language systems focus narrowly on only a *single* language skill. However, Generative Pre-Trained Transformer 3 (GPT3) is a notable exception (Brown et al., 2020). GPT-3 received massive general language training. It was trained on 570 billion megabytes of information (roughly equivalent to 57 billion words). In comparison, the average human processes about half a billion words in their lifetime which corresponds to a minuscule 1% of GPT-3's training. Of most relevance here, GPT-3's text generation was especially impressive with its performance on numerous other language tasks being good (or reasonably good) in spite of the fact that it had not received specifically relevant training.

GPT-3's text generation is often excellent. However, many sceptics have had fun devising situations where its performance is very poor. Here is what GPT-3 produced when Marcus and Davis (2020) gave it the prompt "physical reasoning":

> You are having a small dinner party. You want to serve dinner in the living room. The dining room table is wider than the doorway, so to get it into the living room, you will have to remove the door. You have a table saw, so you cut the door in half and remove the top half.

One take-home message is that you shouldn't ask GPT-3 to assist you with furniture moving! Another is that GPT-3 is "a fluent spouter of bullshit" (Marcus & Davis, 2020, p. 4). More measured criticisms of GPT-3 were made by Sobieszek and Price (2022). They pointed out that GPT-3 had been trained to predict accurately the probabilities of various possible continuations of text. However, it had learned nothing directly about the real world. As a consequence, "While GPT-3 is very good at generating plausible text, it is a bad truth-teller" (p. 361).

The other major problem is that "When GPT-3 speaks, it is only us speaking, a refracted parsing of the likeliest semantic paths trodden by human expression" (Marcus & Davis, 2020, p. 2). In other words, the text generated by GPT-3 is merely a distorted reflection or echo of previous human thinking.

GPT-3 was superseded by GPT-4 in 2023. The general consensus is that it represents a clear improvement over GPT-3 but many of the problematical aspects of GPT-3 remain. For example, as Arkoudas (2023, p. 1) pointed out, "GPT-4 at present is utterly incapable of reasoning".

Summary and conclusions

AI possesses great strengths with respect to several language skills. In addition to those skills discussed earlier, several AI systems have demonstrated excellent translation skills. Google Translate provides reasonably accurate translations between English and over 100 other languages. It is far faster than expert human translators: it can translate an entire page of text in under three seconds. Popel et al. (2020) asked 15 human judges to decide whether news translations from English to Czech were produced by CUBITT (an AI system) or a professional translator. Nine judges (including three professional translators) failed to distinguish between machine and human translations.

In sum, AI systems allow us to access a vast amount of general knowledge with amazing speed and often (but not always) with high accuracy. However, these AI systems are somewhat *inflexible* in their functioning and so it remains disturbingly easy to outwit them by asking questions in a form that does not match the way they have stored information.

Bisk et al. (2020) argued that a central weakness with AI language systems is that they have excessive reliance on internet information but neglect the roles that experience and social interaction play in human use of language. For example, an easy way to fool a chatbot is to focus on personal issues. For example, Sir Roger Penrose, who won the Nobel Prize for Physics in 2020, flummoxed a chatbot by saying to it, "I believe we've met before".

Another example showing that AI language systems are not grounded in experience was reported by Boratko et al. (2020). They asked people questions that were easy for them to answer based on their past experience (e.g., "Name something that people usually do before they leave the house for work"). The ranked list of answers for each question produced by humans and by AI models differed substantially on this experience-based test.

Marcus (2020) suggested that we could give AI language systems the challenging task of watching a YouTube video and then answering questions about it. So far, no AI system comes anywhere near to succeeding on that task even though the overwhelming majority of humans could do so.

Finally, I will briefly extend comparisons between humans and AI beyond language to consider other skills and abilities. AI certainly has some advantages over humans. The supercomputer Frontier can perform one quintillion operations per second (a quintillion is a billion billions or 1,000,000,000,000,000,000). That is numerous billions more operations than any human brain.

Supercomputers and other forms of AI have several stunning achievements to their credit. Examples include beating the world's best human players at complex games such as chess, Go and poker and the ability to detect symptoms of disease from medical images much faster and more accurately than humans. However, most of AI's successes are in relatively narrow and specific areas.

When we compare human brains against AI with respect to general intelligence, human brains are far superior (M. Eysenck & C. Eysenck, 2022). That remains the case even though much progress has been made in artificial general intelligence (AGI). Most AI systems are somewhat brittle and inflexible and are relatively poor at responding appropriately to novel situations. Hendrycks et al. (2021) provided good examples of AI's brittleness. An AI system was trained to categorise images of natural objects with great accuracy. However, its performance collapsed when tiny changes invisible to the human eye were introduced into the images: the AI system was 99% sure that a painting was a goldfish, garlic bread was a hotdog and a motorway was a dam!

M. Eysenck and C. Eysenck (2022) discussed numerous limitations of AI systems. These limitations were summarised succinctly by Booch et al. (2021, p. 15042):

> State-of-the-art AI still lacks many capabilities that would naturally be included in a notion of intelligence. . . . Examples are generalisability, robustness, explainability, causal analysis, abstraction, common sense reasoning, ethics reasoning, as well as a complex and seamless integration of learning and reasoning supported by both implicit and explicit knowledge.

However, it needs to be pointed out that there is a massive amount of research currently being carried out with a view to reducing or eliminating these limitations.

Myth: nudges are very effective at changing people's behaviour

Governments in dozens of countries around the world use insights from psychologists when devising policies to benefit society. By far the most influential of such insights in recent years is the notion that people's decision making can be enhanced by subtle forms of persuasion known as 'nudges', a term popularised by Thaler and Sunstein (2008). What exactly are nudges? They are, "non-regulatory and non-monetary interventions that steer people in a particular direction while preserving their freedom of choice" (Hertwig & Grüne-Yanoff, 2017, p. 973).

Here is an example of a nudge. It involves presenting pictures of eyes ('watching eyes') to encourage people to increase prosocial or helpful behaviour or reduce antisocial behaviour based on the assumption that being watched increases our tendency to behave in socially desirable ways. Wang et al. (2024) confirmed in a meta-analysis on the watching-eyes effect that this nudge has the predicted effects on prosocial and antisocial behaviour.

In 2010, the British government set up the Behavioural Insights Team (the world's first 'Nudge Unit'). One of their first tasks was to use nudges to persuade more people to install loft insulation. An obstacle here was that most people's lofts were full of junk. Accordingly, the Behavioural Insights Team provided low-cost labour to remove this junk. This led to a fivefold increase in the installation of insulation.

Since 2010, over 200 nudge units in over 40 countries have been established. There is widespread enthusiasm for many of the nudges introduced by nudge units. Reisch and Sunstein (2016) asked people in six countries (UK, Italy, France, Denmark, Germany and Hungary) whether they approved of various nudges. Approval ratings across countries varied between 63% and 86% for "requiring calorie labels in chain restaurants" and between 82% and 90% for "a public education campaign for parents promoting healthier food for their children to fight childhood obesity".

The popularity of nudges among members of the public is easy to explain. Most nudges can be used with minimal effort or thinking and people are free to ignore them if they choose to do so.

In 2017, Richard Thaler was awarded the Nobel Prize for Economics in part for his key role in developing the nudge approach (in collaboration with Cass Sunstein) (Earl, 2018). A central idea behind this approach is that most people have deficient decision-making abilities and are strongly influenced by various cognitive biases. However, these cognitive biases and deficiencies can nevertheless lead to effective decision making if the environment is changed appropriately.

Consider status quo bias, a preference for maintaining the status quo (present state) rather than acting to change a decision. Suppose we want to increase organ donation. Most countries have an opt-in system (i.e., people make a deliberate decision to donate their organs). Germany has such a system but only 10% of people are donors. In neighbouring Austria, however, they have an opt-out system (i.e., people are enrolled as donors unless they decide otherwise) and 98% of the people are donors. Arguably, this very high rate of organ donation is due to the fact that their opt-out system benefits from people's status quo bias.

Another simpler possibility is that many people are simply unaware the organ-donation system has changed in their country. For example, the UK changed from an opt-in system to an opt-out system on 20 May 2020, shortly after the start of the first pandemic lockdown. My recollection is that there was very little public discussion of this policy change.

The nudging approach is based in part on dual-process theories of judgement and decision making (Evans & Stanovich, 2013). For example, Kahneman (2003) distinguished between System 1 and System 2 processes. The former are typically fast and relatively effortless, occur without conscious awareness and are hard to control; the latter are relatively slow, flexible and under conscious control. System 1 processes produce intuitive responses which are sometimes modified or corrected by subsequent System 2 processes. The emphasis within the nudging approach is on System 1 processes although nudges can also be produced via System 2 processes. System 1 processing often leads to cognitive biases, but these biases (e.g., status quo bias) can lead to desirable behaviour (e.g., opting in to donation).

Research

We will start by discussing two key predictions from the nudging approach. First, the effectiveness of most nudges should be greater when individuals are not consciously aware their choice is being influenced. This prediction is based on the assumption that many people feel they are being manipulated if they are made aware that others are trying to influence their behaviour.

Second, nudges should be more effective when individuals use System 1 or intuitive processing than when they use System 2 or analytical processing. These two predictions are linked because people are more likely to use System 1 processing when they are unaware that a nudge has been presented.

de Ridder et al. (2022) reviewed research where the presence of a nudge and its purpose were either disclosed to the participants or not disclosed. Nudge effectiveness was typically unaffected by the presence or absence of disclosure, which is contrary to prediction.

The second prediction (i.e., nudges are generally more effective when individuals use System 1 rather than System 2 processing) has also received little support (de Ridder et al., 2022). For example, Blom et al. (2021) asked people to make food choices either as fast as possible or with no consideration of time based on the assumption they would rely more on System 1 processing in the former condition. More participants selected the healthiest choices when they were made more salient (this was the nudge), but time pressure had no effect on their choices.

An attempt has been made in several countries to increase pension enrolment by moving from an opt-in system where workers had to choose to enrol to an opt-out system where they were automatically enrolled unless they chose not to. It has often been reported that the switch to opt-out systems has greatly increased pension enrolment (Chater & Loewenstein, 2023). For example, the UK government in 2012 required private companies to adopt an opt-out system. In 2011, just before the new legislation, only 42% of workers in the private sector were enrolled. However, this figure increased to 63% by 2014 and to 86% by 2019. These figures seem very impressive but they are actually misleading. The increased figures were primarily caused by the legal requirement for companies to provide pension schemes, with the nudge factor (i.e., opting out) being of relatively minor importance.

Several recent meta-analyses have investigated the general effectiveness (or otherwise) of nudges in changing people's behaviour. Mertens et al. (2022) found a small-to-medium effect of nudges in a review of findings from 212 research publications focusing on the effects of nudges on behaviour. Some of the strongest effects occurred with respect to default nudges (i.e., something will happen automatically unless an active decision is made as with opt-out organ donation).

Maier et al. (2022) pointed out that Mertens et al. (2022) discovered evidence of publication bias (i.e., selective publication of positive findings) but had largely ignored it in most of their analyses. As a consequence, Mertens et al. exaggerated the effectiveness of nudging. When Maier et al. re-analysed the data taking full account of publication bias, they concluded that, "after correcting for this bias, no evidence remains that nudges are effective as tools for behaviour change" (p. 1).

More evidence that publication bias often inflates the apparent effectiveness of nudges was reported by DellaVigna and Linos (2022). They focused on two major Nudge Units in the United States that had carried out over 100 trials on a grand total of 23 million individuals. Of crucial importance, DellaVigna and Linos had access to detailed information about *all* the trials (mostly not published in journals) which precludes the possibility of publication bias. On average, the nudges used by these Nudge Units had a 1.4% impact on outcomes (an increase of 8% over the control condition). In contrast, nudges reported in academic journals had an average 8.7% impact on outcomes (a 33% increase over the control condition). Most of this large difference occurred because of publication bias with the research published in academic journals.

Finally, it is highly desirable that the beneficial effects of any given nudge should persist *after* the nudge has been removed and should generalise to situations different from the one in which the nudge was presented. In other words, there should be a spillover effect. Kuhn et al. (2021) gave participants an online shopping task where they selected the organic or conventional option for various groceries. They used a default nudge (one food option had already been ticked) for the first shop but not for the second shop. The nudge was effective for the first shop but there was no spillover effect for the second shop. This is unsurprising given that the default nudge allowed participants to select the nudge-consistent options 'automatically' and without any thinking about the desirability of organic products.

In sum, most nudges have a modest (or no) effect on people's behaviour. In contrast, dramatically greater effects are often produced by government-driven policy changes. For example, the UK government passed a law requiring all car drivers and front-seat passengers to wear a seat belt from 31 January 1983. Before the legislation, 40% of car drivers and front-seat passengers wore seat belts. Shortly after its introduction, this increased to 95%. To the best of my knowledge, no nudge has been remotely as effective in changing behaviour as this rapid 140% increase in compliance.

Summary and conclusions

The entire nudging approach is based on flimsy theoretical foundations. For example, the distinction between System 1 and System 2 processes has been subject to extensive criticism. The assumptions that System 1 processes are unintentional, uncontrollable, unconscious and efficient whereas System 2 processes are intentional, controllable, conscious and inefficient have received minimal empirical support (Melnikoff & Bargh, 2018). Furthermore, it is contrary to much of the evidence to assume that System 1 processes invariably *precede* System 2 processes, and it is simplistic to assign all cognitive processes to only two categories (i.e., System 1 and System 2).

In practice, the few theoretical predictions generated by the nudge approach have attracted little empirical support. Failed predictions include the following: (1) nudges should be more effective when using System 1 processing than System 2 processing and (2) nudges should be more effective when individuals are not aware their decisions are being influenced.

One consequence of deficient theorising is that researchers have used an amazingly heterogeneous ragbag of nudges having little or nothing in common with each other. There is an urgent need to develop a more coherent and principled set of nudges that can be justified theoretically.

In spite of the limited effectiveness of nudges in producing lasting changes in people's behaviour, there is still much enthusiasm for the nudging approach among governments and members of the public. How can this be explained? One major reason is that nudges can often be introduced rapidly and inexpensively. In addition, nudges are typically perceived as a more acceptable way of changing behaviour than alternative approaches (e.g., using fines or increased taxation) which can easily have negative effects on people's views of any government introducing them. Unfortunately, the evidence strongly indicates that large beneficial changes in people's behaviour can generally be produced much more easily when governments introduce systematic changes (e.g., via changes in the law) (Chater & Loewenstein, 2023).

In sum, the enthusiasm for the nudge approach is largely misplaced. The effects of nudges on behaviour are typically small or non-existent when account is taken of publication and selective reporting biases and positive effects rarely generalise to other times or situations. There is little sense of progress over time because there is no overarching theoretical framework within which to make coherent sense of the apparently inconsistent findings reported for the amazingly heterogeneous nudges that have been tested.

What should happen in future? Kuhn et al. (2021) gave participants an online-shopping task where they had to select the organic or conventional option for various groceries. They used a default nudge (one of the two options had already been ticked) for the first shop but not for the second shop. The nudge was effective for the first shop with more organic products being selected when that was the default option. However, there was no spillover effect for the second shop with different groceries to those used in the first shop.

In sum, there is typically little or no evidence for spillover effects when various kinds of nudges are used. This is unsurprising if we consider how nudges work. For example, the default nudge used by Kuhn et al. (2021) allowed participants to select the nudge-consistent options 'automatically' and without any thinking about the desirability of organic products.

What should happen in future? Hertwig and Grüne-Yanoff (2017) argued persuasively that it is often more effective to increase individuals' knowledge and skills if we want to change their long-term behaviour rather than providing nudges to which they respond 'automatically'. Let's return to the Kuhn et al. (2021) study discussed earlier. Suppose we provided people with information about the health and other benefits that would accrue from eating organic produce. It is reasonable to predict that there would be long-term benefits of such knowledge on healthy eating in contrast to the total lack of long-term effects obtained with the use of a nudge.

5 Intelligence

Everyone (including those confessing they have little knowledge about psychology) knows many things about intelligence. For example, they know an individual's intelligence can be summarised by a measure known as the intelligence quotient (IQ). Most people's understanding of key features of intelligence is consistent with the scientific research of psychologists. Warne and Burton (2020) surveyed the opinions of hundreds of American teachers and non-teachers. They found 89% correctly agreed with the statement that "The ability to retain and use learned knowledge is an important aspect of intelligence". The levels of agreement were very similar for two additional true statements: "The ability to think logically is an important aspect of intelligence" and "The ability to think abstractly and solve problems is important to intelligence".

Nevertheless, most people subscribe to various myths about intelligence, many of which have been promulgated by educationalists rather than psychologists. As we will see, the views expressed by educationalists are often in conflict with the research evidence obtained by psychologists.

Myth: there are multiple intelligences in the human mind

Most people believe there are many different forms of intelligence. Furnham and Horne (2021) presented almost 300 British people with the following statement: "There are multiple intelligences in the human mind". They found 90% thought this statement was definitely true (63%) or probably true (27%). In similar fashion, Warne (2020) discovered 84.5% of people accepted the following statement as true: "There are many kinds of intelligence, such as musical-rhythmic intelligence, verbal-linguistic intelligence, and bodily-kinaesthetic intelligence".

The key figure in promoting the notion that there are many different kinds of intelligence is Howard Gardner, an American educationalist. In 1983, he proposed his theory of multiple intelligences. His starting point was to define an intelligence as follows:

> a human intellectual competence must entail a set of skills of problem solving . . . and must also entail the potential for finding or creating

DOI: 10.4324/9781003596677-5

problems. . . . These prerequisites represent my effort to focus on those intellectual strengths that prove of some importance within a cultural context.

(pp. 60–61)

Gardner (1983) identified seven intelligences, some of which are more obvious than others. The obvious ones are logical-mathematical intelligence (used to solve logical or mathematical problems), linguistic intelligence (used in various language activities) and spatial intelligence (used to solve navigational problems and to visualise objects from different angles). The less obvious ones are as follows: musical intelligence (playing and appreciating music), bodily-kinaesthetic intelligence (fine control of bodily movements), intrapersonal intelligence (self-awareness; it "depends on core processes that enable people to distinguish among their own feelings": Gardner et al., 1996, p. 211) and interpersonal intelligence (understanding other people). Note that Gardner (1993, p. 6) argued that "All seven of the intelligences have equal claim to priority".

Perhaps the easiest way to obtain a clearer notion of what is involved in each of these seven intelligences is to consider individuals who were incredibly talented with respect to each one. Gardner (1993) identified Albert Einstein (logical-mathematical intelligence), T. S. Eliot (linguistic intelligence), Pablo Picasso (spatial intelligence), Igor Stravinsky (musical intelligence), the dancer and choreographer Martha Graham (bodily-kinaesthetic intelligence), Sigmund Freud (intrapersonal intelligence) and Mahatma Gandhi (interpersonal intelligence). However, it is hard (and probably unwise) to extrapolate from the fantastic achievements of a very small number of individuals to the broad mass of humanity.

Subsequently, Howard Gardner (e.g., 2006) identified additional intelligences. For example, there is naturalistic intelligence (the ability to understand nature and to take care of plants and animals). Charles Darwin is someone who had outstanding naturalistic intelligence. Another example is existential intelligence. Individuals high in existential intelligence have an interest in complex issues such as the meaning of life and spiritual matters and can discuss these issues seriously and coherently. Socrates and Buddha exemplify individuals with very high levels of existential intelligence.

Gardner assumed that the seven (or nine) intelligences are *independent* of each other even though they are often used in combination when facing real-world problems. In 2013, he argued that "There is strong evidence that human beings have a range of intelligences and that strength (or weakness) in one intelligence does not predict strength (or weakness) in any other intelligences".

According to Gardner, "Each intelligence . . . clearly involves processes that are carried out by dedicated neural networks. No doubt each of the intelligences has its characteristic neural processes" (Gardner, 2020, p. 94). These assumptions are consistent with the notion that the various intelligences are separate or independent of each other.

Gardner's approach has been remarkably popular within education. Its appeal lies in part in the assumption that children lacking high 'traditional' intelligence (i.e., mostly focusing on linguistic and mathematical abilities) may nevertheless have great ability with respect to other forms of intelligence. A major implication of Gardner's theory of multiple intelligences is that teachers should be responsive to their students' abilities and personal preferences. In his own words,

> Seven kinds of intelligence would allow seven ways to teach, rather than one. And powerful constraints that exist in the mind can be mobilised to introduce a particular concept (or whole system of thinking) in a way that children are most likely to learn it and least likely to distort it. Paradoxically, constraints can be suggestive and ultimately freeing.
>
> (Gardner, 1993)

Unsurprisingly, as discussed later, Gardner's multiple-intelligences approach has led to a dramatic increase in matching teaching styles to students' individual patterns of abilities (discussed in connection with the next myth).

Research evidence

Gardner's approach seems reasonable in various ways. His identification of intrapersonal and interpersonal intelligence was far-sighted: emotional intelligence (discussed later) combines those two forms of intelligence and has attracted massive interest in the decades since 1983. In addition, it is certainly true that there are genuine differences among the nine intelligences he identified. It is also true that those individuals who are outstandingly successful within any complex Western culture differ considerably in their most significant abilities or talents. In spite of these strengths of Gardner's theoretical approach, however, most psychologists are unimpressed by it.

We will start by considering Gardner's own research. Clear predictions from his theory are that tasks assessing the same intelligence should correlate highly with each other whereas tasks assessing different intelligences should not. However, Gardner and Hatch (1989) and Gardner and Krechevsky (1993) found that several pairs of tasks allegedly assessing different intelligences correlated strongly and pairs of tasks allegedly assessing the same intelligence often failed to correlate.

However, the most important omission from Gardner's theoretical approach is a factor of general intelligence. One of the most crucial findings produced by psychologists investigating individual differences in intelligence is that nearly all items on intelligence tests correlate positively. That finding strongly suggests there is a general factor of intelligence.

A huge body of research strongly supports the previous suggestion. Carroll (1993) reviewed intelligence-test data from over 130,000 individuals which led to a three-level hierarchical theory (McGrew, 2009). At the top level is a general factor of intelligence (known as "*g*"); 40–50% of individual differences in IQ depend on *g* (Kovacs & Conway, 2019). At the middle level, there are 10 fairly general group factors including crystallised intelligence (based on an individual's accumulated knowledge) and fluid intelligence (ability to reason flexibly on novel problems). At the bottom level, there are numerous very specific factors associated with only one or a few tests.

In fairness to Gardner, a few factors at the middle level resemble some of his intelligences. For example, quantitative knowledge corresponds to his logical-mathematical intelligence and reading and writing corresponds to his linguistic intelligence. However, many of Gardner's intelligences (e.g., linguistic; spatial and logical-mathematical) correlate moderately (about 0.4) with each other and so are *not* independent. Of greatest importance, his failure to recognise the existence of a general factor of intelligence resembles staging a production of the play *Hamlet* leaving out the Prince of Denmark.

Evidence directly relating to the independence or otherwise of Gardner's multiple intelligences was reported by Almeida et al. (2010). They assessed the linguistic, logical/mathematical, spatial, bodily-kinaesthetic, naturalistic and musical intelligences. There were two key findings. First, all six intelligences correlated positively with each other, thereby disproving the notion that they are independent or uncorrelated with each other. Second, a factor based on combining all six intelligences correlated 0.41 with a factor representing general intelligence.

As mentioned earlier, Gardner claimed that each multiple intelligence is associated with its own neural network and brain regions. In spite of several attempts to test this claim, no clear evidence supports it. Typically, each intelligence is associated with many different brain areas and these brain areas often overlap with those associated with several other intelligences. As Waterhouse (2023, p. 6) concluded from her review of the literature, there are many "multi-function brain networks" rather than brain networks specifically dedicated to a single intelligence. Gardner's claim must thus be regarded as a neuromyth (a commonly believed but erroneous assumption about brain function). However, it is a neuromyth subscribed to by 75% of teachers surveyed in the UK, the United States and Canada (Craig et al., 2021).

Gardner's (1993) claim that all seven of his initial multiple intelligences are of equal importance is wildly implausible. For example, many individuals who have outstandingly successful careers and lives are tone-deaf (possessing practically no musical intelligence) or are clumsy (very low bodily kinaesthetic intelligence). In contrast, individuals with very low linguistic intelligence typically find it hard to cope in most Western societies.

Criticisms of Gardner's theory

One of the most problematical features of the theory of multiple intelligences is that it is hard to know when to stop identifying intelligences. Consider the genius-based approach to identifying major intelligences. As Jensen (in Miele, 2002, p. 58) pointed out sarcastically, the logic of this approach is that we could claim that, "Al Capone displayed the highest level of 'Criminal Intelligence', or that Casanova was 'blessed' with exceptional 'Sexual Intelligence'". There are still other potential intelligences. Adams (2004, p. 95): " It could be said that those with the ability to understand and interact with digital information to arrange, manipulate, and display it according to their perceptions possess yet another intelligence". Adams called this 'digital intelligence'.

Another major problem with Gardner's multiple intelligences theory is that it is extremely hard to test thoroughly because of the lack of reliable and valid measures of the various intelligences more than 40 years after the theory was first proposed. Waterhouse (2023, p. 3) accurately described the present situation:

> There are no standard measures of the intelligences, thus individual researchers have to create their own measures for the intelligences. Unfortunately, without standard measures, MI [multiple intelligences] study findings cannot be compared to one another. Also, the lack of standard measures means that no synthesis of MI research findings can be built.

Conclusions

The notion that we possess multiple intelligences (each independent of all the others) must be dismissed as a myth although it is true that individuals differ in the precise pattern of their intellectual strengths and weaknesses across different aspects of intelligence (e.g., quantitative knowledge and language skills). However, these different aspects are by no means strictly independent of each other, and Gardner's failure to acknowledge the crucial importance of a general factor of intelligence invalidates his approach.

On a more positive note, Gardner (1983) was one of the first prominent theorists to argue that traditional theories of intelligence were excessively narrow because of their emphasis on 'academic' aspects of intelligence. As mentioned earlier, what is perhaps Gardner's greatest legacy was that he extended the study of human intelligence to include non-academic aspects relating to awareness of one's own feelings (intrapersonal intelligence) and the ability to understand other people (interpersonal intelligence).

Myth: it is important to match teaching methods to learning styles

We have seen that most people agree with Gardner that humans possess multiple intelligences, which strongly implies that individuals differ dramatically in terms of their intellectual strengths and weaknesses. It seems to follow that teachers should be sensitive to these individual differences in their teaching.

This viewpoint is strongly endorsed by most teachers. Blanchette Sarrasin et al. (2019) found 68% of teachers in Quebec agreed with the following statement: "Students have a predominant intelligence profile, for example logico-mathematical, musical, or interpersonal, which must be considered in teaching".

Perhaps surprisingly, Gardner (2020) rejected the previous statement himself. He would undoubtedly also disagree with this statement: "Adapting teaching methods to the 'multiple intelligences' of students leads to better learning", even though teachers gave it a mean rating of 4.47 on a 5-point scale where 4 = true and 5 = definitely true (Ferrero et al., 2020). In spite of his recent change of heart, Gardner was previously enthusiastic about taking account of students' multiple intelligences when selecting teaching methods.

Striking evidence that the great majority of teachers are convinced of the importance of students' preferred learning styles was reported by Howard-Jones (2014). More than 90% of teachers in the United Kingdom, China, the Netherlands, Greece and Turkey believed students learn better when the information they receive is tailored to their preferred learning styles. More recently, Newton and Salvi (2020) found 89% of educators across 18 countries believed that instruction should be matched to learning style and belief in this myth had not waned in recent years.

Of central importance is the notion of 'learning styles', which "refers to the concept that individuals differ in regard to what mode of instruction or study is most effective for them" (Pashler et al., 2008, p. 105). Most teachers subscribe to the 'meshing hypothesis' (Pashler et al.), according to which learning is most effective when there is a *match* between the individual student's optimal learning style and the teacher's teaching style. The notion that we should tailor educational instruction to individual differences in learning style sounds preferable to an alternative 'one size fits all' approach.

What is required to provide an adequate test of the meshing hypothesis? As Hyman and Rosoff (1984) pointed out, first we need to have a precise notion of what is meant by 'learning styles'. After that, we require a valid way of assessing each student's learning style and each teacher's teaching style. Finally, we may have to persuade teachers to alter their teaching style to make it optimal for students with a given learning style. This could be very hard to implement in practice if a teacher has students with a bewildering variety of different preferred learning styles. Later we will see whether attempts to achieve these goals have been successful.

Research findings: assessment of learning styles

There are substantial differences among teachers concerning the concept of 'learning styles' and the identification of the main categories of learning styles. For example, Papadatou-Pastou et al. (2021) found teachers had widely discrepant views about learning styles: some related them to learning theories, whereas others related them to behaviourism, personality research, motivational theories and developmental theories. Unsurprisingly, these discrepant views have produced a chaotic situation with respect to the identification of learning styles. In their review, Coffield et al. (2004) discovered 71 different categorisations of learning styles with much overlap among them. The two most popular approaches to learning styles were based on Gardner's multiple intelligences (discussed earlier) or the Visual-Auditory-Read/Write-Kinaesthetic (VARK) framework (e.g., Fleming & Baume, 2006).

How can we assess students' learning styles? The most popular approach is to use a self-report questionnaire relating to preferred learning styles. For example, learning styles within the Visual-Auditory-Read/Write-Kinaesthetic approach can be assessed by the 16-item VARK Questionnaire (see Fleming & Bonwell, 2019). The visual learning style involves a preference for observation and visual presentation of information (e.g., diagrams or pictures). The auditory learning style involves a preference for listening and verbal instructions. The read/write learning style involves preferring note taking during lectures and reading texts. Finally, the kinaesthetic approach consists of a preference for doing practicals, gaining experience and manipulating objects.

Suppose we compare visualisers (individuals preferring visual intake of information over verbal intake) and verbalisers (individuals showing the opposite pattern of preferences). Massa and Mayer (2006) did this by giving groups of visualisers and verbalisers a lesson on electronics with additional information provided by text or illustrations. The prediction that visualisers should benefit more from illustrations than text whereas verbalisers should benefit more from text was not supported.

We can distinguish between *preferences* or learning styles (i.e., how one does things) and *abilities* (i.e., how well one does them) (Willingham et al., 2015). It seems likely that individuals' preferences would tend to reflect their specific cognitive abilities. However, Massa and Mayer (2006) found preferences in terms of verbal or visual learning styles failed to correlate with actual verbal and visual cognitive *abilities* assessed by an intelligence test.

An and Carr (2017) reviewed research relating to questionnaire assessment of several popular learning styles. Most questionnaires had low reliability (i.e., inconsistency of measurement) and validity (i.e., failure of questionnaires to measure what they are claimed to measure). In other words, the typical assessment of students' learning styles is seriously deficient.

Another problematical issue is that many people do not have a strong preference for a single learning style. Earlier I mentioned the Visual-Auditory-Read/Write-Kinaesthetic (VARK) framework. Peyman et al. (2014) administered the VARK questionnaire to medical students. Only 42% expressed a preference for a single learning style with 17% preferring two learning styles, 13% preferring three learning styles and 28% preferring all four.

Research: meshing hypothesis

Obtaining strong support for the meshing hypothesis (discussed earlier) is important if the learning-style approach is to be of major usefulness within education. Testing this hypothesis thoroughly requires that participants' preferred learning styles are identified (e.g., visual vs. verbal) and that participants are then randomly assigned to receive instruction delivered by visual or verbal means and finally all participants receive the same learning test (Pashler et al., 2008). The hypothesis is supported only if participants learn *better* when the instructional style is compatible with their preferred learning style but learn *worse* when there is incompatibility between their instructional style and preferred learning style.

Willingham et al. (2015) discussed several meta-analyses providing minimal evidence that the meshing hypothesis is correct. Many studies within these meta-analyses failed to use the experimental approach recommended by Pashler et al. (2008; discussed earlier) and so did not provide an adequate test of the hypothesis. Rogowsky et al. (2020) followed Pashler et al.'s recommendations. Visual learners (i.e., those preferring a visual learning style) performed much better than auditory learners regardless of whether the learning material was presented visually or auditorily. Thus, there was no evidence the effects of learning style on learning were dependent on the instructional style as predicted by the meshing hypothesis.

Research: multiple intelligences

There is an alternative way in which educationalists could take account of individual differences among students in the pattern of their multiple intelligences and preferred learning styles. Consider an intervention where students are exposed to a wide variety of methods of instruction based on multiple intelligence theory. For example, during the teaching of mathematics, Dillihunt and Tyler (2006, p. 139) used "a variety of manipulatives, co-operative student simulations of mathematics scenarios, creating diagrams and illustrations of arrays and patterns, playing multiplication memory games, development of rhythms, songs, raps and chants". It is arguable that such an all-encompassing instructional approach would be beneficial to all students regardless of their preferred learning style and dominant intelligences. Performance on a mathematical test by students exposed to the multiple intelligence instruction described earlier was significantly better than that of students exposed to "traditional instruction".

Ferrero et al. (2021) reviewed research on interventions based on multiple intelligence theory. Such interventions often produced superior academic outcomes compared to a control condition (e.g., "traditional instruction"). However, the quality of most of the research is so low that the findings are generally uninterpretable. Of the 17 criteria Ferrero et al. (2021) identified as required for an adequate experimental design, only 4 were adopted by over 50% of the studies they reviewed. More specifically, many studies had no appropriate control groups, the sample sizes were too small, and the outcome measures were neither reliable nor valid.

Of most importance, the intervention condition typically differed from the control condition in several ways in addition to the presence or absence of varied teaching methods. For example, students exposed to an interesting variety of different instructional methods may learn more effectively than those given traditional instruction because the former approach is more motivating and interesting than the boring old traditional instruction rather than because there is some magic ingredient in the multiple-intelligence intervention.

Summary and conclusions

The learning styles approach remains extremely popular among teachers and students in spite of the lack of empirical support for this approach. Striking evidence was reported by Newton and Miah (2017). They discovered that 32% of British academics working in higher education endorsed the following statement: "Even though there is no 'evidence base' to support the use of learning styles, it is my experience that their use in my teaching benefits student learning". This apparently contradictory position is also evident in many of the publications on learning styles in which educationalists continue to champion the cause of learning styles despite the dearth of supportive research.

One of the main reasons for the continuing approval of the learning-styles approach is that it has considerable intuitive appeal. Gardner (2013) provided the following useful advice to teachers: "Individualise your teaching as much as possible. Instead of 'one size fits all', learn as much as you can about each student, and teach each person in ways that they find comfortable and learn effectively". This can be regarded as the central kernel of truth underlying the learning styles approach although it has proved incredibly difficult to turn it into more effective teaching.

Another plausible reason is based on drawing comparisons between the learning-styles approach and the traditional educational emphasis (over-emphasis?) on academic skills such as reading and mathematics. It is arguable in principle that broadening educational instruction to encompass multiple intelligences such as intrapersonal and interpersonal intelligence might equip students better to handle real-life situations.

Endorsing the learning styles' approach can provide a convenient excuse for students whose educational achievements and examination performance are poor. Instead of accepting responsibility for their for their poor school learning, they can argue that the fault lies with their teachers' failure to provide them with teaching appropriately matched to their learning style.

Here is another argument if you remain unconvinced that we should abandon the notion that teaching methods should be tailored to students' preferred learning styles. Consider the factors determining how well a given student learns some educational material. The most important factor is intelligence or IQ because individual differences in intelligence are closely linked to the rate of learning especially of more complex material (Jensen, 1989). Another key factor is the amount of stored knowledge relevant to a learning task that a given student has available to them. The issue of whether the student will learn better when the learning material is presented visually or auditorily is of much less importance as is the student's expressed preference for visual or auditory presentation.

Finally, it is important to consider the cost implications if teachers decide to match their instruction to students' learning styles. It can be relatively expensive to acquire commercially available tests of learning styles, and it requires additional resources to arrange teaching so that the different learning styles within a class are catered to.

Myth: emotional intelligence is helpful in life

Most psychologists would agree with Sternberg's (1985, p. 45) definition of intelligence: "Mental activity directed towards purposive adaptation to, and selection and shaped of, real-world environments relevant to one's life". This definition implies that coping successfully with life requires an ability to understand oneself and other people as well as the ability to think clearly. While conventional intelligence tests focus on thinking ability in its various guises, they typically do not contain items relating to social abilities.

In 1995, Daniel Goleman set the cat among the pigeons by publishing a book the title of which indicates the essence of his approach: *Emotional intelligence: Why it can matter more than IQ*. The efforts of Goleman and others have influenced most people's beliefs about the nature of intelligence. Furnham and Horne (2021) discovered 59% of people believe the statement "Emotional intelligence is a real ability that is helpful in life" is definitely true and a further 26% believe it is probably true. Thus, 85% of people think emotional intelligence is important.

What exactly is 'emotional intelligence'? Van der Linden et al. (2017, p. 37) argued that emotional intelligence "concerns the extent and manner in which individuals experience and utilise affect-laden information of an intrapersonal (e.g., managing one's own emotions) and interpersonal (e.g., managing others' emotions) nature". Note that this definition closely resembles Gardner's emphasis on intrapersonal and interpersonal intelligences (discussed earlier).

Goleman (1995) identified five relevant factors: self-awareness; self-regulation; motivation; empathy and social skills. However, none of these factors was defined with clarity and Goleman himself has done no systematic research into emotional intelligence and its component factors. However, since 1995, there have been over 5,000 research publications with the term 'emotional intelligence' in the title. As a result, much is now known about the nature and importance of emotional intelligence.

If we took most findings of research on emotional intelligence at face value, the conclusion that emotional intelligence is of real importance for academic achievement, job success and relationship satisfaction plus several other valued outcomes would be inescapable. However, we shouldn't take these findings at face value. Consider academic achievement. It has been known for a long time that IQ and various personality traits (e.g., conscientiousness) predict academic achievement. What we require from a test of emotional intelligence is that it accounts for individual differences in academic achievement *not* accounted for by previous tests. The technical term for what is needed is *incremental validity*: a new test should have predictive power over and above that provided by previous measures.

Another issue needs to be considered before discussing the relevant research evidence. The term 'emotional intelligence' is a hybrid combining elements of personality ('emotional') and cognition ('intelligence') in the same way that zonkeys (zebra + donkey) and ligers (lion + tiger) are hybrids. In practice, however, most tests of emotional intelligence focus either on personality or cognition/intelligence. The former tests assess trait emotional intelligence (EI) and typically use questionnaires and/or ratings relating to our perceptions of our own social and emotional effectiveness.

The latter tests assess ability emotional intelligence (EI) which is an individual's ability to perceive and influence their own emotions and those of other people. One of the best-known tests of ability EI is the Mayer-Salovey-Caruso Emotional Intelligence Test (MSCEIT) (Mayer et al., 2003). Individuals' ability to perceive emotions in faces, to use emotions to facilitate thought and action, to understand emotions and to manage emotions is assessed.

There is evidence that tests of trait EI and of ability EI assess different aspects of emotional intelligence. For example, Newman et al. (2010) found that tests of these two types of emotional intelligence correlated only 0.26 with each other. There is thus a modest overlap between trait and ability EI, but they are not measuring the same underlying entity.

Research evidence: academic performance and job performance

We will start by considering the extent to which ability and trait EI predict outcomes strongly influenced by individual differences in intelligence: academic performance and job performance. MacCann et al. (2020) found in a meta-analytic review that ability EI (especially skill-based tasks measuring understanding emotions and managing emotions) correlated 0.24 with academic performance, whereas for trait EI the correlation was only 0.12. Of importance, both types of EI still predicted academic performance to some extent beyond the effects of intelligence and the Big Five personality factors (openness; conscientiousness; extraversion; agreeableness; and neuroticism; see Chapter 6) indicating that they both possess some incremental validity. MacCann et al. argued that EI enhances academic performance by facilitating the development of social relationships at school or university and by regulating academic emotions (e.g., preventing anxiety from impairing performance).

O'Boyle et al. (2011) reviewed the effects of emotional intelligence on job performance. Ability EI and trait EI both correlated approximately 0.25–0.30

with job performance. The interpretation of these findings was complicated by the further findings that ability EI correlated with traditional measures of intelligence (IQ) and trait EI correlated with major personality dimensions (extraversion and neuroticism). However, there was reasonable evidence of incremental validity. Traditional measures of intelligence and the Big Five personality factors together accounted for 42% of individual differences in job performance, but a measure of emotional intelligence combining ability and trait EI accounted for a further 7% of individual differences in job performance.

Doğru (2022) also carried out a meta-analysis. He discovered that ability EI correlated 0.28 with job performance and trait EI correlated 0.33 with job performance. In addition, ability EI and trait EI both correlated negatively with job stress (−0.42 and −0.45, respectively). However, Doğru provided no evidence concerning incremental validity. As a result, it is unclear whether ability and trait EI have any predictive power over and above that provided by traditional measures of intelligence and personality.

Research evidence: social outcomes

Individual differences in trait EI are important in many real-world social contexts. Malouff et al. (2014) reviewed research on trait EI and relationship satisfaction. There was an average correlation of 0.32 indicating that individuals high in trait EI were more satisfied than low scorers. Jardine et al. (2022) carried out a larger meta-analysis and reported an overall correlation of 0.37 between trait EI and relationship satisfaction.

Trait EI is also positively associated (correlation = 0.30) with happiness ratings (Ye et al., 2019). Zou (2014) reported a correlation of −0.31 between trait EI and loneliness. The main reason for this association was that individuals high in trait EI received more social support than those low in trait EI.

The previous findings apparently demonstrate that trait EI predicts important social outcomes with moderate success. However, there are two major qualifications on that conclusion. First, there is the issue of causality. The discovery that trait EI is associated with several real-world outcomes (e.g., relationship satisfaction; happiness) does not necessarily mean that individuals' level of trait EI influences those outcomes. It is also entirely possible that having a satisfactory relationship and being happy produce increased trait EI. Direction of causality cannot be established from correlational evidence.

Second, we need to consider these findings in the context of other research on the Big Five personality factors (neuroticism; extraversion; openness; agreeableness; and conscientiousness). What is crucial is whether there is still an association between trait EI and various social outcomes when full account is taken of the Big Five personality factors. Wollny et al. (2020) obtained a correlation of approximately 0.30 between trait EI and relationship satisfaction. However, that correlation became non-significant when account was taken of the Big Five personality factors.

The findings of Wollny et al. (2020) (plus many other findings) suggest that the aspects of personality assessed by trait EI closely resemble those assessed by the Big Five factors. We will explore this issue by considering the Big Five factors and then relating them to trait EI. Theoretically, the Big Five factors are supposed to be *independent* of each other (i.e., uncorrelated). However, Rushton and Irwing (2008) found conscientiousness correlated –0.52 with neuroticism and +0.39 with agreeableness, extraversion correlated +0.45 with openness and neuroticism correlated –0.42 with agreeableness.

Some researchers responded to the discovery that the Big Five personality factors inter-correlate by taking the extreme step of reducing the Big Five to the Big One (e.g., Musek, 2007)! The Big One (also known as the General Factor of Personality or GFP) combines high extraversion, agreeableness, openness and conscientiousness and low neuroticism. High scorers on this general factor behave in socially desirable ways and are positively evaluated by other people.

How does the General Factor of Personality relate to trait EI? van der Linden et al. (2017) proposed a simple answer: the General Factor of Personality and trait EI are essentially identical. They supported this answer by finding a very high correlation of 0.85 between the Big One and trait EI, which strongly suggests the near-identity of the two traits. Van der Linden et al. (2018) extended their previous findings. Genetic factors accounted for 45% of individual differences in trait EI and 53% of individual differences in the GFP. Of most importance, the high similarity between the two personality factors depended on a common genetic factor: van der Linden et al. (2018) reported a strong genetic correlation of 0.90 between the trait EI and the GFP.

In sum, findings showing that trait EI predicts several important social outcomes are much less original than often claimed. What we have is an example of old wine in new bottles: trait EI is basically a re-packaging of the Big Five personality factors (see also Chapter 11).

Conclusions

On the face of it, there is plentiful research providing strong evidence that emotional intelligence (both ability EI and trait EI) is helpful in everyday life. Measures of emotional intelligence consistently correlate moderately with many important real-world outcomes such as academic achievement, occupational success, relationship satisfaction and happiness. However, closer examination indicates that there are serious doubts as to whether measures of EI add much to what had already been established by more traditional measures of intelligence and personality. This is especially the case with trait EI which is almost indistinguishable from the General Factor of Personality formed from the Big Five personality factors.

In sum, it is arguable that the notion that emotional intelligence is helpful and important in everyday life is not really a myth. However, it must at the very least be conceded that research on emotional intelligence possesses far less originality than has often been claimed for it.

Myth: IQ scores only measure how good someone is at taking intelligence tests

Numerous intelligence tests have been devised since Alfred Binet and Théophile Simon produced the world's first proper intelligence test (Binet & Simon, 1905). If you have ever taken an intelligence test, you may have felt that the items on the test seemed of marginal relevance to the real world. Here are a few examples of the kinds of questions you have probably encountered:

(1) Which number is the next one in the sequence?

   96; 87; 78; 69;?

(2) If I start walking northward, then turn left and turn left again, what direction will I be facing?

(3) Hat is to head as shoe is to ____?

Perhaps because of the apparently unrealistic nature of many intelligence-test items, there is much scepticism concerning the validity of intelligence tests as a way of assessing intelligence. Strong evidence for such scepticism was reported by Furnham and Horne (2021), who discovered 73% of people thought the following statement was true: "IQ scores only measure how good someone is at taking intelligence tests". In addition, 62% believed the statement "Content on intelligence tests is trivial and cannot measure intelligence" was true. Finally, 62% believed that "Intelligence tests are imperfect and cannot be used or trusted".

Most people's beliefs about intelligence tests indicate they have severe doubts about the relevance of intelligence tests to everyday life. There are various reasons for being sceptical about the relevance of intelligence tests to everyday life. For example, it is arguable that such tests are excessively narrow: they mostly assess individuals' ability to think *on their own* (rather than in social situations) and focus excessively on academic subjects (e.g., language; mathematical skills).

Sternberg et al. (2000, p. 32) encapsulated the views of those sceptical of intelligence tests:

> We see people who succeed in school and fail in work or who fail in school but succeed in work. We meet people with high scores on intelligence tests who seem inept in their social interactions. And we meet people with low test scores who can get along effectively with practically anyone. Laypersons have long recognised a distinction between academic intelligence (book smarts) and practical intelligence (street smarts or common sense).

How can we broaden the scope of intelligence and intelligence tests? Sternberg (2015) argued that intelligence should be defined comprehensively:

> Intelligence is (1) the ability to achieve one's goals in life, given one's socio-cultural context; (2) by capitalising on strengths and correcting or compensating for weaknesses; (3) in order to adapt to, shape, and select environments; (4) through a combination of analytical, creative, and practical abilities.
>
> (p. 230)

If intelligence scores are of direct relevance to everyday life, individuals with high IQs should lead more successful lives than those with low IQs. We can also predict that those with low IQs should experience several important real-world disadvantages compared to those with higher IQs. In the following section we discuss the relevant evidence.

Research evidence: effects of high intelligence

What evidence could be used to assess whether intelligence tests provide a good measure of intelligence? One reasonable approach would be to consider individual differences in student performance at school. Roth et al. (2015) reviewed the evidence and discovered IQ correlated 0.54 with academic performance. That is a moderately strong association indicating that IQ accounts for 29% of individual differences in academic performance.

We could explain the previous finding by assuming that individual differences in intelligence cause differences in academic performance. However, correlational evidence cannot establish causality. Consider the possible role of family socio-economic status (SES). There is a positive correlation between IQ and SES, and Westrick et al. (2015) found in a meta-analysis that there was a correlation of 0.24 between SES and educational attainment. Thus, the relationship between intelligence and academic attainment may depend partly on SES. In fact, however, Haider and von Stumm (2022) discovered that intelligence explains a significant proportion of the relationship between family SES and educational attainment.

Of course, the finding that individual differences in intelligence account for 29% of differences in academic performance means 71% of differences in academic performance remain unaccounted for by intelligence. Students' academic performance is obviously multiply determined (e.g., the quality of teaching is important). As a result, even if IQ were a perfect measure of intelligence, it would not totally account for individual differences in performance at school.

In England, parents have some flexibility concerning the secondary school to which their children are sent. Their decision making is influenced by reports from the Office for Standards in Education, Children's Services and Skills (Ofsted) in which schools are placed in four categories ranging from 'outstanding' to 'inadequate' on the basis of school inspections. Unsurprisingly, house prices in areas close to outstanding schools are inflated by parents desperate to ensure their children have good schooling. However, the impact of Ofsted reports on educational achievement is modest. Only 4% of individual differences in GCSE examination performance at 16 is accounted for by those reports (von Stumm et al., 2021).

Academic achievement is also influenced by individual differences in personality. Vedel (2014) found that academic performance by university students correlated 0.26 with conscientiousness. Other personality factors influencing academic achievement were discussed earlier in the chapter.

We have seen that individual differences in intelligence and personality have a substantial impact on academic achievement. Since individual differences in intelligence and personality both depend on genetic factors, it seems reasonable to predict that heritability of academic achievement should be fairly high. Smith-Woolley et al. (2018) carried out a twin study on English and Welsh university students. Genetic factors accounted for 57% of A-level grades and of university quality and 46% of university achievement.

If individual differences in intelligence are important in everyday life, we would expect those with high IQs to have greater occupational success than those with lower IQs. There is overwhelming support for this expectation. In a comprehensive review, Salgado and Moscoso (2019) found the correlation between intelligence and job proficiency was 0.50, 0.44 and 0.32 for high-, medium- and low-complexity jobs, respectively. These findings are as expected because high intelligence becomes more important as job complexity increases.

As Jensen (1980) pointed out, "A certain threshold level of intelligence is a necessary but not sufficient condition for success in most occupations" (p. 344). The high cognitive demands of high-complexity jobs mean that only a relatively small proportion of the population can perform them successfully, and so the variation in IQ among those individuals having such jobs is relatively small (Wolfram, 2023). In contrast, low-complexity jobs can be performed successfully by a much greater proportion of the population and so there is a wide spread of IQs among those performing them.

Wolfram (2023) considered differences among individuals having 360 different occupations. For several prestigious occupations (e.g., physical scientists; solicitors; doctors), the mean IQ was in excess of 110 (75% of the population have IQs lower than that). In contrast, the occupation associated with the lowest mean IQ (87; 81% of people have higher IQs) was that of packers, bottlers, canners and fillers followed by sewing machinists. Across all 360 occupations, intelligence correlated 0.86 with occupational status, 0.77 with occupational prestige and 0.62 with income.

Strictly speaking, the previous findings indicate only that there is a strong association or correlation between individual differences in intelligence and occupational status or prestige. As a consequence, we cannot be sure that differences in intelligence *cause* differences in occupational success or prestige.

Alternatively, having a high-complexity or prestigious job may increase intelligence to a greater extent than being in a low-complexity or non-prestigious job. Stronger evidence that individual differences in occupational success are caused in part by differences in intelligence was reported by Spengler et al. (2018). Intelligence assessed when participants were teenagers correlated 0.35 with occupational level over the next 50 years. This correlation reduced only slightly to 0.29 when adjusted to control for parental social status.

Finally, Wolfram (2023) found individual differences in IQ were far more important than those in any personality factor in determining occupational status and prestige.

Conscientiousness predicted occupational status and prestige more strongly than any of the other Big Five factors; however, it correlated only 0.14 with occupational status and 0.19 with occupational prestige.

Research evidence: effects of low IQ

We have seen that having an IQ well above 100 greatly increases an individual's chances of performing well academically and having a successful career. The other side of the coin is to consider the potential disadvantages of having an IQ well below 100. Relevant data for white American adults were reported by Herrnstein and Murray (1994). Of those with IQs below 75 (low IQs), 30% lived in poverty compared to 6% of those with average IQs and only 2% of those with IQs over 125 (high IQs). Imprisonment had occurred for 7% of those with low IQs, 3% of those with average IQs and 0% of those with high IQs. Of those with low IQs, 55% were high-school drop-outs compared to 6% of those with average IQs and 0% with high IQs.

Much research on the real-world correlates of IQ has focused on longevity. It has consistently been found that IQ is positively correlated with longevity. Hart et al. (2003) found that the risk of dying in middle-aged individuals was 17% greater for a reduction of 15 points of IQ at the age of 11. It is hard to interpret this finding because IQ is correlated with several other factors. However, when Hart et al. took account of the relationships between IQ and social class and deprivation, the figure of 17% only reduced to 12%.

Why do individuals with low IQs have reduced longevity compared to those with high IQs? One factor that has received much attention is healthy literacy, which "denotes a range of skills and resources associated with the ability to process health-related information" (von Wagner et al., 2007, p. 1086). There are moderately strong relationships between IQ and health literacy and between health literacy and longevity (von Wagner et al.). These findings make sense if you think of the complexities involved in the management of your own health. Those with high health literacy are better at health decision making (e.g., "are my symptoms serious?"), at understanding the advice provided by doctors and at taking prescribed medication as instructed.

Why is IQ so important?

There is no doubt that individual differences in intelligence and IQ are very important in everyday life. However, we need to move beyond a description of the main findings to achieve an understanding of *why* IQ is of such central significance in our lives. One answer was provided by Gottfredson (1997, pp. 92–93): "The heart of the argument . . . is this: for practical purposes, g [general factor of intelligence] is the ability to deal with cognitive complexity-in particular, with complex information processing". Coping successfully with the complexities of everyday life is easier for those having high IQs than for those with low IQs. An implication is that intelligence-test items need to assess complex information processing and that the *content* of those items is essentially irrelevant.

Gottfredson (1997) is correct in arguing that the advantage of individuals with high IQs over those with lower IQs revolves around the greater ability of the former individuals to engage in complex processing. However, her approach is limited because it is basically a re-description of the research findings.

What is also important is that more intelligent individuals have a generally faster learning rate than less intelligent ones. There is much supporting research on training courses (see Gottfredson, 1997). For example, the American military for some time admitted individuals of all ability levels to pilot training. Of those in the top 4% for intelligence and motivation, 95% successfully completed their training whereas only 20% of those in the bottom 4% did so (Matarazzo, 1972), leading to increasingly large effects over time. Revelle et al. (2020) drew an analogy with the effects of differences in stickiness when snowballs roll downhill. Sticky snowballs become increasingly larger than less sticky ones over time in the same way that individuals with high IQs acquire increasingly more information than those with low IQs as they experience life. In similar fashion, more intelligent individuals rapidly acquire more knowledge than less intelligent ones, and this greater knowledge facilitates the task of acquiring still more knowledge.

Another limitation with Gottfredson's (1997) approach is that she largely ignores the cognitive processes underlying the ability of high-IQ individuals to engage in more complex processing than low-IQ ones. Kovacs and Conway (2016, 2019) proposed a process overlap theory. Its key assumption is that "General intelligence [g] is a summary of different but correlated abilities rather than the reflection of a single, unitary ability" (Kovacs & Conway, 2019, p. 255). Kovacs and Conway reported evidence suggesting that individual differences in g depend on processes such as cognitive control, sustained attention, planning and mental flexibility.

An alternative approach with more solid empirical foundations is based on the assumption that individual differences in intelligence depend to an important extent on differences in attentional control. Attentional control was defined by Draheim et al. (2024, p. 2135) as "the ability to manage goal-directed action through a combination of maintaining relevant information and behaviour and, blocking, filtering, or otherwise suppressing irrelevant information and inappropriate thought and behaviour". Draheim et al. found individual differences in intelligence were well predicted by measures of attentional control.

Conclusions

Individual differences in intelligence have been shown to be of major importance with respect to many real-world outcomes (especially academic achievement and career success but also including longevity). It is thus a total myth that intelligence tests are largely irrelevant to everyday life. Some of the relationships between IQ and real-world outcomes depend partly on extraneous factors such as socio-economic status. However, these factors account for only a small fraction of IQ-outcome relationships.

Since individual differences in intelligence depend mostly on cognitive processes relating to attention, thinking, long-term memory and so on, we might expect cognitive psychologists would have devoted much research to identifying the key cognitive processes underlying intelligence. In fact, that has *not* been the case. However, recent research has indicated that attentional control is especially important and other cognitive processes (e.g., planning; mental flexibility; processing speed) have also been implicated.

Myth: intelligence does not depend on genetic factors

One of the most controversial issues with respect to human intelligence is whether it depends mostly (or entirely) on environmental factors or whether genetic factors are also important. Furnham and Horne (2021) found 32% of people agreed with the statement that "Genes are not important for determining intelligence", meaning that one-third of the population believes that an individual's level of intelligence is determined almost entirely by environmental factors. Further support for that belief comes from the additional finding that 65% of Furnham and Horne's participants agreed with this statement: "Social interventions can drastically raise IQ".

Twin studies

How can we assess heritability of intelligence? Easily the most popular approach has been to carry out twin studies although similar findings have been obtained from family and adoption studies. There is a crucial distinction between monozygotic or identical twins and dizygotic or fraternal twins. Identical twins share 100% of their genes whereas fraternal twins share on average only 50% of their genes. If individual differences in intelligence depend in part on genetic factors, then we would expect identical twins to be more similar in intelligence than fraternal twins.

The world's first twin study was reported in 1875 by Sir Francis Galton (1822–1911). He concluded that heredity was more important than environment in influencing people's development. However, he relied mostly on anecdotal evidence and he did not fully understand the difference between monozygotic and dizygotic twins (Waller, 2012).

It is often assumed that the role of genetic factors in influencing individual differences in intelligence is fixed. Indeed, you may well have read that, "Intelligence is 70% due to heredity" or "Intelligence is 50% due to heredity". Such statements are mistaken in two different ways. First, we cannot assess the role of heredity *directly*; instead, we assess it *indirectly* through a focus on causes of individual differences in intelligence. Second, heritability provides a measure of individual differences within *a given population* and so heritability can (and does) vary dramatically from one population to another.

Striking findings were reported in a review of numerous twin and adoption studies by Tucker-Drob et al. (2013). Of key importance, genetic factors accounted for less than 25% of individual differences in intelligence in infant populations compared to 70% in adolescence. We will discuss explanations of this dramatic change in heritability as a function of age shortly. For now, the key point is that the heritability of intelligence from adolescence through to old age is 70% (Plomin & Deary, 2015).

Several criticisms have been made of the value of calculating heritability of intelligence from twin studies (Robette et al., 2022). For example, heritability estimates are typically based on the assumption that the shared environments of monozygotic and of dizygotic twins are very similar. However, this assumption is over-simplified. The environmental conditions are more similar on average for monozygotic than dizygotic twins: they are more likely to have the same friends, to be in the same class at school, to be treated similarly by their parents and to spend more time together.

Does the discovery that monozygotic twins experience more similar environments than dizygotic twins invalidate heritability estimates? The short answer is "No". Suppose we consider monozygotic twins brought up apart (easier said than done given their scarcity in the population at large!). If monozygotic twins brought up apart in different families are more similar in IQ than dizygotic twins brought up together, that would provide striking evidence that genetic factors strongly influence individual differences in intelligence. Bouchard et al. (1990) studied adult monozygotic twins who had been separated at an average of 5 months after birth. These twins typically had more similar IQs than dizygotic twins brought up together in other studies. It was estimated that heritability of intelligence for the monozygotic twins brought up apart was 70%, a finding consistent with those from previous studies on such twins.

Why are the environments of monozygotic twins more similar than those of dizygotic twins? Plomin (1990) identified three main reasons all of which exemplify ways in which individuals' genetic endowment influences their environment:

(1) *Active covariation*: Children varying in genetic ability select situations reinforcing their genetic differences (e.g., those of high genetic ability have more years of education and read more books).
(2) *Passive covariation*: Parents of high genetic ability provide a more stimulating environment than those of lower genetic ability.
(3) *Reactive covariation*: An individual's genetically influenced behaviour influences their treatment by other people (e.g., adults are more likely to discuss complex issues with children of high genetic ability).

Individuals with high IQs have a *direct* advantage over those with low IQs in their genetic endowment. However, they have a further *indirect* advantage in that their genetic endowment also influences their environment. As Plomin (1990; discussed earlier) noted, individuals with high genetic ability are much more likely than those with less ability to read many books, go to university and have cognitively demanding jobs. As a result, "Higher IQ leads one into better environments causing still higher IQ, and so on" (Dickens & Flynn, 2001, p. 347) Thus, to him (or her) that hath shall be given. This combination of direct and indirect advantages explains why individual differences in intelligence are strongly influenced by genetic factors in many populations.

Why are individual differences in intelligence influenced much more strongly by genetic factors in adolescence and adulthood than in infancy and childhood? First, children increasingly find themselves in environments that are reasonably optimal for them because of active, passive and reactive covariation (Plomin, 1990; discussed earlier). Second, answering that question also requires considering environmental influences on intelligence at different ages. Tucker-Drob et al. (2013; discussed earlier) discovered that shared or family environment becomes considerably less important with increased age (from 65% in infancy to close to 0% in adolescence). Thus, the increasing influence of genetic factors on individual differences in intelligence depends in part on the decreasing impact of shared environmental influences as children spend more and more of their time outside the family environment.

Conclusions

One-third of individuals apparently do not believe genetic factors are important in determining intelligence (Furnham & Horne, 2021) in spite of the copious evidence disproving that belief (at least in Western countries). However, other research suggests most people have reasonably accurate knowledge of the role played by genetic factors. Willoughby et al. (2019) asked hundreds of people to estimate the contributions of genetic and environmental factors to variations in intelligence. The mean estimate was that 58%

of individual differences in intelligence depend on genetic factors. This is remarkably close to the actual figure of 63% reported by Polderman et al. (2015) from a meta-analysis involving millions of twin pairs.

How can we explain the differences between the aforementioned findings? The statement used by Willoughby et al. (2019) addressed the issue of the relative importance of genetic and environmental factors in explaining individual differences in intelligence but more explicitly than the one used by Furnham and Horne (2021). Accordingly, it seems reasonable to attach more credence to Willoughby et al.'s findings. In spite of their findings, however, most people have mistaken views about the role played by genetic factors in intelligence. We consider two such mistaken views in the following sections.

Myth: single genes have a strong impact on intelligence

Christensen et al. (2010) found 76% of Americans believe that "Single genes directly control specific humans behaviours". Nothing could be further from the truth. Chabris et al. (2015, p. 305) proposed an important "law" of behavioural genetics, according to which "a typical human behavioural trait is associated with very many genetic variants, each of which accounts for a very small percentage of the behavioural variability".

The above "law" is certainly applicable to human intelligence. Savage et al. (2018) carried out a meta-analysis based on 269,867 individuals and discovered at least 1,016 different genes are involved in human intelligence. Subsequently, Genç et al. (2021) identified genes associated with general, verbal and numerical intelligence. In sum, the role of genes in influencing individual differences in intelligence is considerably more complex than generally believed.

Myth: heredity and heritability mean the same thing

Differences in meaning between the terms 'heredity' and 'heritability' were mentioned earlier. Heredity is the transmission from parents to their children of genetic factors exerting an influence on their children's characteristics and behaviour. In contrast, heritability refers to the *ratio* of genetically caused variation in a characteristic (e.g., intelligence) to total variation (genetic + environmental variation) within a given population. In simple terms, heritability measures the extent to which genetic factors account for *individual differences* in any given human trait (e.g., intelligence) within a particular population. Of crucial importance, heritability is *not* a measure of what causes an *individual's* level of intelligence. It is meaningless for someone to claim their level of intelligence is due 80% to genetic factors.

Heritability of 0.7 indicates that 70% of individual differences in, say, intelligence are due to genetic factors. It is often claimed that heritability of intelligence is approximately 0.7, but this is a gross over-simplification. Heritability can vary dramatically from one population to another.

Superficially, it may seem that heredity and heritability are rather similar. We can see that is *not* the case by considering the heritability of the number of fingers individuals have within a population. Is this heritability high or low? Most people (including, sadly, many psychologists) argue that heritability for the number of fingers is high whereas in fact it is very low! How can this be? Remember that heritability refers to *individual differences* so we must focus *only* on what causes some individuals to have more or fewer than 10 fingers. There are very occasional examples of individuals born with an unusual number of fingers because of some genetic abnormality. However, the overwhelming majority of individuals without the standard 10 fingers lack one or more fingers because of environmental factors (e.g., industrial accidents; car crashes).

The reason so many people answer the previous question incorrectly is that they confuse heritability with heredity. If we ask the question why nearly all of us have 10 fingers, then the answer is indisputably that this is due to heredity in the form of genetic factors.

Twin studies have established that heritability of intelligence (which relates to individual differences in intelligence) is often approximately 0.7 or 70% in adult populations. However, this does *not* mean that 70% of our intelligence is determined by heredity and as yet we do not know the precise impact of heredity on human intelligence.

6 Personality

We all know a fair amount about personality and individual differences in personality based on our knowledge of ourselves and observation of friends, family and strangers. With all this knowledge, it might seem reasonable to assume most of us would have a fairly accurate understanding of personality. However, that is not necessarily the case. In 2021, Donnellan and Lucas published a book entitled *Great myths of personality*, in which they explored numerous myths or misconceptions about personality endorsed by large numbers of people. Here we consider five of the most important personality myths in detail.

Myth: high self-esteem is highly desirable (and low self-esteem very undesirable)

Walk into almost any bookshop and go to the section labelled 'Popular Psychology'. Many of the books on display claim to reveal the secrets of achieving high self-esteem. I have just Googled 'Books on self-esteem' and discovered there are literally thousands of books devoted to ways of enhancing your self-esteem. Here is a random selection of these books: *Six Pillars of Self-Esteem* by Nathaniel Branden, *Overcoming low self-esteem* by Melanie Fennell, *Ten days to self-esteem* by David Burns and *The power of self-confidence* by Brian Tracy. For those requiring even more dramatic improvements in their life, there is a book by Jen Sincero entitled *You are a badass: How to stop doubting your greatness and start living an awesome life*. However, it is just possible that you do not aspire to become a badass.

The fact that numerous books on developing high self-esteem have become best sellers indicates that most people believe high self-esteem is highly desirable. The other side of the same coin is that low self-esteem is thought to be extremely undesirable. According to Lilienfeld et al. (2010, p. 162), large numbers of people believe that "Low self-esteem is a major cause of psychological problems". They exemplify this point of view by quoting Branden's (1994) view that one "cannot think of a single psychological problem – from anxiety and depression to fear of intimacy or of success, to spouse battery or child molestation – that is not traceable to the problem of low self-esteem".

DOI: 10.4324/9781003596677-6

Many forms of therapy are based squarely on the notion that increasing the low self-esteem of individuals suffering from mental disorders involving anxiety and/or depression is of central importance. Client-centred therapy, devised by Carl Rogers (1902–1987), is a prime example. According to him, we all have a self-concept (the self as currently experienced) and an ideal self (the self-concept we would most like to possess). A key goal of therapy is to *reduce* the large discrepancy between the self-concept and ideal self typically found in patients. Achievement of this goal is facilitated when the therapist provides unconditional positive regard (non-judgemental acceptance) and empathy (understanding the patient's feelings). The desired outcome is that the patient develops unconditional positive self-regard (high self-esteem) with a substantial overlap between their self-concept and ideal self.

It seems obvious to most people that low self-esteem is bad and high self-esteem good. However, Lilienfeld et al. (2010) argued that the notion that low self-esteem causes many psychological problems is a myth. In similar fashion, Baumeister et al. (2003) reviewed the findings from over 15,000 studies assessing the effects of high self-esteem on various outcomes (e.g., academic performance; occupational success; antisocial behaviour; depression; coping with stress). They concluded that "Self-esteem is not a major predictor or cause of almost anything (with the possible exception of happiness)" (p. 37).

Why might high self-esteem not be the answer to our prayers? Baumeister and Vohs (2018, p. 137) provided a plausible answer: "Very high self-esteem might create problems, such as arrogance, entitlement, pigheaded stubbornness, and overconfidence". As a consequence, those regarding themselves as markedly superior to most people (i.e., having a 'superiority complex') are likely to be perceived as dislikeable.

Another potential answer to the previous question involves focusing on cross-cultural differences. High self-esteem may be of major importance in individualistic cultures emphasising self-reliance (e.g., the United States) but not in collectivistic societies (e.g., China; Japan) where there is more emphasis on the group and social cohesion. Support for that argument was provided by Zhao and Gong (2019), who found Chinese students had lower self-esteem and greater self-doubt than American ones. However, they regarded self-doubt more positively than American students. Brown (2008) compared American and Japanese students. American students were much more likely to say they had high self-esteem, to believe that people with high self-esteem are happier than those with low self-esteem and to think that low self-esteem is a serious problem facing society.

Research: high self-esteem is not desirable

Baumeister et al.'s (2003) article debunking the notion that high self-esteem is hugely beneficial came as a bombshell to almost everyone (perhaps especially writers of self-help books!). How did Baumeister et al. account for the fact that their views differed so much from the prevailing consensus? First, they pointed out that most research on self-esteem provides only correlational evidence and so does not allow us to determine the direction of causality. Consider the common finding that self-esteem correlates positively with academic performance. Perhaps individuals with high self-esteem work harder and more effectively and so perform better academically. However, causality could easily work in the other direction as well: performing well academically may increase an individual's self-esteem. If so, high self-esteem would be the outcome rather than a causal factor.

Baumeister et al. (2003) pointed out that correlations between self-esteem and academic performance can also occur even if there is no causal relationship between these two variables. They reviewed several studies indicating that the relationship between self-esteem and academic achievement is mostly due to ability (IQ) and socio-economic status.

The optimal way to decide whether self-esteem has a causal impact on academic achievement is to use *interventions* designed to enhance self-esteem. If such interventions increase academic achievement, that would provide strong support for the notion that self-esteem causally influences academic performance. In fact, however, such interventions typically produce only small temporary increases in academic achievement (Scheirer & Kraut, 1979).

Second, Baumeister et al. (2003) noted that most research on self-esteem has relied heavily on self-report measures. That seems reasonable: the easiest way for me to know how much self-esteem you have is to ask you. However, real problems can arise when we start correlating self-esteem with other measures. Baumeister et al. discussed research showing there is a strong positive correlation between self-esteem and self-reported physical attractiveness and a strong negative correlation between self-esteem and self-reported body weight. However, these correlations were markedly smaller when self-esteem was correlated with more objective measures of physical attractiveness and body weight.

The previous findings suggest that individuals with high self-esteem think more highly of themselves than is warranted and this positive bias permeates numerous judgements about themselves. As a consequence, it is preferable to use objective measures to establish accurately the relationships between self-esteem and many other qualities and characteristics.

Third, Baumeister et al. (2003, p. 1) argued that we must recognise the 'heterogeneity of high self-esteem': individuals categorised as having self-esteem vary considerably in their underlying personality and the precise reasons why they possess high self-esteem. Kernis (2003) distinguished between secure and fragile high self-esteem. Secure high self-esteem is genuine: those possessing it have inner as well as publicly presented high self-esteem. In contrast, individuals with fragile self-esteem have grandiose views of themselves but are often aware those views are excessively positive. Zeigler-Hill (2006) found that individuals with fragile self-esteem differed from those with secure self-esteem in being more narcissistic (feelings of superiority, entitlement, vanity and exhibitionism).

Stronge et al. (2019) proposed a similar distinction based on individuals' scores on self-esteem and entitlement (i.e., the extent to which individuals feel entitled to more of everything). Individuals scoring high on self-esteem but low on entitlement were categorised as having optimal self-esteem. In contrast, those scoring high on both self-esteem and entitlement were categorised as having narcissistic self-esteem. Individuals with optimal self-esteem had higher psychological well-being than those with narcissistic self-esteem and their level of self-esteem was more stable over time.

Fourth, Baumeister et al. (2003) reviewed research indicating that individuals with high self-esteem think other people like them more than is actually the case, whereas those with low self-esteem underestimate how much they are liked. Dufner et al. (2019) reviewed research on self-enhancement (unrealistically positive self-esteem and psychological adjustment). Self-enhancement was positively related to strangers' social valuations but not to the evaluations of others following longer acquaintance. As Dufner et al. concluded, "Self-enhancers . . . seem appealing at first sight, but their appeal wanes with the passage of time" (p. 63). Thus, those with high self-esteem may be better at making themselves happy than at making others happy.

Research: high self-esteem is desirable and low self-esteem is undesirable

Even Baumeister et al. (2003) accepted that high self-esteem is associated with two desirable features. First, individuals with high self-esteem are significantly happier than those with low self-esteem. Of course, we can never be sure whether people are accurately reporting their level of happiness. However, virtually all the relevant research has found a positive association between high self-esteem and happiness. Second, individuals with high self-esteem display more initiative than those with low self-esteem: they have more confidence in their own views and are more resilient in the face of adversity.

The largest study ever conducted on the relationship between self-esteem and well-being was reported by Zell and Johansson (2024). They reported the findings from over one million individuals from more than 2,000 studies. Overall, self-esteem correlated 0.31 with overall health/well-being. There were three components to health/well-being: mental health; physical health and psychological adjustment. Self-esteem correlated 0.42 with mental health, 0.29 with psychological adjustment and 0.15 with physical health.

As discussed earlier, subjective or self-report measures of outcomes may be less valid than more objective ones. However, Zell and Johansson (2024) found the correlation between self-esteem and health/well-being was comparable for subjective and objective measures (0.30 and 0.35, respectively). Another concern is that self-esteem may be more valued in some cultures than in others. However, the correlation between self-esteem and health/

well-being was similar in East Asian and other cultures (0.37 and 0.30, respectively).

Most research findings (including those of Zell and Johansson, 2024) are hard to interpret because they are correlational. However, recent research has clarified the causality issue. This research has involved the longitudinal approach where participants are assessed over a considerable period of time. When this approach is applied to self-esteem and social relationships, the key prediction is that self-esteem at a given point in time should predict the future quality of relationships. Harris and Orth (2020) found in a meta-analytic review that self-esteem predicted subsequent relationship quality. The effect size was fairly modest but was found across differences in age, gender and ethnicity.

Orth and Robins (2022) discussed meta-analytic reviews of longitudinal studies focusing on other factors. High self-esteem consistently predicted several future outcomes including academic achievement, job satisfaction, job success, income and reduced job stressors. Such findings strongly suggest that high self-esteem has causal effects on all five academic and job-related outcomes.

If high self-esteem is desirable, then we might predict that low self-esteem would be undesirable. There is plentiful research indicating that low self-esteem is correlated or associated with high levels of anxiety and depression. However, that raises the issue of direction of causality: does low self-esteem cause emotional problems or do emotional problems lead to low self-esteem?

Trzesniewski et al. (2006) assessed self-esteem in adolescents and then followed them up for 11 years. Of those having several problems (e.g., major depressive disorder; anxiety disorder; criminal convictions) in adulthood, 65% had had low self-esteem in adolescence compared to only 15% of those with high self-esteem. Among adults with no problems, 16% had had low adolescent self-esteem but 50% had had high self-esteem. Thus, low self-esteem strongly predicted psychological problems several years later.

Orth and Robins (2022) discussed meta-analytic reviews of longitudinal studies confirming Trzesniewski et al.'s (2006) findings. Low self-esteem was a relatively strong predictor of subsequent depression; it also predicted subsequent anxiety although that effect was somewhat smaller. In another longitudinal study, Zhou et al. (2020) discovered that a key reason why low self-esteem leads to depression is because individuals having low self-esteem are especially sensitive to rejection by others. Wang and Hoe (2023) confirmed in a longitudinal study that low self-esteem leads to depression; they also found depression leads to reduced self-esteem.

Self-esteem, neuroticism or emotional intelligence?

There is ongoing controversy as to whether some of the apparent effects of self-esteem may actually be more due to neuroticism. Neuroticism is a major personality dimension relating to the tendency to have negative emotional experiences (e.g., anxiety; depression); low neuroticism is often referred to as emotional stability. Judge et al. (2002) found in a meta-analytic review that the average correlation between self-esteem and neuroticism was −0.64, indicating there is considerable overlap between measures of self-esteem and neuroticism. Thus, it is hard to distinguish between effects of low self-esteem and high neuroticism on depression and anxiety.

Mu et al. (2019) found there was a strong correlation (0.60) between self-esteem and depression. However, this correlation became much smaller (0.24) when account was taken of neuroticism, suggesting neuroticism may be the cause of self-esteem and depression.

There is a further complication in interpreting the various effects of self-esteem when we consider emotional intelligence (the ability to manage one's own emotions and those of others; see Chapter 5). Emotional intelligence as a personality factor consists largely of high extraversion, agreeableness, openness, and conscientiousness and low neuroticism and there is evidence that emotional intelligence and self-esteem are very similar concepts. Weidmann et al. (2017) discovered that self-esteem correlates positively with extraversion, agreeableness, openness and conscientiousness but negatively with neuroticism, precisely the same pattern as that previously found for emotional intelligence as a personality factor! Cheung et al. (2015) directly related self-esteem and emotional intelligence and found they correlated 0.68 with each other and are thus very similar.

Conclusions

Many psychologists dismiss as myths the popular beliefs that high self-esteem is desirable and low self-esteem is undesirable. It is true that exaggerated claims have been made about the effects of high self-esteem in correlational research where we cannot be sure whether high self-esteem is cause or effect. It is also true that individuals with high self-esteem often express excessively positive views about themselves whereas those with low self-esteem sometimes have excessively negative views about themselves and these tendencies can distort the findings from research relying heavily on self-reports. It is also true that some individuals claiming to have high self-esteem (e.g., those with fragile high self-esteem or narcissistic self-esteem) do not possess the positive characteristics typically associated with high self-esteem; indeed, individuals with fragile self-esteem often possess undesirable characteristics such as entitlement, sense of superiority, vanity and arrogance.

However, plentiful research (e.g., from longitudinal studies; from studies focusing on objective outcomes) demonstrates that high self-esteem is generally desirable (although significantly less so than popularly believed). Baumeister et al. (2003) were dismissive of most of the alleged benefits of high self-esteem. However, they admitted that individuals having high self-esteem are happier and more resilient than those with low self-esteem: who wouldn't want to be happy and resilient?

Much research shows that low self-esteem is a factor in the development of various mental disorders (especially depression). Note, however, the existence of considerable overlap between low self-esteem and high neuroticism. In a meta-analysis, Kotov et al. (2010) found high neuroticism was strongly related to several anxiety disorders and to major depressive disorder, and Lönnqvist et al. (2009) found high neuroticism at age 20 predicted mental disorders by the age of 35. Such findings make it hard to disentangle the adverse effects of low self-esteem from those of high neuroticism.

In sum, we can conclude that the myths that high self-esteem is desirable and low self-esteem undesirable are not myths (which explains why I put the word 'myth' in inverted commas at the start of this section). In other words, the beliefs of most members of the public are closer to the true state of affairs than are those of a significant minority of psychologists!

Myth: situational factors overwhelm personality when predicting behaviour

Everyone's behaviour is influenced by both the current situation and their personality. An important issue in personality research is the *relative* importance of these two factors: can we predict someone's behaviour better by focusing on the situation or on their personality? Furnham and Robinson (2022) discovered that most people believe that the situation is far more important. When presented with the very strong statement "Situational factors *overwhelm* personality when predicting behaviour", (my italics), 55% agreed it was definitely or probably true.

It seems natural to assume that the situation has a major impact on our behaviour. Think of situations you find yourself in on a regular basis. Your behaviour is probably very different when in relaxed and informal social situations (e.g., attending a party; enjoying a holiday) than in more formal settings (e.g., work meetings; interviews). Your behaviour is also influenced strongly by the person or people with whom you are interacting: it makes a real difference whether you are talking with your parents, good friends, work colleagues and someone you dislike.

The notion that individuals' behaviour is much more influenced by the situation than by their personality (an approach known as 'situationism') has been strongly endorsed by social psychologists. Its most prominent advocate was Walter Mischel (1968) (Eysenck, 2019). According to Mischel, those arguing that behaviour is well predicted by personality must necessarily assume that any given individual will behave *consistently* across many diverse situations. For example, someone with an extraverted personality should be consistently outgoing, talkative and sociable. In contrast, introverted individuals should typically exhibit far less of those three features in their behaviour.

Mischel (1968) claimed from his review of the relevant evidence that individuals' behaviour is far less consistent across situations than assumed by personality theorists. This led him to the following conclusion:

> I am more and more convinced, however, hopefully by data as well on theoretical grounds, that the observed inconsistency so regularly found in studies of non-cognitive personality dimensions often reflects the state of nature and not merely the noise of measurement.

Mischel (1968) assessed the ability of personality measures to predict behaviour by reviewing research where correlations between personality and aspects of behaviour had been calculated. He concluded that

> The phrase 'personality coefficient' might be coined to describe the correlation between .20 and .30 which is found persistently when virtually any personality dimension inferred from a questionnaire is related to almost any conceivable external criterion involving responses sampled in a different medium – that is, not by another questionnaire.

(p. 77)

Research evidence

Mischel's (1968) generalisation that personality-behaviour correlations rarely exceed 0.3 often applies but is an overstatement. Gignac and Szodorai (2016) reviewed over 700 such correlations. Overall, 75% of them were 0.29 or less and 90% were 0.41 or less.

Does a 'personality coefficient' of 0.3 indicate that personality has a good or poor ability to predict behaviour? Mischel (1968) was certain that personality-behaviour correlations should be much higher than 0.3 for personality to be regarded as an important predictor of behaviour. He pointed out that a figure of 0.3 implies that a given personality factor accounts for only 9% of individual differences in behaviour, thus leaving 91% unaccounted for.

Mischel's (1968) attack on the notion of personality traits had a devastating effect, leading to a marked reduction in research on personality. Bizarrely, however, Mischel (1968) was convinced that situational influences were much stronger predictors of behaviour than personality in the almost complete absence of any supporting empirical evidence!

Sarason et al. (1975) carried out a meta-analysis to provide a key test of Mischel's position. They calculated the percentage of the variance (differences in behaviour among individuals) accounted for by personality and by the situation across 138 experiments. On average, personality accounted for 8.7% of the variance which is consistent with Mischel's claim that personality rarely accounts for more than 9% of the variance in behaviour. However, the situation accounted for only 10.3% of the variance indicating that behaviour was *not* determined substantially more by situational factors than by personality. In addition, the interaction of personality and situation accounted for a further 4.6% of the variance.

Sarason et al.'s (1975) findings have been replicated and extended. Bowers (1973) carried out a meta-analytic review where he discovered that persons (i.e., individual differences) accounted for 11.3% of the variance in behaviour on average whereas situations accounted for only 10.2%. If we followed Mischel's advice and ignored any factors not accounting for far more than 9% of the variance in behaviour, we would be in danger of finding that nothing is worth studying!

In sum, the assumption that situational factors overwhelm personality when predicting behaviour is wrong. However, it could still be argued that behaviour is poorly predicted by individual differences in personality. In the following paragraphs we consider five counter-arguments.

First, a correlation of 0.3 (or less) can still be important and of practical value (a notion discussed further in connection with the next myth). Consider evidence taken from the field of medicine. In the 1980s, there was a large-scale clinical trial to decide whether aspirin reduces the risk of a heart attack. The correlation between administration of aspirin and reduced risk of death from a heart attack was only 0.02 (Meyer et al., 2001). Nevertheless, aspirin has often been recommended to those at risk of a heart attack, and thousands of lives have been saved as a result.

Second, Mischel (1968) focused on the association between a *single* personality trait and a given aspect of behaviour. However, several personality traits are often associated with a given form of behaviour, and we might well be better able to predict individual differences in that behaviour if we took account of several traits. Nielsen et al. (2024) investigated the relationship between personality and prosocial behaviour (i.e., being kind, co-operative and helpful). No single personality trait accounted for more than 9.3% of individual differences in prosocial behaviour. However, when they combined information from several personality traits, Nielsen et al. could account for 13.9% of the variance in prosocial behaviour.

Third, Mischel's (1968) claim that most people display very limited consistency across different situations was based mostly on studies where consistency was assessed by correlating *single* behaviours in different situations. However, that is only one way that consistency can be assessed. For example, we can assess behavioural consistency across time, situation content or behaviour content (Fleeson & Noftle, 2008).

Of particular importance, we can combine several different single behaviours or experiences into an aggregate. Epstein (1977) asked students to record their most positive emotional experience every day over a period of 2 weeks. After that, he worked out the mean intensity of positive experiences separately for all the odd days and all the even days. The correlation for these two measures of positive emotional experiences was 0.88, which is massively greater than Mischel's claim that consistency measures rarely exceed 0.3. In contrast, when positive experiences were compared on only two days, the correlation was less than 0.2.

Fourth, Mischel (1968) assumed that personality and the situation exert *independent* or *separate* influences on behaviour. That assumption ignores the fact that individual differences in personality influence people's choice of the situations in which they find themselves. For example, extraverts are more likely than introverts to engage in stimulating activities involving other people whereas introverts favour leisure activities involving planning and a sense of order (Ickes et al., 1997).

Wilt and Revelle (2019) studied the chosen situations of individuals varying in personality. They contacted people via their mobile phones and asked them to describe their current company and activity. All the 'Big Five' personality factors (extraversion; neuroticism; agreeableness; conscientiousness and openness) predicted the participants' current situation or environment. High extraversion and agreeableness were associated with being in social situations, high conscientiousness predicted studying, low neuroticism predicted work activities, reduced television watching and not being with friends and openness predicted increased television watching and reduced socialising.

In similar fashion, Skimina and Cieciuchi (2020) recorded what individuals were doing seven times a day for seven consecutive days. Individual differences in personality predicted the situations they were in to some extent. For example, individuals high in openness to change were more likely than low scorers to be listening to music, reading and talking with a friend and less likely to be engaged in religious practices, eating or watching television.

In sum, personality not only has a *direct* impact on an individual's behaviour but also has an *indirect* impact by influencing their preferred situations. In other words, people actively select the situations in which they spend most of their time.

Fifth, Mischel (1968) admitted there is a general belief that individuals have personalities reflecting consistencies in their behaviour. However, he claimed that we construct or imagine these consistencies given that our actual behaviour is inconsistent. We can test Mischel's ideas by comparing individuals' ratings of other people's personality with those same individuals' self-reports of their own personality. If ratings are based on imagined consistency in other people's behaviour, we would expect correlations between ratings and self-reports to be low.

Mischel's predicted minimal relationship between ratings and self-reports has been disconfirmed (Eysenck, 2019). Watson et al. (2000) assessed agreement between personality self-reports and ratings for five personality factors in friends, dating couples and married couples. Of the 15 correlations (5 factors × three samples), 100% exceeded 0.30, 73% exceeded 0.40 and 40% exceeded 0.50. The mean correlation between self-reports and ratings was 0.41 with friends and increased to 0.47 with dating couples and 0.56 with married couples. These findings provide compelling evidence that our ratings of others are based on a reasonably valid assessment of their personality rather than on imagined consistency in their behaviour.

Conclusions

The available evidence indicates very clearly that the notion promulgated by Mischel (1968) and others that situational factors overwhelm personality when predicting behaviour is a myth. The most persuasive evidence supporting that conclusion comes from studies finding that the impacts of situational factors and of individual differences in personality in predicting behaviour are comparable.

It might seem that those who subscribe to the previous myth would also agree with Mischel (1968) that we should discard the notion that personality traits are important. However, that is not necessarily the case. Furnham and Robinson (2022) found that over half of those expressing an opinion agreed with the statement that "People come in discrete personality types".

In fact, there is limited usefulness in focusing solely on *independent* effects of situation and personality on behaviour. Individual differences in personality generally influence the situations any given individual chooses to be in. It is also true that the situation (in the form of general environmental influences) has an impact on personality development. Twin studies have revealed that individual differences in personality depend modestly on shared environmental influences within families and much more on non-shared environmental influences unique to any given individual (Johnson et al., 2008).

Finally, there is the issue of *why* most people believe that individuals' behaviour depends considerably more on the situation than on their personality. One possibility is that their answer is based primarily on their own experiences. In our everyday lives, we all realise that our behaviour changes depends on the situation we are in, the specific people with whom we are interacting and so on. However, we are probably less likely to attribute our behaviour across different situations to our personality. We may then use our own experiences to mistakenly believe that individual differences in behaviour are also mostly due to situational factors rather than to individual differences in personality.

Myth: personality measures do not predict consequential outcomes (like health, wealth and divorce) well enough to be useful

We have seen that a majority of people believe that situational factors "overwhelm" personality when predicting behaviour. It follows that individual differences in personality should have extremely limited predictive power with respect to predicting important life outcomes. That may seem reasonable given that such outcomes are typically influenced by numerous factors. For example, longevity depends on genetic factors, socio-economic status, avoidance of life-threatening situations, smoking, obesity and hundreds of other factors, making it unlikely that personality is an important contributory factor.

Furnham and Robinson (2022) presented 616 people with the following statement: "Personality measures do not predict consequential outcomes (like health, wealth and divorce) well enough to be useful". Virtually half of them (49%) believed this statement was definitely or probably true.

It is harder than might be imagined to obtain clear-cut evidence relating to the impact of individual differences in personality on outcomes such as longevity, divorce and success in work. The most basic approach would be to obtain *correlations* between measures of major personality factors and various life outcomes obtained at the same time. However, correlations do not reveal causality. Suppose we discover that the personality dimension of neuroticism is correlated with divorce. It is possible that neuroticism is a causal factor for divorce. Alternatively, experiencing a major negative life event like divorce may increase neuroticism scores in those who have divorced.

Another major limitation of most correlational studies is that potentially important background factors (e.g., socio-economic status; years of education) have often been ignored. This matters because some correlations between personality factors and life outcomes may occur because a background factor influences personality *and* the life outcome.

The optimal approach when attempting to establish whether personality causally influences major life outcomes is to carry out longitudinal studies over an extended period of time. The focus in such studies is on whether personality assessed at one point in time predicts a given life outcome at a subsequent point in time. As with studies where personality and outcomes are assessed at the same time, the findings are typically subjected to correlational analysis.

The most-used correlational measure is r, which indicates the strength of the correlation between personality and outcome. Cohen (1988) argued that an r of 0.10 is small, one of 0.20 is medium and one of 0.5 is large. However, these guidelines are too stringent. In a study discussed earlier, Gignac and Szodorai (2016) discovered when examining hundreds of correlations from the psychological literature that under 3% of correlations exceeded 0.5, only 25% exceeded 0.29 and only 50% exceeded 0.19. This evidence led them to suggest the following reasonable guidelines: 0.10 is a relatively small correlation, 0.20 is a typical correlation and 0.30 is relatively large. We will mostly follow these guidelines in interpreting the relevant findings. However, as discussed earlier, even relatively small correlations can be useful if they relate to important health or other issues. For example, the correlation between smoking and developing lung cancer within 25 years is only 0.08 (Meyer et al., 2001). Nevertheless, nearly all medical experts argue that smoking poses a very significant health risk and reduces life expectancy by several years.

Research findings

Roberts et al. (2007) reported meta-analytic reviews of relevant longitudinal studies with an emphasis on studies controlling for background factors.

The personality factors of central interest were the Big Five factors (conscientiousness; extraversion; neuroticism; agreeableness and openness to experience) (Costa & McCrae, 1992). Roberts et al. focused on three life outcomes (longevity; divorce; occupational attainment) because they can be measured objectively and are socially valued.

What did Roberts et al. (2007) find? We start by considering longevity. Conscientiousness, extraversion and agreeableness all correlated positively with longevity, whereas neuroticism correlated negatively. Conscientiousness correlated most strongly with longevity ($r = 0.09$) followed by extraversion (0.07), neuroticism (0.05) and agreeableness (0.04). These correlations were relatively small. However, all four personality factors had at least twice the predictive power of socio-economic status ($r = 0.02$) with conscientiousness having more than four times its predictive power. IQ predicted longevity with an r of 0.06; thus, it had comparable predictive power to extraversion and neuroticism but less than that of conscientiousness.

Stephan et al. (2019) confirmed the importance of conscientiousness as a predictor of longevity in a longitudinal study. They also discovered that the most predictive feature of conscientiousness was industriousness (e.g., "I have high standards and work toward them").

Why is conscientiousness a relatively good predictor of longevity? Individuals high in conscientiousness generally choose a healthier lifestyle than low scorers. They are less likely to smoke, to have unhealthy eating habits and to be substantially overweight and more likely to take plenty of physical exercise (Stephan et al., 2019).

Roberts et al. (2007) found that the Big Five personality factors predicted divorce more strongly than they did longevity. More specifically, neuroticism correlated 0.17 with likelihood of divorce, whereas agreeableness and conscientiousness correlated negatively (–0.18 and –0.13, respectively). Beck and Jackson (2022) confirmed the importance of agreeableness and conscientiousness in predicting divorce in a mega-analysis (pooling data from multiple studies).

Why do several personality factors predict divorce? The main reason is probably that they are related to individuals' propensity to experience positive and/or negative emotional states (see Chapter 7). Individuals high in extraversion and agreeableness experience more positive emotion than low scorers, and those high in neuroticism experience more negative emotion than low scorers. In a study of romantic relationships, Solomon and Jackson (2014) found that extraversion, agreeableness and conscientiousness all predicted an individual's relationship satisfaction and neuroticism and openness were negatively correlated with their satisfaction. The findings were similar for partner satisfaction.

Roberts et al. (2007) also considered the impact of personality on educational and occupational attainment. Overall, IQ was the best predictor of educational and occupational attainment, followed in order by personality factors (especially conscientiousness), parental income and socio-economic status. Of particular interest, Judge et al. (1999) found that ratings of neuroticism, conscientiousness, agreeableness and extraversion obtained in adolescence predicted occupational status 46 years later.

Zell and Lesick (2022) synthesised the findings from 54 meta-analyses. All five Big Five personality factors were associated with academic and job performance. Overall, conscientiousness was most strongly associated with performance, with the other four having comparable (but smaller) effects. All the associations (except neuroticism) were positive. Conscientiousness was more strongly associated with academic than job performance (0.28 vs. 0.20, respectively), whereas the opposite was the case for extraversion and neuroticism. Indeed, there was hardly any association between extraversion (or neuroticism) and academic performance.

It is plausible that hard work and motivation are of greater importance with respect to academic performance than job performance, whereas someone's interpersonal skills are more important in work contexts than academic ones. Conscientiousness is closely related to motivation. In contrast, extraversion is positively related to interpersonal skills whereas neuroticism is negatively related.

Asebedo et al. (2022) studied the relationship between wealth and positive emotion. An important issue is whether this relationship occurs because wealth makes people happier or because being happy facilitates the accumulation of wealth. Asebedo et al. addressed this issue in a study where positive emotion and wealth were assessed at three points in time: 2008, 2012 and 2016. Wealth influenced subsequent positive emotion *and* positive emotion influenced subsequent wealth. Of most importance here, the impact of positive emotions on wealth depended in part on all of the Big Five personality factors (conscientiousness; neuroticism; extraversion; openness; agreeableness).

Numerous theorists (including Freud and H. J. Eysenck) have argued there are important relationships between personality and mental disorder. It has typically been assumed that certain personality characteristics (e.g., high neuroticism) constitute a vulnerability factor for various mental disorders especially when individuals experience severe life events or stressors (e.g., divorce; death of a spouse; unemployment). Clear-cut evidence that personality factors are associated with mental disorders was reported by Kotov et al. (2010) in a meta-analytic review (mentioned earlier). They distinguished between distress disorders (e.g., major depressive disorder; generalised anxiety disorder; post-traumatic stress disorder) and fear disorders (e.g., panic disorder; social anxiety disorder). High neuroticism and low conscientiousness were both strongly associated with distress and fear disorders, but the associations were greater for high neuroticism. Low extraversion was also associated with most of the disorders.

Kotov et al.'s (2010) findings were only correlational. That is a major limitation given there are several potential explanations for associations between personality and mental disorder (Andersen & Bienvenu, 2011). In addition to the vulnerability hypothesis (personality predisposes one to mental disorders), there are also the scar hypothesis (mental illness adversely affects personality) and the common cause hypothesis (shared environmental or genetic causes).

Since Kotov et al. (2010) discovered that neuroticism was the personality factor most strongly associated with mental disorders, we will focus on research clarifying that association. Hengartner et al. (2016) assessed personality in 1988 and the subsequent presence of mental disorder was noted between 1993 and 2008. Individuals having high neuroticism initially were 41% more likely than those of average neuroticism to have a subsequent major depressive episode and 32% more likely to have an anxiety disorder.

Hengartner et al. (2018) reported additional findings from their longitudinal study. Neuroticism accounted for 51% of the variance (variation) in the severity of symptoms of mental disorder over the course of the study. Neuroticism also predicted the occurrence and persistence of symptoms, and the combination of high neuroticism and aggressiveness with low extraversion predicted the occurrence of several mental disorders.

In sum, most evidence favours the vulnerability hypothesis over the scar hypothesis. However, research also supports the common cause hypothesis. For example, several studies (e.g., Hettema et al., 2006) have reported that genetic factors associated with neuroticism account for nearly 50% of the genetic risk associated with anxiety and depressive disorders.

Two recent large-scale studies have focused on numerous life outcomes. First, Beck and Jackson's (2022) considered 14 different life outcomes, many of which (e.g., unemployment; retirement; criminality) have not been discussed so far. Since they considered all the Big Five personality factors, they calculated 14 × 5 effects of personality on outcomes. Of these 70 personality-outcome effects, 37% were significant. Of the Big Five personality factors, openness was associated with seven significant effects; conscientiousness, agreeableness and extraversion with five and neuroticism with four.

The previous findings may seem unimpressive. However, most findings remained significant in longitudinal studies where life outcomes were assessed some time after personality assessment. This is important because it suggests that personality had causal effects on life outcomes. In addition, most of the findings were unaffected by background factors (e.g., socio-economic status; parental education; race) indicating that they were of general applicability.

Second, Wright and Jackson (2023) argued we should focus on the impact of *changes* in personality over time on life outcomes. Changes in personality often influence subsequent life outcomes in predictable ways. For example, high neuroticism was associated with negative effects on health, and an increase in neuroticism exacerbated these negative effects.

Finally, the great majority of research on personality and life outcomes has been carried out in English-speaking countries and so may have limited general applicability. Stewart et al. (2024) addressed this issue in a study using English-speaking, Russian-speaking and Mandarin-speaking samples. The findings varied somewhat across the numerous life outcomes they considered. However, Stewart et al. concluded that "individuals with similar trait scores often tended to experience similar outcomes despite their different circumstances" (p. 10).

Summary and conclusions

According to Donnellan and Lucas (2021), personality predicts consequential outcomes well enough to be useful, even though 50% of people disagree (Furnham & Robinson, 2022). Superficially, it appears as if the predictive power of personality factors with respect to important life outcomes is often so small that it is unlikely to be of much use. Most strikingly, Beck and Jackson's (2022) discovery that 63% out of 70 personality-outcome effects were non-significant suggests the effects of personality on life outcomes are typically negligible.

However, the ability of personality to predict consequential outcomes varies considerably across outcomes. For example, personality predicts longevity poorly (Roberts et al., 2007) whereas it has strong predictive power for mental disorders such as depression and anxiety (Hengartner et al., 2016, 2018). The predictive power of personality is intermediate for several other consequential outcomes (e.g., divorce; educational and occupational attainment; wealth).

Why does personality predict longevity so poorly? Longevity is influenced by numerous factors; most almost certainly have nothing to do with personality. Examples are susceptibility to serious diseases; DNA repair; maintenance of the ends of chromosomes and protection of cells from damage caused by free radicals. In contrast, consequential life outcomes depending in part on an individual's interpersonal skills (e.g., divorce; relationship satisfaction) are especially likely to be influenced by personality. The strong relationship between personality and mental disorder is to be expected given the key role played by negative emotions such as anxiety and depression in neuroticism and several mental disorders.

Do the various personality-outcome correlations indicate that personality predicts important life outcome well enough to be useful? As any self-respecting philosopher would agree, it all depends what you mean by 'useful'. My starting point is that it is increasingly recognised that most complex psychological phenomena (e.g., longevity; divorce) are influenced by a bewildering multitude of different causes none of which individually has a large effect (Götz et al., 2022).

Why does it matter that many very important life outcomes are largely (or even entirely) determined by factors each exerting only a very small effect? If we decide that effects below a certain size are unimportant, there is a danger we may find ourselves ignoring all factors and so fail to attain any understanding of the causes of life outcomes. Consider the determinants of individual differences in longevity. Personality factors only predicted longevity to a rather limited extent. However, their contribution was greater than that of socio-economic status and comparable to that of IQ.

There is another reason why the prevalence of small effects of personality factors on life outcomes does *not* prevent these factors being useful. We have focused on research investigating personality effects on specific outcomes. In the real world, however, the effects of a given individual's personality *accumulate* throughout life and across several life domains such as longevity, susceptibility to mental disorders, academic and occupational performance and personal relationships. There can be dramatic long-term cumulative effects of personality on an individual's life even if the effects of any single personality factor on a specific life outcome at any one point in time may be modest.

Here is a simple example illustrating the potential power of cumulative effects (Funder & Ozer, 2019). There is evidence (International Situations Project, 2018) that the correlation between agreeableness and experiencing a single social situation as enjoyable and arousing positive emotions is only 0.07. Suppose, however, we consider individuals high and low in agreeableness engaging in hundreds of social interactions. The cumulative effect is that agreeableness correlates –0.30 with loneliness (Wilmot & Ones, 2022).

The size of the effects of personality on life outcomes is important. However, what is also important is the extent to which personality-outcome associations can be replicated. Soto (2019) successfully replicated 87% of 78 previously published personality-outcome associations.

In sum, the totality of the evidence indicates that major personality factors (e.g., the Big Five) often (but by no means always) predict consequential outcomes well enough to be useful. However, sceptics have some justification for arguing that the impact of personality on life outcomes is typically fairly small and so research in this area is of limited usefulness.

Myth: parenting practices are a major source of personality differences

What were the major influences on the development of your personality? I predict that you probably regard the parenting you experienced as a child as an important (*the* most important?) of such influences. If so, you are certainly in good company. Sigmund Freud was a strong advocate of the importance of parenting in determining adult personality. For example, he argued that young children's development of a superego (sense of morality) crucially involved them identifying with the same-sex parent and incorporating their moral values. Thus, parents have a very strong and direct impact on their children's development.

Bandura (1977) emphasised the importance of observational learning in his social learning theory. In essence, children often learn to behave in ways that are rewarded and to avoid behaving in ways that are punished by observing the outcomes of others' behaviour. According to this theoretical approach, parents act as models whose behaviour is *imitated* by their offspring especially when that behaviour is rewarded or reinforced. The implication of Bandura's theory is that children's behaviour will be substantially influenced by how their parents behave. Supporting evidence for Bandura's theory was reported by Gardner (2011). She studied children's social self-efficacy (their ability to form and maintain interpersonal relationships). There was a significant relationship between social self-efficacy in parents and children suggesting that children's social self-efficacy is influenced by observation of their parents' social behaviour.

Most theoretical approaches (including those of Freud and Bandura) have subscribed to what Harris (1998, p. 2) called the 'nurture assumption': "The use of 'nurture' as a synonym for 'environment' is based on the assumption that what influences children's development, apart from their genes, is the way their parents bring them up". The nurture assumption is also very popular among members of the public. Furnham and Robinson (2022) presented over 600 people with the statement "Parenting practices are a major source of personality differences". They discovered that 72% believed this statement was definitely or probably true. According to Lilienfeld et al. (2010), there is also considerable public support for the related assumption that "Raising children similarly leads to similarities in their adult personalities" (p. 153).

Why do so many people believe that parenting practices have a strong impact on children's evolving personalities? The main reason is that children's behaviour often *correlates* with that of their parents. For example, Knafo and Plomin (2006a) investigated prosocial behaviour (positive behaviour such as co-operation and helping) in young twins aged between three and seven. Parental negativity (negative feelings and punitive discipline towards their children) correlated negatively with prosocial behaviour in their children.

It is tempting to interpret the previous finding as indicating an environmental impact of parents' behaviour on their children. However, we must resist the temptation because that interpretation provides a causal explanation of what are only correlational data. In fact, Knafo and Plomin (2006a) found that this negative correlation is mostly due to genetic factors (negative personality characteristics in the parents inherited by their children).

In a similar study on adolescents, Pike et al. (1996) found that maternal negativity correlated with adolescents' antisocial behaviour. Approximately two-thirds of this correlation was attributable to genetic rather than environmental factors. The take-home message is that it is important to separate out genetic and environmental effects when explaining correlations between the behaviour of parents and their children.

Research evidence

How can we obtain clear-cut research evidence indicating the role of parenting in influencing adults' personalities? We can carry out twin studies using monozygotic or identical twins sharing 100% of their genes and dizygotic or fraternal twins sharing on average only 50% of their genes. It is very desirable to include twin pairs reared apart from birth (or shortly thereafter) so we can compare the similarity of personality between twins reared together vs. reared apart. The data obtained from such a twin study allow us to estimate the roles played by shared environmental factors (common factors within families), by non-shared environmental factors (i.e., those unique to any given individual) and genetic factors. According to the nurture assumption, individual differences in personality should depend mostly on shared environmental factors.

Tellegen et al. (1988) carried out a study on adult twins along the above lines. Overall, between 39% and 58% of individual differences in personality were accounted for by genetic factors. For present purposes, however, our focus is primarily on shared environmental factors. The overwhelming majority of theories of personality development would predict that twins brought up together would have more similar personalities than those brought up apart.

In fact, Tellegen et al. (1988) reported only minimal support for the aforementioned prediction in a study on adult twins. For the 11 personality scales of the Multidimensional Personality Questionnaire, the mean correlation for identical twins brought up apart was 0.49 which was only marginally less than that for twins brought up together (0.52). For fraternal twins, the mean correlation for those brought up apart was 0.20 compared to 0.22 for those brought up together. Tellegen et al. concluded that, "Contrary to widely held beliefs, the overall contribution of a common family-environment component [shared environment] was small and negligible" (p. 1031).

Subsequent research has produced similar findings. Nguyen et al. (2021) estimated that individual differences in personality traits are on average 47% due to genetic factors, 53% due to non-shared environmental factors and 0% due to shared environmental factors. Plomin and Daniels (2011, p. 579) concluded their review of the relevant research as follows:

Children in the same family experience practically no shared environmental influence that makes them similar for behavioural traits. In other words, the effective environments of siblings are hardly any more similar than are the environments of strangers who grow up in different families.

From what has been said so far, it appears that shared environmental influences on the personalities of children growing up together are non-existent or of minimal importance. In fact, however, the totality of the evidence is more nuanced in several ways.

First, the conclusion that shared environment is unimportant is mostly based on twin studies. Such studies provide somewhat limited information. For example, twins can resemble each other because of shared genetic influences or shared environmental influences and it is hard to identify the precise contribution made by each influence. Progress can be made by broadening the scope of research. Hahn et al. (2012) investigated personality in grandparent-child pairs, non-twin sibling pairs, mother-child pairs, as well as identical and fraternal twins to provide a more complete picture.

What did Hahn et al. (2012) find? They confirmed that shared environmental effects are negligible when only identical and fraternal pairs are considered. However, they discovered much evidence of small (but significant) shared environmental effects on personality within the other pairings. For example, shared environmental effects accounted for 15% of the variance in Agreeableness and 12% of the variance in Conscientiousness with non-twins.

Second, another alternative approach to twin studies is the adoption approach where unrelated children (either two adopted children or one adopted and one biological child) growing up in the same family are studied. If shared environmental factors are important, these unrelated children should resemble each other in personality to some extent. Loehlin et al. (1981) found that biologically unrelated children brought up within the same family had only minimal personality resemblance. When these children were followed up with 10 years later (Loehlin et al., 1987), the findings still showed "a near-zero influence of shared family environmental factors" (p. 961).

Matteson et al. (2013) compared the effects of shared environment on personality in twin and adoption studies. The effects were slightly largely with the adoption pairs than the twin pairs, suggesting that the twin approach is less sensitive to the detection of small shared environmental effects.

Third, most research has focused on relatively *broad* personality traits. That raises the possibility that shared environmental factors have greater impact on narrower or more *specific* traits (e.g., social and political attitudes; coping styles). Nguyen et al. (2021) briefly reviewed the relevant research. Genetic factors typically accounted for a smaller percentage of the variance with narrow than broad traits allowing more scope for environmental factors (shared and non-shared) to influence individual differences. Of most importance, shared environmental factors often played a significant role in accounting for individual differences in narrow traits (especially socio-political attitudes such as stereotyped masculinity and intolerance of ambiguity).

Fourth, most research has focused on *adult* monozygotic and dizygotic twins. However, we might expect any effects of shared environment on personality to be greater in children and adolescents because they are more likely than adults to be living at home and so much more exposed to the family environment. Relatively strong effects of shared environment on narrow traits have been found in several studies on young children. Knafo and Plomin (2006b) focused on the narrow trait of prosocial behaviour in twins assessed between the ages of two and seven. At the age of two, genetic factors accounted for 32% of individual differences in prosocial behaviour but shared environment accounted for 47%. The situation was very different when the children were aged seven: genetic factors accounted for 61% of individual differences whereas shared environment accounted for only 3%.

Similar findings were reported by Wesseldijk et al. (2018) in a study on conduct problems (e.g., aggression; violation of rules; theft) in monozygotic and dizygotic twins. At the age of nine or 10, genetic factors explained 43%

of the variance in conduct problems, shared environment accounted for 44% of the variance and non-shared environment accounted for the remaining 13%. The findings were strikingly different for adolescents (aged 13 to 18): genetic factors remained important (49% of the variance), but shared environment accounted for 0% of the variance and non-shared environment for 51%. This collapse in the impact of shared environment may reflect factors such as reduced parental monitoring and/or the increased influence of peers (friends of the same age).

Summary and conclusions

The findings from most twin and adoption studies are apparently clear: there is very limited evidence for shared environmental influences on the personalities of children within any given family. However, shared environmental influences are generally present during early childhood but decrease thereafter (Plomin et al., 2001). The key reason is that children within the same family increasingly find themselves in different social environments as they grow up. For example, in the late 1990s, 79% of 4-year olds but only 35% of 3-year olds in England were in daycare. In adulthood, shared environmental influences often totally disappear.

The overall picture is somewhat more complex and nuanced than is generally assumed to be the case in several ways. First, parental influence on narrow personality traits or aspects of behaviour may be somewhat larger (Nguyen et al., 2021). Second, most research has involved the use of twin studies, and there is evidence (discussed earlier) that the influence of shared environment is sometimes underestimated in such studies. Third, there are strong parental influences on childhood and adolescent antisocial behaviour. Among identical or monozygotic twins, the twin experiencing the harsher parenting generally exhibits more antisocial behaviour (Burt et al., 2021).

Fourth, it is important to consider family dynamics. Shared environmental effects occur when parental behaviour impacts on their children's personality development. However, it would be simplistic to assume children are *passively* receptive to parental behaviour. In fact, there are *bi-directional* influences between parents and children, with children's behaviour often influencing their parents. For example, parents give thanks/praise, encouragement and both in response to their infant's helping behaviour in 80% of situations (Dahl, 2015) indicating that parents are responsive to their child's prosocial behaviour. The effects were bi-directional because children who received thanks/praise and encouragement behaved more prosocially thereafter.

Fifth, if we are to achieve a complete understanding of the factors influencing adolescent and adult personality, we must consider non-shared environmental influences (i.e., environmental influences unique to any given individual). Johnson et al. (2008) found non-shared environmental influences accounted for 44% of individual differences in the Big Five personality factors. It has proved surprisingly difficult to identify the most important non-shared environmental influences (Burt, 2024). Harris (1998) argued that children's peer group (other children of a similar age) is the most important non-shared environmental influence. However, the evidence indicates that children and adolescents *seek out* peers having similar personalities (e.g., young people prone to antisocial behaviour seek out friends also prone to antisocial behaviours) (Burt, 2024).

Sixth, the great majority of research has involved samples consisting of white, educated, industrialised, rich, democratic (WEIRD) individuals and so we know very little about the determinants of individual differences in personality in non-WEIRD societies. Of potential relevance is a study by Gidziela et al. (2023). Genetic factors accounted for a greater percentage of individual differences in conditions such as attention-deficit/hyperactivity disorder and autism spectrum disorder in WEIRD samples than in non-WEIRD ones. No definitive explanation for this finding is available. However, it is likely that environmental conditions are more similar for individuals living within a WEIRD society than a non-WEIRD society (e.g., nearly everyone in WEIRD societies receives several years of formal schooling). That would make environmental influences relatively less important in WEIRD societies while increasing the relative influence of genetic influences.

Myth: Men are from Mars, women are from Venus (men and women have dramatically different personalities)

There has been much controversy about the extent of gender differences across a vast range of psychological characteristics. At one extreme we have John Gray who published a popular book called *Men are from Mars, women are from Venus* in 1992. As you undoubtedly guessed from the title, this book presents a grossly exaggerated (and oversimplified) view of the nature and magnitude of gender differences. Gray focused especially on alleged differences between men and women in their preferred communication style (e.g., women want men to listen; men want to solve problems).

A much more measured viewpoint (subscribed to by most psychologists) is the gender similarities hypothesis, according to which, "males and females are alike on most – but not all – psychological variables" (Hyde, 2005, p. 590).

Arguably, more nonsense has been written about gender differences than almost any other topic in psychology. Millions of people have very fixed stereotypical views about gender differences often based on nothing other than wishful thinking or gender bias. For example, you have probably seen or heard the 'fact' that women talk much more than men. Brizidine (2006), in a book entitled, *The female brain*, quantified the difference, claiming that women say about 20,000 words a day whereas men content themselves with a mere 7,000. Many people simply accepted her word for it since it squared with their own preconceptions.

When Brizidine was challenged to justify the previous claim, she replied, "The real phraseology of that should have been that a woman has many more communication events a day – gestures, words, raising of your eyebrows".

That is an entirely different point to the one made in her book and is equally lacking in firm empirical evidence. James and Drakich (1993) examined the evidence from 56 studies. The notion that women talk more than men was supported by two studies. However, the opposite finding was reported in 34 studies.

The remaining 20 studies reported no gender difference in talking. In one of the most thorough studies, Mehl et al. (2007) used electronically activated recorders to monitor talking. Women spoke marginally more words than men each day on average (16,515 vs. 15,669, respectively) but the difference was non-significant.

Another stereotypical view held by many people is that men and women's personalities are very different. Furnham and Robinson (2022) found 32% of their respondents agreed with the statement that 'Men are from Mars, women are from Venus (men and women have dramatically different personalities)', with only just over one-third indicating it was definitely false. Is this stereotypical view also false?

Research

The most common way to measure gender differences in personality is to use a measure known as d, which assesses the magnitude of differences between two groups. As discussed earlier, Cohen (1988) proposed that a d value of 0.20 is small, one of 0.5 is medium and one of 0.8 is large. These guidelines are arbitrary but facilitate our interpretation of d values relating to gender differences in personality.

In spite of many strong stereotypes about gender differences, most such differences are actually very modest. Zell et al. (2015) carried out a meta-synthesis based on the findings from over 12 million individuals! Across the 386 comparisons between males and females they reported, the mean d value was 0.21, which is small. More specifically, 46% of the differences were small and a further 39% were very small.

We start by considering gender differences with respect to the well-established Big Five personality factors (neuroticism, conscientiousness, extraversion, openness and agreeableness). What would we expect to find based on stereotypical views? Löckenhoff et al. (2014) found there was fairly general agreement among Americans that women have higher mean scores on all five factors, with the greatest differences being for agreeableness followed by neuroticism and the smallest differences being for extraversion and conscientiousness. These stereotypical views correspond reasonably closely to the actual gender differences identified by Kajonius and Johnson (2018). Women scored higher on all factors, with agreeableness showing the largest difference ($d = 0.64$) followed by neuroticism ($d = 0.40$) with extraversion and conscientiousness showing the smallest differences (both d's = 0.23).

The previous findings based on American samples are broadly consistent with those in numerous other countries. Schmitt et al. (2008) in a study of gender differences in 55 countries found women outscored men on all factors except openness, with neuroticism (d = 0.40) and agreeableness (d = 0.15) having the largest effects.

Löckenhoff et al. (2014) found across 26 countries that the stereotypical view was that women have higher scores than men on all five personality factors, with the greatest differences being for agreeableness (d = 0.40) and neuroticism (d = 0.26) and the smallest difference for extraversion (d = .06). They compared these stereotypical views with actual gender differences in the Big Five factors across numerous countries based on self-report data. The findings were similar: the largest gender difference were for agreeableness (d = 0.45) and neuroticism (d = 0.40).

Suppose we explicitly focus on aspects of personality where it was strongly suspected there would be marked gender differences. Precisely this was done in a meta-analysis by Twenge (1997) on gender differences related to masculine vs. feminine personality traits (e.g., assertive and independent vs. gentle and understanding of others). The d value for this gender difference was 0.73 (close to the figure of 0.80 that Cohen, 1988, identified as indicating a large effect). Of the 386 gender differences analysed by Zell et al. (2015), this was the largest gender difference.

Hsu et al. (2021) carried out a meta-analysis on gender differences in 'masculine traits' (agency) and 'feminine traits' (communion) based on over 500,000 participants. They used a statistic g (closely resembling d) to assess these differences. Women were more communal than men (g = 0.56) whereas men were more agentic than women (g = 0.40). Note that these gender differences have been decreasing over time probably as a result of social and cultural changes. Note also that these gender differences were smaller in gay, lesbian and bisexual samples.

Galinsky et al. (2024) that focusing on power differences between men and women allows us to obtain some understanding of sex/gender differences in personality. They reviewed numerous studies and discovered that high-power individuals and men typically displayed high agency and low agency whereas the opposite was the case for low-power individuals and women. These findings suggest that social power contributes to sex/gender differences in personality. Decreasing differences in masculine and feminine traits between men and women very likely reflects the decreasing imbalance of power between men and women in Western society.

The picture so far is one where there are smallish (but easily replicated) gender differences in major personality factors such as agreeableness and neuroticism plus somewhat larger gender differences in 'masculine' and 'feminine' traits. However, nearly all these gender differences involved the participants providing *self-reports* of their personality, and they may have exaggerated how 'masculine' or 'feminine' their personality actually is. We can deal with that issue by using *ratings* (i.e., each individual's personality is assessed by someone who knows them well). When Löckenhoff et al. (2014) did this for the Big Five personality factors, they obtained findings comparable to those they reported with self-reports. For example, d for neuroticism was 0.43, for agreeableness it was 0.25 and for extraversion it was only 0.12.

In fact, the predominantly small effects described earlier underestimate what is actually the case, because the research on which it is based is limited in several respects. First, questionnaires provide imperfect measures of personality factors. For example, when the same personality factor is assessed by the same questionnaire on the same people on two occasions close together in time, the typical correlation is only about 0.75. As a consequence, gender differences in personality have probably been underestimated. This issue can be addressed by correcting the scores for measurement errors.

Second, most research has focused on large major personality factors (especially the Big Five). It is arguable that gender differences may be greater among narrower personality traits (identified as 'facets' in questionnaires assessing the Big Five factors).

Third and most important, research on gender differences in personality has nearly always focused on only *one* personality factor at a time. Much larger gender differences might be obtained if we considered *several* related personality factors at the same time. For example, men on average differ from women in being taller and having a larger waist size. Gender differences would be more pronounced if we took account of both factors together rather than treating them separately.

Del Giudice et al. (2012) carried out the first systematic study of gender differences in personality taking account of the third limitation discussed earlier. In their initial analysis of the findings from a large American sample on Cattell's 16PF [Personality Factor] questionnaire, the average d value when each personality factor was considered individually was only 0.26. After that, they combined information from the various personality factors using a measure known as D (conceptually very similar to d except that it reflects differences in several variables rather than only one). D was 2.71 for this global gender difference, indicating there was an overlap of only 10% between the male and female personality distributions.

Kaiser (2019) considered gender differences in over 800,000 individuals from 50 countries rectifying all three major limitations of previous research. He assessed all 30 facets of the Big Five factors (e.g., agreeableness consists of trust, morality, altruism, co-operation, modesty and sympathy facets) and then corrected the resultant scores for measurement errors. The mean value for D across all 50 countries was 2.11, ranging from 1.49 (Pakistan) to 2.48 (Russia). These findings indicate there are very large gender differences in personality in all 50 countries (remember that $D = 0.80$ is generally regarded as a large effect). Note that when Kaiser considered personality facets one at a time, the mean d value was only 0.25 (indicating a small effect).

It could be argued that "One swallow doesn't make a summer", and so a single study producing dramatic findings does not prove that gender differences in personality are large. Reassurance was provided by Kaiser et al. (2020), who studied gender differences in personality across several English-speaking countries using items assessing 15 related personality traits based on Cattell's 16 PF (Personality Factor) test. They combined information from all 15 traits which produced a D of 2.10. That means we could correctly guess the gender of someone 85% of the time based only on knowing their personality profile.

Around the world

So far I have focused mostly on the overall picture with respect to gender differences in personality. However, the extent of such gender differences has been found to vary across countries in several studies and so we can identify factors associated with larger or smaller differences. What would we expect to find? According to social role theory (Eagly & Wood, 1999), gender differences in personality depend mostly on social norms about traditional sex roles. It would be predicted from this theory that gender differences in personality would be larger in gender-unequal countries in which sex role stereotypes are strong.

Falk and Hermle (2018) proposed an alternative theoretical approach. According to their resource hypothesis, there are substantial differences across countries in access to material and social resources. Countries with high levels of economic development (material resources) and greater gender equality (social resources) will exhibit the largest gender differences in preferences and personality because those living in such countries can express themselves freely without restriction. Intriguingly, predictions from the resource hypothesis are diametrically opposite to those from social role theory.

Falk and Hermle (2018) compared the two theories by assessing several preferences (e.g., willingness to take risks; patience; altruism; trust) in 76 countries. As predicted by the resource hypothesis, gender differences in preferences were strongly predicted by high levels of material and social resources.

Similar findings with respect to personality were reported by Costa et al. (2001) in a study on the Big Five personality factors across 26 countries. Gender differences in personality correlated 0.47 with GDP (gross domestic product), 0.57 with women's life expectancy and –0.46 with women's illiteracy rates. Thus, gender differences were greater in countries that are prosperous and healthy and where women have good educational opportunities.

Kaiser (2019) found gender differences in D were larger in countries with high food consumption, cultural individualism and low historical prevalence of pathogens (organisms causing disease). Speculatively, men and women in such countries have more freedom to exhibit their 'natural' personalities because of the favourable environmental conditions in which they live. Similar findings were reported by Herlitz et al. (2024) in a review based on 27 meta-analyses. Gender differences in personality were greater in countries with higher living conditions (e.g., economy; gender equality; education).

Summary and conclusions

The distance between Mars and Venus varies between 75 and 209 million miles. It would be an exaggeration to claim that the personalities of men and women are that far apart or that their personalities are "dramatically different". Indeed, most research until comparatively recently reported only modest gender differences in personality. However, such research was limited because it typically focused on only one personality trait at a time. Gender differences become greater when several personality traits are considered jointly. For example, del Giudice (2023) found that individuals' personality scores could be accurately identified as male or female 68% of the time when five personality traits were considered but 74% of the time when 30 personality traits were considered.

Kaiser (2019) and Kaiser et al. (2020) obtained very large gender differences across many different countries when they focused on personality patterns (or profiles) across related traits. More specifically, they reported D values (closely resembling d values) of 2.11 and 2.10, respectively. We can put these values in context. The average d value in psychology is 0.4 and only 17% of d values exceed 0.8. Thus, D values greater than 2.0 are very unusual.

In sum, it remains a myth that men and women have "dramatically different" personalities. However, what are probably the greatest gender differences relating to psychological characteristics have been found with respect to personality profiles. Thus, men and women can be regarded as having "substantially different" personalities. Since Herlitz et al. (2024) found that sex differences in personality are mostly larger in countries that enjoy better living conditions, it is likely that these differences will increase in magnitude over time.

7 Social psychology

Social psychology is responsible for some of the best-known research in the entire history of psychology. Nearly everyone has heard of Stanley Milgram's research in which he apparently discovered that most ordinary decent people were prepared to administer potentially lethal electric shocks to a middle-aged man with a heart condition when ordered to do so by someone in authority. You are probably also familiar with Philip Zimbardo's Stanford Prison Experiment in which mock prison guards treated their mock prisoners in cruel and degrading ways.

In this chapter, we discuss some of these famous classic studies in social psychology. We also consider some other major myths whose origins go back several decades or centuries. Regrettably, the origins of most of these myths lie in the mistaken theories and biased research of social psychologists and sociologists (see also Chapter 11)! The full story of what actually happened is told throughout the rest of this chapter.

Myth: Milgram proved that most people will obey immoral orders

An important feature of nearly all societies is that some individuals are given power and authority over others. Examples include managers and their staff, parents and their children and doctors and patients. A system requiring some obedience to authority makes sense when the authority figure possesses relevant expertise, knowledge and experience. However, it can go disastrously wrong as in the much-cited case of Nazi Germany, where obedience to the Nazi party forced (or encouraged) millions of Germans to carry out appalling atrocities.

To what extent can ordinary people be persuaded to behave immorally when ordered to do so by an authority figure? This was the intriguing question addressed by Stanley Milgram (1974) in one of the most famous (or notorious!) research programmes in the history of psychology. In Milgram's (1963) original research, a learner (a middle-aged man with a heart condition) performed a simple learning task and a teacher administered electric shocks of increasing intensity every time he produced a wrong answer. At 180 volts, the learner yelled, "I can't stand the pain!" and by 270 volts his response was an agonised scream. The maximum shock was 450 volts.

DOI: 10.4324/9781003596677-7

This original experiment was carried out at Yale University and the experimenter was present throughout.

Suppose you had been the teacher in this situation. Do you think you would have been prepared to deliver the maximum (and potentially fatal) 450-volt shock in this situation? Psychiatrists predicted only 0.125% of participants would do so (Milgram, 1965) and students produced a figure of 1.2% (Milgram, 1963). In fact, Milgram (1963) found 65% of his participants gave the maximum shock: 520 times as many as the expert psychiatrists had predicted and 54 times more than the students' average estimate! The obvious interpretation of these findings is that we all have profoundly mistaken views about our willingness to obey authority even when it is immoral to do so.

Milgram (1974) carried out further experiments manipulating various aspects of his experimental situation. Fewer participants showed total obedience (giving all the shocks) when the learner's plight was made more obvious. For example, when the teacher had to force the learner's hand onto the shock plate, only 30% were fully obedient. Only 20% were totally obedient went the experimenter gave his orders by phone and so his impact was reduced. The setting also made a difference: when the experiment was carried out in a run-down building rather than prestigious Yale University, only 48%. of participants administered all the shocks.

Milgram (1974) provided a theoretical account of his dramatic findings of strong (or very strong) obedience to authority. He claimed humans are susceptible to becoming the instrument of an authority figure by entering the agentic state and so abandoning their sense of personal responsibility. According to Milgram, the tendency to adopt the agentic state is, "the fatal flaw nature has designed into us".

The previous account closely resembles that given in most textbooks. However, the finding that total obedience was 520 times more common than psychiatrists would have predicted should perhaps have set off some alarm bells within the fraternity of textbook writers (and psychologists in general). Can you think of any potential problems with Milgram's research on obedience to authority? Suppose you were a participant in one of Milgram's studies. How plausible would you have found it that a research psychologist at a prestigious university would try to persuade you to administer potentially lethal electric shocks to someone with a heart condition? You would need to have a very low opinion of psychologists if you believe they might expose you to the possibility of killing someone!

In fact, as you have probably guessed or already knew, no actual shocks were administered. Note also that the learner and the experimenter were both confederates who simply behaved as Milgram had instructed them to behave.

Criticisms of Milgram's research

Milgram repeatedly claimed that any of us might be willing to be fully obedient to authority. However, in one of his earliest publications on obedience to authority (Elms & Milgram, 1966), he used the California F-Scale (F stands for Fascist) to assess the authoritarian personality (respect for authority, conventionalism, toughness and authoritarian aggression). High scorers on the F-scale were significantly more likely than low scorers to be fully obedient to authority. Thus, we need to take account of personality as well as Milgram's experimental situation.

Serious doubts about Milgram's interpretation of his findings were raised by Hollander and Turowetz (2018). They tracked down interviews given by 91 people who were questioned immediately after they had taken part in one of Milgram's experiments. In these interviews, participants were asked to explain their behaviour. Of most importance were the responses given by the 46 participants who had been fully obedient. As Milgram would have predicted, 59% of the fully-obedient participants responded that they were following instructions, consistent with the notion that they were in an agentic state during the experiment. However, 72% of them indicated they did not believe the learner was being harmed, a finding that undermines Milgram's research and how he interpreted his findings.

Perry et al. (2020) discussed further evidence of the prevalence of participants harbouring doubts about Milgram's research procedure. Close examination of the data reported by Milgram indicated that 44% of his participants harboured doubts that the learner had received any electric shocks. Does this matter? Clear-cut evidence that it does was reported by Perry et al. Of those who believed fully that shocks were given, 38% were totally obedient, compared to 65% among those harbouring the most doubts. Only the findings from those participants who fully believed they were administering potentially lethal shocks are surprising and of theoretical interest. Among those participants, only just over one-third were totally obedient.

Other problems present themselves if we consider Milgram's (1963) article on obedience to authority. A crucial requirement when reporting an experiment is to ensure *all* the relevant details of the procedures used are made explicit so another experimenter could in principle replicate the study. Milgram failed to do this. He did not make it obvious that the experimenter and the teacher were in one room with the learner in an adjacent room. This is important: there is much less obedience when the teacher and learner are in the same room so the teacher can experience the learner's suffering at first hand. Also of relevance, the learner did not protest until the tenth shock had been administered which means that the teacher in another room had no idea that the learner might be suffering.

Milgram claimed that the experimenter responded to a reluctance on the part of the teacher to continue to administer electric shocks with prods such as, "You must continue" or "You must go on". Such prods indicated that the experimenter behaved like an authority figure ordering the subordinate figure (i.e., the teacher/participant) to obey. Milgram's claim was often falsified. When Laurens and Ballot (2021) analysed in detail what actually happened in Milgram's research, they discovered the experimenter sometimes said, "We must continue" or "We must go on". This changes the situation from one of authority figure-subordinate to one of two people co-operating with each other. Of most importance. the use of "we" also means that the responsibility for what happens is not solely that of the teacher but is also shared by the experimenter.

There is another major omission. The experimenter told participants who protested at what they were being asked to do that he would accept full responsibility if anything went wrong but this is not stated in the article. It only became clear that the experimenter often went off-script in this way when Gina Perry (2013) discovered numerous audiotapes of Milgram's research. These off-script statements loaded the dice in favour of Milgram's theory that obedient participants lose their sense of responsibility and enter the agentic state. In essence, the participants were being instructed to lose their sense of responsibility!

We are now in a position to go back to Milgram's (1965) startling finding that the percentage of participants being fully obedient was more than 500 times greater than predicted by psychiatrists. In the article, Milgram fails to indicate at all what these psychiatrists were told about the experimental situation: this makes it impossible to interpret the psychiatrists' predictions.

Mixon (1971) carried out a more adequate study. He presented individuals with the Method section of Milgram's (1963) article and asked them to estimate how many participants would have been fully obedient. Females estimated that 33% of participants would be totally obedient whereas the estimate for males was 44%. Thus, Milgram's findings are not especially surprising when people are provided with relevant information about the procedures he adopted. Of course, as we have seen, the Method section from Milgram's (1963) article does not contain complete information about what he did. People would probably guess fairly accurately the percentage of fully obedient participants if provided with a full and accurate account of Milgram's experimental situation.

One of the main reasons Milgram's research attracted a huge amount of media attention was that he claimed his findings on obedience to authority were directly relevant to the appalling and inhumane treatment of the Jews by the Nazis during the Holocaust. This claim is absurd for various reasons. First, the values underlying Milgram's research were positive (e.g., understanding more about human learning) whereas those of Nazi Germany were vile and totally immoral (e.g., racial superiority).

Second, Milgram's participants had to be watched closely by the experimenter to ensure their obedience, but this was unnecessary in Nazi Germany. Indeed, many Nazis continued to kill Jews even when offered the opportunity to stop doing so. Third, many participants experienced strong conflict between the experimenter's demands and their own conscience and were clearly upset and distressed. In contrast, most Nazis were unconcerned about moral issues and carried out atrocities without any qualms.

Ethical concerns

We have seen that there are multiple issues with Milgram's research which were largely ignored for decades. However, it was recognised immediately that Milgram's research posed serious ethical problems. Indeed, these problems are so great that no one for several decades has carried out research closely resembling that of Milgram. A fundamental requirement of ethical research is that participants are free to leave the experiment without giving any reason. In contrast, participants in Milgram's research were told they had to continue with the experiment even if they did not want to.

Another serious ethical problem with Milgram's research is the agonised state many participants found themselves in. Here is an observer's description of one participant (Milgram, 1974): "I observed a mature and initially poised businessman enter the laboratory smiling and confident. Within 20 minutes he was reduced to a twitching, stuttering wreck, who was rapidly approaching a point of nervous collapse. He constantly pulled on his earlobe and twisted his hands. At one point, he pushed his fist into his forehead and muttered 'Oh God, let's stop it!'" Research having that sort of impact cannot be ethically acceptable.

Milgram attempted to defend himself against the previous criticisms of his research by claiming that all the participants had been carefully debriefed about its true nature at the end of the experiment, with 84% of them indicating they were glad to have been involved. In fact, Milgram's claims were dishonest: he only debriefed some of the participants. The reason he gave for that was that the research was carried out in a small town (New Haven, Connecticut) and he did not want too many people to be forewarned about the deceptions involved in it.

Conclusions

The take-home message from Milgram's research programme used to be that non-psychologists do not understand how easily most people can be persuaded to behave unethically and immorally if ordered to do so by an authority figure. In contrast, psychologists realise how prone we are to abandon our sense of responsibility and threaten the existence of others if that is what we are ordered to do.

Ironically, the truth is essentially the opposite! Non-psychologists can estimate very accurately how people will respond in the Milgram situation if provided with complete information about it. In contrast, most psychologists believed for several decades that Milgram's research was among the most important ever carried out within psychology. Griggs and Whitehead (2015) analysed the coverage of Milgram's research in 10 social psychology textbooks published 50 years after his original study on obedience to authority. In spite of the fact that numerous valid criticisms of this research had been published during those 50 years, these textbooks almost ignored them: "Although more space is devoted in current textbooks to coverage of the

Milgram study than in previous generations of textbooks, the coverage of criticisms of the Milgram study . . . remains minimal" (Griggs & Whitehead, 2015, p. 390). One exception not discussed by Griggs and Whitehead is a 2008 textbook of mine in which eight serious criticisms of the study are discussed.

Milgram was well aware of key ethical issues: "My own view is that deception for any purposes [in psychology] is unethical and tends to weaken the fabric of confidence so desirable in human relations" (Milgram, 1959). Why, then, did he misrepresent the procedures he had used and the findings he obtained? He was strongly motivated by the prospect of becoming famous and one way to do that was by producing totally unexpected findings. As Nicholson (2011, p. 246) pointed out,

> The 'counterintuitive' quality of the research findings became a central part of the obedience narrative. . . . Not surprisingly, Milgram himself developed a strong emotional attachment to the idea that he had made a psychological 'discovery', and a former graduate student recalled that 'he would become furious if a student suggested that it was all common sense'.

Milgram's determination to make his findings appear very surprising explains why he left out crucial details of his experimental procedure when reporting his research. As discussed earlier, his findings did not appear very surprising to people given the limited information provided in the Method section of his 1963 study. As Mixon (1990, p. 25) concluded, "Given enough detail . . . people are quite good at judging what happens in Milgram's study".

In sum, the myth that most people will obey immoral orders is believed by millions of people in large measure because of Milgram's research on obedience to authority. This research achieved mythical status for two main reasons. First, as we have seen, he distorted his reporting of that research to make the findings appear more remarkable than was actually the case. Second, his research also attracted massive attention because of the way that Milgram explicitly linked his findings to the horrors of Nazi Germany. This linkage was especially clear in an unpublished note he wrote: "Let us stop trying to kid ourselves. What we are trying to understand is obedience of the Nazi guards in the prison camps, and that any other things we may understand about obedience is pretty much of a windfall, an accidental bonus" (cited in Nicholson, 2011, p. 243).

Myth: crowds typically panic in threatening situations

Do you believe that crowds panic in threatening situations? If your answer is "Yes", you are in good company because approximately 80% of people share that belief (Dezecache, 2015). Papp (2020) reported data showing that students in Hungary, the United States and Italy all strongly agreed that panic is a common reaction when disaster strikes.

We must put some of the blame for these highly unflattering views of our responses to danger on Hollywood and the way it portrays crowds. As Drury and Reicher (2010, p. 60) pointed out, "Hardly any self-respecting Hollywood disaster movie would be complete without one scene of people running wildly in all directions and screaming hysterically". Prime examples are movies such as *Independence Day* and *Earthquake in New York*: nearly everyone responds to danger by panicking and trampling other people underfoot in their selfish desire to save themselves at the expense of others.

Many academics buy into this negative view of crowd behaviour. Schweingruber and Wohlstein (2005) identified the following characteristics often ascribed to crowds: (1) spontaneous; (2) irrational; (3) highly emotional; and (4) suggestible. Across 20 textbooks, 65% of the authors agreed that crowds are spontaneous, 50% that crowds are somewhat or totally irrational, 50% that they are highly emotional and 60% that they are suggestible.

The most famous advocate of the notion that crowds are dangerous and irrational was Le Bon, who wrote *Psychologie des foules* (1895). The word *'foules'* is generally translated as 'crowds' but can also mean 'mobs'. Le Bon was a reactionary whose political views led him to claim that crowds behave like "lower forms of evolution" (Le Bon, 1895, p. 39). According to him, when individuals are in a crowd, their conscious personality is gradually replaced by the group unconscious personality. Fear spreads throughout an entire crowd like a contagious disease to produce panic and then the anonymity of individuals in a crowd or mob removes normal social constraints and so leads to violence.

The focus on anonymity remains important. In their review of textbooks, Schweingruber and Wohlstein (2005) found 40% of authors emphasised the role of anonymity in explaining crowd behaviour. Under the cloak of anonymity, individuals have a reduced sense of responsibility and so feel much freer to behave aggressively and violently. A term that has often been used in this context is deindividuation, which Baumeister et al. (2016, p. 10) defined as "a temporary reduction in self-awareness, personal responsibility, and evaluation apprehension, usually brought about by immersing the self in a group".

Zimbardo (1969) obtained evidence that deindividuation can lead to aggressive behaviour. Female participants were instructed to give electric shocks to other women. Deindividuation was produced in half the participants by having them wear laboratory coats and with hoods covering their faces. These deindividuated women gave electric shocks twice as intense as those of other participants who simply wore their own clothes. There is an issue with this study because the clothing worn by the deindividuated individuals resembled that worn by the Klu Klux Klan, a secret organisation that carried out numerous violent acts against Americans of colour. Johnson and Downing (1979) found that individuals who were deindividuated by being dressed as nurses actually gave fewer electric shocks than those wearing their own clothes.

Evidence suggesting that crowds readily turn into rioting mobs comes from a consideration of major incidents such as those following the killing of George Floyd by a policeman (Derek Chauvin) in the United States on 20 May 2020 or the killing of Mark Duggan by police in Tottenham Hale, London on 4 August 2011. In both cases, crowds in many different cities engaged in prolonged rioting and violence. In the case of Mark Duggan, riots in London were followed by "copycat violence" in several cities including Birmingham, Manchester, Wolverhampton and Bristol. More recently, several riots in England followed the mass stabbing in Southport on 29 July 2024 in which three children were killed.

Some of the available evidence is certainly consistent with the negative views of crowd behaviour expressed by Le Bon (1895). Mann (1981) analysed newspaper reports of crowds watching someone threatening suicide by jumping from a bridge, building or tower. We might anticipate that crowds in those circumstances would attempt to dissuade the suicidal individual from jumping. In many cases, however, the crowd encouraged the victim to jump; this is what Mann termed a 'baiting crowd'. His findings suggested that the probability that a crowd would engage in baiting was greater when the individuals in the crowd were more anonymous (or deindividuated) because the crowd was large and/or because the incident took place after dark. However, Mann only considered 10 cases of baiting and 11 of non-baiting, and so the effect of crowd size was non-significant.

Smith et al. (2019) attempted to replicate Mann's (1981) findings based on a much larger sample of 152 public suicide attempts. There was no support for earlier findings. Instead, baiting behaviour was predicted by crowd frustration: it was more likely to happen when the event lasted for a long time, when the traffic was blocked and pedestrian walkways were cordoned off. These findings are consistent with the frustration-aggression hypothesis (Berkowitz, 1989), according to which frustration caused by unexpectedly thwarted goals is often a trigger for aggressive behaviour.

Contemporary evidence: reactions to fires

How do people react when there is a fire in a theatre or other building? Media reports typically claim that those affected by the fire reacted irrationally and in a panic-stricken way, which coincides with most people's expectations. In the following paragraphs we evaluate these claims in the context of several examples of life-threatening fires in theatres and other contexts.

Using transcripts of interviews with survivors, Johnson (1988) investigated what happened during the 1977 Beverly Hills Supper Club fire in Southgate, Kentucky in which 165 people died. Although people were afraid and some were screaming, most occupants leaving the building walked out calmly. Johnson found that queuing, routine courtesy and helping were widespread.

Even at the moments of greatest urgency and when there was more individual competition, social bonds did not collapse entirely. For example, people were more likely to help the elderly than others, and family units continued to function.

Similarly, Donald and Canter's (1992) study of the 1987 King's Cross Underground fire also found that people were often unwilling to deviate from familiar patterns of behaviour. For example, some commuters continued to follow their accustomed routes even when this meant delaying their exit or exposing themselves to danger.

In sum, the speed with which fires can spread means that by not acting immediately upon the potentially urgent need to evacuate, any delays can have fatal results. Such considerations led Townsend, a Senior Officer in the London Fire Rescue Service, to conclude that "When people die in fires, it's not because of panic, it's more likely to be the lack of panic" (cited in Kemp, 2003). Admittedly, some reports of theatre fires provide apparent support for the notion that crowds are inclined to panic. However, careful analysis indicates that the inadequate structure of the theatres and insufficient emergency exits played a much larger role than panic (Chertkoff & Kushigian, 1999).

Contemporary research: other disasters

Numerous disasters occur every year. In Europe alone, there were 899 natural and technological disasters during the decade between 2000 and 2009 and there were further major man-made disasters such as the bombings in Madrid in 2004 and in London in 2005 (Grimm et al., 2014). Drury and Reicher (2010) interviewed many of those present during the bombings in London on 7 July 2005. Most experienced a sense of togetherness and used numerous positive terms (e.g., 'unity'; 'affinity'; 'part of a group'; 'warmness') to describe their feelings. I was working in central London when the bombings occurred (and actually heard the bomb that went off in Tavistock Square) and witnessed first-hand the solidarity and calm exhibited by most Londoners.

Similar findings were obtained in research on other disasters. For example, Proulx and Fahy (2004) analysed the reports of 435 survivors of the attacks on the World Trade Center in New York on 11 September 2001. Mutual help was highlighted in 46% of the reports and 57% of the survivors perceived other people as behaving calmly in reaction to the situation. Here is the testimony of an architect who arrived by subway underneath the Trade Centre when the first plane crashed: "I'm looking around and studying the people watching. I would say that 95 percent are completely calm. A few are grieving heavily and a few are running, but the rest were very calm. Walking. No shoving and no panic" (Clarke, 2002, p. 24).

It could be argued that the previous reports by witnesses of the aftermath of the plane crashes reflected their partial awareness of how people behaved and possibly also reflected their own biases. However, there is objective evidence indicating that nearly everyone who was in the Trade Center Towers survived if they were on floors below where the planes struck. This strongly suggests that nearly everyone behaved calmly and rationally rather than becoming hysterical and trampling other people underfoot.

Dezecache et al. (2021) provided a more nuanced account of how individuals respond in very threatening situations. They focused on the mass shooting by three gunmen at Le Bataclan concert theatre on 13 November 2015. Ninety people were killed at the theatre and hundreds more were injured. Dezecache et al. interviewed 32 survivors, all of whom recalled observing, initiating or participating in supportive actions including emotional support and physical support (e.g., assisting someone who was wounded). However, the survivors also recalled 69 unsupportive actions (e.g., pushing others out of the way; ignoring calls for help; ordering others to stop crying or complaining about their wounds).

What determined whether responses to the mass shooting were supportive or unsupportive? Socially supportive behaviour was more likely than unsupportive behaviour when individuals could not escape, were under fire by the gunmen and felt interpersonal closeness with others. Note, however, that supportive actions were relatively common even when individuals had the opportunity to flee leaving others to their fate.

In sum, the findings were generally consistent with previous research in that most actions were supportive and co-operative. However, individuals' reactions depended on the precise situational circumstances (e.g., possibility of escape) and there was more evidence of self-focused or selfish behaviour than was found in most previous research.

What is 'panic'?

A theme running through research on reactions to fires and other disasters is that there was relatively little evidence of panic. In general, the behaviour of those exposed to disasters was mostly highly appropriate in the circumstances. Note, however, that the term 'panic' has no precise scientific definition – many different behaviours (including rational ones) exhibited by members of a crowd could be interpreted as indicating panic (Haghani et al., 2019). In fact, such claims based on the assumption that most people overreact to a life-threatening emergency are generally well wide of the mark.

Social identity model

There is consensus that individuals within crowds often become deindividuated

According to traditional theoretical accounts (e.g., Le Bon, 1895), individuals within a crowd become deindividuated and anonymous, and they lose self-awareness, as a consequence of which their behaviour becomes uninhibited and freed from social constraints. In the words of Baumeister et al. (2016, p. 10), "The primary effect of deindividuation [is] to reduce accountability, especially in enabling people to take illicit selfish benefits (e.g., cheating, stealing)".

The obvious problem with this theoretical approach is that it fails to explain why most crowds behave rationally and co-operatively. A prominent explanation was provided by Reicher et al. (e.g., 1995, 2016) in their social identity model. According to this model, deindividuation is, indeed, an important consequence of individuals being in a crowd. However, the behaviour of such deindividuated individuals is strongly influenced by the group's social norms (standards of behaviour). These norms are of central importance in determining whether crowd behaviour is desirable or undesirable.

As Reicher et al. (2016, p. 36) argued,

> When groups are more antisocial, it is not the result of a loss of individual identity per se, but rather because of the specific norms of the groups with which people identify. . . . Anonymous members of groups neither lose accountability nor act selfishly . . . there is a shift whereby the group rather than the individual becomes the basis of both accountability and interest. We become accountable for our performance as group members; we act for the collective gain rather than our personal benefit.

Norms are very important within the social identity model. However, we need to distinguish between *situational* group norms (what most people regard as appropriate behaviour in a given situation or context) and *general* social norms (standards of behaviour *not* tied in to a given context). Deindividuation of individuals in crowds increases responsiveness to (and conformity with) situational group norms but not general social norms.

Postmes and Spears (1998) carried out a meta-analysis of 60 studies concerned with group and crowd behaviour. Manipulations designed to produce deindividuation (e.g., anonymity; large groups) were associated with behaviour breaking general social norms (e.g., aggression; violence). However, the mean correlation was only 0.09, indicating the effect was very modest in size.

As predicted by the social identity model, factors thought to increase deindividuation *increased* adherence to situational group norms (Postmes & Spears, 1998). In contrast, most other theories predict that deindividuation would *reduce* adherence to group norms.

Conclusions

The stereotypical view is that the behaviour of crowds faced by a disaster or other threatening situation is highly undesirable. As discussed earlier, Schweingruber and Wohlstein (2005) found that many people believe crowds are spontaneous, irrational, highly emotional and suggestible. In fact, it would generally be more accurate to use adjectives such as rational, supportive and calm to describe their behaviour.

Three qualifications need to be put on the aforementioned summary. First, how individuals respond to a disaster often depends in part on their personality. For example, individuals low in agreeableness will be less likely to provide supportive behaviour than high scorers and those high in neuroticism will be more likely to panic when confronted by a disaster than low scorers.

Second, it is important to assess the motives leading individuals to behave in certain ways. As Dezecache et al. (2021, p. 11) pointed out, "Reassuring others to promote one's own safety (i.e., reassuring someone else to make him/her quiet and avoid detection by the terrorists) crucially differs, motivationally speaking, from comforting others for their welfare".

Third, most of the evidence consists of the self-reports of individuals interviewed some time after a given disaster. It is possible that these self-reports exaggerate the extent to which individuals actually behaved co-operatively and unselfishly in disaster situation. It is also possible that these self-reports are somewhat distorted by failures of memory.

Myth: Zimbardo proved that the power structure in prisons makes guards aggressive and violent

One of the best-known and renowned studies in the entire history of psychology was conducted by Philip Zimbardo and colleagues at Stanford University in California between 14 and 20 August 1971. It was designed in the attempt to understand why there were so many brutal attacks by guards on prisoners in America's prisons. Unsurprisingly, this study became known as the Stanford Prison Experiment. Coincidentally, there was a prison riot at Saint Quentin prison in California the day after the end of the experiment leading to the deaths of two prisoners and three guards.

Zimbardo argued there were two main potential reasons why this brutality was occurring. One reason is that prison guards tend to have aggressive or sadistic personalities; in other words, they are self-selected for this job because they like the prospect of exerting power over the inmates. The other reason is that the social environment in prisons (e.g., a rigid power structure; cold and forbidding atmosphere) is mostly responsible for the aggressive behaviour of prison guards.

The Stanford Prison Experiment is so well known that I will just briefly indicate the highlights. At the outset, emotionally stable students agreed to act as 'guards' and 'prisoners' in a mock prison. The two groups were clearly distinguished by their clothing. The guards wore plain khaki shirts and trousers, a whistle, a police nightstick and reflecting sunglasses whereas the prisoners wore a loose-fitting muslin smock with an identity number on the front and back, a light chain and lock around one ankle and a cap made from a nylon stocking.

The mock prison was deliberately designed to be as unpleasant as possible. There were three small cells (9 ft by 6 ft) with three prisoners assigned to each cell. According to the official account of the study (Haney et al., 1973), the mock guards were instructed to maintain a reasonable degree of order but were prohibited from using any physical aggression.

The happenings within the mock prison rapidly became so potentially dangerous that the entire experiment was brought to a premature close. Violence and rebellion were both present within two days of the start of the experiment. The guards repressed the rebellion by the prisoners by using fire extinguishers, removing many of the prisoners' rights and systematically harassing the prisoners and treating them violently. After only one day, one prisoner became so emotionally disturbed (e.g., uncontrollably crying and screaming) that he had to be released.

Over subsequent days, some guards seemed to take great pleasure in behaving sadistically towards the prisoners, and there was a steady increase in their use of force and aggression. As a result, two more prisoners were released because they became very emotionally disturbed. Finally, the experiment was brought to an end when Zimbardo's girlfriend, Christina Maslach, burst into tears and said, "It's awful what you are doing to those boys!"

How can we interpret these findings? According to Haney and Zimbardo (2009, p. 807), the following conclusions are justified: "Certain very powerful social situations, settings, and structures can shape and transform the behaviour of the persons who enter them, suppress individual differences, and compromise deeply held values". In essence, "The inhumanity of the 'evil situation' totally dominated the humanity of the 'good' participants" (Zimbardo, 1983, p. 62).

What you have just read is the original account of the Stanford Prison Experiment provided by Zimbardo and his colleagues. This account was accepted by many people (at least until comparatively recently). For example, Zimbardo was awarded the American Psychological Association's prestigious gold medal in 2012 for producing "one of the most famous demonstrations in psychology that situational factors can powerfully shape human behaviour".

Griggs (2014) analysed the coverage of the Stanford Prison Experiment in 11 introductory psychology textbooks. There were no criticisms of it in five of them and the others had minimal criticisms mostly centring on ethical problems associated with the distress caused to the mock prisoners (although a textbook of mine published in 2008 but not discussed by Griggs contained four detailed criticisms of Zimbardo's study). The picture is similar in the seven social psychology textbooks analysed by Griggs and Whitehead (2014). Three contained no criticisms at all, and two more made only very minor criticisms.

In spite of all these endorsement of the Stanford Prison Experiment and the acclaim it has received over several decades, it actually reveals practically nothing of any value about the causes of violence in prisons. Thus, the notion that Zimbardo showed that violent behaviour by guards is 100% down to the situation is a myth and nothing more.

What is wrong with the Stanford Prison Experiment?

As discussed shortly, Zimbardo's original account of what happened during the experiment is grossly deficient. I will start by considering criticisms based on the original account, followed by many additional ones based on information about the experiment that only became public knowledge several decades afterwards.

It might be better to ask "What *isn't* wrong with the Stanford Prison Experiment?" rather than what is wrong with it. Of central importance, even the original account in no way justifies the conclusion that anyone who became a mock guard would have behaved aggressively and violently. For example, Zimbardo (1989, p. 154) pointed out that about one-third of the guards "became tyrannical in their arbitrary use of power", with a single brutal guard who stood out. In contrast, other guards were reasonably friendly in their dealings with the prisoners. These findings are totally inconsistent with a purely situational account of the guards' behaviour.

There is a more fundamental reason why Zimbardo's experiment did not indicate that individual differences among guards are irrelevant in explaining their behaviour: no attempt was made to investigate individual differences in a systematic fashion! The guards used in the experiment were all young emotionally stable male adults. Does anyone really believe the findings would have been exactly the same if the guards had been elderly nuns or young men with sadistic and psychopathic personalities? Nevertheless, the whole tenor of Zimbardo's approach is that the answer must be "Yes".

There are multiple ethical issues with the Stanford Prison Experiment. It is unacceptable to submit participants in an experiment to humiliation and distress of such intensity that three of the mock prisoners became so emotionally disturbed they had to be released. More specifically, one of the most crucial requirements of ethical research is that participants are told *in advance* what will happen in an experiment and then provide full informed consent. Zimbardo did not adhere to this requirement.

There was a marked *increase* in criticisms of the Stanford Prison Experiment in the decades after the Stanford Prison Experiment. Why was this? One major reason was that Zimbardo began to admit that several crucial features of the study had been omitted from his original account. Another reason was that Zimbardo donated very extensive files and tapes to the Stanford University Archives relating to the study in 2011.

In the time period before 2011, Zimbardo revealed he had been very proactive in trying to make the guards behave aggressively. He instructed the guards as follows:

> You can create in the prisoners . . . a sense of fear to some degree, you can create a notion of arbitrariness that their life is totally controlled by us, by the system, you, me – and they'll have no privacy . . . they can do nothing, say nothing that we don't permit. We're going to take away their individuality.
>
> (Zimbardo, 1989)

Note that his references to 'we' and 'us' means he was explicitly identifying himself as the leader of the guards rather than a bystander simply observing what happened. This is a vivid example of experimenter bias.

Haney et al. (1973) claimed the guards had dreamt up nearly all the humiliations they heaped on the prisoners (e.g., putting bags over their heads; forcing them to use buckets rather than toilets). This claim was false as was made clear in 2005 by Carlo Prescott, a consultant for the study who had spent 17 years in San Quentin prison. In his role as consultant, he had told Zimbardo about all these humiliations several months ahead of the study based on his own prison experiences (discussed by Knowles, 2018).

As mentioned earlier, much more information about the Stanford Prison Experiment became available in 2011. Le Texier (2019) spent years analysing all this information and made several startling discoveries refuting the claim that the guards had spontaneously behaved in aggressive and hostile ways. Of most relevance, the testimony of the guards revealed very clearly how Zimbardo applied pressure to the guards to behave as he wanted them to. For example, according to John Mark (one of the guards),

> Zimbardo went out of his way to create tension. Things like forced sleep deprivation . . . he knew what he wanted and then tried to shape the experiment – by how it was constructed, and how it played out – to fit the conclusion that he had already worked out.
>
> (Mark, 2011)

More damning evidence came from David Jaffe, the warden in charge of the guards. Here are his views at the end of the experiment:

> Even before I arrived, Dr. Zimbardo suggested that the most difficult problem would be to get the guards to behave like guards . . . I was given the responsibility of trying to elicit 'tough-guard' behaviour.
>
> (Le Texier, 2019, p. 829)

Here is David Jaffe talking to one of the guards who was deemed to be too soft:

> Generally, you've been kind of in the background. . . . But we really want to get you active and involved. Because the guards have to know that every guard is going to be what we call a 'tough guard'.
>
> (Le Texier, p. 829)

Finally, we consider what happened to James Peterson. He was a guard who was asked to leave the experiment prematurely. When Zimbardo was asked what had happened, this is what he said:

> It might have been that Peterson just didn't want to get into the role. That is, you know, just didn't want to force the prisoners to do push-ups and jumping jacks and all the other things. . . . The only reason we would let a guard go is if he was not playing his role.
>
> (Knowles, 2018)

In other words, Peterson was removed from the experiment because he was not behaving as Zimbardo wanted him to!

Replication?

In spite of all the previous criticisms of the Stanford Prison Experiment, it could still be argued that the study might have produced similar findings if it had been carried out without the experimenter pressuring the guards to behave in certain ways. Precisely this was done in an attempted replication study carried out in 2001 by Reicher and Haslam for the British Broadcasting Corporation (BBC) and shown on television in 2002.

The findings were very different (Reicher & Haslam, 2006). The guards failed to identify with their role whereas the prisoners increasingly identified with theirs. As a result, the guards were reluctant to impose their authority on the prisoners and so were overcome by them. The findings were very different to those in the Stanford Prison Experiment because the pressure Zimbardo applied to the guards to act aggressively was missing from the BBC study. However, it may also be relevant that the guards in the BBC prison study knew their actions would be seen by millions on television which may have had an inhibiting effect on their behaviour.

Summary and conclusions

The notion that Zimbardo's Stanford Prison Experiment demonstrates how the power structure in prisons leads to violence by the guards is simply a myth carefully constructed by Zimbardo. In fact, the study tells us nothing at all about the reasons why prison guards are sometimes aggressive and violent. Of crucial importance, Zimbardo's role in the study was that of a theatre director ensuring that the cast said the lines he wanted them to say rather than as a researcher remaining scrupulously neutral and unbiased. Zimbardo more or less admitted as much when discussing the removal of the guard James Peterson from the experiment: "The point is, it's a drama. . . . You have to play the role in order for the whole thing to work" (Knowles, 2018).

If you think I am exaggerating, consider another way in which Zimbardo disingenuously attempted to distort the guards' behaviour. He told the guards that it was desirable for them to behave very aggressively because this would generate huge publicity leading to reform of the terrible American prison system (Reicher et al., 2020).

Myth: individual differences in attitudes are mostly learned

The study of attitudes and attitude change is one of the most important topics within social psychology. An attitude can be defined as "a person's evaluation of an object on a favourable to unfavourable continuum" (Albarracin &

Shavitt, 2018, p. 300). It is very clear from this definition that we all possess huge numbers of attitudes: we have attitudes about products (e.g., Marmite), health (e.g., desirability of a healthy lifestyle), people we know and attitudes about ourselves. Here we will mostly be concerned with relatively general attitudes relating to political attitudes, prejudice and ideology.

Historically, it was nearly always assumed that attitude formation depends primarily on experience and learning. In essence, your positivity or negativity towards any given object develops as a result of your personal experiences with that object and the information that you read or hear about it.

In the study of attitudes, we can focus either on specific attitudes or clusters of attitudes. For example, we can ask whether people are in favour of – or opposed to – the death penalty. Alternatively, we can consider clusters or groupings of related attitudes which can be regarded as forming an ideology. One of the most researched ideologies is conservatism which refers to traditional values and opposition to change. For example, Henningham (1996) devised a 12-item conservatism scale asking individuals' views on issues such as legalised abortion, stiffer jail terms and multiculturalism.

There has been much more research on general attitudes or ideologies than on specific attitudes. A key reason is that individuals exhibiting conservatism with respect to one issue tend to exhibit conservatism on many other issues, which justifies regarding it as a general factor. Another reason is that an individual's attitude on a given issue may be strongly influenced by their idiosyncratic experiences. For example, someone who is generally low in conservatism may nevertheless favour longer jail sentences for criminals because someone in their family was violently attacked and the culprit received only a short prison sentence.

Most researchers and theorists in social psychology have assumed (explicitly or implicitly) that individual differences in attitudes depend entirely or almost entirely on environmental factors. Most non-psychologists agree that genetic factors are of little or no relevance to individual differences in attitudes (Willoughby et al., 2019; discussed further later in the chapter). As we are about to see, these assumptions by psychologists and non-psychologists are mythical.

Authoritarian attitudes and personality

Probably the most famous psychological research on the factors responsible for people's general social attitudes or ideology was produced by a group of researchers centred on Theodor Adorno, a German Jew who spent the Second World War in exile in California. Their research represented an attempt to understand the appalling atrocities committed by the Nazis. In their book *The Authoritarian Personality* (1950), Adorno et al.'s central argument was that individuals having authoritarian attitudes and personality (characterised by rigid beliefs, hostility towards other groups and submissiveness to authority) were those most likely to be attracted to fascism.

What factors are responsible for the development of authoritarian attitudes and the authoritarian personality? According to Adorno et al. (1950), authoritarian adults had been treated harshly as children, causing them to have high levels of hostility towards their parents. This hostility was largely or entirely unconscious, with children apparently idealising their parents; in Freudian terms, children identify with the same-sexed parent. In adulthood, authoritarian individuals act submissively towards authority figures and displace their hostility onto minority groups. Adorno et al. claimed authoritarian individuals are strongly inclined to follow the orders of authority figures. Thus, the appalling atrocities committed by the Nazis were greatly facilitated by the authoritarian personalities possessed by millions of ordinary German citizens.

One limitation with Adorno et al.'s (1950) approach was that it attached too much importance to mistaken Freudian views about childhood (e.g., exaggerating the parental impact on children: see Chapter 6). Another limitation was that the questionnaires they used to assess the authoritarian personality (e.g., the F (Fascism) Scale) were poorly designed. Altemeyer (1981, 1988) dealt with these limitations in his development of some of Adorno et al.'s (1950) ideas. His Right-Wing Authoritarianism Scale represented an improved version of the F Scale. It assessed three components of right-wing authoritarianism: submissiveness towards authority figures; authoritarian aggression; and conventionalism (strict adherence to social norms).

Altemeyer jettisoned some of the Freudian ideas espoused by Adorno et al. (1950). However, he basically agreed with them that an individual's home environment during childhood was crucially important in determining whether they develop right-wing authoritarianism. He cited Mark Twain, the American author, who had been influenced by a preacher who said "You tell me whar a man gits his corn pone [unleavened maize bread], an I'll tell you what his 'pinions is". Altemeyer (1988) agreed with this preacher, arguing we "get our opinions where we get our corn pone – at home" (p. 63).

Altemeyer (1988) discussed evidence supporting his 'corn-pone theory' in his book, *Enemies of Freedom*. He discovered there was a moderately high correlation of 0.40 between right-wing authoritarianism in parents and their adult offspring, which is as expected if parental attitudes influence those of their children. There were also more modest correlations (never exceeding 0.24) between retrospective ratings of parental behaviour and right-wing authoritarianism in their adult children.

In spite of the fact that *Enemies of Freedom* was awarded the American Association for the Advancement of Science's Prize for Behavioural Science Research, it is seriously flawed. As we have seen numerous times in this book, researchers are often far too eager to interpret correlational evidence as indicating a causal relationship. McCourt et al. (1999) obtained findings that convincingly demolished the theoretical position adopted by Adorno et al. (1950) and Altemeyer (1981, 1988).

They carried out a complex study based on monozygotic (identical) and dizygotic (fraternal) twins brought up together or apart (i.e., in separate families). This twin study allowed them to disentangle the roles of environmental and genetic factors in producing individual differences in authoritarian attitudes assessed by Altemeyer's Right-Wing Authoritarianism Scale.

What did McCourt et al. (1999) find? Their key findings were that individual differences in authoritarian attitudes depended 50% on genetic factors and 35% on non-shared environmental factors (i.e., those differing between twins). That means a maximum of 15% of individual differences in authoritarianism could possibly depend on family or shared environment, the factor regarded as of pre-eminent importance by Adorno et al. (1950) and by Altemeyer (1981, 1988). Limitations in the data collected mean the 'true' percentage is somewhat less than 15%.

McCourt et al. (1999) apparently provided some support for the notion that the rearing or family environment is important by replicating Altemeyer's (1988) finding that parental behaviour correlated with adult authoritarianism in their biological children. However, they also found that authoritarianism in adult adoptees failed to correlate with parental rearing behaviour allegedly producing authoritarian children. This finding is totally at variance with predictions from Altemeyer's theoretical approach.

Role of genetic factors

We have seen that Adorno et al. (1950) and Altemeyer (1981, 1988) grossly exaggerated the impact of parental behaviour on the development of authoritarianism in children. I imagine that you feel that this is entirely excusable and understandable in a new area of research. In fact, however, reality is more complicated and fascinating than that.

Let us turn the clock back to 1974 when Eaves and Eysenck published an important article on factors relating to social attitudes. They carried out a twin study and discovered that individual differences in social attitudes have a fairly strong genetic influence. More specifically, genetic factors accounted for approximately 65% of individual differences in radicalism-conservatism and 54% of individual differences in toughmindedness-tendermindedness. These findings were of relevance to the views of Adorno et al. (1950) given that authoritarian attitudes correlate strongly with the conservatism and also correlate with toughmindedness (Ray, 1973).

What was the reaction to Eaves and Eysenck's (1974) bombshell discoveries? It was extremely muted. According to *Web of Science*, that article was cited only 12 times in the 10 years following its publication by researchers other than those responsible for the original research. In the following 10 years (1984–1994), there were only 19 citations by other researchers.

This lukewarm reception is merely illustrative of the mindset of most researchers in social psychology. As McGuire (1969, p. 161) pointed out, "Even theorists who agree on little else are in complete accord on the extreme and undemonstrated notion that all attitudes are developed through experience".

Amazingly, this strong emphasis on the notion that attitudes are learned persists to this day. From time to time, the *Annual Review of Psychology* publishes reviews of the current state of knowledge with respect to social attitudes. The most recent such reviews (both entitled 'Attitudes and attitude change') were by Bohner and Dickel (2011) and Albarracin and Shavitt (2018). Neither review contains *any* mention of words such as 'genetic', 'heredity' and 'genes'. This total neglect of the role played by genetic factors in influencing individual differences in attitudes is also found in most social psychology textbooks.

Superficially, this neglect of genetic factors may seem unsurprising since it would be absurd to suppose that we have specific genes determining our views about abortion or *Love Island*. However, such neglect is bizarre given that genetic factors have been convincingly shown to influence individual differences in attitudes in dozens of studies over the past 50 years (Dawes & Weinschenk, 2020). For example, Hatemi et al. (2014) analysed data on political ideology (grouping of political attitudes) from over 12,000 twin pairs obtained from five countries over four decades. Genetic factors consistently accounted for between 20% and 60% of individual differences in political ideology (averaging 40%).

As mentioned earlier, non-psychologists also drastically underestimate the role played by genetic factors. Willoughby et al. (2019) found that members of the public believed on average that genetic factors account for 18% of individual differences in political attitudes. In fact, the 'true' figure of 40% (taken from Hatemi et al., 2014) is 120% greater than that.

How can we explain the selective blindness and bias of social psychologists (and many lay people) that has prevented them from acknowledging that individual differences in attitudes depend in part on genetic factors? According to Tooby and Cosmides (1992), most social scientists adhere to 'the standard social science model', which is based on the assumption that human behaviour is influenced almost exclusively by environmental factors (e.g., socialisation). As a consequence, "What is organised and contentful in the minds of individuals comes from culture and is socially constructed . . . [leading to] a flexibility in human behaviour that belies any significant 'instinctual' or innate component" (p. 32). Belief in the standard social science model has also led social psychologists to ignore or de-emphasise the fact that family members are related genetically as well as having a shared environment.

The evidence discussed earlier may seem to show that theorists such as Adorno et al. (1950) and Altemeyer (1981, 1988) were totally wrong when they emphasised the role played by the parental or family environment in producing individual differences in attitudes. However, there is a missing piece in the jigsaw puzzle. Research demonstrating that genetic factors strongly influence individual differences in attitudes has typically involved *adult* samples and it is not necessarily the case that the same is true for *child* or *adolescent* samples. This gap in the available evidence was filled by Hatemi et al. (2009) (discussed in the following paragraph).

Hatemi et al. (2009) carried out a longitudinal twin study where they obtained information about the political attitudes (liberalism-conservatism) of their sample between the ages of nine and 17. They also obtained data from a twin study using samples across the adult life span. Family or shared environmental factors accounted for a progressively greater percentage of individual differences in political attitudes between the ages of nine (approximately 25%) and 17 (60%+), whereas genetic factors had *no influence* on political attitudes throughout childhood and adolescence. In stark contrast, genetic factors accounted for between 40% and 60% of individual differences in political attitudes in adults between the ages of 20 and 75 with family or shared environment accounting for 0% to 20% of the variance.

It is unsurprising that family or shared environment has a diminishing impact in adulthood when offspring have left the family home. It is harder to interpret the finding that genetic factors exert greater influence on political attitudes during adulthood than childhood. What is noteworthy, however, is that there is a halving in the similarity of political attitudes between dizygotic or fraternal twins in adulthood compared to childhood. It is as if the reducing impact of family environment provides more scope for genetic factors to influence political attitudes.

Why and how do genetic factors influence attitudes?

Many criticisms have been made of the use of twin studies to investigate factors influencing individuals' attitudes. It is often claimed monozygotic or identical twins are treated more similarly than dizygotic or fraternal twins. This provides an alternative environmentally based explanation of the greater similarity in attitudes between identical twins than fraternal ones.

There are several reasons why this explanation is implausible. First, it implies that the parents of identical twins are more enthusiastic about their children having the same political beliefs than parents of fraternal twins. Second, it cannot explain why the similarity in attitudes between fraternal twins is at least as great as that between identical twins during the years of childhood and adolescence (Hatemi et al., 2009). Third, Hatemi et al. (2010) considered data from non-twin siblings, spouses and parents as well as from twins. Over 40% of individual differences in political attitudes stemmed from genetic factors, and there was some evidence that twin studies may slightly *underestimate* genetic influences.

It is generally agreed that the influence of genes on political attitudes is *indirect*. However, there have been various attempts to clarify the underlying mechanisms involved. Research so far strongly suggests that numerous genes are involved rather than a strictly limited number (Dawes & Weinschenk, 2020).

Kalmoe and Johnson (2022) pointed out that individuals only realise their genetic potential under favourable conditions. For example, genetic influences on height are greatest when individuals are well nourished. In similar fashion, they argued that genetic influences on political attitudes would be greatest among those possessing the greatest political knowledge. In a twin study, Kalmoe and Johnson found genetic factors accounted for 57% of individual differences in socio-political conservatism. However, as predicted, this figure was much higher for those having the greatest political knowledge (74%) than for those having the least knowledge (29%).

It is highly probable that there are important gene X environment interactions, meaning that the extent to which genetic factors impact on attitudes depends on various environmental factors. For example, we saw in the study by Hatemi et al. (2009) that genetic factors influence attitudes massively more during adulthood than during the years of childhood and adolescence spent living in the family environment.

Many theorists (e.g., Adorno et al., 1950; Eaves & Eysenck, 1974) have assumed that there are important relationships between personality and attitudes. There is clearly a relationship between them. For example, Mondak and Halperin (2008) investigated personality correlates of liberalism-conservatism. Individuals high in openness and neuroticism were more liberal-minded than low scorers, whereas individuals high in conscientiousness were high in conservatism.

It has often been hypothesised that the main reason for correlations between personality traits and political attitudes is because the former cause the latter. This hypothesis seems plausible if we assume that personality traits are more basic and fundamental than political attitudes or ideology. We can test this hypothesis by carrying out a longitudinal study where personality traits and attitudes are both assessed at two points in time. If the hypothesis is correct, we would predict that changes in personality should predict subsequent changes in attitudes. Hatemi and Verhulst (2015) carried out such a study with the personality and attitudes of twins and siblings being measured at two points approximately 10 years apart.

What did Hatemi and Verhulst (2015) find? There was no support for the hypothesis: changes in personality traits and political attitudes over the 10-year period were minimally related or not related. Instead, their findings indicated that correlations between personality traits and political attitudes reflect a common underlying genetic influence. As Hatemi and Verhulst (2015, p. 17) concluded, "Both personality traits and political attitudes are independently part of one's psychological architecture".

Summary and conclusions

There is compelling evidence that individual differences in attitudes (specifically, ideology) throughout adult life depend to a moderate extent on genetic factors. However, it remains for future research to clarify precisely how the numerous genes involved interact with environmental factors to produce the observed individual differences in adult attitudes and ideology. Horwitz et al. (2023) identified one important factor. They discovered in a large-scale review that married couples on average are more similar to each other with respect to political attitudes than any of the major personality traits. This similarity may increase the impact of genetic factors on the political attitudes of their offspring.

Earlier I discussed some reasons why social psychologists have largely (or entirely) ignored all the evidence on the role played by genetic factors. Another reason is that most research on attitudes by social psychologists has involved investigating environmental factors producing attitude change. This perhaps allows us to achieve some reconciliation between the genetic and social psychological approaches. Ludeke and Krueger (2013) found in a longitudinal twin study on middle-aged people that there was a high level of stability of authoritarian attitudes over a 15-year period, with most of this stability being attributable to genetic factors. In addition, however, the typically smallish changes in attitudes over that time period were due to individuals' unique or non-shared environmental influences.

As mentioned earlier, there are various reasons why most people underestimate the contribution made by genetic factors to individual differences in political attitudes. For example, it is likely that your political attitudes are fairly similar to those of your parents. The 'natural' assumption is that this similarity reflects the environmental influence provided by your parents. In fact, however, much of that similarity reflects genetic similarities within families.

Myth: happiness is influenced most strongly by what happens to us

An interesting and important question that most of us have considered from time to time is the following: what determines whether someone is happy or not? Evidence that millions of people are eager to discover the secrets of happiness comes from the bewildering number of best-selling books focusing on answers to that question. When I did a Google search, I instantly discovered the existence of hundreds (if not thousands) of relevant books with titles ranging from *The Happiness Factor* (Kirk Wilkinson) to *The How of Happiness* (Sonja Bomirsky) to *The Happiness Project* (Gretchen Rubin).

At a very general level, we can distinguish between bottom-up and top-down theories of happiness. According to bottom-up theories, individual differences in happiness depend predominantly on the emotional experiences (pleasant and unpleasant) we have had during the course of our lives. In contrast, top-down theories emphasise the importance of internal factors (including genetic factors, especially those relating to personality). Of course, individual differences in happiness probably involve complex interactions of bottom-up and top-down factors.

Furnham and Cheng (2000) gave individuals aged between 15 and 35 a questionnaire designed to identify the factors they believed are most important for happiness, with every item starting with "People tend to be happy if. . . ." These individuals gave a rating for each item between one (unimportant) and seven (important). Having close friends/confidants produced an average score of 5.90 (the highest score out of 38 causes of happiness), doing the work they like averaged 5.67 and being financially well off averaged 4.03. In contrast, being born with 'happy genes' scored only 2.58. These findings suggest most people believe much more strongly in the bottom-up approach to understanding individual differences in happiness than the alternative top-down approach.

'Happy genes'?

How can we assess the notion that "happy genes" play an important part in determining individual differences in happiness? The best way of assessing the role of genes in influencing happiness is by twin studies with monozygotic (identical) twins and dizygotic (fraternal twins). Lykken and Tellegen (1996) discovered identical twins are much more similar in well-being (feeling good about oneself) than fraternal twins. They estimated that between 44% and 52% of individual differences in well-being or happiness were due to genetic factors.

Bartels (2015) carried out a meta-analytic review of twin studies on well-being involving a total of over 55,000 individuals. On average, genetic factors accounted for 36% of individual differences in well-being. In a further meta-analysis, genetic factors accounted for 32% of individual differences in satisfaction with life. The influence of genetic factors on well-being is maximal in adolescence (approximately 40%) and declines slowly to 24% in old adulthood (De Vries et al., 2024). The increased impact of environmental influences on well-being in old adulthood occurs in part because there are marked individual differences in severe life events (e.g., chronic ill health; death of one's spouse).

Many types of genetic factors jointly contribute to individual differences in happiness or life satisfaction. However, Røysamb et al. (2018) found in a twin study that genetic factors relating to personality are of special importance. Overall, genetic factors accounted for 31% of individual differences in life satisfaction and 65% of those genetic factors were personality-related. The personality factors of extraversion and neuroticism were of special importance: the former correlated 0.30 with life satisfaction and the latter correlated –0.48. These findings are readily explained (Costa & McCrae, 1980): extraversion relates to experiencing high levels of positive emotions whereas neuroticism relates to experiencing high levels of negative emotions (e.g., anxiety; depression). Individuals high in extraversion and low in neuroticism experience much positive emotion but little negative emotion and so are generally happy. As an old expression has it, "Accentuate the positive, eliminate the negative".

How does the influence of genetic factors on individual differences in happiness or well-being compare to the impact of environmental factors? Lykken and Tellegen (1996) addressed this issue. Socio-economic status accounted for 3% of individual differences in well-being, income for 2% and marital status for less than 1%.

'Hedonic treadmill'

How can we explain the surprisingly small effects of most environmental factors on our level of happiness or well-being? An influential answer is based on the notion that we typically adjust or adapt to the circumstances in which we find ourselves. If you have ever gone swimming in an outdoor swimming pool or in the sea in England, you have probably experienced a very common example of this. Initially, the water feels incredibly cold and you feel it was a daft idea to go swimming. Surprisingly rapidly, however, the water mysteriously seems to warm up.

Helson (1948) argued in his adaptation-level theory that we interpret and respond to our current experiences in the light of our prevailing adaptation level. This adaptation level form represents a point of indifference or neutrality corresponding to our *expectations* based on past experience. Suppose someone who is relatively poor wins £10,000,000 in a lottery. They would initially be elated because they would suddenly have access to far more money than they ever expected. Over time, however, they adapt to having huge amounts of money and the elation associated with their windfall disappears.

Brickman and Campbell (1971) applied the previous ideas to the psychology of happiness by proposing the notion of the 'hedonic treadmill'. In a treadmill, you always end up at the same place no matter no rapidly you move. By analogy, you gradually adapt to winning a massive sum of money in a lottery so that eventually you are no happier than beforehand. That sounds dispiriting. More optimistically, the notion of the 'hedonic treadmill' also leads to the prediction that if you suffer some major misfortune (e.g., paralysis), the unhappiness it causes will gradually reduce until you become as happy as you were prior to the misfortune.

Brickman et al. (1978) tested predictions based on the assumption that there is a 'hedonic treadmill'. They contacted winners of the Illinois State Lottery, nearly all of whom had won at least one hundred thousand dollars and one-third of whom had won one million dollars (equivalent to five million dollars or four million pounds today). Even though the great majority regarded winning as a highly positive event, they did not feel any happier after winning than beforehand and did not expect to feel happier in 2 years' time.

Smith and Razzell (1975) interviewed 88 individuals who had won at least £75,000 (equivalent to nearly £2,000,000 today) on the football pools. While 77% of these winners claimed the money won on the pools had made them happier, what was most striking was the relatively modest effect winning such a large sum had on many of them. One winner said, "The mortgage was the main thing, and little luxuries we'd never been able to have – a washer, save one doing it by hand, different little things like that". One winner, John Sellens, claimed, "I haven't changed, ask any of the lads – they'll tell you. It's silly to change really, it don't make any difference to me . . . because I still go out with the same people".

More surprisingly, Smith and Razzell (1975) discovered that there were *disadvantages* associated with winning large sums of money. Most of the pools winners gave up their jobs almost immediately, which often led to boredom and excessive drinking. For example, Richard Taylor reacted in the following unfortunate way:

> I was an alcoholic, I went to hospital with it, it crippled me, really crippled me. For about two and a half years I was a total drunk from morning to night . . . I used to drink through boredom, bloody boredom that's all, and misery.

There were two other problems associated with winning the pools. First, it often disrupted individuals' social identity because of the conflict between their previous working-class existence and their comfortable middle-class lifestyle after their win. Only 28% of pools winners were definite about their social class compared to over 50% of non-winners. Second, sudden wealth typically had what Smith and Razzell (1975) called an 'amplification effect': it amplified or exaggerated important aspects of the winners' behaviour. For example, a very shy and retiring winner stopped work and had even fewer social contacts than before his win. Another winner who enjoyed practical jokes began to carry out more elaborate ones after his win such as arranging for someone he had argued with to discover a dead horse in his garden (shades of *The Godfather*).

The most dramatic prediction based on the hedonic-treadmill assumption is that individuals suffering some great misfortune will eventually regain the level of happiness they experienced prior to their misfortune. This assumption is summed up in the excessively optimistic Arab proverb, "Throw a man into the sea, and he will become a fish". Brickman et al. (1978) tested this assumption with accident victims. Two-thirds of them were quadriplegics having practically no use of their arms and legs, and the remainder were paraplegics having paralysis of the legs and part or all of the trunk. They reported having been happier than others before their accident and they expected to be as happy as other people in 2 years' time. However, their current happiness level was significantly lower than that of other people. Note that these individuals had been disabled for less than 1 year, so it could be argued that the adaptation process was still incomplete.

Schulz and Decker (1985) studied paraplegic and quadriplegic individuals 20 years after their injury. Their average psychological well-being was only slightly lower than that of healthy individuals. Those disabled individuals having good social support from family and friends were as happy as healthy individuals. However, 66% of the disabled individuals indicated they were less happy now than when they were younger.

The findings discussed so far were based on relatively small samples of individuals who experienced a serious misfortune. Lucas (2007) discussed his findings from very large-scale studies where information about individuals' life satisfaction was available for 5 years prior to their misfortune and 7 years thereafter. Severe disability caused an immediate drop in life satisfaction from 6.8 to 5.3 on a 10-point scale with no evidence of recovery over the subsequent 7 years. The pattern was very similar with respect to less severe disability with the main difference being that life satisfaction dropped to 6.2 followed by a plateau. Death of a spouse led to a marked reduction in life satisfaction from 7.2 to 6.0. However, widowhood was followed by a small increase in life satisfaction year by year until it reached 7.0, which was only slightly less than during the pre-widowhood period.

In sum, there is qualified support for the notion of a hedonic treadmill. More specifically, individuals typically show the predicted adaptation following great good fortune. However, they often show rather limited (or no) adaptation following great misfortune (Diener et al., 2006).

Summary and conclusions

We saw earlier that evidence suggests most people believe individual differences in happiness can be better explained by bottom-up theories focusing on our experiences than by top-down theories emphasising personality and genetic factors (Furnham & Cheng, 2000; Lilienfeld et al., 2010). However, other findings reported by Furnham and Cheng indicate that people's beliefs are more complex and nuanced. For example, most agreed that people tend to be happy if "they have high self-esteem" and if "they have a pleasant personality (friendly and good sense of humour)".

Most research on the factors determining individual differences in happiness does not allow us to establish causality. For example, Satici et al. (2016) discovered that loneliness correlated –0.52 with happiness, indicating that lonely individuals tend to be much less happy than those who are not lonely. The crucial issue is whether loneliness causes unhappiness or whether unhappiness causes loneliness. If unhappiness causes loneliness, we would predict that individuals with a 'happy' personality (e.g., high extraversion + low neuroticism) should be less inclined to loneliness than those with low extraversion + high neuroticism. In a meta-analytic review (combining findings from many studies), Buecker et al. (2020) found loneliness correlated –0.37 with extraversion and .36 with neuroticism.

Stronger evidence that top-down factors play a major role in determining individual differences in loneliness was provided by Boomsma et al. (2005). Monozygotic or identical twins were much more similar than dizygotic twins with respect to loneliness. Overall, Boomsma et al. discovered genetic factors accounted for 48% of individual differences in loneliness.

In similar fashion, the positive correlation between marital satisfaction and happiness does not show that the former necessarily causes the latter. The reason is that individual differences in marital satisfaction depend in part on genetic factors (Spotts et al., 2005).

In sum, the finding that several factors (e.g., loneliness; marital satisfaction; good friends) correlate positively with happiness is easily (but mistakenly) interpreted to mean that these factors cause happiness. That is partially true. For example, Folk and Dunn (2024) reviewed research showing that most individuals who used the strategy of becoming more sociable became happier (in part because it reduced loneliness). However, the causality also operates in the opposite direction: individual differences in genetic factors relevant to happiness partially determine the likelihood that any given individual will be lonely, experience marital satisfaction, have good friends and so on. The overall findings can only be explained by taking full account of the role of genetic factors in influencing happiness levels while acknowledging that experienced events also affect happiness (Eysenck, 1990).

8   Mental disorders and their treatment

More than 50% of American adults experience at least one mental disorder in their lives (Centers for Disease Control and Prevention, 2018), and comparable figures have been reported for most other countries (including the United Kingdom). That means the vast majority of individuals have experienced mental illness themselves and/or observed it in one or more family members. As a consequence, we might imagine most people would have reasonably accurate beliefs about mental illness and about the effectiveness (or otherwise) of therapies designed to treat it.

In fact, misconceptions about mental illness are surprisingly prevalent. Basterfield et al. (2023) identified 20 misconceptions about mental illness and its treatment believed by at least two-thirds of psychology students. However, these misconceptions were less prevalent among those knowing a close friend or immediate family member who had received clinical treatment. Some of the most important misconceptions are discussed in this chapter.

Myth: mental illnesses are due almost entirely to people's life experiences

Basterfield et al. (2023) reported that 85% of psychology students endorsed the misconception that "Mental illnesses are due almost entirely to people's life experiences". The key words in this statement are "almost entirely" since it is indisputable that life experiences play a role in triggering virtually every mental disorder. Consider social anxiety disorder, which is characterised by extreme fear of social situations (especially those involving unfamiliar individuals or scrutiny by others). Parental rejection (making children feel unloved) and/or parental overprotectiveness (giving children little control over their social lives) both play a significant role in triggering social anxiety disorder (Norton & Abbott, 2017).

Holmes and Rahe (1967) developed the Social Readjustment Rating Scale on which individuals indicate which of 43 life events have happened to them over a period of time (usually the previous 6 or 12 months). Each event is assigned a life-change value up to 100 based on its likely impact. Here are some examples: death of a spouse (100); divorce (73); marital separation

DOI: 10.4324/9781003596677-8

(65); death of a close family member (63). Individuals experiencing several stressful life events producing a total of more than 300 life-change units are more likely than those experiencing relatively few such events to develop various mental disorders (especially depression and anxiety disorders: Martin, 1989).

However, we should not focus on severe life events in isolation – their impact varies considerably across individuals. An important factor is the quality of the social support they receive. Brown and Harris (1978) studied women who had recently experienced a serious life event. Of those without an intimate friend, 37% became depressed compared to only 10% of those having an intimate friend.

Diathesis-stress model: genetic factors

The dominant approach to understanding the factors causing any given mental disorder is the diathesis-stress model. According to this model, diathesis is a vulnerability or predisposition within an individual and stress refers to severe and distressing life events (e.g., divorce; death of a loved one). The key assumption of the model is that the occurrence of a mental illness depends on the joint and interactive influences of diathesis and stress.

The origins of the diathesis-stress model go back at least as far as the nineteenth century when many psychiatric textbooks discussed the predisposition-excitation framework (Kendler, 2020). According to this framework, mental illnesses are jointly determined by predisposition (or vulnerability) and by excitation (or stress). This approach was described by the English psychiatrist Henry Maudsley (1867):

> Two persons are exposed to a similar heavy mental shock:
> one of them is driven mad by it, but the other is not. Can we say then that the madness has been produced by a moral [psychological] cause? Not accurately so; for in the former case there has been some innate vice of nervous constitution, some predisposition of it to disease, whereby insanity has been produced by a cause which has had no such ill effect in The latter case. . . . It will be most expedient to adopt the time-honoured division of predisposing or remote and of exciting or proximate [immediately preceding] causes.
>
> (pp. 488–489)

Supporting evidence was reported by Sbarra et al. (2013). They focused on the impact of divorce on individuals who prior to separation or divorce had (or did not have) a major depressive episode. Those without such an episode beforehand rarely had a major depressive episode following separation or divorce. In contrast, those having experienced a depressive episode prior to separation or divorce had almost a 60% chance of having another major depressive episode following separation/divorce. Thus, a severe life event (separation/divorce) and individual vulnerability (indicated by a prior depressive episode) jointly determined the probability of a post-separation/divorce depressive episode.

Colodro-Conde et al. (2018) tested the diathesis-stress model with respect to major depressive disorder (depressed mood, tiredness, lack of pleasure in activities and worthlessness). Their twin study confirmed there is a genetic vulnerability for depression. Colodro-Conde et al. also found the number of stressful life events experienced predicted the onset of depression. Of central importance, individuals having genetic vulnerability *and* experiencing many stressful life events were at greater risk of major depressive disorder than would be expected if we simply added the separate risks from genetic vulnerability and many life events. Thus, the findings fully supported the model.

Genetic factors are an important determinant of individual differences in vulnerability with respect to many mental disorders. The strongest evidence comes from studies comparing monozygotic or identical twins and dizygotic or fraternal twins. The key measure is the concordance rate: the probability that if one twin has a mental disorder the other twin has the same disorder. Since monozygotic twins share 100% of their genes but dizygotic twins share only 50% on average, the concordance rate should be significantly higher for monozygotic than fraternal twins if genetic factors partially determine the occurrence of a mental disorder.

The evidence from twin studies of schizophrenia (a very serious disorder involving hallucinations, delusions and grossly impaired social functioning) was reviewed by Hilker et al. (2018). The concordance rate was much higher for monozygotic than dizygotic twins (33% vs. 7%, respectively). Hilker et al. estimated that genetic factors accounted for 79% of individual differences in susceptibility to schizophrenia.

We can extend the twin-study method by considering the concordance rate for other family relationships. Gottesman (1991) did that for schizophrenia. The concordance rate was 48% for monozygotic twins. Between first-degree relatives sharing 50% of their genes on average the concordance rate was 17% for dizygotic twins, 13% for children and 9% for siblings. The concordance rate for second-degree relatives sharing 25% of their genes on average was 5% for half-siblings, 4% for grandchildren and 3% for nephews/nieces and for uncles/aunts. The lifetime incidence of schizophrenia is 1% in most countries and so *all* these concordance rates indicate a strong intra-familial vulnerability for schizophrenia.

The importance of genetic factors varies considerably across the various mental disorders. Polderman et al. (2015) carried out a heroic study where they analysed the data from over 14 million twin pairs with respect to 17,804 human traits or characteristics. Strikingly, genetic factors accounted on average for 49% of individual differences across all these traits (i.e., heritability was 49%). Among the mental disorders, heritability was higher for schizophrenia (77%) and bipolar disorder (76%) than for attention-deficit/hyperactivity disorder (58%) or depression (44%).

It is perhaps natural to assume that different genetic factors are associated with each mental disorder. However, the number of mental disorders identified by the *Diagnostic and Statistical Manual of Mental Disorders (DSM)*, a highly influential diagnostic system produced by American psychiatrists, was 541 in its most recent edition (DSM-5; American Psychiatric Association, 2013). It seems improbable (or virtually impossible) that each of these 541 disorders has its own specific genes associated with it.

Consider anxiety disorders. DSM-IV (American Psychiatric Association, 1994) identified 10 anxiety disorders and this more than doubled to 23 in DSM-5 (American Psychiatric Association, 2013). Can it really be true that there are almost two dozen distinctively different anxiety disorders? The short answer is "No". One strong reason for doubt is extensive *comorbidity* (the presence of two or more mental disorders at the same time) with respect to anxiety disorders. Approximately 50% of individuals with an anxiety disorder also have one or more others.

Twin studies have assisted in the task of making sense of comorbidity. Hettema et al. (2006) discovered that several anxiety disorders (generalised anxiety disorder; panic disorder; agoraphobia; social anxiety disorder) as well as major depressive disorder are all triggered in part by common genetic factors.

In sum, most mental disorders are determined by individual differences in vulnerability as well as by the prior occurrence of severe life events. Genetic factors typically play an important role in influencing these individual differences in vulnerability. However, even though the diathesis-stress model is undoubtedly a step in the right direction, it is nevertheless oversimplified. Of particular note, its implicit assumption that stressors or life events and genetic or other vulnerabilities are *independent* of each other is mistaken (see the following section).

Independent vs. dependent life events

We have seen that individuals developing mental disorders have on average experienced more severe life events than those who do not. How should we interpret this finding? It may seem obvious (as assumed within the diathesis-stress model) that experiencing many stressful life events helps to cause mental disorder. However, what we have here is correlational evidence: the number of stressful life events experienced *correlates* positively with the probability of developing a mental disorder. It is ill-advised to claim there is always a direct causal link from life events to mental disorder on the basis of such evidence.

It has often been assumed implicitly that stressful life events occur *randomly*, like being struck by lightning. That assumption only applies to some stressful life events. Consider these life events: imprisonment for a crime; abortion; attempted suicide; shooting or stabbing someone. These stressful life events are (at least to some extent) under an individual's control and so can be regarded as *dependent* events. In contrast, other events (e.g., miscarriage; suicide of a friend; death of a romantic partner) are mostly outside the individual's control and so are *independent* events.

Kendler et al. (1999) demonstrated the importance of the distinction between dependent and independent stressful life events. They studied the relationship between stressful life events and major depressive disorder in monozygotic (identical) twin pairs and dizygotic (fraternal) twin pairs. Independent stressful life events had a clear causal relationship with the onset of major depression. However, one-third of the relationship between stressful life events and depression onset was *not* causal: it occurred because individuals genetically predisposed to major depression *selected* high-risk environments leading to the occurrence of dependent stressful life events.

Boardman et al. (2011) focused on depression in adolescent twin pairs. Genetic factors accounted for 43% of individual differences in dependent life events but only 12% for independent life events. Of most importance, much of the relationship between dependent life events and depression was due to common genetic factors influencing both those events and depression rather than the environmental impact of those life events on depression.

Conclusions

The stressful life events that individuals experience undoubtedly influence the probability they will develop a mental disorder, and so there is a grain of truth in the myth that mental illnesses are due almost entirely to people's life experiences. However, it is a myth because the extent to which life events directly cause mental disorder is greatly exaggerated. This exaggeration occurs for two main reasons. First, the large individual differences in vulnerability to stressful life events are ignored or de-emphasised. For example, Kendler et al. (2004) found that individuals high in neuroticism (a personality dimension associated with negative emotional states) were *four* times as likely as those low in neuroticism to develop major depression following severe life events.

Second, stressful life events may occur shortly before the onset of a mental disorder without the former being causally responsible for the latter. Dependent life events are partially under an individual's control and so reflect their vulnerability rather than having a direct influence on their subsequent mental disorder.

The finding (Basterfield et al., 2023) that 85% of students believe mental illnesses are due almost entirely to people's life experiences strongly (or even necessarily) implies that genetic factors play a very modest (or no) role in triggering mental illnesses. However, that leaves us with an interesting paradox (discussed further in Chapter 10). When people indicated the extent to which genetic and environmental factors contribute to differences in various mental disorders, they fully appreciated the role played by genetic factors (Willoughby et al., 2019). More specifically, they slightly underestimated the role of genetic factors in schizophrenia and bipolar disorder and slightly overestimated the role of genetic factors in depression.

How can we resolve the previous paradox? Here are two possible answers. First, when people decide whether mental disorders are due almost entirely to people's life experiences, this may lead them to focus on environmental influences without considering that genetic influences might also be important. Second, stressful life experiences strongly influence *when* someone develops a mental disorder, whereas genetic factors strongly influence *whether* any given individual will have a mental disorder. Basterfield et al.'s (2023) items may focus people's attention on the *when* issue whereas Willoughby et al.'s (2019) items may focus their attention on the *whether* issue. Whatever the correct explanation of the paradox, there is clearly more general awareness of the role played by genetic factors in mental illness than appears from their endorsement of the statement that mental disorders are almost entirely due to people's life experiences.

Myth: psychiatric diagnoses or labels stigmatise people

The great majority of clinical psychologists and psychiatrists agree it is important to provide a psychiatric diagnosis for individuals with mental disorders. Nearly all therapeutic approaches are based on the assumption that accurate diagnosis facilitates optimising treatment. That assumption is supported by meta-analyses showing all major forms of therapy are reasonably or very effective under typical clinical conditions (Shadish et al., 1997).

In spite of the acknowledged value of psychiatric diagnoses, it has often been argued that individuals diagnosed or labelled with a psychiatric disorder are stigmatised (viewed negatively) as a result. Most people believe stigmatising is a genuine phenomenon: Basterfield et al. (2023) found 85.6% of psychology students disagreed with the following statement: "Psychiatric labels do not cause harm by stigmatising people". Basterfield et al. identified the notion that psychiatric labels stigmatise people as a myth, as had Lilienfeld et al. (2010) in their book *50 great myths of popular psychology*.

The Scottish psychiatrist R. D. Laing strongly believed that psychiatric labels stigmatise those labelled. According to him, a scientist claiming that "All men are machines" might receive a Nobel Prize. In contrast, someone labelled a schizophrenic who said "I am a machine" might easily be dispatched to a psychiatric hospital. Laing famously argued that we should blame society rather than troubled individuals: "Insanity – a perfectly rational adjustment to an insane world".

Rosenhan (1973) study

Rosenhan (1973) carried out the best-known study designed to demonstrate how psychiatric labels can stigmatise perfectly sane individuals. In his study, eight individuals without any abnormalities (one of whom was Rosenhan) attempted to gain admission to 12 different psychiatric hospitals. They asked for (and obtained) appointments at these hospitals. Upon arrival, they claimed mistakenly that they heard voices that seemed to be saying '*empty*', '*hollow*' and '*thud*'. The voices were unfamiliar but matched the sex of the individuals concerned. This was the *only* psychiatric symptom they displayed. Nevertheless, they were all judged to be insane and were admitted to hospital. Seven were diagnosed as suffering from schizophrenia and the other one was diagnosed with manic-depressive psychosis (now called bipolar disorder).

After these eight pseudo-patients were admitted to a psychiatric ward, they stopped showing any symptoms of abnormality. They were hospitalised for between 7 and 52 days (average = 19 days), which suggests the psychiatrists and psychologists rapidly recognised the pseudo-patients were sane rather than insane. However, what actually happened was more complex. All those originally diagnosed with schizophrenia were discharged with the unusual diagnosis of 'schizophrenia in remission'.

The fact that these eight individuals had been labelled as suffering from a serious mental disorder caused them to be poorly treated. When the pseudo-patients made courteous requests for information, they were ignored 71% of the time by psychiatrists and 88% of the time by nurses and attendants. Rosenhan concluded as follows:

> Psychiatric diagnoses . . . carry with them personal, legal, and social stigmas . . . the data speak to the massive role of labelling in psychiatric assessment. Having once been labelled schizophrenic, there is nothing the pseudo-patient can do to overcome the tag. The tag profoundly colours others' perceptions of him and his behaviour.
>
> (pp. 252–253)

In sum, "the label sticks, a mask of inadequacy forever" (p. 257).

Most textbook writers were impressed by Rosenhan's research. Bartels and Peters (2017) discovered two-thirds of textbooks on abnormal psychology voiced no criticisms of it, and the remaining one-third made only minor criticisms. However, I expressed many criticisms of Rosenhan's research in books starting in 1981.

There are several serious criticisms of Rosenhan's research. First, it is misleading to claim the pseudo-patients exhibited only a *single* symptom (i.e., hallucinating voices). For example, no sane person would contact a psychiatric hospital and try to gain admission as a patient. Kety (1974) drew an analogy with physical disease:

> If I were to drink a quart of blood and, concealing what I had done, come to the emergency room of any hospital vomiting blood, the behaviour of the staff would be quite predictable. If they labelled and treated me as having a bleeding peptic ulcer, I doubt that I could argue convincingly that medical science does not know how to diagnose that condition.
>
> (p. 959)

Second, it is untrue that the pseudo-patients behaved normally following admittance to the psychiatric hospital. As Hunter (1973, p. 361) pointed out, "Had their behaviour been normal, they would have walked to the nurses' station and said, 'Look, I am a normal person who tried to see if I could get into the hospital by behaving in a crazy way or saying crazy things. It worked and I was admitted to the hospital, but now I would like to be discharged from the hospital'".

Third and most seriously, Rosenhan's (1973) account is very inaccurate. Cahalan (2019) spent years investigating the records relating to Rosenhan's study, concluding he was 'the great pretender'. Rosenhan used the alias 'David Lurie' in the study. He was examined by a psychiatrist F. L. Bartlett, whose medical records referred to David Lurie's distress: "His mood was depressed. He felt his wife really did not know how disturbed and helpless and useless he was and that 'everybody would be better off without me'" (Scull, 2023, p. 192). This goes far beyond merely claiming to hear voices.

Cahalan (2019) interviewed two pseudo-patients used in Rosenhan's (1973) research. One (Harry Lando) found his stay in a psychiatric hospital to be calming, uplifting and supportive. Since this did not fit Rosenhan's preferred narrative, he was simply dropped from the study. Inspection of the medical records indicated that neither he nor the other interviewed pseudo-patient (Bill Underwood) was discharged with the diagnosis 'schizophrenia in remission'. Finally, the fact that Calahan could not track down any more pseudo-patients in spite of massive efforts strongly suggests they did not exist.

Psychiatric labels or diagnoses do not cause stigma

Lilienfeld et al. (2010) put forward several reasons (including the debunking of Rosenhan's study) for disagreeing with the notion that psychiatric labels or diagnoses cause those so labelled to be stigmatised. They argued diagnostic labels are valid because they provide us with a reasonable ability to predict someone's behaviour. Negative reactions to individuals diagnosed with a mental disorder are due to the *behaviour* exhibited by those individuals rather than the psychiatric label itself. Ruscio (2004) also argued that the information provided by psychiatric diagnoses overlaps substantially with the observable behaviour of those labelled. For example, it is arguable that the label 'major depressive disorder' applied to a given patient provides similar information to that available from their sad and unhappy behaviour.

Lilienfeld et al. (2010) argued that there has been greater public understanding of mental illness and significant improvements in therapeutic techniques over time. As a result, there is less evidence of stigmatisation of patients now than previously.

Most psychiatric diagnoses possess reasonable validity and predictive power. However, we must distinguish between negative beliefs about individuals with mental disorders justified by their behaviour and negative beliefs that involve stigmatising due to *exaggerated* beliefs based on cultural stereo-types or other mistaken assumptions.

Before proceeding, we should discuss the term 'stigma' in more detail. We can distinguish among three somewhat separate components of stigma: (Ottati et al., 2006). First, there is *cognitive* stigma (e.g., negative stereotypes relating to the alleged incompetence, dangerousness and blameworthiness of mental patients). Second, there is *affective* stigma (or prejudice) involving negative emotions (e.g., anger; fear) towards mental patients. Third, there is *behavioural* stigma (or discrimination) including social distancing from patients and treating them unfairly with respect to employment and housing. These components often influence each other. For example, the belief that mental patients are dangerous (cognitive stigma) may trigger anger (affective stigma), and fear of mental patients (affective stigma) may lead to social dis-tancing and discrimination (behavioural stigma).

The previous three components all relate to public stigma (negative beliefs that members of the public have about mental patients). We also need to consider self-stigma, which occurs when patients with mental disorders inter-nalise the negative stigmatising stereotypical views of society. According to Corrigan and Rao (2012), the development of self-stigma goes through four stages: awareness (recognising negative public views of mental disorder); agreement (acceptance of those negative views); application (applying those negative views to oneself); and harm (becoming self-defeatist).

The negative effects of self-stigma among schizophrenic patients were explored by Sarraf et al. (2022). Those with high levels of self-stigma had more depressive symptoms, a lower quality of life and reduced self-esteem compared to those with low levels of self-stigma.

Psychiatric labels or diagnoses do cause stigma

The belief that mentally ill patents are inclined to be violent has a long history. Gray (1857; cited in Nederlof et al., 2013) wrote about violent behaviour in psychiatric patients: "It [violent behaviour] is exhibited in every conceivable manner, from harsh words to suicide and the most cruel and brutal murders, and is found in every form of insanity" (p.1).

Evidence that this belief remains very common was reported by Baster-field et al. (2023): 72% of psychology students agreed with the statement "Most patients with severe mental disorders have a history of violence". An even higher percentage (89%) agreed that "Most people with schizo-phrenia are violent". These statements are myths because the true figures concerning the dangerousness of mentally ill patients are considerably lower than most people's beliefs. Fewer than 10% of patients with serious men-tal illnesses (psychoses such as schizophrenia and bipolar disorder) commit violent acts (Hodgins et al., 1996). This is at least five or six times lower than the dominant view that "most schizophrenics" are violent (Basterfield et al., 2023). Indeed, psychiatric patients taking their medication regularly are no more likely than the general population to behave violently (Stead-man et al., 1998).

Lilienfeld et al. (2010) discussed these myths about the strong association between mental disorder (or schizophrenia) and violent behaviour as if they were totally separate from the myth that psychiatric diagnoses or labels cause stigma. In fact, they are strongly intertwined. If most people greatly exaggerate the likelihood of mentally ill patients being violent (and do so even more with schizophrenics), this indicates they have stereotyped views or beliefs going well beyond patients' actual behaviour.

Why do almost three-quarters of the population associate mental illness with violence? A key reason relates to the depiction of mentally ill patients on television, in the movies and in newspapers. On American television, 25% of them killed someone and 50% hurt other people (Stuart, 2006). In addition, the offence rate among mentally ill characters was 10 times greater than that among other characters (30% vs. 3%, respectively). Strikingly, 83% of schizophrenic characters in films engaged in violent behaviour, almost one-third killed someone else and 25% killed themselves (Owen, 2012).

Newspaper coverage of mental illness reveals a similar picture (Wahl, 2003). Two-thirds of articles in the UK press linked mental illness and violence. Important themes such as the patients' perspective, their recovery and their achievements were rarely mentioned.

The portrayal of mentally ill patients in the media influences people's views (and perhaps also reflects those views). Link et al. (1999) found the percentages of people believing schizophrenics are likely to be violent was 61% compared to 33% for those with major depressive disorder. Of real concern, those perceiving patients as potentially violent were more likely to want to socially distance themselves from them. Of those questioned, 63% were reluctant to interact with a schizophrenic and 47% with someone having major depressive disorder.

Most members of the public worried about being violently attacked by someone with a serious mental illness imagine mistakenly think they are likely to be attacked by a complete stranger in a frighteningly unpredictable way. In fact, most acts of violence committed by psychotic individuals are directed towards a member of their own family or someone well known to them (Ahonen et al., 2019).

Changes over time

Earlier I mentioned that Lilienfeld et al. (2010) claimed that stigmatising of patients with mental disorders has steadily reduced over time. Relevant evidence was reported by Pescosolido et al. (2021) in a study where participants were presented vignettes describing individuals with the symptoms of schizophrenia, depression or simply daily troubles in 1996, 2006 and 2018.

There was a much greater tendency to reject individuals with mental disorders than those with daily troubles at all three time periods with only modest changes between 1996 and 2018. Only 20% were unwilling to work closely with someone having daily troubles compared to 35% for the depressed person and 60% for the schizophrenic. Only 10% were unwilling to have a person with daily troubles as a neighbour, but this figure increased to 20% for the depressed individuals and over 40% for the schizophrenic. Stigmatisation of depressed individuals reduced modestly over time. However, the perceived danger that schizophrenics would be violent *increased* between 1996 and 2018.

Disclosure

There is an element of ambiguity with respect to interpreting the findings from some of the research discussed earlier. More specifically, the high levels of social rejection of individuals with mental disorders could be due to exaggerated reactions to their somewhat unusual behaviour and/or their psychiatric diagnosis. We can obtain clearer evidence by considering the reactions of others to those with mental disorders *before* and *after* their mental disorder was disclosed. If psychiatric diagnoses stigmatise individuals, they should experience significantly more negative reactions following such disclosure.

Wahl (1999) found that disclosure often led to a significant increase in social rejection. Many patients reported that friends were less likely to call round, there were fewer visits to neighbours and they received fewer social invitations. Overall, disclosure increased patients' feelings of isolation.

Thornicroft et al. (2009) explored the impact of their diagnosis on schizophrenics in 27 different countries. There were consistently high levels of discrimination in every country. The diagnosis of schizophrenia most often led to discrimination with respect to making or keeping friends (47% of respondents), followed by discrimination by family members (43%), keeping a job (29%), finding a job (29%) and in intimate or sexual relationships (27%). Unsurprisingly, 72% of the schizophrenics had concealed their diagnosis when seeking training or work and 55% had done so when looking for a close relationship.

More evidence that disclosure has a negative impact on mental patients' ability to find a job was reported by Rüsch et al. (2018). Those individuals more willing to disclose their psychiatric diagnosis during their search for a job were less likely to be re-employed 6 months later than those unwilling to disclose.

Conclusions

Lilienfeld et al. (2010) argued that the negative reactions of members of the public to patients with mental disorders reflect patients' actual behaviour rather than their psychiatric label or diagnosis. As predicted, there is more stigmatisation of patients with more serious mental illnesses (e.g., schizophrenia; antisocial personality disorder; bipolar disorder) than those with less serious ones (e.g., depression; generalised anxiety disorder) (Hazell et al., 2022). Such findings indicate that people are responsive to patients' symptoms.

However, many or most members of the public have grossly exaggerated views concerning the potential dangers and threats posed by patients with mental disorders (especially their tendency to be violent). As a result, people are inclined to distance themselves from individuals with mental disorders and to discriminate against them (e.g., when they seek employment) much more than would be warranted by their actual behaviour. This is especially clear in research on disclosure. Patients' behaviour is unlikely to change much before and after the disclosure of their psychiatric diagnosis to those with whom they interact. Nevertheless, disclosure typically leads to a significant increase in discrimination.

As discussed earlier, the negative effects of stigmatisation on patients with psychiatric disorders are often exacerbated by self-stigma. In essence, many patients come to believe the distorted stigmatising views of the public leading to a worsening of their symptoms.

In sum, the alleged myth that psychiatric diagnoses or labels stigmatise is actually true (perhaps it is a non-mythical myth?). In spite of Lilienfeld et al.'s (2010) claims that any stigmatisation of patients with psychiatric diagnoses has reduced markedly in recent times, stigmatisation has changed relatively little in recent decades (Pescosolido et al., 2021).

Myth: The Rorschach Inkblot test is a very useful way of diagnosing most mental illnesses

One of the best-known psychological tests for diagnosing individuals with mental disorders is the Rorschach Inkblot Test invented by the Swiss psychiatrist Hermann Rorschach (1921). The test's development was strongly influenced by a nineteenth-century game called *Klecksographie* or Blotto in which players produced inkblots and then described what they saw. Rorschach was so keen on this game when he was a boy that he was given the nickname 'Klecks' meaning a blob or inkblot.

The Rorschach Inkblot Test in its original form consisted of 10 symmetrical inkblots, five in black-and-white and the other five in colour (two in black and red and three entirely colourful). Rorschach discovered there were clear-cut differences in inkblot interpretations between schizophrenic patients and healthy Swiss individuals. The test is very simple: those taking it report whatever they see in each of the inkblots; this can involve a single response or more than one response to any given inkblot.

The Rorschach Inkblot Test is one of numerous so-called 'projective' tests. The underlying rationale of all such tests is that individuals *project* their own personality onto ambiguous stimuli (e.g., inkblots). This rationale appears reasonable given that the information provided by the stimulus is insufficient to identify or classify it easily. More dubiously, it has often been assumed that the Rorschach test circumvents individuals' conscious defences and so reveals important hidden aspects of their personality. No convincing evidence supports this assumption.

Very large numbers of people believe the Rorschach Inkblot Test (and other projective tests) are very valuable for diagnosing and understanding mental disorders. Basterfield et al. (2023) found 76% of university students agreed that "Rorschach inkblots are a very useful way of diagnosing most mental illnesses". In the 1990s, 43% of American clinical psychologists said they used the test frequently or all the time and many more used it occasionally (Watkins et al., 1995). Worldwide, the Inkblot Test is administered to several million people every year.

An indirect measure of the popularity of Rorschach's test is the very large number of cartoons devoted to it. For example, one cartoon in the *New Yorker* was entitled 'Narcissus takes a Rorschach test' and has the patient saying to successive inkblots: "Me . . . Me . . . Me . . . Me . . . Me . . . Me. . . ." Another cartoon in the same magazine has a patient saying, "I'm a sexual deviant?! You're the one with all the dirty pictures!" Another way the Rorschach test has impinged on the public consciousness is through films. For example, *The Master* (1982) stars Joaquin Phoenix as Freddie Quell, a World War Two veteran with post-traumatic stress disorder. He is a sex-obsessed deviant who produces sexual interpretations of innocuous Rorschach inkblots.

Research

There have been many changes over the past century to the ways the Rorschach is administered and scored. There was a major sea of change in 1974 when Exner introduced his Rorschach Comprehensive System which provided clear and detailed instructions for the administration and scoring of the Rorschach test. He subsequently developed and extended this Comprehensive System (e.g., Exner, 2003).

Prior to Exner's (1974) introduction of the Rorschach Comprehensive System, the situation with respect to the Rorschach test resembled the Wild West (i.e., it was characterised by a general lawlessness). Those taking the test were totally free to say whatever they liked, and their perceptions or interpretations of the inkblots could be scored for over 100 characteristics. Some characteristics related to *content* (e.g., was food perceived?; was blood perceived?). Others related to *location* (e.g., is the blot perceived as a whole or is only part of it perceived? and *determinants* (e.g., colour; movement; shading). Investigators focused on different characteristics and the imprecise definitions of most of the characteristics meant there was much confusion among them as to the appropriate interpretation of individuals' responses.

Harrower (1976) presented Rorschach experts with the Rorschach responses of Nazi war criminals including Hermann Goering (head of the

Luftwaffe) and Rudolf Hess (Deputy Führer) obtained in 1945 plus the responses of other people (e.g., ministers, military officers and psychiatric patients). These experts were unable to identify which sets of responses came from the Nazi war criminals which sheds considerable doubt on the validity of the test.

A likely reason for the poor performance of the Rorschach experts is that they had no background information about the respondents. This points to a substantial problem with the Rorschach test: examiners' interpretations of inkblot responses are often influenced (or contaminated) by their assessment of respondents' personalities based on their interactions with them rather than solely by the respondents' responses to the test.

Overall, in the pre-1974 era, there was very little evidence that the Rorschach inkblot test was reliable (provided consistent findings) or valid (measured what it was claimed to measure). Exner's (1974) development of the Comprehensive System meant the Rorschach test became more scientific and replicable. Lilienfeld et al. (2000) assessed the Comprehensive System's strengths and limitations. Many studies suggested high levels of reliability and validity were sometimes achievable with the Comprehensive System but most of them lacked sufficient detail to assess their adequacy. Lilienfeld et al. concluded that only half of the Rorschach variables can be assessed with good reliability.

The evidence on validity is also very mixed. Wood et al. (2010) carried out a meta-analysis of studies where the Rorschach Comprehensive System was used to distinguish between psychopaths (individuals who are aggressive, dishonest and lacking in remorse) and non-psychopaths. Of the 37 Rorschach variables considered, 32 were not significantly related to psychopathy and the other five variables were only weakly predictive.

The most thorough attempt to assess the validity of the Rorschach test was reported by Mihura et al. (2013). They reviewed all the relevant research on the extent to which 53 of the main variables included in the Comprehensive System predicted external criteria such as observer ratings and psychiatric diagnosis. Validity was excellent for 13 of these variables and good for 17 more (many of these variables related to cognitive and perceptual processes). However, there was only modest validity for 10 variables and little or no validity for the remaining 12. Wood et al. (2015) accepted that these findings accurately reflected *published* research. However, Mihura et al.'s failure to consider unpublished studies led them to overestimate the validity of many variables.

There are various kinds of validity. A test such as the Rorschach inkblot may possess validity in the sense of having some ability to identify psychological characteristics (e.g., psychopathy). However, what is often more important is *incremental validity*: does the test have predictive power additional to that provided by other information (e.g., life history; questionnaire data)? The Rorschach has typically been found to lack incremental validity (Lilienfeld et al., 2010).

The Comprehensive System differed from previous approaches because it provided extensive normative data on non-patient American adults and children. That means that any given individual's response pattern to the inkblots can be compared against those of a representative sample of the population. However, the norms are deficient. Wood et al. (2001) carried out a meta-analysis of studies where the Rorschach test had been used with non-patient groups. The Rorschach responses of these groups on 14 different Comprehensive System variables differed significantly from those of the non-patients used to produce norms for the test. More specifically, the non-patient groups included in the meta-analysis appeared pathological (abnormal) with respect to all 14 variables when compared against the norms! Thus, the norms failed to indicate clearly whether an individual or group is normal or abnormal.

Another issue with the Rorschach norms is that they are based only on American individuals. However, there are various cross-cultural differences in response patterns (Areh et al., 2022). For example, envy is associated with black, red and green in the United States but with black, purple and yellow in Russia. Only French individuals often see a chameleon in inkblot 8 and only Scandinavians often see Christmas elves in inkblot 2.

Another important issue is that psychiatrists and clinical psychologists who use the Rorschach test generally have spent some time beforehand with the patients whose Rorschach responses they are interpreting. As a result, their interpretations of those responses are influenced by their personal knowledge of the patients as well as by the responses themselves. In fact, the Rorschach test's validity can only be assessed accurately if those scoring respondents' responses have no other information available about them.

Finally, there is the issue of whether it is possible for respondents taking the Rorschach test to fake good or bad. Most Rorschach experts claim the test is immune from faking. However, the research evidence tells a different story. Rorschach experts generally perform poorly when attempting to discriminate between the Rorschach responses of patient groups with mental disorders such as schizophrenia, depression or PTSD and those of healthy individuals faking those disorders (Areh et al., 2022).

In sum, the Rorschach inkblot test has had a huge impact: over 1,700 articles with 'Rorschach' in the title have been published, as well as numerous books. In spite of all this research effort, its achievements are few and far between, and it has not established itself as a reliable and valid measuring instrument. In addition, the Rorschach test lacks any clear underlying theoretical rationale. As a result, it has proved very difficult to explain *why* some of the main variables assessed by the test appear to have good validity whereas others do not.

Why has the Rorschach Inkblot Test remained so popular?

It seems puzzling that millions of people continue to believe in the Rorschach test given its many limitations and poor ability to diagnose mental disorders. One reason for its continuing popularity is that it possesses face validity: superficially it appears to measure what it claims to measure. It seems believable that individuals suffering from mental disorders would give more bizarre and offbeat responses to the inkblots than members of the general public.

However, the most likely reason why the Rorschach inkblot test is still popularly believed to be an excellent clinical tool is because of 'illusory correlation' (Lilienfeld et al., 2010). This is a phenomenon where individuals perceive a relationship between two variables (e.g., a mental illness and scores on the Rorschach test) even when there is no actual relationship. Illusory correlations typically occur when individuals have a prior *expectation* that the two variables will be correlated.

Chapman and Chapman (1969) showed that the Rorschach test was susceptible to illusory correlation in a study focusing on homosexuality (illegal in the United States at the time). Initially, they found Rorschach experts mistakenly believed that certain inkblot responses (e.g., feminine clothing; humans with sex confused) were valid indicators of homosexuality even though they were actually invalid. They then presented students with Rorschach cards providing information about a patient's alleged response to a given inkblot plus two symptoms. The linkage between Rorschach responses and symptoms was entirely random. However, most students showed an illusory correlation: they misremembered what they had seen as indicating a frequent association between the invalid indicators and homosexuality. Their prior expectations led them to believe mistakenly that the Rorschach test was a valid measure of homosexuality.

There is another major reason why the Rorschach test is still widely used. This reason relates directly to an experiment carried out by Forer (1949). He gave students a personality test and then subsequently presented each of them with a personality profile. All the students agreed their profile described their personality very accurately. The ingenious twist in the experiment was that all the students received an identical personality profile!

Why were the students fooled? The personality profile consisted of very vague general statements applicable to most people (e.g., "At times you are extraverted, affable and sociable, while at other times you are introverted, wary and reserved"; "You have a great deal of unused capacity which you have not turned to your advantage"). This phenomenon is known as the Barnum effect, after the American showman P. T. Barnum who famously said, "There's a sucker born every minute".

Prince and Guastello (1990) found the Rorschach test is susceptible to the Barnum effect. Psychiatrists were provided with two reports for each of their patients allegedly based on the patients' performance on the Rorschach test. One report was genuine and the other was a bogus report consisting of information taken at random from other patients' genuine reports. The psychiatrists assessed how well each report described the patient named on it. The descriptions in the bogus reports were rated as being almost as accurate as those contained in the genuine report. It appears that most of the interpretations contained within the reports were sufficiently general that they applied to all the patients.

Myth: people with multiple personality disorder (dissociative identity disorder) have more than one distinct personality

Numerous individuals have been diagnosed with 'multiple personality disorder'. These individuals allegedly have two or more separate personalities. This notion may seem strange given that the overwhelming majority of people manage to make do with only one. However, 78.5% of psychology students believe people with multiple personality disorder have more than one distinct personality (Basterfield et al., 2023).

The notion that individuals can have two or more totally separate personalities goes back a long way. A famous example is Robert Louis Stevenson's novel, *The Strange Case of Dr. Jekyll and Mr. Hyde* (1886). It focuses on Henry Jekyll (who has many friends and a friendly personality) and Edward Hyde (who is murderous, cruel and evil). It is revealed towards the end of the book (spoiler alert!) that Jekyll and Hyde are the same person.

Interest in the possibility of multiple personalities was greatly fuelled in 1957 by a film called *The Three Faces of Eve*. The film was about Chris Sizemore, who had three very different identities: Eve White was timid and self-effacing, Eve Black was wild and fun-loving and Jane was stable and sensible.

The case of alleged multiple personality disorder that had the greatest impact was that of Sybil Dorsett (a pseudonym for Shirley Ardell Mason). Her story was discussed in a book by Schreiber (1973) entitled *Sybil*. According to this book, Sybil suffered childhood trauma causing her to develop no fewer than 16 different personalities! The enormous success of *Sybil* led to a huge increase in the number of patients diagnosed with multiple personality disorder. Its sensational story was turned into a TV movie in 1976 and then another TV movie in 2007.

The true story is less sensational (Nathan, 2011). Cornelia Wilbur, the Freudian psychoanalyst who treated Shirley Ardell Mason, persuaded her to claim to believe she had numerous personalities. The most compelling evidence was contained in a letter Shirley Ardell Mason wrote to Wilbur. In that letter, she admitted she was, "none of the things I have pretended to be . . . I do not have any multiple personalities . . . I do not even have a 'double'. . . I am all of them. I have been essentially lying". In addition, she had not suffered childhood trauma, which had allegedly instigated her development of multiple personalities.

The fourth edition of the *Diagnostic and Statistical Manual of Mental Disorders* (American Psychiatric Association, 1994; DSM-IV) replaced the previous 'multiple personality disorder' with 'dissociative identity disorder'. There are close similarities between the two mental disorders. However, the emphasis within dissociative identity disorder is more on a splintering or fragmentation of an individual's identity rather than a proliferation of different identities or personalities.

In DSM-5 (American Psychiatric Association, 2013) the crucial criterion for dissociative identity disorder is the following: "Two or more distinct identities or personality states are present, each with its own relatively enduring pattern of perceiving, relating to, and thinking about the environment and self". In addition, there is amnesia for recall of important personal information and traumatic events, and the individual's life must be adversely affected by the disorder.

A history of trauma is *not* a criterion for a diagnosis of dissociative identity disorder. However, 70% of individuals diagnosed with dissociative identity disorder suffered childhood abuse and/or neglect or suffered some other form of childhood trauma (e.g., medical trauma; war) (Lynn et al., 2019).

The precise number of identities (and the nature of those identities) vary considerably among patients. However, there is much evidence for two fundamental types of identities (Boon et al., 2011): trauma identities (fixated on the individual's traumatic experiences) and avoidant identities (avoidance of trauma-related painful memories).

Dissociative identity disorder and schizophrenia

As you read about the symptoms of dissociative identity disorder, you may have wondered about the relationship between that disorder and schizophrenia. Many people believe schizophrenics have multiple personalities. Stuart and Arboleda-Flórez (2001) found 47% of Canadians agreed that "schizophrenics suffer from split or multiple personalities", and similar estimates have been obtained in other studies (Lilienfeld et al., 2010). This is actually a myth. Patients with schizophrenia exhibit only occasional dissociative symptoms which are much less severe than those of patients with dissociative identity disorder (Steinberg et al., 1994).

Where did the mistaken notion that schizophrenics have split or multiple personalities originate? In 1908, the Swiss psychiatrist Eugen Bleuler coined the term 'schizophrenia' derived from two Greek words ('schizo' meaning 'split' and 'phrene' meaning 'mind'). Bleuler (1911/1950, p. 8) used this term because "the 'splitting' of the different psychic functions is one of its most important characteristics". What Bleuler probably meant was that schizophrenics have a single personality that has split or shattered (e.g., thoughts and emotions are disconnected). However, he hinted at the notion that schizophrenics can have more than one personality (Moscowitz & Heim, 2011).

Many psychiatrists and clinical psychologists in the early twentieth century believed there were close links between schizophrenia and multiple (or dissociated) personalities. Rosenbaum (1980) discovered there was a dramatic reduction in the number of reports of multiple personality after the diagnosis of schizophrenia became increasingly popular. Detailed examination of numerous case reports indicated that patients with multiple personalities were increasingly diagnosed and treated as schizophrenics.

Trauma model vs. the socio-cognitive model

Few mental disorders are as controversial as dissociative identity disorder. One reason for scepticism concerning the genuineness of dissociative identity disorder is that there was a huge percentage increase in patients diagnosed with it following the worldwide publicity given to the disorder by books such as *Sybil* (1973) (discussed earlier). The number of reported cases in the United States increased from 79 in 1970 to approximately 6,000 in 1986 and tens of thousands by the end of the twentieth century (Lilienfeld et al., 1999).

The enormous publicity relating to Sybil Dorsett's alleged 16 personalities triggered a marked increase in the number of separate identities patients claimed to have. As sceptics have pointed out, the ready accessibility of detailed information about dissociative identity disorder makes it relatively easy for individuals to claim to have many of the symptoms of that disorder.

Sceptics argue that patients can have various motives for pretending to possess two or more identities. For example, they may claim amnesia for their criminal behaviour because it was committed in an identity that is now inaccessible. Loewenstein (2020) discussed the case of Ms. Doris Neely, a 50-year-old woman who had set fire to the home of her former therapist. She suffered from dissociative identity disorder and claimed she could not recall what happened during a 3-hour period of time during which the arson occurred. According to her defence lawyer, she should not be held accountable for behaviour she cannot recall when she is in her main identity.

There are two apparently starkly different theoretical accounts of the development of dissociative identity disorder (Dodier et al., 2022). According to the trauma model, the disorder is genuine and is typically a fairly direct consequence of traumatic childhood experiences. According to the socio-cognitive model, individuals exhibit the symptoms of dissociative identity disorder because of various social and cognitive factors. These factors include fantasy proneness, a tendency to exaggerate symptoms, media influences, suggestions from therapists and motives to feign multiple identities.

It is hard to assess the validity of these two models. However, one valuable approach is to focus on the relationship between traumatic experiences and dissociative symptoms. This relationship is typically relatively modest and many patients with dissociative identity disorder have not suffered traumatic experiences (Dodier et al., 2022). Patihis and Lynn (2017) found the number of dissociative symptoms correlated much more strongly with fantasy proneness and cognitive failures than with traumatic experiences. Overall, these findings support the socio-cognitive model more than the trauma model.

Another approach to investigating the two models is to compare the symptoms displayed by patients with dissociative identity disorder with those of malingerers (healthy individuals simulating the symptoms of that disorder after receiving relevant training). The findings are somewhat mixed and inconsistent.

Barth et al. (2023) used the Miller Forensic Assessment of Symptoms Test to ascertain the number of uncommon symptoms of dissociative identity disorder possessed by patients and malingerers. The malingerers claimed to have more than three times as many of these symptoms as patients with dissociative identity disorder. Of key importance, the test corrected identified 91% of malingerers as malingerers but misclassified 17% of patients as malingerers. These findings provide more support for the trauma model than the socio-cognitive model because they suggest the symptoms reported by patients are genuine.

If individuals with dissociative identity disorder possess two or more totally separate identities or personalities, they should exhibit *inter-identity amnesia:* when they are in one identity they should have no access to autobiographical memories experienced and stored when in another identity.

Marsh et al. (2018) investigated inter-identity amnesia in patients with dissociative identity disorder. The patients were initially presented with an embarrassing scenario (e.g., being berated in a supermarket for hitting a child with your trolley) and instructed to engage with it using one of their identities (avoidant or trauma identity). They were then instructed to switch to their other identity and engage with a different embarrassing scenario.

All the patients denied conscious awareness of anything that had happened when engaging with the first scenario following the switch of identities. Thus, they exhibited *subjective* inter-identity amnesia. However, Marsh et al. (2018) also assessed inter-identity amnesia using the autobiographical Implicit Association Test (aIAT) which assessed the speed with which participants decided whether statements relating to the scenarios were 'true' or 'false'. The patients showed clear evidence of memory for the scenario experienced in the other identity. Thus, there was no inter-identity amnesia on this less direct measure.

Additional evidence that patients with dissociative identity disorder lack full inter-identity amnesia was reported by Marsh et al. (2021). Patients performed two behavioural tasks (e.g., part of one task involved taking our their mobile phone, putting it on silent and then placing it close to a pot plant), one in each of two contrasting identities.

The key findings related to forced-choice recognition performance for the actions performed on the behavioural tasks. The patients exhibited some recognition memory for the behavioural task performed in another identity, which indicates that patients with dissociative identity disorder lack inter-identity amnesia. However, all the patients with dissociative identity disorder reported having amnesia for the events experienced in the other identity. How can we reconcile the apparent discrepancy between that finding and the recognition-memory findings? Marsh et al. (2021) speculated that patients with dissociative identity disorder are motivated to limit their memory searches to events and experiences consistent with the current identity's sense of self. That explains why they claim to have inter-identity amnesia. When they are required to focus on information relevant to another identity (as in the forced-choice recognition test used by Marsh et al., 2021), it becomes clear that their reported inter-identity amnesia is perceived rather than actual.

Summary and conclusions

Can we resolve the controversy between those who refuse to believe dissociative identity disorder is a genuine mental disorder and those subscribing fully to it? One possibility is to opt for a compromise between these two apparently incompatible positions. The eleventh edition of the International Classification of Diseases (ICD-11) (World Health Organisation, 2018b) distinguishes between the 'classical' view of dissociative identity disorder (i.e., patients have no conscious awareness of their other identity or identities) and partial dissociative disorder described as follows in ICD-11:

> Partial dissociative identity disorder is characterised by disruption of identity in which there are two or more distinct personality states (dissociative identities). . . . One personality state is dominant and normally functions in daily life, but is intruded upon by one or more non-dominant personality states (dissociative intrusions). . . . They are experienced as interfering with the functioning of the dominant personality state and are typically aversive . . . there may be occasional, limited and transient episodes in which a distinct personality state assumes executive control to engage in circumscribed behaviours, such as in response to extreme emotional states or during episodes of self-harm or the re-enactment of traumatic memories.

Partial dissociative identity disorder is far removed from the high drama of numerous different identities each totally oblivious of the existence of any of the other identities. However, it corresponds much more closer to what is observed in clinical practice (Tyrer, 2019).

In sum, the belief that patients with dissociative identity disorder have "more than one distinct personality" is not borne out by most of the evidence. More specifically, patients with dissociative identity disorder do not have two or more 'distinct personalities', each unaware of the existence of the other personalities. However, there is considerable support for the weaker notion of partial dissociative disorder. In other words, patients with dissociative identity disorder have two or more distinct personality states.

Theoretically, it is increasingly clear that multiple factors contribute towards dissociative identity disorder. We do not need to choose between the trauma and socio-cognitive models: both identify factors influencing the development and maintenance of that disorder.

Myth: most psychotherapy requires lying on a couch and recalling one's childhood

Sigmund Freud, the bearded Austrian *Wunderkind*, has had far more impact on how non-psychologists think about psychology than anyone else. His most influential ideas relate to mental illness (especially the anxiety disorders) and to a form of treatment (psychoanalysis) designed to treat patients suffering from mental disorders. The most distinctive feature of psychoanalysis is that it emphasises that it is essential for patients to develop insight into their childhood problems if they are to be cured. Psychoanalysis has developed and changed over time, and the term 'psychodynamic therapy' is often used to encompass several variants of psychoanalysis as practised by Freud.

According to Freud, repression (meaning the motivated forgetting of traumatic experiences especially those occurring in childhood and involving physical and/or sexual abuse) is of central importance. The development of insight involves forcing painful, threatening or unacceptable repressed thoughts and memories out of the unconscious mind into consciousness (see Chapter 3).

It is generally supposed that Freud believed that the traumatic memories recalled by patients were nearly all genuine recollections of childhood experiences. However, that is *not* correct. As Sprengnether, 2012, p. 215) pointed out, Freud (1899),

> makes the startling claim that memories from childhood vividly recalled in adult life bear no specific relationship to what happened in the past. Rather, they are composite formation – elements of childhood experience as represented through the distorting lens of adult wishes, fantasies, and desires.

Freud argued that the way to cure neuroses or anxiety disorders was to allow the patient to gain access to their repressed ideas and conflicts from childhood and to face up to them. Of special importance, patients should focus on the emotions associated with their repressed ideas rather than simply regarding them in an intellectual fashion. However, gaining genuine insight into one's conflicts and problems dating from children is very hard to achieve. When the therapist attempts to persuade the patient to uncover repressed ideas:

> The patient attempts to escape by every possible means. First, he says nothing comes into his head, then that so much comes into his head that he can't grasp any of it. At last he admits that he really cannot say something, he is ashamed to . . . one continually replies that telling everything really means telling everything
>
> (Freud, 1917, p. 289).

Most people imagine that the psychoanalytic approach remains dominant to this day. Basterfield et al. (2023) found 79% of psychology undergraduates agreed that "Nowadays, most psychotherapy involves lying on a couch and recalling one's childhood". Presumably most people who believe psychoanalysis has been a dominant therapeutic approach for well over 100 years think that is because it has proved itself an especially effective way of treating mental disorders. Indeed, Lilienfeld et al. (2010, p. 236) argued that a prominent myth believed by millions of people is the following: "All effective psychotherapies force people to confront the 'root' causes of their problems in childhood".

Psychoanalysis is the only major therapeutic approach where the patient lies on a couch during treatment. Freud's famous couch was given to him in about 1890 by a patient and treasured by him until his death in 1939. It was a relatively short, old-fashioned couch with a richly detailed rug on top of it. Why Did Freud attach such importance to having his patients recline on a couch? This is what he had to say on the matter:

> I hold to the plan of getting the patient to lie on a sofa while I sit behind him out of his sight . . . it deserves to be maintained for many reasons . . . I cannot put up with being stared at by other people for eight hours a day (or more). . . I do not wish my expressions of face to give the patient the material for interpretations or to influence him in what he tells me.
>
> (Freud, 1913, pp. 133–134)

There are other possible benefits of using a couch. Patients may feel less inhibited when talking about sensitive issues if they cannot see the therapist, and they may feel less pressure to maintain a non-stop dialogue. Bizarrely, there has been no systematic attempt to obtain any evidence that Freud's preferred therapeutic set-up is more effective than simple face-to-face interaction between therapist and patient.

How dominant is the psychoanalytic approach?

How accurate is the widespread view that psychoanalysis (with its emphasis on exploring patients' childhood) remains the dominant therapeutic approach when treating mental disorders? Since a remarkably high percentage of all the world's clinical psychologists work in the United States, we will start there. Norcross and Karpiak (2012) found the percentage of psychoanalytically informed clinical psychologists had decreased from 35% in 1960 to 18% in 2010. In contrast, the number of clinical psychologists favouring cognitive-behavioural therapy had increased from 2% in 1973 to 31% in 2010.

Similar findings were reported by Jaimes et al. (2015). Between 1993 and 2013, the percentage of clinical psychologists in Quebec having psychoanalytic or psychodynamic therapy as their main orientation decreased from 26% to 21%. In contrast, cognitive-behavioural therapy increased in popularity from 18% of clinical psychologists to 38%.

However, there are some areas of the world in which psychoanalytic and psychodynamic therapy remain popular. For example, this form of therapy is much used in most of South America (especially Argentina and Brazil). For example, an amazing 1% of the population of Buenos Aries (capital of Argentina) consists of psychotherapists (Moncada, 2024).

Most people believe there are various "schools" of therapy (e.g., Freudian; cognitive; behavioural). For example, Basterfield et al. (2023) found 67% of psychology students thought the best predictor of treatment effectiveness for most mental disorders was the "school" of therapy used by the therapist. This school-based view is promulgated by most textbooks on abnormal psychology in which each "school" is discussed separately (although it is typically mentioned that reality is more complex).

The notion that there are schools of therapy greatly oversimplifies matters. As Kopta et al. (1999) pointed out, "The long-term dominance of the major psychotherapies has ended and integrationism and eclecticism [using ideas from several different forms of therapy] are now the direction for technical advances in treatment" (p. 455). For example, Jensen et al. (1990) found 68% of American therapists used an eclectic approach often spanning three or four types of therapy.

Why do so many people exaggerate the dominance of psychoanalysis?

Why do so many people believe that psychotherapy is predominantly psychoanalytic in orientation? According to Wedding and Niemiec (2003, p. 209):

> Psychologists, psychiatrists, and the process of psychotherapy have been portrayed in films for nearly a century, and it is obvious the film industry has been profoundly influenced by stereotypes of psychotherapy as classical psychoanalysis.

Examples include several of Woody Allen's films (e.g., *Annie Hall*, 1977) and the *Seven-Per-Cent Solution* (1976). In the latter film, Sherlock Holmes is treated by Sigmund Freud for his cocaine addiction. It emerges in the final therapy session that Sherlock Holmes had witnessed his father murdering his mother for adultery and that the arch-villain Moriarty was his mother's lover.

Wahl et al. (2018) focused on 22 films about psychotherapy from the twenty-first century. Psychoanalytic or psychodynamic therapy involving a focus on recalling childhood memories was the most common form of treatment: it was used by 33% of therapists shown on screen compared to 0% for cognitive and 0% for behavioural therapists. Note that it was unclear what type of therapy was being used by 54% of therapists. Successful therapy involved recall of traumatic events (typically from childhood) in 64%

of cases. Finally, 58% of therapists had a couch in their office, but only one-third of clients reclined on it when it was present.

There are other reasons why it is generally believed that most psychotherapy focuses on patients' childhood experiences and memories. Members of the public exaggerate the impact of childhood experiences on adult behaviour and mental disorders. Basterfield et al. (2023) found 67% of psychology students believe that most people sexually abused in childhood develop severe personality disturbances in adulthood. Childhood sexual abuse is associated with a significantly higher incidence of adult severe personality disturbances. However, a clear majority of adults who experienced childhood sexual abuse do not subsequently develop personality disturbances (Shrivastava et al., 2017).

Furnham and Robinson (2022) reported further evidence that most members of the public exaggerate the impact of childhood experiences: 72% of people believe parenting practices are of major importance in producing individual differences in personality (see Chapter 6). In fact, Nguyen et al. (2021) reviewed the relevant literature and concluded that shared environmental influences provided by parents to their children accounted for 0% of individual differences in adult personality! In contrast, genetic factors accounted for 47% of such individual differences.

Is confronting childhood problems necessary for psychotherapy to be effective?

The short answer is a resounding No!" There are over 500 approaches to psychotherapy (Eisner, 2000), the great majority of which focus predominantly on resolving patients' current problems and concerns rather than dredging through their childhood problems.

As we saw earlier, cognitive-behavioural therapy is used increasingly in the Western world to treat a wide range of mental disorders (especially anxiety disorders and depression). The central focus of this form of therapy is to change patients' current irrational beliefs and behaviour without considering their childhood experiences. For example, patients with social anxiety disorder often avoid social situations because they mistakenly believe they are less socially skilled than is actually the case (Rapee & Lim, 1992). Avoidance behaviour is reduced via exposure therapy (placing patients repeatedly in feared social situations). Patients' exaggerated concerns about the inadequacy of their social behaviour are addressed by providing them with videotaped feedback of their own behaviour. This decreases anxiety and enhances their social behaviour (Laposa & Rector, 2014).

It has proved surprisingly difficult to compare the effectiveness of different forms of therapy for mental disorders because successful treatment depends on numerous factors. These factors include the nature of the mental disorder, the initial severity of patients' mental disorder, the presence or absence of comorbidity (i.e., the presence or absence of additional mental disorders), the length of treatment and the measures used to assess treatment effectiveness. With respect to measures, therapeutic effectiveness can be assessed from the patient's own perspective, their subjective well-being, from society's perspective (the patient's ability to function in society) or the therapist's perspective (Strupp, 1996).

In spite of the many problems, there have been numerous attempts to assess the effectiveness of the various major therapies (e.g., psychodynamic therapy; cognitive behavioural therapy). Matt and Navarro (1997) combined the findings from 63 different meta-analyses and found 75% of patients receiving therapy improved more than the average untreated client. Of importance, moderately beneficial effects were found with all forms of therapy. Their findings are reasonably representative of other studies, although there has been a general tendency for psychodynamic therapy to be somewhat less effective than other major therapies.

Lilliengren (2023) provided a comprehensive review of research studies on the effectiveness of psychodynamic therapy. Overall, psychodynamic therapy was more effective than no treatment in 90% of studies. However, it was more effective than cognitive behavioural therapy in only 7% of studies and was significantly less effective than cognitive behavioural therapy in 24% of studies.

In sum, psychodynamic therapy is generally moderately effective. However, the greater effectiveness of cognitive behavioural therapy convincingly indicates that confronting childhood problems is not required for therapy to be effective.

Is confronting childhood problems sufficient for psychotherapy to be effective?

This is a surprisingly hard question to answer. As we have seen, psychoanalysis and other psychodynamic therapies stemming from it are moderately effective in treating many mental disorders. However, it is much harder to identify how and why they are effective. Of importance here is the fallacy known as post hoc ergo propter hoc (after this, therefore because of this). Patients are exposed to psychodynamic therapy with its emphasis on patients facing up to their childhood problems and subsequently (at least in many cases) they recover from mental illness. It is tempting to conclude that confronting childhood problems causally enhances patients' psychological well-being, but we need to be beware of the aforementioned fallacy.

Why might psychodynamic therapy be effective other than because it focuses on resolving childhood problems? The starting point is to distinguish between factors *specific* to any given form of therapy and those *common* to most or all therapies (Cuijpers et al., 2019). The most important common factors include the following: therapeutic alliance (a warm relationship between therapist and client with mutual agreement on how to achieve therapeutic goals); patient expectations concerning the likely success of treatment and therapist empathy.

The discovery that a given common factor correlates with therapeutic success does not prove the common factor causally influenced that success. For example, Flückiger et al. (2018) found in a meta-analysis that the quality of the therapeutic alliance correlated +0.28 with therapeutic effectiveness. It is possible that a strong therapeutic alliance directly enhances therapeutic effectiveness. Alternatively, it could be that early signs that therapy is proving effective enhance the quality of the therapeutic alliance. However, if therapeutic alliance has a causal impact on patient outcome, then therapeutic alliance early in treatment should predict subsequent reduction of symptoms. Flückiger et al. discussed much evidence supporting that hypothesis.

Conclusions

Psychoanalysis and psychodynamic therapy have been declining in popularity in many parts of the world. Accordingly, the great majority of therapy nowadays does not involve any focus on childhood problems. Even though psychodynamic therapy is moderately effective in treating many mental disorders, the comparable (or superior) effectiveness of other therapies demonstrates conclusively that therapy can be very effective even when no attempt is made to resolve the patient's childhood problems.

It might appear that we are on stronger ground in claiming that focusing on resolving patients' childhood problems is a valuable therapeutic approach. However, even Freud was sceptical of the genuineness of many of the traumatic memories 'recalled' by patients and much research indicates that these alleged memories are often implanted by the therapist (see Chapter 3).

In addition, we know remarkably little about the precise mechanisms causing any given form of therapy to be successful. There is an ongoing controversy as to the involvement of common factors in explaining the success of therapies of all kinds (Cuijpers et al., 2019). In sum, we know for certain that a therapeutic emphasis on resolving childhood problems is not necessary for therapeutic success and it may well not be sufficient either.

Myth: antidepressants are much more effective than psychotherapy for treating depression

Historically, it was generally assumed that what we call 'mental disorders' were caused by demons or other supernatural forces. On that assumption, what needed to be done was to make life as difficult as possible for these demons. Popular techniques (but presumably not popular among those on the receiving end!) included immersing the patient in boiling hot water, flogging, starvation and torture. It was erroneously believed these 'cures' would persuade the demons to leave the patient's body and thus remove their disorder. This is an excellent example of the treatment being worse than the disease.

It has been estimated that 350 million people worldwide suffer from clinical depression (World Health Organisation, 2018a). Between 2020 and 2023, the number was even higher because of the negative impact of Covid and lockdowns on people's ability to interact with others and pursue normal lives. Antidepressant drugs are the commonest way of treating depression. More than 8 million people in the UK are on antidepressants, and prescriptions for antidepressant drugs increased by over 100% between 2005 and 2016. There are numerous antidepressant drugs, but the most popular ones are selective serotonin reuptake inhibitors (SSRIs). The first SSRI was Prozac (fluoxetine) approved for use in 1987.

Most people are very positive about the value of antidepressants. Basterfield et al. (2023) found 71% of psychology students agreed that "Antidepressants are much more effective than psychotherapy for treating depression". Most people (72%) also agreed with this statement: "Because Prozac, which increases the activity of serotonin in the brain, has been shown to effectively treat depression, we can conclude that depression is caused by a deficiency of serotonin in the brain". Thus, almost three-quarters of the population believe they understand the mechanism by which anti-depressants like Prozac have their beneficial effects.

Research evidence

You might imagine it would be easy to establish whether depression can be treated more successfully by antidepressants than by psychotherapy. You have two groups of depressed patients, one of which receives antidepressants and the other of which receives psychotherapy (e.g., cognitive therapy or cognitive-behavioural therapy. Following treatment, you simply compare the percentages of patients who have recovered. When DeRubeis et al. (2005) compared the effectiveness of antidepressants (SSRIs) and cognitive therapy in treating major depressive disorder, they discovered 58% of patients showed considerable improvement with each form of treatment. Thus, antidepressants were not "much more" effective than psychotherapy but seemed comparably effective.

The previous conclusion is flawed. In order for any given form of therapy to be regarded as effective, it needs to satisfy two criteria: (1) *remission* (i.e., disappearance of most or all the symptoms) and (2) *no relapse* (i.e., no return of the symptoms following treatment). DeRubeis et al. (2005) focused only on remission. Hollon et al. (2005) studied those depressed patients who had responded well to therapy in DeRubeis et al.'s study for 12 months after treatment. Of those patients who had received drug therapy, 76% suffered a relapse compared to only 31% of those receiving cognitive therapy.

The previous findings are typical. Hollon et al. (2021) reviewed eight studies (including Hollon et al., 2005): the risk of relapse following successful cognitive therapy was less than half that following successful drug therapy in seven of them. The risk of relapse is reduced (but remains high) when antidepressant drugs continue to be administered after remission. Kishi et al. (2023) found in a meta-analysis that the relapse rate 39 weeks after remission was 69% when the drugs were discontinued but 40% when anti-depressants were continued.

Hollon et al. (2021) reviewed several studies where the relapse rate following cognitive therapy was compared against that when antidepressant drugs were administered throughout with no discontinuation. Overall, the relapse rate following cognitive therapy was much lower than that for medication continuation.

There is more bad news for those believing antidepressant drugs are highly effective in treating depression. It is important to take account of the placebo effect, which occurs when patients respond positively to an inactive substance based on their belief it will be effective. The optimal way to investigate the placebo effect is to treat some depressed patients with antidepressant drugs and others with a placebo without them knowing which form of treatment they are receiving. In a review, Sanchez-Lafuente et al. (2021) found there was a substantial placebo effect when antidepressant drugs were used to treat major depressive disorder.

There are two main reasons why a placebo effect is observed (Curkovic et al., 2019). First, placebos can facilitate recovery from depression if patients *expect* them to reduce their symptoms. Second, there is often a reduction in symptoms of depression over time even in the absence of therapy (Curkovic et al., 2019); this is known as spontaneous remission.

Kirsch (2019, p. 1), a long-term opponent of antidepressant drugs, has claimed that, "Most (if not all) of the benefits of antidepressants in the treatment of depression and anxiety are due to the placebo response, and the difference in improvement between drug and placebo is not clinically meaningful". However, improvement with antidepressant drugs is often greater than with placebos. Kirsch argues that much of this difference occurs because patients often guess correctly whether they are taking antidepressants or placebos, and this knowledge inhibits the placebo effect.

Why is the relapse rate much higher for antidepressants than psychotherapy?

We have seen the long-term beneficial effects of antidepressants are typically much smaller than those of cognitive therapy. Why is that? To answer this question, we must first consider the reasons why individuals become depressed in the first place and the mechanisms responsible for the progressive reduction of their depressive systems.

On the face of it, depression is an extremely negative emotional state and one we would be much better (and happier) without. Many clinical psychologists and psychiatrists agree, arguing that depression weakens the motivation to pursue adaptive goals and reduces cognitive functioning. However, the notion that the evolution of the human species has led very large numbers of people to suffer a useless and unpleasant emotional state is perplexing and implausible.

An alternative approach is to argue that depression causes severe short-term costs but is often adaptive and functional in the long-term. Genetic factors play a major role in explaining individual differences in depression. However, depression is frequently triggered by a major loss (e.g., death of a loved one; divorce), and depressed individuals need to adjust to their lost goal and replace it with a new one. More specifically, depressed individuals need to go through the following processes: "Biasing cognition to avoid losses, conserving energy, disengaging from unobtainable goals, signalling submission, soliciting resources, and promoting analytical thinking" (Durisko et al., 2015, p. 316).

The crucial limitation with using antidepressants to treat depression is that they do nothing to promote the deliberate and analytical thinking required to resolve the problems causing depression in the first place. Instead, they simply anaesthetise the depressed individuals' distress. As Hollon (2020, p. 1212) pointed out, "Putting someone on ADMs [antidepressant medications] is analogous to holding a blow dryer up to a thermostat to turn the furnace down, an effect that lasts for as long as the blow dryer stays on". In view of this limitation, it is unsurprising that over 85% of depressed patients are prescribed antidepressants for over 2 years.

What underlying mechanism determines the impact of cognitive therapy (and cognitive behavioural therapy) on depressed individuals? According to Hollon et al. (2021), all forms of cognitive therapy facilitate the patient's ability to address the complex problems they face with effective deliberate thought. It is this direct focus on resolving patients' major problems that prevents relapse. More specifically, cognitive and cognitive-behavioural therapy focus on the 'cognitive triad': patients' unrealistic negative thoughts about themselves, the world and the future.

One of the most influential cognitive approaches to the treatment of depression was proposed by Beck (e.g., Beck & Dozois, 2011). It is based on three key hypotheses:

(1) *Access hypothesis*: if depressed individuals receive appropriate training, they become aware of the content of their own thinking.
(2) *Mediation hypothesis*: how depressed individuals think about and interpret life's events influences their emotions and behaviour.
(3) *Change hypothesis*: individuals can recover from depression by intentionally modifying their cognitive and behavioural reactions to life's events.

In the absence of therapy, most depressed individuals spend much of their time engaged in rumination; this is,

a pattern of responding to distress in which an individual passively and perseveratively thinks about his or her upsetting symptoms and the

causes and consequences of those symptoms, while failing to initiate the active problem solving that might alter the cause of that distress.
(McLaughlin & Nolen-Hoeksma, 2011)

In sum, cognitive therapy is effective because it replaces the patients' initial ineffective thinking style involving rumination and negative irrational thinking into a much more effective problem-solving thinking style.

If this analysis of the underlying mechanisms responsible for the successful treatment of depression by cognitive therapy is correct, it offers a potential explanation for the high relapse rate following antidepressant therapy. More specifically, antidepressant therapy is not designed to promote a rational problem-solving approach to patients' major concerns.

Serotonin hypothesis

According to the serotonin hypothesis, depression is caused by a deficiency of serotonin in the brain. As we saw earlier, 72% students believe this hypothesis is supported by evidence that Prozac, a selective serotonin reuptake inhibitor (SSRI) that increases the activity of serotonin in the brain, is an effective treatment for depression. Since the SSRIs increase serotonin levels in the brain, there is apparent logic in the earlier belief argument and it is consistent with the common assumption that serotonin is the 'happy chemical'.

However, it has proved extremely difficult to assess serotonin levels in the brain. Moncrieff et al. (2023) recently carried out an 'umbrella review' based on surveying existing reviews and meta-analyses to gain an overview of the research evidence relating to the serotonin hypothesis. Here are their conclusions:

> The main areas of serotonin research provide no consistent evidence of there being an association between serotonin and depression, and no support for the hypothesis that depression is caused by lowered serotonin activity or concentrations. Some evidence was consistent with the possibility that long-term antidepressant use reduces serotonin concentration.
>
> (p. 1).

Some experts are less pessimistic about the serotonin hypothesis. Jauhar et al. (2023) argued there are reliable abnormalities in serotonin activity in depressed individuals including suggestive evidence for reduced serotonin levels. It may thus be premature to discard the serotonin hypothesis altogether. However, even if depressed individuals tend to have low levels of serotonin it would not necessarily follow that these low serotonin levels are *causally* involved in the development of depression. At the very least, "The role of serotonin in depression will need to be integrated into more complex neurobiological models than those originally envisaged" (Jauhar et al., p. 240).

Conclusions

The belief that antidepressants are much more effective than psychotherapy in the treatment of depression is profoundly mistaken. Antidepressants are no more effective than psychotherapy (e.g., cognitive therapy) in producing remission of symptoms during the course of treatment and there is a much greater risk of relapse with drugs than with psychotherapy. Some (or much) of the apparent effectiveness of antidepressants in producing remission of symptoms is due to the placebo effect (discussed further in Chapter 10).

The high relapse rate when antidepressants are discontinued is easily explicable: the drugs alleviate the symptoms of depression but don't address directly the factors causing depression in the first place. It is possible that depressed individuals have low levels of serotonin in the brain. However, it is a fallacy to assume that because SSRIs (e.g., Prozac) that increase serotonin levels in the brain are moderately effective in treating depression, a deficiency of serotonin was the cause of the depression. We can see the fallacy clearly in the following example (McLeod, 2001): aspirin cures a headache, but that does not mean a lack of aspirin caused the headache in the first place!

In view of the compelling evidence that anti-depressant drugs are significantly less effective than psychotherapy, why are so many people convinced the opposite is the case? The short answer is that most easily accessible information about anti-depressant drugs greatly exaggerates their effectiveness (see also Chapter 10). Demasi and Gøtzsche (2020) discovered that 92% of websites in 10 countries contained misleading information exaggerating the benefits of anti-depressant drugs and minimising their limitations.

9 Psychology and the law

Psychologists play an increasing role in the legal process. One of the most prominent of these psychologists (especially within the United States), is Elizabeth Loftus, a Professor of Psychology at the University of California Irvine. She has appeared as a witness in numerous high-profile cases because of her expertise in the field of memory. More specifically, her research has indicated that human memory is often much less accurate and more error-prone than generally assumed (see Chapter 3). Loftus has presented evidence in over 300 court cases including those involving Michael Jackson, Harvey Weinstein and Ghislaine Maxwell.

In this chapter, we discuss how psychologists have dispelled myths about numerous aspects of the legal system, some of which have had negative effects on the administration of justice. This is especially the case with respect to eyewitness testimony. Gross and Shaffer (2012) examined 873 cases in the United States where someone convicted of a crime was subsequently exonerated. In three-quarters of these cases, eyewitness misidentifications were involved. Wise and Safer (2010) found American judges' knowledge of the factors causing eyewitness testimony to be inaccurate was no greater than that of undergraduate students. This ignorance is shared by lawyers, jurors and law officers (Wise et al., 2014).

Myth: an eyewitness's confidence is never a good predictor of their identification accuracy

Imagine you are a juror in a court case where the most important evidence provided by the prosecution lawyers is the identification of the culprit by an eyewitness. If that eyewitness seems very confident, would you regard their identification as sufficient evidence to convict the defendant? Kassin and Barndollar (1992) found only 49% of members of the public agreed that "An eyewitness's confidence is not a good predictor of his or her identification accuracy". Thus, half believed eyewitness confidence is a good predictor of their identification accuracy. In contrast, Kassin and Barndollar found 87% of eyewitness experts argued eyewitness confidence does not predict their identification accuracy.

DOI: 10.4324/9781003596677-9

More evidence that members of the public attach much more importance than experts to eyewitness confidence was reported by Simons and Chabris (2011). They asked laypeople to indicate whether they agreed with the following statement: "In my opinion, the testimony of one confident eyewitness should be enough evidence to convict a defendant of a crime". As many as 37% of the respondents agreed with the statement compared to 0% of memory experts.

Recent research indicates that members of the public have become more sceptical of the predictive value of eyewitness confidence. Brewin et al. (2019) found 82% of undergraduates agreed that "An eyewitness's confidence is never a good predictor of his or her identification accuracy".

How can we explain this increased scepticism? There is growing awareness that DNA evidence has recently been used to exonerate numerous innocent individuals falsely convicted of crimes they did not commit. In approximately 70% of these cases, misidentification by eyewitnesses was a significant factor in their conviction (Innocence Project, 2021). This has understandably led millions of people to doubt the accuracy and trustworthiness of eyewitness testimony.

Intriguingly, many experts have moved in the opposite direction and now believe eyewitness confidence is often of great value! Here is the conclusion reached by two leading eyewitness experts:

> With few exceptions, the results of studies conducted in the lab and in the real world show that confidence is highly predictive of accuracy [with one important exception discussed shortly], and high confidence often implies high accuracy.
>
> (Wixted & Mickes, 2022, p. 67)

Research evidence: negative

I will start with a whistle-stop tour of early research on the relationship between eyewitness confidence and accuracy (Wixted & Wells, 2017). Most early studies involved a staged event following by presenting eyewitnesses with a lineup of individuals; the suspect was present in 50% of the lineups and absent in the remaining 50%. Eyewitnesses either chose a given individual (choosers) or did not choose anyone (non-choosers). The typical overall finding based on the combined data from choosers and non-choosers was that there was a decidedly modest correlation of 0.20 or less between confidence and accuracy. Such findings led numerous psychologists to conclude eyewitness confidence has little predictive value. Wilson et al., 2013 (p. 98) maintained that "One surprising lesson that psychologists have learned about memory is that the confidence of an eyewitness is only weakly related to their recognition accuracy".

Early evidence from cases where DNA evidence indicated that individuals convicted on the basis of eyewitness identification were actually innocent apparently supported the notion that eyewitness confidence does not predict their identification accuracy. For example, Ronald Cotton was found guilty in 1985 of raping Jennifer Thompson on the basis of her very confident identification of him as the culprit. He was subsequently exonerated by DNA evidence having spent over 10 years in prison. Garrett (2011) investigated 161 such cases. Almost without exception, the mistaken eyewitnesses claimed at trial they were totally confident they had correctly identified the culprit.

Research evidence: positive

The aforementioned laboratory and real-world findings apparently provide compelling evidence that it is a myth to assume eyewitness confidence predicts accuracy of identification. However, that conclusion is unwarranted. Let's start by re-considering the laboratory evidence based on staged events. Sporer et al. (1995) made the important point that only eyewitnesses who choose (i.e., identify someone) testify in court. Accordingly, it makes sense to analyse the data from choosers only (ignoring the findings from non-choosers). The confidence-accuracy correlation was 0.41 for choosers, demonstrating that eyewitness confidence among choosers is a moderately strong predictor of their identification accuracy. For non-choosers, in contrast, the confidence-accuracy correlation was a mere 0.12.

We saw earlier that Garrett (2011) found eyewitnesses who identified the wrong person as the culprit were typically very confident at trial in their mistaken identification. However, when Garrett delved more deeply into such cases, he discovered serious problems with the evidence presented in court. For example, he gained access to Jennifer Thompson's initial identification of Cotton from a photo line-up. She hesitated for nearly five minutes before finally saying, "I think this is the guy". More generally, 57% of the 161 eyewitnesses studied by Garrett had reported a lack of certainty about their previous identifications. In fact, 40% of these eyewitnesses failed to identify the innocent defendant on their first try!

Why did these eyewitnesses have increasing confidence in their identifications as the time since the crime increased? Jennifer Thompson became more confident because she received positive feedback from the police when she initially identified Ronald Cotton as the rapist. Positive police feedback also played a major role in the increased confidence of other eyewitnesses in their mistaken identifications. This phenomenon is the 'post-identification feedback effect'.

Systematic research has confirmed the strength of the post-identification feedback effect and, worryingly, has also shown that eyewitnesses typically forget they initially had little confidence in their identification (Steblay et al., 2014). Wells and Bradfield (1998) uncovered another concern. When eyewitnesses were asked if post-identification feedback might have influenced their level of confidence, most said "No". However, those who said "No" were as susceptible to post-identification feedback as those who said "Yes".

How much weight should we attach to an eyewitness's confidence in their *initial* attempt to identify the culprit? Wixted et al. (2016) addressed this issue in a real-life study where eyewitnesses identified culprits from photo lineups in the Houston Police Department over a 1-year period. Eyewitness confidence proved to be a very good predictor of eyewitness accuracy: 80% of identifications were correct when eyewitness confidence was high compared to only 20% when it was low.

Are jurors aware of subtleties such as the greater validity of an eyewitness's initial identification confidence than their courtroom confidence? In a study using mock jurors, high eyewitness confidence increased the likelihood of a guilty verdict regardless of whether the high confidence occurred initially or in the courtroom. This was the case even when low confidence initially was followed by high courtroom confidence (Key et al., 2023).

The plot thickens

As discussed earlier, Garrett (2011) apparently discovered that eyewitnesses who very confidently identified the wrong person as the culprit in court had been much less confident at the time of their initial identification of that person. However, this narrative is oversimplified in two key ways (Berkowitz et al., 2022). First, we often have very limited evidence concerning eyewitnesses' confidence in their initial identifications that may have happened several months or even years prior to trial. In only 21% of the cases studied by Garrett did eyewitnesses report at trial that they had initially lacked confidence in their identification and such retrospective memories may be inaccurate.

Second, the problem may be less an issue of eyewitness misidentification and more one of mistaken eyewitness memory (Berkowitz et al., 2022). The National Registry of Exonerations in the United States documented over 700 exonerations where innocent individuals had been imprisoned due in part to mistaken eyewitness identification. In 46% of these cases, the police initially came to regard an innocent person as the suspect because of eyewitness testimony (e.g., an eyewitness's description of the culprit or informal identification) (Kenchel et al., 2020).

It is now clear that the extent to which a high level of eyewitness confidence reflects accuracy of eyewitness identifications depends on several factors involved in the lineup. Sauer et al. (2019) re-analysed previous data focusing on two factors: (1) degree of match between the witness's memory of the culprit and the suspect in the lineup: high or low; and (2) plausibility of the innocent suspect (based on identification rates in pilot testing): high vs. low.

When the task was 'easy' (high match + low innocent suspect plausibility), accuracy was 80% at the highest level of confidence. In contrast, when the task was 'hard' (low match + high innocent suspect plausibility), accuracy at the highest confidence level was only 20%. The enormous difference between these accuracy rates associated with high confidence means we must avoid strong generalisations about the predictive value of high confidence by eyewitness in their identifications.

Conclusions

The history of research on the extent to which eyewitnesses' confidence predicts the accuracy of their identification of the culprit has been decidedly chequered. For a long time, memory experts were highly sceptical of the predictive value of eyewitness confidence. However, much recent evidence suggests that high eyewitness confidence is often associated with high accuracy, which caused many experts to change their minds.

Finally, it has become clear that the predictive value of eyewitness confidence depends on the precise circumstances in which it is assessed. For example, eyewitnesses expecting the suspect to be present in a show-up (single person in lineup) are more likely to adopt a lenient response criterion for deciding the suspect is present leading to increased false identifications and over-confidence. As predicted, Eisen et al. (2017) found that high eyewitness confidence was more likely to be wrong when eyewitnesses were persuaded to adopt a lenient response criterion.

The overwhelming majority of research on eyewitness testimony has been carried out in Western, Educated, Industrialised, Rich, Democratic (WEIRD) countries. As a consequence, it is entirely possible that the findings would be rather different in non-WEIRD countries. For example, Vredeveldt and de Bruïne (2022) reviewed research conducted in predominantly oral cultures such as Sierra Leone, Rwanda and East Timor. Individuals in those cultures often describe events they have heard about from a family member or friend as if they had actually witnessed those events themselves. As a consequence, they may be over-confident in their memory because its accuracy depends on the accuracy of the memory described by their informant and the accuracy with which they remember what that informant said.

In sum, the notion that we should believe a confident eyewitness's identification of the culprit can be regarded as a myth. However, it is less of a myth than memory experts used to believe but more of a myth than some memory experts continue to believe. What is required of future research is to identify more clearly the boundary conditions under which eyewitness confidence is (and is not) predictive of eyewitness accuracy.

Myth: experts can nearly always identify the culprit from fingerprinting evidence

Fingerprinting evidence has been used extensively by the legal system in North and South America, Europe and around the world. Tens of thousands of defendants have been found guilty based mainly on such evidence. Most people believe fingerprints typically allow the police to identify the culprit.

Illsley (1987) surveyed 978 jurors 93% of whom believed fingerprint identification is a science. Almost as many (85%) argued it was the most reliable means of identification (this was before DNA evidence was widely used). An important reason for the strength of their belief in the value of fingerprint evidence is that most people believe no two fingerprints are the same. As a result, experts should be able to match a suspect's fingerprint against a large database of stored fingerprints with great accuracy.

Koehler (2017) obtained a more precise estimate of people's views of the reliability of fingerprint evidence. When asked what were the chances that a qualified and experienced fingerprint examiner would mistakenly claim that fingerprints taken from two different individuals came from the same person, their average estimate was 1 in 5,500,000.

Unsurprisingly, fingerprint assessors are also convinced of its value. According to McMurtrie (2010, pp. 273–274),

> Many in the latent fingerprint community . . . testify that the ACE-V [Analysis, Comparison, Evaluation, Verification] method [the most-used approach] has a 'zero error rate.' They claim that when the method is used by well-trained and experienced examiners, no errors are ever made, so that the method itself is error free.

Findings concerning the validity of fingerprint evidence will be discussed shortly. First, however, I will provide a whistle-stop tour of how fingerprinting became a major weapon in the police armoury.

History of fingerprinting

Human beings realised many centuries ago that we all have interesting patterns on our fingertips. However, a German anatomist, Johann Mayer, made a giant step forward when he claimed in 1788 that, "The arrangement of skin ridges [on fingertips] is never duplicated in two persons". This alleged discovery became important many years later when the police were finding it increasingly difficult to verify the identities of criminals in crowded cities like London. Since first-time offenders typically received much lighter sentences than repeat offenders, habitual criminals had a vested interest in giving false names so the police did not realise they had previously committed numerous other crimes.

During the nineteenth century, the police tried various approaches to establish an individual's identity. For example, photographs of a suspect's face could be compared against stored photographs of known criminals. However, that method was laborious and imprecise. Alphonse Bertillon, a French police official, devised a technique based on 11 bodily measurements which also proved of limited efficacy.

Fingerprints were initially used to establish identity by Sir William Herschel (1833–1917). However, the most influential figure was Sir Francis

Galton (1822–1911). He established that an individual's fingerprints remain the same over many years. He also produced a system for categorising fingerprints based on *loops* (curves backing onto themselves), *whorls* (circular or spiral patterns) and *arches* (wave-like curves). Approximately 60% of individuals' fingerprints are loops, 35% are whorls and 5% are arches. In addition, unique identification of a fingerprint requires an emphasis on minutiae (ridge endings and ridge bifurcations or forks).

Harry Jackson was the first criminal in England found guilty of a crime on the basis of fingerprints. Some billiard balls were stolen from a house in Denmark Hill, south London, on 27 June 1902. The police noticed fingerprints not belonging to any of those living in the house on a freshly painted windowsill. Richard Muir, the prosecution lawyer, used the fingerprint evidence to convict Harry Jackson and have him imprisoned for 7 years (28 months per billiard ball).

The rapidly increasing success of the police in imprisoning criminals on the basis of fingerprint evidence alarmed the criminal fraternity. The American gangster John Dillinger (1903–1934) applied acid to his fingers in the attempt to remove his fingerprints. Unfortunately for him, his fingerprints subsequently re-appeared identically to his original fingerprints.

Many criminals failed to learn the lesson that it was vitally important to ensure the police did not have access to their fingerprints. On 8 August 1963, 15 criminals carried out the Great Train Robbery in which £2,600,000 (£75,000,000 in today's money) was stolen from a Royal Mail train. The criminals used a nearby farmhouse as a hideout after the robbery. Before they left it, they attempted to wipe away their fingerprints. In spite of that, the police harvested 311 fingerprints, which led directly to 12 of the train robbers being caught and imprisoned.

Research evidence

It is probable that no two individuals have exactly the same fingerprints (although it would be incredibly difficult to prove the point). You might think monozygotic (identical) twins would have the same fingerprints but this is *not* the case. Identical twins have slightly different fingerprints because the development of fingerprints in the womb is influenced by factors such as umbilical cord length, nutrition and position in the womb. The likelihood that everyone has a unique fingerprint is obviously a great advantage when it comes to using fingerprints for forensic purposes. However, all is not plain sailing.

In real-world settings, the police start with latent fingerprints (the impressions left by the criminal at the scene of the crime). After that, automatic fingerprint identification systems (AFISs) scan huge databases of stored fingerprints. These fingerprints were collected deliberately from known individuals under controlled conditions. Use of AFISs typically produces a relatively small number of possible matches to the fingerprint obtained at the crime scene ranked by similarity to the criminal's fingerprint. A fingerprinting expert then decides which known print (if any) matches the culprit's latent print.

The FBI's AFIS contains the fingerprints of over 162,000,000 individuals. Ironically, the more fingerprints stored in this (or any other) database, the greater the probability of 'close non-matches'. These are fingerprints that are extremely similar even though obtained from two different individuals. Koehler and Liu (2021) asked 125 fingerprint agencies to indicate whether pairs of fingerprints were from the same or different individuals (two pairs consisted of close non-matches). The false-positive error rate was 16% with one of the close non-matches and 23% with the other. If we average across the two close non-matches, the false-positive error rate was more than *one million times* higher than the estimated false-positive error rate reported by members of the public (Koehler, 2017; discussed earlier)!

Koehler and Liu (2021) required DNA analysts to make very difficult decisions, and so typical false-positive error rates should be much lower than the ones they reported. Sikorski (2022) reviewed four experimental studies where the false-positive error rate ranged between 0% and 4.2%.

Optimal performance would occur when matching fingerprints are identified as matching ("hits") rather than non-matching ("misses") and when non-matching fingerprints are identified as non-matching ("correct rejections") rather than matching ("false alarms"). Thompson et al. (2014) compared the performance of experts and novices using genuine crime-scene fingerprints. The experts had more hits than the novices (72% vs. 49%) when the fingerprints matched. When the two fingerprints were similar but did not match, experts had massively fewer false alarms than the novices (1.65% vs. 57%). Thus, the experts were much more cautious than the novices in deciding there was a match.

The fingerprint experts in Thompson et al.'s (2014) study performed impressively when deciding whether there was an overall match between two fingerprints. However, experts often vary among themselves to a surprisingly large extent when asked whether two fingerprints share the same minutiae (features). Evett and Williams (2015) asked 130 fingerprint experts to compare pairs of fingerprints. The range in the number of minutiae shared by two fingerprints taken from the same person varied between 10 and 40 with one pair and 14 to 56 with a different pair.

Accurate fingerprint detection depends on two main factors. First, there is the completeness of the latent fingerprints left at the scene of the crime. Inconsiderately, criminals try not to leave complete fingerprints and so the fingerprints available to the police are often somewhat or very incomplete. Second, there is the expertise of the person assessing the fingerprints. However, even experts are subject to various biases when making matching judgements about fingerprints (Dror, 2020). Confirmation bias is of particular importance: the fingerprint expert's expectations, motives and beliefs and the situational context in which the fingerprint task is conducted distort their decision making.

Fingerprint matching obviously depends on the completeness of the latent prints. Kellman et al. (2014) identified several aspects of latent prints influencing how easy or hard it was for fingerprint experts to match them with known prints. Identification performance was determined by information quantity (fingerprint area), information quality (e.g., intensity and contrast of the print) and global features (e.g., ridge patterns). Overall, matches were detected 86% of the time and non-matches 97% of the time. However, the experts were correct 100% of the time with the easiest 59% of the fingerprint pairs.

We turn now to the ways experts exhibit bias. FBI fingerprint experts were brought in to identify the bomber involved in the terrorist attack in Madrid on 11th March 2004. Four of these experts decided that a fingerprint taken from Brandon Mayfield, an innocent American lawyer who was falsely arrested and jailed, was from the same person as a fingerprint taken from the actual bomber (Ouhane Daoud). These fingerprint experts were probably unduly influenced by the fact that Mayfield had converted to Islam some years earlier: this is an example of confirmation bias.

Dror et al. (2006) obtained more evidence of confirmation bias. Fingerprint experts judged whether two fingerprints matched having been told incorrectly they were the ones mistakenly matched by the FBI as the Madrid bomber. In fact, these experts had judged these fingerprints a clear and definite match several years earlier. The misleading information given to the experts caused 60% of them to be definite non-matches! Thus, expectations triggered by confirmation bias can distort fingerprint identification.

Studies such as the one by Dror et al. (2006) are somewhat artificial and may not reflect what happens with fingerprint identifications for real-life crimes. Kassin et al. (2012) considered 241 cases where someone convicted of a crime was subsequently exonerated on the basis of DNA evidence. They compared cases where the accused had made a false confession and those where there was no confession. There were more evidence errors (including false fingerprint matching) with the confession cases than the non-confession ones. Kassin et al. hypothesised that confessions are perceived as so incriminating that they taint other forms of evidence. As predicted, the first evidence error was false confession in 65% of cases with multiple errors.

How can we improve fingerprint identification?

Fingerprint identification (especially given the typically incomplete nature of latent fingerprints) is prone to error. Of most concern, even fingerprint experts are often susceptible to confirmation bias when other forms of evidence suggest the accused is guilty.

How can we improve this worrying state of affairs? First, fingerprint experts typically make categorical decisions (i.e., match; inconclusive; non-match). However, there are many cases where the evidence is insufficient to make a definitive decision. In such cases, it is useful for experts to have other categories available (e.g., 'probable match'; 'highly probable match') (Dror & Langenburg, 2019).

Second, fingerprint experts differ considerably in the amount of evidence they require to make a specific decision (Hicklin et al., 2020). As a consequence, some experts are much more likely than others to mistakenly decide that matching fingerprints do not match. Training could enhance experts' ability to adopt optimal decision thresholds.

Third, Growns et al. (2022) argued that statistically rare fingerprint features are of special value in analysing fingerprints. Accordingly, they trained novices and experienced fingerprint examiners to focus on these rare features. This training programme significantly improved the fingerprint-matching performance of both groups.

Fourth, many experts exaggerate their own ability to make accurate, unbiased decisions about fingerprint matches. Kukucka et al. (2017) carried out a study on cognitive bias defined as being influenced by contextual information (e.g., the accused's criminal history; an eyewitness; a detective's opinion). Even though 64% of fingerprint experts accepted that cognitive bias was a cause for concern, only 25% admitted their own judgements were influenced by cognitive bias. Across several branches of forensic science including fingerprinting, 37% of experts estimated that their accuracy rate was 100%!

Cuellar et al. (2022) provided a plausible explanation of why many fingerprint examiners believe their judgements are better than is actually the case. Suppose an examiner mistakenly claims the defendant's fingerprint matches the one found at the crime scene. This claim makes it likely that the innocent defendant will be found guilty. (Loeffler et al., 2019, estimated that 6% of defendants are wrongly convicted). Since the examiner's mistake will probably never come to light, they will regard the guilty verdict as vindicating their (mistaken) judgement about the fingerprint evidence.

Potential jurors can be taken in by experts' exaggerated claims. Kukucka et al. (2020) used a hypothetical court case where the defendant had confessed to the crime and a fingerprint expert claimed the defendant's fingerprint matched evidence from the crime scene. When the fingerprint expert was aware of the defendant's confession and admitted that could have influenced his judgement, potential jurors discounted his testimony. However, when he denied that his awareness of the confession could have influenced his judgement, potential jurors were as impressed by his testimony as they were by the testimony of an expert unaware of the confession. Thus, potential jurors mistakenly accepted the expert's claim that his judgement was uninfluenced by bias.

The way forward is to shield fingerprint experts from irrelevant contextual information that might bias their decision making. Reassuringly, experts provided training in cognitive bias are more accepting of the need for shielding than untrained experts (Kukucka et al., 2017).

Fifth, when fingerprint evidence is presented in court cases, the individual presenting that evidence is typically described as an 'expert'. However, while all so-called fingerprint experts have had relevant training, there is no clear and precise definition of 'fingerprint expert' based on performance level. It would obviously be useful if jurors in court cases had a clearer notion of the precise level of expertise provided by 'fingerprint experts'.

Sixth, Neumann et al. (2014) asked 146 fingerprint examiners to compare 15 pairs of fingerprints and to indicate their thought processes throughout this task. There were substantial differences across examiners in the fingerprint features they used and the extent to which the various features contributed to their decisions (i.e., match or mismatch).

Neumann et al. (2014) discovered examiners' decision-making processes are subjective because they required examiners to be open and transparent about how they set about the task of comparing fingerprints. For the future, increased openness and transparency would make it easier to assess the value of any examiner's decisions. It might also lead to identification of the optimal strategies for reliable and valid fingerprint analysis.

Conclusions

Many fingerprint examiners achieve very high levels of performance when matching fingerprints under ideal conditions: they have a high level of expertise, the fingerprints in question are complete and detailed and they are not exposed to any contextual information that might bias their judgement. In the real world, however, fingerprints are often very incomplete and lacking in many details, fingerprint examiners do not have great expertise and their judgement is often biased by contextual information.

Most people believe the myth that fingerprint evidence is almost invariably accurate because they de-emphasise the messiness and complexities involved in using such evidence in real-world conditions. If they were aware that fingerprints taken from crime scenes are often very fragmented and indistinct, it seems improbable they would continue to argue that the chances of a fingerprint expert erroneously claiming that two fingerprints match when they do not are as low as 1 in 5,500,000 (Koehler, 2017).

Myth: DNA tests are almost infallible for identifying culprits

DNA testing has a very high reputation as a reliable and valid method to establish whether any given individual is guilty of a particular crime. As discussed earlier, there are numerous cases where individuals convicted of serious crimes primarily on the basis of eyewitness testimony were subsequently exonerated because of DNA evidence. One such example is Eddie Joe Lloyd, who spent 16 years in prison for a crime he had not committed until DNA evidence indicated a mismatch between his DNA profile and the one established from the crime science. He described DNA testing in the following terms: "That's God's signature. God's signature is never a forgery".

There are at least 10 different forensic sciences. Airlie et al. (2021) asked over 500 forensic scientists from over 20 countries to indicate how valuable they perceived these various sciences to be. Several forensic sciences (e.g., fibre analysis; bloodstain pattern analysis) were rated as 'very valuable' by between 25% and 35% of the respondents. In third place was firearms identification (rated as 'very valuable' by 59% of respondents), with the top two places being filled by DNA analysis and fingerprint analysis with 'very valuable' ratings from over 80% of respondents.

DNA testing has also received the rubber stamp of approval from most members of the public, who believe it provides scientific and objective evidence and is almost infallible. In a study mentioned earlier, Koehler (2017) asked members of the public to estimate the probability that a qualified and experienced DNA analyst would make a false-positive judgement by deciding that samples of DNA taken from two individuals actually came from the same person. Their average estimate was that the probability was 1 in 10,000,000. This represents an extraordinarily high level of performance and is twice as impressive as the estimated probability of 1 in 5,500,000 for false positives with fingerprinting evidence (discussed earlier).

What does the figure of 1 in 10,000,000 mean in the context of court cases in England and Wales? One might imagine that the outcomes of numerous court cases would depend on DNA analysis. In fact, DNA analysis contributes to judicial outcomes in under 1% of recorded crimes in England and Wales (Amankwaa & McCartney, 2021). That means that a court case involving a false positive identification based on DNA should occur less than once every century in England and Wales!

Research evidence

Experts in DNA analysis have sometimes disingenuously argued that the test is infallible but errors occur because of experts' mistakes. The truth or falsity of the belief in infallibility of DNA tests is discussed later. The starting point is that the accuracy of DNA analysis is typically much lower when there is a DNA mixture (i.e., the DNA profile contains DNA from more than one person) than when all the DNA is from the same person.

Butler et al. (2018) reported the findings of two major studies involving DNA mixtures from up to four individuals. Accuracy levels were high with two-person DNA mixtures (especially with respect to the major contributor to the mixture). However, there was much more variability in performance when more than two individuals contributed to the mixture. In one case, 30% of the analysts at a particular laboratory claimed the DNA of a given individual was not there, 50% said they didn't know whether it was there and 20% argued that the individual was in the mixture and that they could exclude more than 99.9% of the population!

There are other reasons why DNA analysis can be very complex. For example, there may be a limited quantity of DNA, there may be degradation of the sample or the DNA sample may contain contaminants.

We saw earlier that fingerprint experts often exhibit confirmation bias (i.e., their expectations distort their decision making). DNA analysts are also prone to confirmation bias. Informal findings were reported by Thompson (2009). He gave two talks where he presented a slide showing DNA taken from a crime scene and DNA evidence from four suspects (Tom, Dick, Harry and Sally). When Tom was identified as the defendant, expert DNA analysts in the audience argued there was a good match between his DNA sample and the one from the crime scene dismissing contrary evidence as due to 'artefacts' in the data. When Dick was identified as the defendant, the DNA analysts exaggerated the goodness of the match between his DNA and the sample from the crime scene.

Thompson (2009) argued that some of the practices of DNA analysts exemplify the Texas sharpshooter fallacy. This fallacy comes from the story of a Texan who allegedly fired shots randomly into the side of a barn and then painted a target very precisely around each of the bullet holes. After that, he impressed his neighbours by showing them that he could apparently hit every target dead centre.

Research evidence of confirmation bias in the interpretation of DNA mixtures was reported in a ground-breaking study by Dror and Hampikian (2011) based on a real case of gang rape. One defendant testified against the other suspects in return for receiving a more lenient sentence in a plea-bargain deal. However, these other suspects all denied any involvement in the gang rape. The DNA analysis experts who examined the DNA mixture concluded that one of these suspects could not be excluded from being a contributor to the mixture.

The key issue addressed by Dror and Hampikian (2011) was whether the DNA experts' conclusion was influenced by their knowledge of the plea-bargain deal. Accordingly, they presented 17 experts with the original DNA evidence from the trial but without providing them with information about the court case. Only one of these experts agreed with the conclusion of the original analysts (i.e., 'cannot be excluded'), 12 concluded 'exclude' and two concluded 'inconclusive'. Thus, experts' judgements on mixture DNA can be influenced by biasing contextual information (i.e., knowledge of the plea-bargain deal). They also demonstrate that subjective factors can play a role in interpreting DNA evidence.

Many people exaggerate the relevance of DNA evidence because they subscribe to the prosecutor's fallacy (Thompson & Newman, 2015). A prosecutor (or member of the public) argues that if the suspect is guilty, then the probability of stored DNA from that person matching DNA taken from the crime scene would be extremely high. From that reasonable assumption, they conclude that the existence of a match between an individual's known DNA and DNA from the crime scene indicates the probability of the suspect's guilt is very high. This conclusion is fallacious because it is crucially important to consider questions of *how* and *when* as well as *who*. All DNA analysis can demonstrate with high probability is that individual X's DNA was found at the crime scene. However, that does *not* reveal how or when that DNA sample was created. As Gill (2019) pointed out, DNA samples do not have a date or time stamp on them.

Ironically, the increasing sensitivity of DNA techniques means more DNA samples recovered from crime scenes were not produced during the crime itself. Examples include *background* DNA (deposited ahead of the crime and irrelevant to it) and *secondary transfer* DNA (DNA from someone who was never there but whose DNA was transferred to the crime scene by another person because they shook hands or had some other form of contact) (Gill, 2019). Recent evidence indicates that secondary transfer can occur even in the absence of direct contact (van Oorschot et al., 2021).

There have been several miscarriages of justice involving confirmation bias by DNA examiners and their reluctance to consider the possibility that an individual's DNA at the crime scene could be interpreted in non-incriminating ways. In the following paragraphs we discuss two such cases.

Consider a notorious case where three individuals (Rudy Guede, Amanda Knox and Raffaele Sollecito) were all initially convicted of the murder of Meredith Kercher, who was stabbed to death in Perugia, Italy in 2007. Guede's conviction was confirmed, but Knox and her boyfriend Sollecito were eventually found not guilty. Amanda Knox was Meredith Kercher's flatmate. A knife retrieved from her boyfriend's flat had small traces of Meredith Kercher's DNA on the blade and a sample of Amanda's DNA was discovered on the handle.

Prosecutors claimed Ms. Knox's DNA was transferred to the knife when Ms. Kercher was stabbed with it even though no blood was detected on the knife. Amanda Knox was eventually found not guilty in part because Ms. Knox could have used the knife to cut bread, and in fact starch grains were discovered on the blade. Since Ms. Knox lived in the same flat as Ms. Kercher, there were several totally innocent explanations for the presence of her DNA on the knife. Thus, the prosecutors' interpretation of the DNA evidence is a clear example of confirmation bias.

This case contains another even more obvious example of confirmation bias (Gill, 2016). There were numerous samples of Rudy Guede's DNA on Kercher's clothes and in her room. However, no traces of Amanda Knox's DNA were found on the clothes or in the room. The DNA experts for the prosecution suggested Amanda Knox might have selectively removed her DNA. That is absurd. DNA samples are invisible and it is impossible to selectively remove one person's DNA samples while retaining those of another person.

Gill (2019) discussed another miscarriage of justice revolving around the DNA of an innocent person found at the crime scene. The victim was Anne Marie Foy, a sex worker murdered in Liverpool in September 2005. David

Butler was a local taxi driver known to use sex workers in that area and his distinctive striped taxi was captured in the area on CCTV. In addition, Mr. Butler's DNA was recovered from her fingernails. The prosecution said it was, "more than a thousand billion times" more likely that it was David Butler's DNA than anyone else's which is a ridiculous exaggeration. All this incriminating evidence made it seem virtually certain that Ms. Foy had had extensive contact with Mr. Butler's skin as he hit and strangled her before he deposited her body in a nearby park. Accordingly, Mr. Butler was charged with murder and taken to court.

Mr. Butler denied ever having met the victim. He also argued that, since he suffered from emphysema, he would have been unable to strangle Ms. Foy or to drag a dead woman's body. The defence team established there was a mixture of different DNA profiles under Ms. Foy's fingernails and the match with David Butler's DNA was only partial. They also discovered his nickname was "flaky" because of the dry skin condition from which he suffered. As a consequence, it was possible the presence of his DNA under Ms. Foy's fingernails could have been due to innocent contact or secondary transfer (e.g., transfer via bank notes used to pay Ms. Foy). In view of the uncertain nature of the evidence against him, Mr. Butler was acquitted.

Improving DNA analysis

As discussed earlier, reliability in the sense that findings can easily be replicated is at the heart of all the forensic sciences (Sikorski, 2022). That means that expert DNA analysts should typically make the same judgements when deciding whether any two DNA samples form a match or a mismatch. There have been surprisingly few thorough research attempts to assess the reliability of DNA analysis.

However, there are some cases where DNA analysts' judgements proved to be unreliable (e.g., Thompson, 2009; Dror & Hampikian, 2011).

Unreliable findings are most likely to occur when DNA analysis produces results interpretable in more than one way. It is not known how often that is the case. However, suggestive evidence was reported by Thompson and Ford (1991). They reviewed 20 forensic cases where DNA evidence had been used to incriminate the defendant. There were potential sources of ambiguity in 14 of these cases. In four cases, a laboratory decided there was a match between the defendant's DNA sample and the sample from the crime scene even though the decision should have been 'mismatch' based on their own standards and guidelines!

How could DNA analysts' judgements attain a higher level of reliability? First, there needs to be standardisation (agreed standards for analysing and interpreting DNA evidence (Dror, 2023). Unfortunately, such standardisation has not been achieved. Consider the following guidelines for the conduct of DNA analysis proposed by The Scientific Working Group on DNA Analysis Methods (SWGDAM, 2017). These guidelines state that each DNA laboratory is essentially free to decide how to conduct DNA analyses. This is problematical because there is a real danger that a lack of standardisation leads to excessive flexibility in decision making, and this in turn leads to unreliable judgements.

Another way DNA analysis could be improved is by increased openness and transparency (Sikorski, 2022). Detailed information about how DNA analysts conduct their examination of the DNA evidence and the precise criteria they use in decision making are often lacking. Absence of such information makes it much harder to decide how much confidence we should have in DNA analysts' judgements.

Another way of improving DNA analysis would be to require DNA analysts to evaluate DNA samples without any pre-knowledge of contextual information (e.g., other evidence apparently incriminating the defendant). This would eliminate (or at least greatly reduce) any confirmation bias DNA analysts might otherwise display. However, consider the 'criminalist's paradox' (Thompson & Newman, 2015). If DNA analysts take account of task-irrelevant information (e.g., eyewitness identification; defendant's confession), they may make more accurate judgements. However, it is preferable for DNA analysts to have no knowledge of other sources of information so that the strength (or otherwise) of the DNA evidence on its own can be assessed.

Conclusions

There are four main reasons why the common belief that DNA analysis provides almost infallible evidence of guilt and innocence is misplaced. First, the DNA sample obtained from the crime scene may be of limited value because of degradation of the sample or the presence of contaminants or because it contains DNA from two or more individuals. Second, DNA analysis is often unreliable because the absence of agreed-upon standards means it can be subjective and excessively flexible. Third, DNA experts often exhibit confirmation bias because they are influenced by their knowledge of the defendant. Fourth, even if the DNA analysis is excellent, it does not directly indicate how and when a given individual's DNA came to be present at the crime scene.

Most members of the public exaggerate the value of DNA evidence because they implicitly assume that the DNA samples taken from crime scenes contain a reasonable quantity of DNA from a single individual. They also mistakenly assume that all that is required to prove guilt is to show there is a match between the suspect's DNA and the DNA sample obtained from the crime scene. In so doing, they ignore the importance of establishing how and when the crime-scene DNA came to be there.

Myth: the polygraph test is very good at detecting lying

Contrary to popular belief, there is no *single* polygraph or lie-detector test but rather a bewildering variety of somewhat similar tests. William Moulton

Marston (1893–1947) was an American psychologist who played a decisive role in the test's initial development. The story goes that Elizabeth Marston, his wife, told him one day that "when she got mad or excited, her blood pressure seemed to climb". This led him to develop the systolic blood pressure test (systolic blood pressure is the amount of pressure an individual's blood is exerting against their artery walls when their heart beats).

Marston (1917) published an article showing that his assessment of systolic blood pressure enabled him to decide whether someone was lying. The 10 male participants responded to a mock examination by a prosecution lawyer by answering questions honestly or dishonestly. Systolic blood pressure was higher for all the participants when lying than when telling the truth. In contrast, it was much harder to detect lying among mock jurors who only witnessed the participants' behaviour.

Marston's research was discussed in several popular magazines. In an article in *Look* magazine, he argued that suspicious husbands could use the lie detector test to ascertain their wife's trustworthiness. In those sexist times, he did not also point out that suspicious wives could use the lie detector to assess their husband's faithfulness!

You have probably never heard of Marston's research on lie detection. However, you have probably heard of *Wonder Woman*, a character he created. Marston (1943) gave the following explanation for creating *Wonder Woman*:

> Not even girls want to be girls so long as our feminine archetype lacks force, strength, and power. . . . The obvious remedy is to create a feminine character with all the strength of Superman plus all the allure of a good and beautiful woman.

There is a link between Wonder Woman and Marston's systolic blood pressure test: *Wonder Woman* has a lasso of truth compelling anyone captured by it to tell the truth always.

Marston recorded only a *single* physiological measure. In principle, we could assess more accurately whether a suspect is lying by using a test including several measures. This was done in 1921 by John Larson, who was a policeman and physiologist working in California. His polygraph assessed changes in blood pressure, heart rate and respiration rate (Synnott et al., 2015). It was assumed that someone lying would experience anxiety or fear, which would lead to increased blood pressure, heart rate and respiration rate. Contemporary polygraphs closely resemble Larson's. However, they often include skin conductance (electrical resistance of the skin) which assesses sweating in the palm of the hands.

Members of the public are consistently much more convinced of the validity and accuracy of the polygraph test than experts. Myers et al. (2006) found 68% of members of the public agreed that polygraph tests are 85% accurate when used to detect guilty suspects and over 70% agreed the tests are 85%

accurate when used to detect innocent suspects. The corresponding figures for experts were 27% and 22%, respectively.

The dangers of using the polygraph test were vividly demonstrated on the *Jeremy Kyle Show*, a television programme shown for several years in the UK. Steve Dymond was scheduled to appear on that show in 2019 in an attempt to persuade his fiancée, Jane Calaghan, that he had not cheated on her. However, he failed the polygraph test and shortly thereafter committed suicide. As a result, that episode of the *Jeremy Kyle Show* was never shown.

Comparative Question Test

The Comparative Question Test is the most common way of using the polygraph to assess guilt and innocence (especially in the United States). Individuals are asked three different kinds of question. First, there are *relevant* questions relating directly to the crime being investigated (e.g., "Did you attack her with a Bowie knife?"). Second, there are *irrelevant* questions (e.g., "Do you believe in global warming?). Third, there are *comparison* questions relating to the individual's moral character (e.g., "Have you ever broken the law?").

The irrelevant questions provide a baseline indicating an individual's general physiological responsiveness. Of crucial importance, it is assumed that someone who is guilty will respond more strongly physiologically to the relevant questions than the comparison questions, whereas the opposite will be the case with someone who is innocent.

There are several problems with the Comparative Question Test. The most serious one relates to the questions directly relevant to the crime being investigated. Imagine you are suspected of having murdered someone even though you are totally innocent. If you are asked the question "Did you murder Sophie Smith?" you would realise that your emotional response to that question could be perceived as incriminating. That realisation might easily make you very anxious. The key point is that the Comparative Question Test assesses an individual's general level of arousal but high arousal is not specifically or uniquely associated with deception.

The validity of the Comparative Question Test can best be assessed by calculating two measures: (1) *sensitivity* (the probability of accurately detecting individuals who are lying) and (2) *specificity* (the probability of accurately detecting truthful individuals). We want sensitivity and specificity to be high. However, this is not straightforward. We can increase sensitivity by adopting a lower threshold of evidence for someone to be categorised as lying. However, this increases the probability of misclassifying an honest person as a liar (i.e., specificity decreases).

Many polygraph examiners claim the Comparative Question Test has a sensitivity of 90%. When Iacono and Ben-Shakhar (2019) re-analysed the data from several studies, they discovered a sensitivity of 90% can only be achieved by accepting a false-error rate of 27% (specificity of 73%). Thus, the approach advocated by many polygraph examiners has the unacceptable consequence that over one-quarter of innocent suspects would be classified as guilty!

Alternatively, we could emphasise having a low false-positive rate. However, Iacono and Ben-Shakhar (2019) found that reducing the false-positive rate to 10% (specificity = 90%) would mean that sensitivity was reduced to 74%. Thus, one-quarter of guilty suspects would be classified as innocent. Thus, it is currently impossible to achieve high sensitivity *and* high specificity at the same time because increasing one measure decreases the other measure.

Another problem is that the Comparative Question Test is not a standardised test. Standardised tests (e.g., most intelligence tests) are ones where the administration of the test, the precise questions on the test and the method of scoring are the same for everyone taking the test. In contrast, the polygraph test lacks all the key features of a standardised test. Before the test starts, the examiner will typically attempt to persuade the individual being tested that the polygraph is extremely good at detecting any deception on their part but there is no set way of presenting this information.

The relevant questions on the Comparative Question Test necessarily depend on the precise crime details. However, the irrelevant and comparison questions also typically differ across examiners. Finally, the precise scoring of the polygraph data varies considerably across examiners. For example, the physiological responses to some questions may or may not be weighted more heavily than others, and the cut-off point for deciding that an individual's physiological responses to relevant questions are significantly greater than those to comparison questions also varies.

Another problem with the Comparative Question Test is that the examiner's *expectations* concerning the guilt or innocence of the individual being tested may influence their behaviour during the test and/or their subsequent interpretation of the data. This effect is an example of 'forensic confirmation bias' (Kassin et al., 2013). Evidence for such a bias was reported by Elaad et al. (1994). Experienced polygraph examiners made judgements of ambiguous criminal polygraph records. They were significantly more likely to decide a suspect was guilty when told he/she had eventually confessed than when told someone else had confessed. In sum, "There is no objective lie detection device; ultimately, the examiner is the lie detector" (Iacono & Ben-Shakhar, 2019, p. 91).

Finally, guilty individuals may attempt to increase their physiological responses to the comparison or control questions to avoid being identified as guilty by the test. Iacono and Lykken (1997) asked members of the Society for Psychophysiological Research (who would mostly be knowledgeable about the polygraph test) whether they agreed that "The CQT [Comparative Question Test] can be beaten by augmenting one's response to the control questions". They discovered that 99% agreed with the statement and 75% agreed that they could personally learn how to defeat the test.

Honts et al. (1987) investigated whether two countermeasures (biting the tongue; pressing the toes against the floor) were effective in defeating the Comparative Question Test. Participants were tested after carrying out a mock crime, which involved entering a professor's office and stealing an examination paper from their desk. The findings were striking: there were 0% false negatives (i.e., deciding that a 'criminal' was innocent) in a control condition but 47% false negatives when countermeasures were used.

Concealed Information Test

Some limitations associated with the Comparative Question Test are absent or less evident with the Concealed Information Test (Ben-Shakhar, 2012). Someone undergoing this test is presented with multiple-choice questions, each having one relevant alternative or probe (e.g., some aspect of the crime being investigated) significant only for the culprit. There are also about five neutral or control alternatives selected so innocent suspects cannot discriminate them from the probe. For example, words such as '*gun*', '*poison*', '*rope*' and '*knife*' might each be presented several times and the expectation is that only the murderer will respond to the probe (i.e., the murder weapon).

The Concealed Information Test is more theory-based than the Comparative Question Test. The basic assumption is that significant stimuli produce a physiological reaction (the orienting response), which is greater when stimuli are significant and/or novel. Thus, the key prediction is that guilty individuals will show greater orienting responses than innocent ones to probes. Orienting responses can be assessed in several ways including skin conductance response, respiration, changes in heart rate and the P300 component of the event-related potential (a positive wave in the brain starting approximately 300 ms after stimulus presentation).

Meijer et al. (2014) reviewed research on the Concealed Information Test using the above measures of orienting responses. Large differences in orienting responses to probe items by guilty and innocent individuals were found for all four measures. The most impressive findings were obtained with skin conductance response and the P300.

Ogawa et al. (2015) reviewed studies testing the validity of the Concealed Information Test. Sensitivity (correct detection rate) ranged between 76% and 88% and specificity (correct rejection rate) varied between 83% and 97%. We can compare these figures against those of the Comparative Question Test which is typically scored to produce sensitivity of 90%. As we saw earlier, a consequence is that specificity is only 73% indicating that the false-positive rate is much higher for the Comparative Question Test than the Concealed Information Test.

A limitation of the Concealed Information Test is that it assesses recognition of crime-scene information rather than guilt. In the real world, totally innocent individuals may possess considerable information about the details of a crime (e.g., the victim was stabbed with a knife) because of what they have heard on the media or via rumours. One way of dealing with this limitation is to use more specific or detailed probes than usual. Precisely this was done by Geven et al. (2022). The Comparative Question Test worked as well with specific probes (e.g., *switchblade* with control words such as *Swiss knife* and *dagger*) as with more general ones (e.g., *knife*).

The validity of the Concealed Information Test can be reduced if individuals being tested use countermeasures. As discussed earlier, countermeasures are most effective at camouflaging guilt when individuals being tested produce enhanced physiological responses to neutral items (Ben-Shakhar, 2012). This can be done by physical means (e.g., biting the tongue to inflict pain) or by mental means (e.g., thinking about emotional or exciting memories). Physical countermeasures have the disadvantage from the individual's perspective that they are easier for the examiner to detect.

The great majority of relevant studies were carried out under artificial laboratory conditions involving a mock crime. Such conditions are obviously very different from the often highly stressful conditions in which individuals accused of a serious crime receive the test. However, the test has been used especially in Japan but also in Israel to investigate real-life crimes and (as we have seen) it has proved reasonably successful in Japan (Ogawa et al., 2015).

Conclusions

The polygraph test as typically used in forensic investigations (i.e., the Comparative Question Test) is seriously flawed. It lacks any clear theoretical rationale and typically has an unacceptably high false-positive rate. It has not been subject to proper scientific investigation and the key validity measures (sensitivity and specificity) are rarely assessed.

Findings from real-world research are worrying. Ginton (2023) analysed the data from over 50,000 polygraph tests conducted by Israeli police using the Comparative Question Test (see also Chapter 10). He estimated that suspects who were lying were detected 94% of the time, which sounds impressive. However, Ginton also reported that only 65% of those categorised as lying were actually guilty. Thus, large numbers of innocent individuals were deemed to be lying on the basis of the test, which makes it of very limited use. The most worrying consequence is that many innocent individuals who are categorised as lying on the allegedly 'fail-proof' polygraph test are persuaded to plead guilty to crimes they did not commit.

The opposite problem, namely, guilty individuals not being detected by the polygraph test, has occurred numerous times. There are many examples of American criminals each responsible for the deaths of dozens of people who successfully cheated the test. They include Ted Bundy, who murdered at least 30 girls and young women; Gary Ridgeway (the Green River Killer) who killed at least 48 women and deposited some of their bodies in the Green River and Aldrich Ames, a CIA officer who was a Russian mole and probably responsible for hundreds of deaths. It is probable that all these murderers used countermeasures to cheat the polygraph test.

In the face of all this evidence that the polygraph test is seriously flawed, why do some many people continue to believe in its accuracy and validity? Of most importance, many people misinterpret the finding emphasised by polygraph examiners, namely, the claimed 90% success rate. What they mean is that a guilty individual has a 90% chance of failing the polygraph test, which is often true. However, as we have seen, it is totally unwarranted to draw the conclusion that the test is highly accurate: the reason is that many innocent individuals also fail the test. Here is a hypothetical example. You know for certain that one person out of a group of 100 committed a given crime. You give them all the polygraph test and discover 26 of them fail the test and so appear to be guilty. There is a 90% chance the culprit is one of those 26 individuals but you have no know idea which one is the culprit.

In sum, "Polygraph theory and research support continue to rest on shaky ground while practice continues unfettered by valid criticism" (Iacono, 2024, p. 1). That conclusion is especially applicable in the United States where numerous potential employees are not hired because they failed a polygraph test and many innocent individuals languish in prison for the same reason. In contrast, polygraph evidence is not admissible in court in the United Kingdom, which is as it should be.

Myth: hypnosis enhances eyewitnesses' memory

It is often believed that hypnosis is a very valuable technique for increasing the ability of eyewitnesses (and others) to retrieve memories from the past. Simons and Chabris (2011) reported that 55% of members of the American public (but 0% of memory experts) mostly or strongly agreed that "Hypnosis is useful in helping witnesses accurately recall details of crimes". Belief in the value of hypnosis remains remarkably high. Basterfield et al. (2023) discovered 81% of college students agreed that "People cannot lie under hypnosis".

Historically, hypnosis was mostly used within therapy as a method for treating patients with mental disorders. Its origins go back to Franz Mesmer (1734–1815), a Viennese doctor. He claimed to have cured his patients by applying magnets to various parts of their bodies and inducing in them a trance-like state. Subsequently, early psychologists and psychiatrists such as Pierre Janet, Joseph Breuer and Sigmund Freud also claimed hypnosis helped their patients to recall traumatic childhood events. Yapko (1994) found 75% of psychotherapists endorsed the notion that hypnosis enables people to remember things they could not otherwise remember. Many hypnotherapists and psychiatrists still believe the hypnotic state enhances memory: "The individual is often unable to recall old memories when awake, but can clearly narrate them in the hypnotic state" (Chan et al., 2023, p. 2).

The notion that hypnosis involves putting someone into a very strange and mysterious trance-like state depends in part on a famous novel (*Trilby* by du Maurier) published in 1894. In this novel, Svengali is an evil person who seduces and dominates a young half-Irish girl called Trilby. She is initially tone-deaf but Svengali uses hypnosis to turn her into a great singer. To this day, the term 'Svengali' is used to describe someone exerting excessive control over others.

Numerous films have emphasised the power of hypnosis. Barrett (2006) identified 230 films featuring hypnosis and pointed out

> When a hypnotist appears on screen, expect evil. . . . Hypnosis in cinema has a dark and lascivious history. For nearly a century, celluloid mesmerists have swung watches, twirled spiral discs, and transfixed the unsuspecting with their piercing gaze. Maidens surrendered their virtue and good men staggered away, glassy-eyed, to steal and kill.
>
> (p. 13)

Occasionally, hypnosis is used to compel people to harm themselves. In Orson Welles' film *Black Magic*, Count Cagliostro learns the secrets of hypnosis from Mesmer and uses its power to force his enemies to commit suicide.

The common theme running through the overwhelming majority of films focusing on hypnosis is that it gives hypnotists total control over other people's lives. For example, hypnosis is used to persuade someone to commit an assassination in *The Manchurian Candidate* (1962) and to lead someone to disfigure themselves with scalding water in *The Hypnotic Eye* (1960). This theme is also prevalent in television portrayals of hypnosis (Barrett, 2006). We will discuss whether hypnosis really possesses the magical powers often attributed to it after considering its impact on eyewitness memory.

Eyewitness memory

The extent to which hypnosis is used in the legal process has varied over time, as is aptly captured in the title of an article by Winter (2013): "The rise and fall of forensic hypnosis". In the heyday of forensic hypnosis (1960s and 1970s), police made apparently effective use of hypnosis in the attempt to track down two serial killers. One was Albert DeSalvo, the Boston Strangler, who killed at least 11 women in the Boston area after sexually molesting them. Under hypnosis, DeSalvo provided details about one of his victims (Evelyn Corbin) that he could not have known unless she had given him the information.

Ted Bundy was another serial killer who murdered more than 30 young women. Nita Neary was returning home when she saw the man who had just brutally attacked four women running down the stairs. Initially, she told the police she had seen a man at the scene. One week later, however, she was put into a hypnotic state and provided further information (e.g., he had dark hair). She subsequently identified a photograph of Ted Bundy from a photo line-up. About a month later, a man abducted and killed 12-year-old

Kimberly Keach. Clarence Anderson, who was the only eyewitness, underwent hypnosis on two occasions and subsequently identified the killer as Ted Bundy. Ted Bundy eventually confessed to these and many other murders.

It is hard to evaluate the direct contribution made by hypnosis with respect to identifying the culprit in the cases just discussed (as well as numerous others). Hypnotists may bias the information obtained under hypnosis because of their prior beliefs about the culprit. Orne (1979) provided several examples. In one case, the defendant (Jeffrey Alan Ritchie) was accused of killing a 2-year-old child in California in 1977. There were videotape recordings of the defendant's preliminary statement and of his subsequent questioning under hypnosis. Orne discovered many inconsistencies between the tapes. He concluded that the defendant had been influenced by the hypnotist and that some of what he said under hypnotism was untrue. As a result, the court dismissed the evidence obtained under hypnosis.

Research evidence

Research findings have been somewhat inconsistent. Geiselman et al. (1985) asked eyewitnesses to watch police training films showing simulated violent crimes followed by interviews with law-enforcement personnel. Those receiving the standard police interview correctly recalled an average of 29.4 items of information but also incorrectly recalled 6.1 items. Hypnotised eyewitnesses performed better averaging 38.0 correct items plus 5.9 incorrect items.

Other research is less supportive of hypnosis. Scoboria et al. (2002) assessed the impact of hypnosis and misleading questions on recall of a taped narrative. Hypnotised participants recalled more correct items than non-hypnotised ones and had fewer 'Don't Know' responses. However, they also had more recall errors than non-hypnotised participants. Thus, hypnosis caused participants to be less cautious when deciding whether they had accurately recalled the answers to questions about the narrative they had heard.

Lynn et al. (2009) reviewed research on the effects of hypnosis on memory. In 23 studies, hypnotised individuals were more confident than non-hypnotised individuals in the information they recalled or they exhibited confidence in inaccurate memories concerning events they had previously denied had ever happened. Lynn et al. reviewed nine other studies where hypnosis had no effect on participants' confidence in their recollections. In five of these studies, hypnosis either led to increased errors or the recollection of less accurate information.

There are various possible interpretations of the tendency for hypnotised individuals to be less cautious and more confident in their memory retrieval than non-hypnotised individuals. The most plausible explanation is that reduced cautiousness and increased confidence occur because most hypnotised individuals *expect* hypnosis will increase their ability to remember information accurately while reducing memory errors.

In sum, the research evidence demolishes two widely held myths about hypnosis. First, it is a myth that hypnosis reliably produced enhanced recall of past events. Second, it is also a myth that individuals cannot lie under hypnosis. If anything, hypnotised individuals produce *more* inaccurate memories and are also more confident about their accuracy.

Age regression

A fanciful notion about hypnosis and memory is that it permits individuals to return to their infancy: 'hypnotic age regression'. It has often been assumed this is a genuine phenomenon. However, Nash (1987) concluded in a comprehensive review that "Hypnotically regressed subject response does not resemble that of children, and when it does, waking control subjects can do just as well" (p. 50). Some researchers have reported significant findings but these findings came from poorly controlled studies.

It is unsurprising there is no convincing evidence of hypnotic age regression given the well-established phenomenon of infantile amnesia (the inability of adults to recall any memories from before about 2 1/2 or 3 years of age). Several theories of infantile amnesia have been proposed (Eysenck & Keane, 2020). However, hippocampal neurogenesis is of central importance. The hippocampus is a brain structure crucially involved in the formation of episodic memories of personal events. Hippocampal neurogenesis is a process in which new neurons are generated within the hippocampus early in development. These new neurons inhibit infants' ability to form lasting episodic memories (Madsen & Kim, 2016) and thus produce infantile amnesia. This makes the notion of hypnotic age regression highly implausible.

Why do most people exaggerate the ability of hypnosis to enhance memory?

As discussed earlier, a key reason why most people believe that hypnosis is an effective way to enhance memory is because that is how it is portrayed in most films, TV shows and novels. Another reason (also influenced by media coverage) is that most people greatly overestimate the difference between the hypnotic and everyday conscious states. For example, 70% of people in four countries agreed that hypnosis is "an altered state of consciousness quite different from normal waking consciousness" (Green et al., 2006). In the same study, 49% of respondents agreed that "I am wary of becoming hypnotised because it means giving up free will to the hypnotist". The term 'trance' is often used to refer to the allegedly very different state that individuals enter when hypnotised.

Most evidence indicates the hypnotic and non-hypnotic states are much more similar than typically assumed. For example, Braffman and Kirsch (1999) reported evidence indicating that hypnosis does not necessarily increase suggestibility: 54% of their participants were no more suggestible or less suggestible following hypnotic induction. They also found individual differences in hypnotic suggestibility were best predicted by *non-hypnotic* suggestibility. In a study by Kirsch et al. (2008), all participants received a hypnotic induction but some were given additional instructions to remain fully alert and not slip into hypnosis. Participants' subjective experiences were comparable in both conditions.

Gandhi and Oakley (2005) reported particularly interesting findings. A hypnotic procedure produced a much greater increase in suggestibility when labelled 'hypnosis' than when labelled 'relaxation'. These findings can be explained by assuming that many people have prior expectations about the likely effects of hypnosis on their thinking and behaviour (Lynn et al., 2020). However, there is one major difference between the hypnotic and non-hypnotic states: hypnotised individuals have a reduced sense they are responsible for their own experience and actions because they are less consciously aware of their own intentions (Terhune & Hedman, 2017).

Strong support for Terhune and Hedman's (2017) views was reported by Palfi et al. (2021). Their participants indicated the colour in which a word describing a different colour was presented (e.g., the word RED in the colour blue). Performance is typically slow (this is the Stroop interference effect). However, there was reduced interference when participants were instructed to experience the words as a meaningless foreign script. Participants simply given that instruction believed they had greater control over experiencing the words as meaningless than those given that instruction as a post-hypnotic suggestion. However, there was no performance difference between those two conditions. Thus, hypnosis reduced participants' sense of control over their own experience but did not influence their performance.

Processes involved in hypnosis

Several processes are involved in hypnosis. Even though hypnosis has proved ineffective in enhancing memory, it is possible that some processes associated with hypnosis facilitate recall. For example, hypnotised individuals typically have their eyes closed when remembering a crime or other event. Eye-closure might enhance recall because it eliminates the potentially negative effects of distracting visual information when the eyes are open.

Wagstaff et al. (2011) investigated the impact of eye-closure on memory. Participants listened to an audio recording of two men planning a robbery. Subsequently, they were instructed as follows: "Please describe as many details as you can remember about the robbery planned by the two men". Participants who had their eyes closed and engaged in focused meditation produced more correct details (with no increase in incorrect details) than those in a control condition.

Wagstaff et al.'s (2011) study is limited because we cannot disentangle the impact of eye-closure and focused meditation on memory performance. However, other research has indicated more clearly that eye-closure enhances memory. For example, Parker and Dagnall (2020) found eye-closure improved correct recognition memory without increasing false recognition.

Conclusions

There are more misconceptions and myths about hypnosis than most other phenomena in psychology. Lynn et al. (2020) identified 21 such myths and misconceptions. What underlies nearly all these misconceptions is the mistaken assumption that the hypnotic state differs radically from the non-hypnotic state and involves 'blind obedience' to the therapist or other person. Film makers have fostered that assumption because it produces far more dramatic situations than would be the case if they assumed correctly that the hypnotic state is almost indistinguishable from the non-hypnotic state in most ways.

As discussed earlier, we can understand most of the effects of hypnosis on memory by assuming it leads people to expect their memory to be enhanced. That expectation leads them to produce more memories (including more incorrect ones) and to have more confidence in their incorrect memories.

More generally, Stein et al. (2023, p. 1) provided a succinct summary of our current knowledge:

> There is no robust neurophysiological evidence to demonstrate that hypnosis is a special or unique state . . .'conscious unconsciousness' is an inaccurate depiction of hypnosis, because even the most highly suggestible individuals remain fully conscious when responding to hypnotic suggestions . . . hypnosis is a set of procedures in which verbal suggestions are used to modulate awareness, perception and cognition rather than to unnecessarily invoke 'special states'.

Myth: offender profiling is (very) useful in identifying culprits

Offender profiling (or criminal profiling) is used by forensic psychologists and law-enforcement agencies to identify the key personality, demographic and other characteristics of criminals based on a detailed analysis of crime-scene evidence. Many people with knowledge of offender profiling are enthusiastic about its value in crime investigations. Torres et al. (2006) discovered 86% of psychologists and psychiatrists knowledgeable about the law believed that offender profiling "is a useful tool for law enforcement". Kagee and Breet (2015) found 89% of psychologists agreed that "Criminal profiling is helpful in solving cases". In another study (Trager & Brewster, 2001), 38% of U.S. police officers claimed offender profiling is helpful in identifying suspects especially in cases of rape or murder.

Many members of the public are also positive about the value of offender profiling. Greiwe and Khoshnood (2022) found most people agreed that offender profiling is accurate, useful and that the police can benefit from its use as an investigative tool. When Basterfield et al. (2023) presented college students with the statement "Criminal profilers do not consistently do much better than non-experts at solving crimes", 70% of them disagreed. Thus, more than two-thirds of individuals have a touching faith in criminal profiling.

Since most people have had no direct involvement in police investigative procedures, the media and books are typically their main source of information about offender profiling. This started over 100 years ago when members of the public first became aware of offender profiling through the dramatic (and almost invariably successful) predictions made by the fictional detective Sherlock Holmes.

Many films have featured offender profilers, of which the Academy Award winning *The Silence of the Lambs* (1991) is perhaps the best known. In that film, Jodie Foster plays a young woman training to become an FBI profiler. She teams up with Hannibal Lecter (played by Anthony Hopkins); he is a brilliant psychiatrist who has been incarcerated because he is also a cannibalistic serial killer. Between them, they manage to track down "Buffalo Bill", a serial killer who specialises in skinning his female victims.

The greatest media coverage of offender profiling has been on television. In the UK, there was a very popular series in the 1990s called *Cracker*. It starred Robbie Coltrane as a criminal psychologist (Eddie 'Fitz' Fitzgerald) who admits he drinks, smokes and gambles too much. However, he is a brilliant offender profiler and uses his skills to assist the Manchester police to catch numerous killers. Offender profiling has figured more strongly on American television, where numerous series such as *Hannibal, Criminal Minds, Crime Scene Investigation* and *Profiler* have achieved considerable success.

All these films and television series would serve a useful function (rather than merely providing entertainment) if their portrayal of offender profilers and other investigative professionals were accurate. However, that is not the case. Donovan and Klahm (2015) analysed the performance of investigative teams including profilers on three crime series shown on American television in the 2011–2012 season: *Criminal Minds, NCIS (Naval Criminal Investigative Service)* and *The Mentalist*. The success rate of these teams averaged 92% across the three series, reaching a perfect 100% for *Criminal Minds*! In addition, they practically never mistakenly suspect innocent individuals. These figures for identifying criminals are gross exaggerations, being far more than double the actual figure. As a result of the excessively positive impression of offender profiling and other investigative techniques created by television shows, over 40% of American citizens believe these techniques are somewhat or very accurate (Dowler & Zawilski, 2007).

Offender profiling: evidence

Offender profiling is based on two fundamental assumptions. First, there is the assumption of *behavioural consistency*: any given offender's behaviour is similar across several crimes. Second, there is the assumption of *behavioural distinctiveness*: any given offender's behaviour across different crimes is sufficiently distinctive that it can be distinguished from other offenders' behaviour patterns.

Offender-profiling research has improved over time (Fox & Farrington, 2018). Earlier research was often methodologically unsound and relatively unscientific. Snook et al. (2007) considered all peer-reviewed studies on offender profiling. Anecdotal inferences were used in 60% of the studies, 23% involved intuition and only 42% had some reliance on scientific evidence (the percentages exceed 100% because more than one approach was adopted in some studies). These deficiencies have been corrected to some extent in more recent research.

Of crucial importance when evaluating the performance of offender profilers is whether their ability to predict characteristics of offenders significantly exceeds that of individuals lacking knowledge of offender profiling. Here is a concrete example. Suppose the police are investigating several murders apparently carried out by a serial killer. The murderer typically used a heavy axe to kill their victims after having tortured them. You wouldn't need to have spent years studying offender profiling to guess that the murderer probably has the following characteristics: male; poor anger control; sadistic; well-built. Thus, offender profilers need to demonstrate they can accurately predict non-obvious characteristics of criminals as well as obvious ones.

Snook et al. (2007) reviewed studies comparing the performance of offender profilers and those lacking knowledge of profiling (e.g., students; detectives). The offender profilers were slightly better than non-profilers at predicting the culprit's physical attributes but somewhat *worse* than non-profilers when predicting the culprit's social habits and cognitive processes. Profilers correctly identified the culprit on 62% of occasions compared to only 38% accuracy for the non-profilers. This suggests profiling has some value even though the profilers were wrong 38% of the time. However, all the relevant studies were very artificial and so the findings may well not generalise to real-life situations.

Case linkage

One relatively successful use of offender profiling is in case linkage analysis (i.e., the ability to link different crimes to a single offender based on behavioural evidence at the various crime scenes). The basic rationale is that most criminals exhibit their own specific signature (or trademark) behaviours while committing crimes and these idiosyncratic signatures permit successful case linkage analysis.

Fox and Farrington (2018) reviewed research on case linkage analysis based on 40 findings from 18 studies. This form of analysis was moderately accurate with respect to 57% of the findings, strong for a further 18%, but weak for the remaining 25%. Accuracy was highest for murder and sexual offences and somewhat lower for robbery and burglary. There was some evidence that different crime types were associated with different profiles. For example, the profile of those who committed sexual homicide included the following: sadistic; anger/fury; power-control; sexual.

Fox and Farrington (2018) did not address the key issue of whether the accuracy of trained profilers exceeds that of non-trained individuals, which considerably complicates the task of evaluating how successful offender profilers have been. For example, no one is hugely surprised to discover that individuals committing sexual homicide are sadistic, angry, furious and determined to exert power and control over others! Tonkin (2012) compared the performance of profilers and students in linking cases of commercial robbery or residential burglary. The profilers outperformed the students when linking commercial robbery cases but not when attempting to link residential burglary cases.

Why might experienced profilers be significantly better than untrained individuals? Untrained individuals are often oblivious of certain behaviours forming part of a criminal's signature. For example, Davies et al. (2012) studied case linkages among serial car thieves. Profilers had previously identified factors such as geographical distance (i.e., car thieves generally steal cars from a given area), car selection (i.e., old vs. new) and car acquisition (e.g., forced entry vs. using keys). These factors are all reasonably obvious. However, temporal proximity was also important: car thieves tend to steal cars at a given time of day and including this factor increased the accuracy of case linkage.

Even though the use of case linkage analysis by profilers has generally proved useful, there are three unresolved issues. First, evidence demonstrating serial criminals have their own signature behaviours is based on those who are caught. It is arguable that one reason why they are caught is precisely because they exhibit repetitive patterns of criminal behaviour. This is an important point: in the UK, only 8% of crimes are solved by the police and so offenders who are caught may be very unrepresentative of offenders in general.

Second, when case linkage analysis identifies the wrong person, this can lead to an expensive misallocation of police resources. Yokota et al. (2017) considered the use of profiling in 296 crimes committed in Japan. In 15% of cases, offender profiling produced incorrect links between crimes (i.e., analysis indicated incorrectly that two crimes were committed by the same culprit).

Third, we need much more evidence that case linkage analysis by expert profilers is substantially better than the predictions made by members of the public. To date, this important issue remains relatively unexamined.

Culture clash

The best way to understand controversies surrounding offender profiling is to regard it as a clash between two cultures. On the one hand we have practitioners (e.g., profiling experts) with a strong vested interest in emphasising the positive achievements of offender profiling and playing down or ignoring failures. On the other hand we have research psychologists critical of the relatively weak empirical evidence for the value of offender profiling and who are especially interested in scientific testing of different interpretations of this evidence.

As mentioned earlier, an overarching assumption made by offender profilers is that criminals exhibit consistent patterns of behaviour when committing their crimes. This assumption is closely related to trait theories of personality assuming that any given individual will tend to behave in a fairly consistent fashion across situations. However, as discussed in Chapter 6, individuals typically exhibit only relatively modest consistency and environmental factors are as important as personality traits in determining behaviour.

Bateman and Salfati (2007) adopted a scientific approach to investigate the assumption of behavioural consistency in serial killers. Remember that to identify a given individual as the culprit of a crime, what is required is that that individual behaves consistently *and* that their pattern of behaviour is distinctively different from that of other culprits. This latter requirement led Bateman and Salfati to ignore forms of behaviour common to more than half of serial murderers: the body is hidden (68%) and the body is moved after the murder (61%).

Bateman and Salfati (2007) found considerable inconsistency with respect to most forms of behaviour exhibited by serial murderers. The only exception occurred with respect to four aspects of planning and control: bringing a crime kit to the scene; destroying evidence; weapon brought to the scene; and restraining the victim. In spite of this limited positive evidence, Bateman and Salfati concluded that "Serial homicide offenders are not consistently performing the same crime scene behaviours throughout their series of homicides" (p. 543).

There are several plausible explanations of the behavioural inconsistency exhibited by serial murderers (and other criminals). When convicted of an offence, they may decide to change their criminal behaviour to minimise the chances of being caught again. In addition, the environmental conditions in which crimes are committed vary considerably. For example, a criminal who prefers to commit crimes very carefully and meticulously may sometimes be forced to proceed much faster than usual if in imminent danger of being discovered in mid-crime.

Another major problem that has not received sufficient attention is what Snook et al. (2008) call 'after-the-fact reasoning'. Suppose the police have arrested the person suspected of having carried out a serious crime. There is a natural temptation for offender profilers to go back over their predictions concerning the culprit's characteristics and be overly generous in assessing the accuracy of those predictions.

Alison et al. (2003a) analysed 21 criminal profiles used in the course of major criminal investigations. These profiles contained 3,090 statements mostly repeating details of the offence already known to be true. Only 880 statements (29%) made genuine *predictions* about the unknown criminal's characteristics. Of those statements, 82% were unsubstantiated (i.e., unsupported by any evidence), 55% were unverifiable (e.g., "the offender will have fantasised about the act in the weeks leading up to offence"), 24% were ambiguous and only 28% were falsifiable. After-the-fact reasoning is most likely to occur with ambiguous statements such as the following: "the offender will have poor heterosocial skills". That is so vague that any evidence that the suspect has imperfect 'heterosocial skills' can be chalked up as a successful prediction.

Alison et al. (2003b) investigated after-the-fact reasoning in more detail. Police officers and forensic professionals were presented with the offender profile allegedly describing a man who had mutilated and brutally murdered a young woman. Some were presented with a description of the actual offender whereas others received a made-up description of a very different offender. Amazingly, police officers and the forensic professionals both gave very similar accuracy ratings to the profile regardless of whether it was compared to the description of the actual offender or the imaginary one. This happened because they focused primarily on the apparent 'hits' in the profile and largely ignored mismatches.

In sum, the strongly-held belief that profilers can predict a culprit's characteristics from evidence obtained from the crime scene is 'the criminal profiling illusion' (Snook et al., 2008). Practitioners typically interpret their success rate as being almost entirely attributable to their expert skills. However, they fail to consider other possible explanations (e.g., after-the-fact reasoning; a similar success rate can be achieved by non-experts reliant only on general knowledge). The fundamental point (and the reason why the culture clash decisively favours scientific researchers over practitioners) is that only scientists are dedicated to the task of accurately identifying the factors underlying practitioners' success rate. Until there is compelling evidence that offender profilers consistently outperform non-experts in conditions precluding after-the-fact reasoning, the validity of offender profiling will remain unproven.

Conclusions

It would be wrong to argue that offender profiling has no value because there is evidence it can be of modest usefulness (e.g., case linkage). However, most of the available evidence lacks scientific rigour. For example, it is almost meaningless to report the success rates of expert offender profilers in the absence of any information about the success rates of non-experts provided with the same information. Generally speaking, the more scientifically rigorous the research, the less evidence there is that offender profiling is effective.

10 How to become a mythbuster

We have seen throughout this book that there is reasonable evidence that most members of the public accept numerous psychological myths. We start this chapter by considering *why* they believe various myths. After that, we focus on what can be done to reduce belief in these myths: this is 'mythbusting' to borrow a term used by Lilienfeld et al. (2010). There is also a more general discussion of ways to evaluate psychological research critically and how to minimise biased perceptions of ourselves.

Why do people subscribe to myths?

If 20 psychologists answered the previous question, they would probably produce 20 different answers. However, nothing daunted, here is my answer. We all obtain information and knowledge from multiple sources and so my starting point is to identify those sources providing inaccurate or misleading information. First, there is media coverage including films, television, newspapers, magazines, YouTube and Google. Second, evidence obtained by psychologists can be accessed by reading the original research articles or second-hand accounts on Google or elsewhere.

Third, members of the public have access to general knowledge they have acquired over the years and to their own personal experiences. They may also be influenced by wishful thinking or confirmation bias or they may accept intrinsically improbable beliefs.

Many of the strongest myths in psychology are influenced by two or more factors. Table 10.1 provides a summary of the factors relevant to each myth. When more than one factor is relevant, I list the factors in decreasing order of importance based on my subjective judgement. I will discuss all eight factors with an emphasis on those myths most clearly exemplifying each factor. Since many myths are multiply determined, some myths are discussed with respect to two or more different factors.

Inaccurate media coverage: sensationalism

The most obvious way the media misrepresent and distort psychological phenomena is by making them appear far more dramatic and sensational

DOI: 10.4324/9781003596677-10

Table 10.1 Factors influencing myths

Key
1 = Inaccurate media coverage: entertainment
2 = Inaccurate media coverage: reflecting commercial interests
3 = Distorted research: inadequate theory and/or experimentation + distorted reporting of findings
4 = Biased textbook coverage: one-sided presentation of research
5 = Members of the public: confirmation bias or wishful thinking
6 = Members of the public: deficient or slipshod thinking about intrinsically improbable beliefs
7 = Members of the public: mistaken extrapolation from limited personal experience
8 = Members of the public: plausible belief based on general knowledge (kernel of truth) but ignoring other relevant knowledge

?????? = non-mythical myth (i.e., arguably not really a myth at all)

Chapter 2: Perception and attention					
Myth 1: Subliminal perception influences behaviour	1	3			
Myth 2: We generally detect changes in objects	7				
Myth 3: Visual perception provides precise information	7				
Myth 4: Everyone agrees on the colour of a dress	7				
Myth 5: We are all face experts	7	3			
Chapter 3: Memory					
Myth 1: Memory is like a video camera	5	6			
Myth 2: Memories are permanent					
Myth 3: Repression and return of the repressed are common	2	3			
Myth 4: Amnesic patients have forgotten their pasts	1				
Myth 5: Only function of memory is to recall the past	7	8	3		
Myth 6: Forgetting is a bad thing	1	7	6	8	
Chapter 4: Thinking and cognition					
Myth 1: 10,000 hours of practice produce outstanding performance	1	3	2	7	8
Myth 2: Brain training enhances thinking/intelligence	1	2	6		
Myth 3: We only use 10% of our brains	1	6			
Myth 4: AI will soon be much more intelligent than humans	2	3	1		
Myth 5: Nudges are very effective at changing behaviour	2	1	8		
Chapter 5: Intelligence					
Myth 1: There are multiple intelligences	2	4	6	1	8
Myth 2: Teaching methods should reflect learning styles	2				
Myth 3: Emotional intelligence is helpful in life	??????				
Myth 4: Intelligence tests do not measure intelligence	5	6			
Myth 5: Intelligence does not depend on genetic factors	5	6			

(Continued)

Table 10.1 (Continued)

Chapter 6: Personality				
Myth 1: High self-esteem is desirable and low self-esteem is undesirable	??????			
Myth 2: Situation overwhelms personality in behaviour	7	3	5	6
Myth 3: Personality doesn't predict major outcomes	2	8		
Myth 4: Parenting strongly influences personality	3	1	7	8
Myth 5: Men are from Mars, women are from Venus with respect to personality	1	8		
Chapter 7: Social psychology				
Myth 1: Milgram proved most people will obey immoral order	3	4	1	
Myth2: Crowds typically panic in threatening situations	8	1		
Myth 3: Zimbardo proved that the power structure in prisons causes guards to be brutal	3	4	1	
Myth 4: Individual differences in attitudes are mostly learned	3	4	8	
Myth 5: Happiness is mostly determined by our experiences	1	5	7	8
Chapter 8: Mental disorders				
Myth 1: Mental disorders are almost entirely due to life experiences	1	3		
Myth 2: Psychiatric labels stigmatise people	??????			
Myth 3: Rorschach inkblots are valid at diagnosing many mental disorders	2	3	5	8
Myth 5: Multiple personality disorder exists	2	3	8	
Myth 6: Most psychotherapy requires lying on a couch and recalling one's childhood	3	1		
Myth 7: Anti-depressants are better than psychotherapy at treating depression	3	2	4	5
Chapter 9: Psychology and the law				
Myth 1: Eyewitness confidence is never a good predictor of their identification accuracy	??????			
Myth 2: Experts can nearly always identify the culprit from fingerprinting evidence	2	6	8	
Myth 3: DNA tests are almost infallible for culprit identification	2	6	8	
Myth 4: The polygraph test is very good at detecting lying	2	3	8	
Myth 5: Hypnosis enhances eyewitnesses' memory	2	3	8	
Myth 6: Offender profiling is very useful in identifying culprits	2	3	8	

than is actually the case. Consider the myth that amnesic patients have forgotten their past (Chapter 3). According to this, amnesia typically occurs when someone receives a serious bang on the head causing a loss of identity and a total personality change. However, amnesics in films generally have no problem with remembering information acquired after the onset of amnesia. Finally, amnesics in films regain their previous identity and memory powers because of a second bump on the head.

Everything is wrong with the previous depiction of amnesia. Most amnesics have much greater problems with learning and remembering new information than remembering the past. However, it would be boring for movie audiences to see someone struggling to learn. What is much more exciting is to see someone experiencing a total personality transformation with a subsequent massive bump on the head restoring them instantly to their previous self.

Many other myths in psychology owe much to the desire of those working in the media to make psychological phenomena appear exciting and dramatic. In Chapter 8, I discuss the myth that patients with mental disorders are violent. Fewer than 10% of individuals with severe mental disorders (e.g., schizophrenia) commit acts of violence but 83% of schizophrenic characters in films behave violently. In fact, the most prevalent symptoms among patients with mental disorders are depression and anxiety. However, moviegoers would find it boring to watch someone sitting around having negative thoughts about the past and themselves and/or being very worried about what might happen in the future.

Evidence that watching films increases negative views of those with mental disorders was reported by Poulgrain et al. (2022). Participants watched the film *Joker* (2019), in which the central character Arthur Fleck (played by Joaquin Phoenix) suffers from several disorders including schizophrenia, psychopathy and narcissism. Afterwards, the participants reported an increased desire to avoid mentally ill people.

Finally, consider the myth that crowds nearly always panic. What individuals in crowds typically do when faced by disasters or highly threatening situations (e.g., fires; bombings) is to respond rationally and co-operatively (see Chapter 7). However, movie makers believe (probably correctly) that audiences would not turn up to watch disaster movies which accurately portrayed crowds' reactions. It is much more lucrative to sensationalise crowds' reactions by buying into the myth that people respond to disasters by running around like headless chickens. A prime example of this is the film *Armageddon* (1998) where an enormous asteroid is about to hit the Earth and most people respond in a terrified and totally irrational way.

Commercial and political interests

We have seen that inaccurate media coverage is often due to attempts to sensationalise psychological phenomena to increase the numbers of viewers or readers. However, strong commercial and political interests can also systematically distort media coverage.

We start with commercial interests. Anti-depressant drugs are the drugs most prescribed by psychiatrists. In the United Kingdom, NHS prescriptions for a *single* anti-depressant drug (sertraline) in the year 2020–2021 cost £156 million. As a consequence, we will focus on such drugs. However, the situation with respect to other drugs is similar.

As discussed in Chapter 8, most people believe anti-depressant drugs are much more effective than psychotherapy in treating depression although relapses are far more common following anti-depressant drugs. These drugs also increase the risk of suicide and can cause withdrawal symptoms (e.g., insomnia; anxiety).

Most people also hold another incorrect belief about anti-depressant drugs. They believe depression is caused by a deficiency of serotonin in the brain and that anti-depressant drugs are effective because they increase serotonin levels. In fact, depression is *not* caused by low levels of serotonin, and most depressed individuals do not have unusually low serotonin (Moncrieff et al., 2023).

The main reason so many people believe the above myths is that most readily accessible information is misleading and inaccurate, in part because drug companies have a strong vested interest in persuading potential patients of the advantages of drug therapy. Demasi and Gøtzsche (2020) analysed the information about anti-depressant drugs on the Internet available on 39 websites in 10 countries, many promoted by drug companies. Overall, 92% contained misleading information. More specifically, 56% of the websites claimed anti-depressant drugs can prevent relapse, 74% argued that depression is caused by a "chemical imbalance" which can be resolved by drugs and only one website admitted that anti-depressant drugs can be addictive. The mistaken notion that depression is caused by a "chemical imbalance" can have negative consequences. Depressed patients believing depression is caused by a chemical imbalance had poorer treatment expectations and also reported more depressive symptoms following treatment (Schroder et al., 2020).

Commercial interests also influence the available information about many tests used by psychologists. Two examples are the Rorschach inkblot test (Chapter 8) and the polygraph or lie test (Chapter 9). The Rorschach test is commercially available through Hofgreve Publishing at a cost of approximately £220 for the original 10 coloured inkblots, scoring manual, recording blanks and so on. With respect to the polygraph test, there are 2,800 members of the American Polygraph Association, many of whom earn their living from administering the test. The existence of these commercial forces means we should be cautious about claims concerning the validity of these tests.

We turn now to the role played by political interests in creating myths about psychological phenomena. Consider the myth that crowds nearly always panic in threatening situations (Chapter 7). This myth had its origins in politics and was popularised by Le Bon (1895). The ruling classes in numerous countries over the centuries have feared "mob rule" because it might overturn the established order. This political idea goes back to Plato, who compared the behaviour of crowds to a mob of quarrelling sailors overrunning the ship of state (Keum, 2023). Le Bon himself believed society should be organised hierarchically and he strongly disapproved of egalitarianism and even democracy. His extremely negative views of crowds were based on very meagre evidence and he hardly considered whether rioting crowds might have legitimate grievances.

Political interests have also distorted the public's perception of nudges (small environmental changes designed to steer people's behaviour gently in a socially desirable direction) (Chapter 4). Beneficial changes in people's behaviour can be produced via direct government intervention (e.g., rules or taxes) or via nudges. For example, politicians often argue that individuals become overweight or obese because they lack self-control or a sense of personal responsibility. On that argument, nudges designed to persuade people to eat healthier food or simply less food might prove successful. However, such nudges have proved ineffective in part because highly processed foods trigger strong urges or cravings and can be addictive (Gearhardt & DiFeliceantonio, 2023). The only plausible solution to the obesity pandemic is government legislation requiring food companies to produce more nutritious and less addictive foods.

Distorted research: biased experimental design, reporting and interpretations of findings

Embarrassingly, we have seen repeatedly that psychologists themselves have created and then disseminated many myths. It follows that they should accept responsibility for setting the record right.

The research process consists of a series of stages. Researchers typically start with an experimental hypothesis followed by producing an experimental design to test the hypothesis (or hypotheses). The findings are then analysed statistically and reported. Finally, conclusions are drawn based on the match (or mismatch) between the hypotheses and the findings. There is an ever-present danger of experimenter bias (the experimenter's beliefs and/or expectancies influencing the research process). Experimenter bias can distort all stages of research (Bishop, 2020) and several examples are discussed in the following sections.

Biased experimental design

The design of experiments in psychology can be systematically *biased* by experimenters or researchers to increase the probability of obtaining the desired findings. Consider the hypothesis that brain training designed to enhance working-memory processes such as attentional control increases intelligence (see Chapter 4).

A crucial criterion when designing an experiment is to ensure we can provide a definitive explanation of its findings. In this case, the experimental condition must provide training in the working-memory skills theoretically relevant to intelligence. In addition, the control condition should provide training very similar in every respect (e.g., length; complexity) except that it should not involve any working-memory processes.

In the previous example, participants in the control condition must receive very similar training to those in the experimental condition. However, that is insufficient. In most research studies on brain training, recruitment methods emphasised that brain training would produce enhancement and/or improvement of cognitive functioning. That matters in two ways. For example, Foroughi et al. (2016; discussed in Chapter 4) used a suggestive recruitment poster focusing on the beneficial effects of brain training on intelligence and a control recruitment poster not mentioning brain training or its potential beneficial effects.

While both groups received an identical very short training programme, only those given the expectation that their intelligence would increase showed enhanced IQ after training. Parong et al. (2022) gave participants a brain-training intervention or a control intervention (general knowledge task) after being given explicit information that the intervention would increase or decrease their cognitive functioning. Cognitive functioning increased more following positive expectations regardless of whether brain training was received.

Two meta-analyses of research on brain training (Au et al., 2015; Karbach & Verhaeghen, 2014) concluded that brain training enhances intelligence. However, Melby-Lervåg and Hulme (2016) found both meta-analyses included several studies of very poor quality (e.g., no control group; control intervention very different from the experimental intervention; ignoring potential expectation effects). When they took account of the quality of the studies included in the meta-analyses, Melby-Lervåg et al. concluded that, "there is no convincing evidence that working memory training produces general cognitive benefits" (p. 324).

We turn now to the biased research designs used by offender profilers constructing a profile of an offender's characteristics from evidence found at the crime scene (see Chapter 9). Offender profilers often claim their profiles are very accurate and the FBI stated that the accuracy rate of its profiles exceeds 80%.

The high success rates claimed by the FBI and other offender profilers are essentially meaningless in the abstract. It is crucial to demonstrate that their performance is substantially better than that of members of the public presented with the same evidence. No one would be impressed by the FBI's claimed 80% success rate if individuals with no knowledge of offender profiling obtained the same success rate.

Snook et al. (2007) identified 130 studies on offender profiling. Amazingly, there was no attempt to compare profilers' performance against that of non-experts in 92% of these studies! Only four studies made a reasonable attempt to decide whether profilers outperform non-experts. Across these four studies, profilers' performance slightly exceeded that of non-experts. However, even that modest achievement is unimpressive: many predictions made by offender profilers are inherently ambiguous and so can be claimed to be 'correct' almost regardless of the culprit's actual characteristics.

Regression to the mean and spontaneous remission

Consider this real-life research carried out in Flanders. Various measures were taken to increase the safety of 'black spots' (road intersections where there had been several injuries). The number of injuries at these black spots subsequently reduced by 20%. We might conclude the safety measures taken *caused* the reduced number of injuries.

However, De Pauw et al. (2011) showed the previous conclusion is wrong. They identified numerous 'black spots' comparable to those receiving traffic-safety measures (i.e., there had been a large number on injuries) but which had not received any traffic-safety measures. The number of injuries reduced almost as much at black spots *not* receiving any traffic-safety measures as those that received such measures! These findings can be explained by regression to the mean: black spots are identified because there has been an *atypically* high number of injuries there in recent years. As a result, we would expect the number of injuries to reduce as injuries move back to more typical or representative numbers in the absence of traffic-safety measures.

We turn now to regression to the mean in psychological research. Yesavage et al. (2018) gave military veterans with very severe major depression (e.g., 61% were regarded as suicidal) genuine treatment (transcranial magnetic stimulation) or a sham treatment (pretending to administer transcranial magnetic stimulation). The results were amazing: within 5–12 days, 41% of patients receiving the genuine treatment and 37% of those receiving sham treatment showed remission (a virtual absence of symptoms). Easily the most plausible explanation of these findings is that they are due to regression to the mean.

Additional evidence for the role played by regression to the mean in therapy for depression was discussed by Hengartner (2020). In a study on the use of anti-depressants to treat major depression, the remission rate after 12 weeks of anti-depressant therapy was 28% (Trivedi et al., 2006). This finding apparently indicates the efficacy of the drugs. However, we need to consider how many patients with major depression would show remission *without* treatment. Whiteford et al. (2013) reviewed research on individuals with major depression receiving no therapy. After 3 months, 23% were in remission. The finding that, over 3 months, the spontaneous remission rate (23%) is close to the remission rate with anti-depressant drugs (28%) strongly suggests that regression to the mean plays a major role.

Spotting bias in experimental designs

We have seen that much research on techniques such as brain training and offender profiling has been biased because there were several differences between the experimental and control conditions or even no control condition at all. However, experimenter bias is often more subtle. Consider Ekman's very influential research on facial expressions of emotion. This research was based on the hypothesis that facial expressions can communicate only six basic emotions and that these emotions are universal (i.e., found worldwide). This research provides strong evidence of experimenter bias because Ekman's experimental design maximised the probability of obtaining support for his position.

A survey by Ekman (2016) indicated that 80% of emotion researchers believe universal signals of emotion are displayed facially and a substantial majority agreed with Ekman that *anger, fear, disgust, sadness* and *happiness* are basic emotions with over 40% agreeing that Ekman's sixth emotion (*surprise*) is a basic emotion. Ekman's research has proved so influential among experts and members of the public alike that it is the "common view" (Barrett et al., 2019, p. 2).

See if you can spot any problems or biases in Ekman's research (discussed in Box 10.1).

Box 10.1   The myth that there are six basic facial expressions of emotion

Ekman and Friesen (1971) presented posed and spontaneous photographs of faces to pre-literate New Guinea villagers. Each photograph had been judged by over 70% of American observers to show one of the following six emotions: *happiness; sadness; anger; surprise; disgust or fear*. On each trial, the villagers heard a very short story illustrating a given emotion. For example, "His (her) friends have come, and lie (she) is happy" relates to happiness. They were then shown three photographs and selected the one most relevant to the story. The participants selected the appropriate photograph on 80% of trials (chance performance = 33%). Ekman and Friesen concluded the six emotions they studied are universal since they were found in a culture that had had essentially no contact with the Western world.

Ekman et al. (1987) showed observers in 10 countries photographs that were good examples of the six basic emotions previously studied by Ekman and Friesen (1971). After each photograph had been presented, observers decided which of seven emotion terms (the six basic emotion terms plus *contempt*) was most appropriate. Overall, observers selected the appropriate emotion label 78% of the time, thus apparently demonstrating there are six basic universal emotions.

What are the main biases and problems with Ekman's research? First, in everyday life you practically never see a face on its own with no accompanying body or *context*. The immediate context typically dominates our interpretation of someone's facial expression (Barrett et al., 2019). The Soviet film-maker Lev Kuleshov found the emotional expression ascribed to an actor's neutral face was strongly influenced by an immediately preceding emotional scene. The Kuleshov effect was demonstrated by Calbi et al. (2017): the same neutral face was interpreted very differently depending on whether it was preceded by a scene evoking happiness or fear.

Second, in Ekman et al.'s (1987) study, observers viewed photographs of posed and exaggerated facial expressions and decided which emotion was being expressed by choosing a single emotion word from only three options. Unsurprisingly, this approach produced unrealistically neat-and-tidy findings.

Srinivasan and Martinez (2021) used similar photographs to Ekman's, but observers provided their own emotional labels. There was substantial variability in the labels observers applied to any given facial expression. Only 35% of participants labelled an allegedly fearful face as expressing fear, whereas 19% said it expressed surprise, 4% said sadness and 4% said happiness. In similar fashion, the allegedly angry face was identified as angry by only 40% of participants and the allegedly sad face was identified as sad by only 37%.

Third, there is Ekman's bizarre claim that only *one* positive emotion (i.e., *happiness*) is observable in facial expressions. Cowen and Keltner (2020) asked observers to respond to 1,500 naturalistic photographs in various ways (e.g., generating their own emotion label). They replaced Ekman's solitary positive emotion (*happiness*) with ten (*love*; *awe*; *desire*; *amusement*; *pride*; *interest*; *contentment*; *ecstasy*; *elation* and *triumph*).

Fourth, Cowen and Keltner (2020) identified 28 different emotions in facial expressions using 1,500 naturalistic photographs. Emotions identified by Cowen and Keltner (but not by Ekman) included *relief*, *confusion*, *doubt* and *embarrassment* as well as the ten positive emotions discussed earlier. It could be argued that Ekman's six facial emotions are more common or important than the 28 identified by Cowen and Keltner. However, the participants in Cowen and Keltner's study said they encountered facial expressions indicating *awe, contempt, interest, love* and *sympathy* more often in their everyday lives than facial expressions indicating the six emotions emphasised by Ekman and Friesen (1971).

Fifth, there are greater cultural differences in interpreting facial expressions than acknowledged by Ekman. For example, a wide-eyed gasping face is typically interpreted as expressing fear in the Western world. However, the Maori of New Zealand and the Trobriand Islanders in Papua New Guinea interpret that facial expression as indicating anger (Crivelli et al., 2016).

In sum, Ekman's research has an element of self-fulfilling prophecy about it. He decided six universal emotions are expressed facially and then designed research maximising the probability of obtaining confirmatory evidence. He achieved this by using carefully selected photographs and requiring observers to decide which emotion was being expressed by selecting an emotion from a very limited number of possibilities.

The problems caused by experimenter bias in research design are so important and prevalent that it is worth considering another example. Researchers often want to assess the effectiveness of a given therapy. Many people think you can do this simply by assessing patients before and after treatment. The logic is simple: if symptoms are substantially reduced after treatment, the therapy is effective. What has often been regarded as the 'gold standard' is the randomised controlled trial: patients are assigned at random to receive a given therapy or to a control group not receiving it. The therapy is effective if the patients receiving therapy have a greater reduction in symptoms.

Suppose you have developed a form of therapy (e.g., a new anti-depressant drug). You decide the optimal way to convince psychiatrists they should prescribe this drug is by carrying out a randomised controlled trial comparing the effectiveness of your drug against a control group. How might you bias your experimental design to maximise the likelihood that your new drug will appear to be very effective? Think of your answers to that question before reading the answers in Box 10.2

Box 10.2   Loading the dice in a randomised controlled trial

Cuijpers and Cristea (2016) provide an excellent guide to therapists/researchers showing how to load the dice to ensure they obtain findings from a randomised controlled trial that make even ineffective therapies appear effective. Below are five ways used extensively in clinical research. Since the effectiveness of drug therapy is measured by the *difference* between the drug and control conditions following treatment, you can artificially increase the extent of recovery in the drug condition (points 1–4) or artificially reduce recovery in the control condition (point 5).

(1) Strongly encourage patients to have high expectations that the therapy will be effective. This often enhances the effectiveness of therapy through a placebo effect.
(2) Ignore the data from patients receiving therapy who drop out of treatment. These patients tend to be those benefiting least from therapy and so ignoring drop outs increases its apparent effectiveness.
(3) Use numerous outcome measures to assess therapeutic effectiveness. Report findings only from outcome measures indicating therapy was effective and ignore the others.
(4) The therapist/researcher should conduct the randomisation process themselves. This may inadvertently (or even deliberately) lead to patients most likely to benefit from therapy being allocated to the therapy condition.
(5) Use a waiting list control group (patients who only receive therapy after patients in the drug condition). Michopoulos et al. (2021) compared four different control conditions in a meta-analysis of therapy for depression and found that waiting-list patients (those waiting some time before receiving therapy) consistently had the poorest outcomes.

Cuijpers et al. (2010) carried out a meta-analysis of 126 studies where the effectiveness of psychotherapy in the treatment of depression was compared against a control group. Only 9% of the studies did not resort to any of the dubious practices listed earlier. Psychotherapy was apparently much less effective in the high-quality studies than the others. Plessen et al. (2023) replicated these findings in a comprehensive meta-analytic study including over 70,000 depressed patients. However, the great majority of psychotherapy studies (including high-quality ones) had clearly beneficial effects on patients' depression.

Biased reporting of research findings: under-reporting

Some myths discussed in this book owe their origins to the fact that the psychologists conducting the original research providing the basis for the myth omitted crucial details when reporting it. Consider Zimbardo's Stanford Prison Experiment (discussed in Chapter 7). It is a poorly designed experiment; indeed, it is not really an 'experiment'. Zimbardo's central claim that it demonstrated individual differences play no part in explaining the aggressive behaviour of prison guards is totally unsubstantiated because he failed to study individual differences!

The Stanford Prison Experiment was carried out in 1971 and reported in a very misleading fashion by Haney et al. (1973). It was 17 years later before Zimbardo provided a fuller account of what had actually happened and 39 years later before he provided complete information. This is unacceptable.

Another culprit is Milgram (1963, 1974) (Chapter 7) who allegedly found most individuals will obey immoral orders. His finding that two-thirds of ordinary people were willing to administer potentially lethal electric shocks to a middle-aged man with a heart condition has often been regarded as the most surprising and important finding in the history of psychology. However, it becomes much less surprising when we consider experimental details omitted or camouflaged by Milgram. For example, 44% of Milgram's participants had doubts as to whether any shocks were actually being administered. In addition, Milgram failed to point out that participants protesting at what they were asked to do were explicitly told the experimenter would accept full responsibility if anything went wrong.

Biased reporting of research findings: misinterpretations

Another form of experimenter bias occurs when researchers provide distorted interpretations of their findings. The polygraph test (or 'lie test'; see Chapter 9) provides a clear example. Expert polygraph examiners typically claim the polygraph test is extremely accurate: a review of real-life cases concluded the accuracy of the polygraph test was between 92% and 98% (Forensic Research Incorporated, 1997).

Ginton (2023) thoroughly analysed over 50,000 polygraph tests conducted by the Israeli police. The estimated probability that guilty individuals were detected as liars by the polygraph test was 94% (comparable to the success rate claimed by polygraph examiners). However, only 65% of those individuals categorised as lying on the polygraph were actually guilty.

Why are the earlier findings very impressive or very unimpressive depending on how the data are analysed? The polygraph test is *overly sensitive* so it classifies many innocent individuals as guilty. More specifically, one-third of those appearing as liars on the test are innocent which undermines claims that the polygraph is accurate and valid.

We can see why the finding that 94% of guilty individuals failing the polygraph test is misleading by considering an extreme example. Suppose we devised a polygraph that classified everyone (guilty or innocent) as liars. It would correctly classify 100% of guilty individuals as liars. However, the test would be useless because it would also incorrectly classify 100% of innocent individuals as liars!

Biased interpretation of findings: correlational evidence

Hundreds of thousands of research studies in psychology produce correlational evidence. Most people know you cannot infer causality from correlational evidence. The finding that A correlates with B can potentially be explained in three different ways: A causes B; B causes A; or some third factor (C) causes A and B. However, very large numbers of people commit what Seifert et al. (2022) call the causal theory error (i.e., misinterpreting correlational evidence in causal terms). According to Seifert et al., "It is arguably the most ubiquitous and wide-ranging error found in science literature, classrooms, and media reports" (p. 14).

We find causal theory errors wherever we look. Sumner et al. (2014) discovered that 33% of academic press releases contained exaggerated causal claims of health-related research, as did 81% of news stories based on those press releases. For example, it is often claimed that eating large quantities of highly processed food can cause numerous diseases although the claim is based on correlational evidence. Dietary quality is positively associated with socio-economic status (Alkerwi et al., 2015) and so some of the negative correlation between quantity of highly processed food eaten and various diseases is probably due to social class differences in financial resources, access to good medical care and so on.

Causal theory error is surprisingly prevalent in published research. For example, Schellenberg (2020) reviewed 40 correlational studies where musicians and non-musicians or individuals with or without music training were compared with respect to non-musical behaviour (e.g., language abilities; cognitive abilities). Invalid causal inferences were drawn in 47% of these studies. Individuals receiving music training differ in many ways from those who do not: they have higher IQs, come from families of higher socio-economic status and have more innate musical ability than those who do not (Schellberg). Thus, the differences in language and cognitive abilities found between those receiving or not receiving music training cannot be ascribed to the presence or absence of music training.

Another example of the causal theory error is found in research allegedly demonstrating that 10,000 hours of deliberate practice in any given domain is all that is required to produce exceptional performance (Ericsson et al., 1993; see Chapter 4). Most of the evidence is correlational: Hambrick et al. (2020) reported across numerous studies that the number of hours of practice correlated on average about 0.50 with performance. Since practice typically improves performance, it may seem that Ericsson et al.'s (1993) theory has received strong support.

We can see the flaw with the previous interpretation by asking a question: who would choose to devote 10,000 hours to the acquisition of a given skill? It is primarily individuals with innate talent. In other words, those devoting huge amounts of time to practising a skill differ from those who do not *before* they start practising it (Ullén et al., 2016).

There is considerable evidence that most people make causal theory errors when presented with correlational findings. Bleske-Rechek et al. (2015) asked their participants to read the description of research on the relationship between playing video games and aggressive playground behaviour. The research involved either an experimental design with *random* assignment to the video-playing and non-video playing groups or a non-experimental survey design without random assignment. In both cases, video-game playing was positively associated with aggression.

Participants should have drawn the causal inference that video games cause increased aggression with the experimental but not the non-experimental research. In the non-experimental research, it is entirely possible that aggressive individuals are more likely than non-aggressive ones to engage in video-game playing. With the experimental research, *random* assignment to groups means the initial levels of aggression should be similar in the two groups. Strikingly, 63% of participants drew the valid causal inference from the experimental research and 63% drew the invalid causal inference that aggressiveness causes video-game playing from the non-experimental research. Thus, they failed to appreciate the crucial difference made by random assignment.

We can relate these findings to Schellenberg's (2020) study on music training. The causal inference that music training enhances various cognitive abilities would be valid if a *random* process had been used to decide which individuals received such training. That would have produced a situation where the groups receiving or not receiving music training differed *only* in terms of the amount of music training.

Why do so many people (including advanced college students in the study by Seifert et al., 2022) make the causal theory error? One important factor is whether it seems plausible that causality is involved. For example, it is plausible to infer that music training causes enhanced cognitive abilities on the basis of correlational evidence. However, if correlational evidence indicated that music training is associated with reduced cognitive abilities, it seems much less likely that people would draw the inference that music training had impaired cognitive abilities.

Reducing causal theory errors

Seifert et al. (2022) developed an intervention designed to reduce causal theory errors. It included an emphasis on creating as many causal theories as possible of research findings and producing diagrams to illustrate each causal theory. Of importance, correlational findings are typically consistent with several different causal explanations and so we should not accept any given causal explanation as valid. This intervention was effective in reducing causal theory errors.

Irving et al. (2018) used a simple intervention to reduce invalid causal inferences. Participants read a fictitious news story including the following invalid causal explanation for correlational data: "watching television for more than 3.5 hr a day causes an increased rate in cognitive decline". Some participants subsequently read a correction providing alternative explanations for that finding (e.g., *cognitive decline is responsible for an extended time spent watching television*). This correction halved the number of invalid causal inferences and increased sixfold the number of valid correlational inferences.

Grosz et al. (2020) pointed out that there is a "taboo" against drawing *explicit* causal inferences from correlational evidence in research articles. However, most correlational research tests theories predicting causal relationships, and numerous correlational studies contain *implicit* causal inferences. It might be thought that people would be less likely to draw causal inferences from correlational evidence if those inferences are implicit rather than explicit but this does not seem to be the case (Alvarez-Vargas et al., 2023). The optimal approach is for researchers to discuss openly potentially causal interpretations of their data combined with acknowledging the limitations in the data.

In sum, it is concerning that most people fail to realise that causal explanations cannot validly be made from correlational data. However, correlational data are not valueless. At the very least, discovering that two variables correlate with each other (e.g., aggressiveness and video game playing) suggests it is probably worth investigating the relationship by experimentation permitting causation to be ascertained. Conversely, if two variables fail to correlate, it is less likely to be worthwhile to investigate their relationship experimentally.

Biased reporting of research findings: neglect

Genetic factors influence almost all human traits or characteristics. For example, Polderman et al. (2015) found in a meta-analysis of 14 million twin pairs on almost 18,000 human traits that *all* these traits were influenced by genetic factors. However, the reporting and discussion of research findings often involve totally ignoring the potential relevance of genetic factors.

Evidence that individual differences in attitudes depend to a considerable extent on genetic factors was established by Eaves and Eysenck (1974) (see Chapter 7). Many subsequent twin studies have confirmed the key role played by genetic factors but such factors are totally ignored by most researchers. For example, Briñol and Petty (2019) reviewed research on attitudes in a handbook chapter entitled 'The impact of individual differences on attitudes and attitude change'. Incredibly, the authors failed to mention genetic factors even though such factors explain approximately 40% of individual differences in attitudes!

Biased textbook coverage

So far I have focused on biases that experimenters have introduced into the design and reporting of their research findings. However, most textbook writers also engage in biased reporting. Consider famous (or notorious) studies such as Zimbardo's Stanford Prison Experiment (Chapter 4), Milgram's research on obedience to authority (Chapter 7) and Rosenhan's research on the stigmatising effect of psychiatric labels (Chapter 8). All three studies are badly flawed and yet most textbook coverage of them (at least until recently) mentions only one or two of the numerous valid criticisms of these studies.

The failure of most textbook writers to provide a balanced account of psychological research is not limited to the previous three examples. Ferguson et al. (2018) discussed textbook coverage of 12 other well-known controversial issues in psychology. What was said about these issues was typically either totally biased or partially biased (predominantly one-sided but with a brief acknowledge that there was another side to the issue).

Another important controversial issue relates to unconscious or implicit racial prejudice, which is typically assessed by the Implicit Association Test (IAT). In its original version (Greenwald et al., 1998), there were two conditions. In one condition, participants pressed one key if a black face or a positive word (e.g., *love*) was presented and a different key if a white face or bad word (e.g., *terrible*) was presented. The white participants had slower reaction times in this condition than when a black face was paired with a negative word and a white face with a positive word.

Greenwald et al.'s (1998) findings have frequently been replicated (Kurdi et al., 2018). Millions of people have done the IAT, and it is claimed that most white people exhibit 'unconscious racial bias'. However, the findings are open to alternative explanations. For example, the white participants may simply be more *familiar* with some face-word combinations than others. It is also possible that white participants have strongly positive views of white people and positive but less strongly positive views of black people. Surprisingly, the findings from African American participants are typically very similar to those from white ones (Bartels & Schoenrade, 2021) and these findings cannot plausibly be attributed to racial bias.

Bartels and Schoenrade (2021) reviewed the coverage of the IAT in 17 introductory psychology textbooks. None indicated that it is hard to interpret the findings from the IAT and only two mentioned that African Americans apparently exhibit the same unconscious racial bias as white people. Overall, 42% of the textbooks failed to mention any problems with the IAT and another 42% only briefly mentioned any criticisms. In conclusion, it is worth emphasising that racial bias is a real and serious problem regardless of the strengths and limitations of the IAT.

Why are textbooks biased?

Why do most textbook writers provide biased and uncritical accounts of psychological research? Several answers have been proposed. First, they may want to "sell" psychology to undergraduate students and one way to do this is to pretend that psychological research provides clear-cut answers on important issues. Second, textbook writers have strictly limited space to discuss any given topic in psychology leading them to de-emphasise criticisms of the research they discuss. Third, the simplified views presented in most psychology textbooks may be desirable: "Giving a full account of the entire scholarly discourse surrounding a particular study may overburden students as long as they do not possess a solid (broad) knowledge base" (Gollwitzer et al., 2023, p. 246).

A more controversial answer to the previous question was provided by Bartels (2023a, 2023b). He argued the great majority of psychologists have liberal or left-wing attitudes and this ideological bias may explain the biased accounts of research found in introductory textbooks. For example, most liberal thinkers in the 1960s believed the American prison system was excessively harsh and Zimbardo's Stanford Prison Experiment apparently supported their beliefs. Bartels' conclusion was that the biases of textbook writers "indoctrinate" students who read their textbooks.

It is certainly true that most psychologists have liberal views. Research on self-reported political ideology among American academic psychologists indicates that 85%–90% are liberals (Reinero et al., 2020). Does this imbalance matter? Raneiro et al. found 74% of politically relevant research had no clear political slant. They argued that if a liberal bias were present in evaluating research, it would follow that liberal-leaning research would be flimsier and harder to replicate than conservative-learning research. In fact, however, liberal findings were as easy to replicate as conservative ones.

In sum, there is very little evidence that introductory psychology textbooks are distorted by the political leanings of textbook writers. Note that only a relatively small fraction of topics in psychology (especially within social psychology) can be regarded as politically sensitive, so ideological indoctrination could have no more than a modest effect. As a textbook writer myself, I suspect the main reason for one-sided and inaccurate presentation of research findings is the motivation to provide a simple and easily understood account.

Whatever textbook writers' precise motivations, "Students' beliefs about human behaviour and mental processes are about the same at the end of the course as at the beginning, that is to say, no more accurate than those of the general public" (Bernstein et al., 2023, p. 2). More specifically, Bernstein et al. discovered across eight institutions that students who had completed an introductory course endorsed 55% of 40 common misconceptions or myths.

What can be done?

I don't accept the argument that the limited space available to discuss any given topic means textbook writers cannot avoid providing distorted one-sided accounts of psychological research. For over 30 years, all my textbooks have contained evaluation sections associated with each topic in which the major strengths and limitations of theory and research on that topic are presented succinctly. For example, in my book *AS Level Psychology (5th ed)* (Eysenck, 2012), I include four criticisms of Zimbardo's Stanford Prison Experiment and five of Milgram's obedience to authority research. Most of these criticisms consist of only two sentences each.

More generally, there is consensus that the development of critical and scientific thinking is of central importance in the teaching of psychology. For example, the American Psychological Association's Introductory Psychology Initiative (IPI) identified scientific thinking as one of the major student learning outcomes (Altman et al., 2021). Among IPI's recommendations were to "examine how psychological science can be used to counter unsubstantiated statements, opinions, or beliefs" (p.182).

Bernstein (2023) made the interesting suggestion that the teaching of each topic in psychology should involve students asking themselves the following questions:

(1)   What am I being asked to believe or accept? (2) What evidence is available to support the assertion? (3) Are there alternative ways of interpreting that evidence? (4) What additional evidence would help evaluate the alternatives? (5) What conclusions are most reasonable given the evidence available so far?" (p. 266).

Members of the public: confirmation bias or wishful thinking

People are often reluctant to change their opinions because of confirmation bias. This is the tendency to search for (and overweight) information supporting one's beliefs and to avoid (and discount) information inconsistent with those beliefs: this is known as selective search. Confirmation bias provides a partial explanation for many myths in psychology: if you already believe a myth, that reduces the probability you will consider subsequent evidence that might invalidate it. Yang et al. (2022) discovered that people find it easier to start believing in something than to stop believing in it (this is 'asymmetry of belief revision'). More specifically, people are more likely to believe a claim they once thought was false than to disbelieve a claim they previously thought was true.

Psychologists are also subject to confirmation bias. Scientists rate the quality of a piece of research more highly if its findings agree with their prior beliefs (especially strong beliefs) (Koehler, 1993). We have also seen (Chapter 9) that expert forensic scientists (e.g., fingerprint and DNA analysts) are susceptible to confirmation bias.

The conventional view is that confirmation bias is undesirable because it causes individuals to become increasingly entrenched in their (often mistaken) views. However, Rollwage and Fleming (2021) argued that confirmation bias can be adaptive for individuals having high meta-cognitive ability (the ability to reflect accurately on their own cognitions). These individuals generally have high confidence in their correct decisions and low confidence in their wrong decisions. Rollwage and Fleming found selective information processing driven by confirmation bias improved decision making compared to the unbiased collection of evidence in such individuals.

Other rather similar biases also distort people's thinking and make them susceptible to psychological myths. One example is wishful thinking, "where beliefs are updated in the direction of desired outcomes rather than what the evidence implies" (Melnikoff & Strohminger, 2024, p. 1). Another example is myside bias, "which occurs when people evaluate evidence, generate evidence, and test hypotheses in a manner biased toward their own prior opinions and attitudes" Stanovich et al., 2013, p. 259). Some people regard the terms myside bias and confirmation bias as synonymous whereas others regard myside bias as a specific form of confirmation bias. I prefer the latter approach: myside bias is especially likely to apply to issues of great personal importance to an individual.

Egalitarian ideology and/or wishful thinking: changing intelligence

Most people believe intelligence or IQ is easy to change (Chapter 5). Furnham and Horne (2021) found popular support for several myths based on that belief (percentage agreeing with each myth in brackets): "Environmentally driven changes in IQ mean that intelligence is changeable/malleable" (69%); "Social interventions can drastically raise IQ" (77%); "Brain training programs can raise IQ" (65%); "A pupil's environment and personality has powerful effects on academic achievement" (88%).

Warne and Burton (2020) asked people to indicate how many IQ points an average person's IQ would increase permanently if they received each of 20 environmental interventions. All 20 interventions were predicted to increase IQ. Here are the findings from what were regarded as the most powerful interventions (mean number of points IQ would increase is in brackets):

- Parents reading to a child daily (11.22 points)
- An effective teacher every year in elementary school (10.22 points)
- Well-funded schools with small class sizes (9.54 points)
- Watching educational programmes on TV (9.10 points)
- A high-quality preschool programme (9.09 points)
- Brain-training games (8.80 points)
- Talking to a child in the womb regularly (7.94 points)
- Ensuring a person stays in school 1 year longer (7.19 points)

It would be predicted that a child of average IQ (100) would move to an IQ of 182 if they were fortunate enough to receive all eight interventions mentioned earlier! The odds against having an IQ that high are more than 4 million to one (e.g., Bill Gates has an estimated IQ of 160). In fact, most of the previous interventions produce very small or negligible increases in IQ. An extra year of schooling probably has the greatest effect on IQ. Ritchie and Tucker-Drob (2018) discovered each additional year of education added an average of 3.4 points of IQ (under half the predicted amount).

How can we explain the dramatically exaggerated views of the impact of environmental factors on IQ possessed by many people? One plausible hypothesis is that these views stem from an egalitarian ideology (Warne & Burton, 2020). As Arneson (2013, p. 1) pointed out, "An egalitarian favours equality of some sort. . . . People should be treated as equals, should treat one another as equals, should relate as equals, or enjoy an equality of social status of some sort".

According to most versions of egalitarianism, the notion that some individuals are destined to be more intelligent than others is 'unfair' and 'unjust'. From such a perspective, the belief that numerous environmental interventions can produce significant increases in intelligence or IQ in almost anyone is very appealing. As predicted, liberals and egalitarians believe the role of genetic factors in influencing intelligence is smaller than do conservatives (Suhay & Jayaratne, 2013).

Most people's excessively optimistic view of the ease with which environmental interventions can increase IQ is probably indicative of wishful thinking as well as an egalitarian ideology: it would be highly desirable to increase our intelligence substantially with apparent ease. Indeed, it is hard to disentangle the effects of egalitarian ideology and wishful thinking on beliefs about the malleability of intelligence.

We might expect that wishful thinking would lead people to have various other beliefs about intelligence minimising the perceived 'unfairness' of some people being more intelligent than others. For example, they would disagree with the statement "People with lower intelligence are more likely to die at younger ages". Warne and Burton (2020) found 41% of people disagreed. In fact, however, it is correct: Iveson et al. (2018) discovered that each 15-point increase in IQ is associated with a 24% decrease in mortality.

Egalitarian ideology and/or wishful thinking: genetic influences

We have seen that liberals are less likely than conservatives to endorse genetic explanations for differences in intelligence (Suhay & Jayaratne, 2013). Is there a similar difference between liberals and conservatives with respect to genetic explanations for other psychological differences? Willoughby et al. (2019) found that liberals generally estimated the genetic influence on psychological traits (intelligence, personality, musical talent, violent behaviour and athleticism) as less than conservatives. The modest size of this relationship (and its reversal with respect to psychiatric traits (including schizophrenia, bipolar disorders and depression) indicate that ideology has only small and inconsistent effects on the estimated impact of genetic factors on human behaviour.

Myside bias

There is considerable evidence for myside bias with respect to the issue of direct relevance to the individual. Stanovich and West (2007) asked students to rate the accuracy of contentious (but factually accurate statements such as the following:

(1) College students who drink alcohol while in college are more likely to become alcoholic in later life.
(2) The gap in salary between men and women generally disappears when they are employed in the same position.

Students who regularly drank alcohol rated the accuracy of statement (1) lower than those who did not, and women rated the accuracy of statement (2) lower than men. Thus, there was strong myside bias. The extent of myside bias was unrelated to intelligence suggesting the students made little use of analytical thinking.

Similar findings were reported by Roozenbeek et al. (2022) in a study using the Misinformation Susceptibility Test consisting of real (e.g., Attitudes Toward EU Are Largely Positive, Both Within Europe and Outside It) and fake (e.g., New Study: Left-Wingers Are More Likely to Lie to Get a Higher Salary) headlines. Misinformation susceptibility was strongly related to myside bias but only modestly related to analytical thinking skills.

Wishful thinking: misconceptions about the self

Wishful thinking is of central importance in explaining why the shelves of most large bookshops are groaning under the weight of self-help books promising to make us irresistibly sexually attractive, enhance our self-esteem enormously, give us a fantastic personality, make our memory perfect and equip us with the motivation and drive to earn huge amounts of money. Presumably these books only sell in large quantities because millions of people believe they could potentially achieve great things.

Wishful thinking about the self leads to more (and stronger) misconceptions or myths than does wishful thinking about other people. Zell et al. (2020) reviewed research from almost one million participants on the better-than-average effect, which is "the tendency for people to perceive their abilities, attributes, and personality traits as superior to those of their average peer" (p. 132). There was a consistently strong better-than-average effect for personality traits (especially positive traits). There was also a weaker better-than-average effect for abilities. The lower effect for abilities probably occurs because it is generally easier to confirm or verify one's abilities (e.g., exam performance) than one's personality traits.

Wishful thinking is also involved in optimism bias (the tendency to underestimate the probability of negative events happening to oneself but overestimating the probability of positive events). For example, Weinstein (1980) asked university students to assess the probability of events happening to them and to their classmates. They thought the probability of positive events (e.g., living past 80; graduating in top third of their class; owning their own home) was greater for them than their classmates whereas the probability of negative events (e.g., having a drinking problem; having a heart attack; being fired from a job) was less for them than their classmates.

How can we explain optimism bias? Klein and Helweg-Larsen (2002) found that optimism bias correlated 0.31 with perceived control. This suggests the possibility that individuals exhibit optimism bias because they perceive their ability to control future events is greater than that of most other people.

The better-than-average effect and optimism bias may be of some value. For example, Zell et al. (2020) found that the extent of the better-than-average effect correlated with higher self-esteem and overall life satisfaction. However, excessive optimism can be dangerous. For example, most smokers deny that the overwhelming evidence that smoking reduces life expectancy by several years. Heikkinen et al. (2010) discovered that smokers rationalised their behaviour in several ways: smoking in moderation is not harmful; they engage in physical exercise to offset any risks from smoking; they claim that smoking is no riskier than coffee or a glass of wine.

There is also evidence of excessive optimism bias in recent research on alcohol consumption (Morris et al., 2024). Participants provided a measure of optimism bias (a reduced likelihood they would develop a drinking-related problem than the average person). Bizarrely, optimism bias *increased* in line with alcohol consumption; in other words, those with the highest alcohol consumption were the ones who were most confident that they were much less likely than the average person to have a drinking-related problem in future!

Obesity is a big problem and is becoming bigger every year: 50% of the English adult population will probably be obese by 2050. It is widely known that obesity increases the probability of numerous serious diseases and can greatly reduce life expectancy. How do obese individuals respond? Truesdale and Stevens (2008) found only 7% of obese men accepted they were obese and 20% thought their weight was healthy and normal! Such massive self-deception can prove very costly to health.

What can be done?

We have seen that most people exhibit various cognitive biases (confirmation bias; myside bias; wishful thinking) leading them to believe psychological myths and to be generally susceptible to misinformation. How can these biases be reduced? Perspective taking is an especially useful strategy. This consists in thinking about a psychological myth or other issue from a perspective very different from one's own. McCrudden et al. (2017) found students exhibited reduced myside bias with respect to climate change when they adopted the perspective of a climate scientist.

Sternberg et al. (2023) advocated that people engage in a different from of perspective taking when evaluating psychological research. For example, they could adopt the role of a critical reviewer of a research article or of an objective reviewer who is looking for valid positive and negative points. Of central importance, adopting such perspectives broadens the reader's thinking and so reduces biased and distorted thinking.

The biases we have been discussing can involve selective search for information, selective interpretation of evidence and selective recall of information. However, selective search appears to be of most importance (Vedejová & Čavojová, 2022). Accordingly, we will focus on selective search. There is convincing evidence that most people will search selectively for information supporting their beliefs or decisions rather than disconfirming information (Jonas et al., 2001).

How can we reduce selective search for confirmatory information? In a review, Hart et al. (2009) identified accuracy motivation as important: if individuals are motivated to make the optimal decision or hold the most accurate belief, they exhibit reduced selective search. If students believe that good examination performance requires accurate accounts of theory and research, they should exhibit reduced selective search.

How can students eliminate selective search and their erroneous beliefs in numerous psychological myths? Ironically, in view of increasing doubts about the validity of information provided by Google, it provides what is often the fastest and best route to mythbusting. All you need to do is to type in the following: "Criticisms of [fill in essence of a psychological myth]". I have just done this for four myths chosen at random: memory is like a video camera (Chapter 3); 10,000 hours practice is all you need for outstanding performance (Chapter 4); Milgram's research proved that we are obedient to authority (Chapter 7) and criminal profiling is very accurate (Chapter 9). In every case, I was immediately presented with several valid criticisms of each myth.

Members of the public: deficient thinking about intrinsically improbable beliefs

Members of the public believe numerous myths about psychological phenomena. Some of these commonly held myths exemplify the dangers of failing to think clearly about issues. Consider the myth that our memory is like a video camera, which implies that memories are typically very detailed and accurate, are not subject to any bias and change very little over time (discussed earlier in this chapter and in Chapter 3). You don't have to spend much time thinking about the limitations of your own memory to realise that it is considerably more limited and error-prone than a video camera.

We turn now to the myth that we use only 10% of our brains (Chapter 4). Evolutionary changes typically occur over long periods of time and the human brain is no exception. It took 6 to 8 million years for the human brain to attain its current size (1,400 cc) and it did so in response to the environmental challenges faced by our ancestors. The notion that the human brain has enormous powers we don't use is ludicrous. It is about as likely as discovering that humans have the ability to fly but for some reason have never made any use of it.

Another myth depending on slipshod thinking is that brain training can enhance our intelligence or IQ (Chapter 4). Most brain training consists of tasks based on working memory (a cognitive system involved in attentional control). Research studies typically involve about 8 hours of training (Noack et al., 2014) and allegedly increase IQ by about 4 points (Au et al., 2015). Thus, someone with an IQ of 100 who had 8 hours of brain training would finish up with an IQ of 104. Miraculously, their IQ would have moved from being higher than that of 50% of the population to being higher than that of 60%. If that person were a citizen of the United Kingdom, 8 hours of brain training would have allowed them to overtake the IQs of 6,500,000 of their fellow citizens!

There is another reason why endorsing the myth that brain training enhances intelligence is based on slipshod thinking. Most people spend thousands of hours a year using working memory to deal with everyday issues and problems. The notion that devoting a minute fraction of that time performing a brain-training task would enhance their intelligence is wildly improbable.

A clear majority of people believe that intelligence tests don't measure intelligence (Furnham & Horne, 2021; Chapter 5). For example, 73% agree that, "IQ scores only measure how good someone is at taking intelligence tests", which strongly implies that performance on intelligence tests is totally irrelevant to real life. However, Furnham and Horne also found 71% believe that intelligence is important in the workplace. It is conceivable that intelligence is important in the workplace but that the only prominent and well-established way of assessing intelligence (i.e., the intelligence test) provides a totally inadequate measure of intelligence. However, it is surely improbable.

Most people who believe intelligence tests don't measure intelligence are aware that the amount of money that individuals with high IQs generally earn more than people with low IQs. They are also probably aware that most individuals living in very deprived and impoverished circumstances have IQs well below 100.

Deficient thinking also partially explains why so many people believe culprits can nearly always be identified correctly by experts on the basis of fingerprint or DNA evidence (Chapter 9). More specifically, Koehler (2017) found that on average people believed that the probability an expert would mistakenly claim that fingerprints from two different individuals came from the same person was 1 in 5,500,00. The probability that the same mistake would be made by an expert assessing DNA evidence was 1 in 10,000,000.

Why are these beliefs highly improbable? First, fingerprints or samples of DNA found at the scene of the crime are often fragmentary, degraded or contaminated. Second, fingerprints and DNA samples are intrinsically complex. The FBI has fingerprints from over 160 million individuals and DNA samples from 22 million individuals. As a consequence, there are typically several fingerprints or DNA samples from non-culprits that closely match the evidence from the crime scene, thus providing plenty of scope for experts to decide mistakenly that two fingerprints or DNA samples come from the same person. Third, experts are fallible and are likely to be prone to error given the complexity of the judgements they are required to make. There is no task (even very simple ones) anyone would perform with essentially perfect accuracy over millions of trials.

Everyone sometimes engages in inadequate thinking about psychological findings. I plead guilty with respect to Asch's (1951, 1956) famous research on conformity. Imagine you were a participant in one of his studies. You were in a group of participants viewing a visual display and then indicating which of three lines was the same length as a standard line as the experimenter worked his way around the group members ending with you. This is a very easy task and so you were very surprised when all the other participants give the same wrong answer on some trials.

What would you think? There is surely a sporting chance you would imagine that something highly suspicious was going on. If so, you would have been right because all the other group members were confederates of the experimenter instructed beforehand to give the same wrong answers on some trials. However, I have never encountered any such questioning of Asch's research in spite of having read numerous accounts of it.

I decided to read Asch's (1956) thorough account of his research. I discovered that an unspecified number of participants strongly suspected the experimental situation was a fake, and their data were eliminated. Adair (1972) carried out a conformity study using a task resembling that of Asch and discovered 44% of his participants were suspicious.

Asch (1956) admitted that,

It crossed the minds of many subjects in the course of the experiment that the majority might be deliberately misleading, or that the group was following the first member who, for some unknown reason, was in error. However, this belief had the form of a fleeting hypothesis. . . . The best evidence for this is that such expressions did not prevent subjects from yielding heavily [showing conformity]" (p. 29). It could equally well be argued that participants suspicious of Asch's situation decided they would "play the game" by pretending to agree with the majority. Indeed, Asch (1956, p. 26) admitted that some of their comments were consistent with that argument.

Griggs (2015) criticised textbook writers for their misleading coverage of Asch's research. However, he focused solely on the fact that textbook writers emphasised the extent of conformity in that research even though participants failed to conform approximately two-thirds of the time. Ironically, he said nothing about the failure of textbook writers to consider participants' suspicions about the experimental set-up and the likely impact of those suspicions on their behaviour.

Individual differences in gullibility

Psychological myths are often believed because of a general tendency to accept one's initial thoughts about an issue rather than to think about it in more detail. According to the influential dual-process theoretical approach (e.g., Evans & Stanovich, 2013), there are two major modes of thinking: Type 1, which is fast and intuitive with a reliance on heuristics (rules of thumb) and Type 2, which is slower and more effortful and involves rational, analytic processing. The natural prediction is that individuals preferring Type 1 processing will be more likely to believe psychological myths than those preferring Type 2 processing. The distinction between Type 1 and Type 2 processing is useful even though it oversimplifies the complexities of human cognition (Melnikoff & Bargh, 2018).

Bensley and Lilienfeld (2015) obtained support for the aforementioned prediction. They used the Test of Psychological Knowledge and Misconceptions where each item requires participants to choose between a psychological misconception or myth and a scientifically supported alternative. Students endorsing the most psychological misconceptions were overconfident because they failed to use Type 2 processes involved in monitoring (and reflecting on) their answers. Supporting evidence was reported by Bensley et al. (2020): a preference for an intuitive cognitive style was associated with increased beliefs in psychological myths.

Bensley et al. (2020) found that individuals believing numerous psychological myths also believe in conspiracy theories and parapsychology. They assessed individuals' ability to distinguish between *science* (astronomy; chemistry; cognitive behavioural therapy; evolutionary biology; neuroscience; physics and psychology) and *pseudoscience* (alchemy; astrology; creation science or intelligent design; Freudian psychoanalysis; parapsychology; phrenology and scientology). Individuals who strongly believed in numerous psychological myths, conspiracy theories and parapsychology were less able than other individuals to distinguish clearly between science and pseudoscience. Bensley et al. (2022) found that individuals exhibiting a general tendency to endorse several unsubstantiated claims (including psychological myths; conspiracy theories and paranormal beliefs) often have an intuitive cognitive style.

What can be done?

According to the Chinese philosopher Confucius, "Real knowledge is to know the extent of one's ignorance". Unfortunately, most people don't seem to follow his excellent advice. Consider the Dunning-Kruger effect (Kruger & Dunning, 1999): incompetent and ignorant individuals often greatly exaggerate their own competence and knowledge. Dunning and Kruger explained this lethal combination as the 'double curse': incompetent individuals perform poorly and have incorrect beliefs and their incompetence prevents them from evaluating their own performance and beliefs correctly. In crude terms, stupid people are too stupid to know how stupid they are.

There are numerous striking examples of the Dunning-Kruger effect. For example, those knowing the least about the actual causes of autism are the ones most likely to believe they know more than doctors and scientists about its causes Motta et al., 2018). In similar fashion, expert scientists agree that genetically modified foods are safe to eat and could greatly reduce starvation around the world. In contrast, the most extreme opponents of genetically modified foods know the least about them (but mistakenly believe they know the most) (Fernbach et al., 2019).

Burgess et al. (2022) considered the relevance of the Dunning-Kruger effect to the endorsement of psychological misconceptions. The worst-performing students were as confident as the best-performing ones in the accuracy of their answers. In addition, the worst-performing students had *more* confidence in their wrong answers (i.e., endorsement of myths) than the correct ones.

The first step in combating the Dunning-Kruger effect with respect to psychological myths and facts is to question your knowledge base: do you really have enough information about a given topic to be confident in your views about it? The second step is to imagine that someone else gave different answers to you. What reasons might they have had for doing this? The third step is to discuss scientific issues in psychology with other people without trying too hard to defend your initial viewpoint.

Note that the Dunning-Kruger effect is often open to various interpretations. For example, McIntosh et al. (2022) argued that much of the effect is due to a statistical artefact. Suppose students performing a task are asked to guess how their performance relates to 99 other students. If they have very little evidence to go on, they will probably guess their performance is average (i.e., better than about 50% of other students). Poor performers (those doing better than, say, only 10 other students) will necessarily appear very over-confident even though they are vaguely aware their performance was not very good. That is exactly what McIntosh et al. found.

If we are to find ways of reducing people's susceptibility to psychological myths, it is useful to consider individual differences in the ability to think clearly and effectively about issues. There is strong evidence that more intelligent individuals subscribe to fewer psychological myths or misconceptions than less intelligent ones (Bensley, 2023). However, it can be argued that critical thinking ("reasonable, reflective thinking focused on deciding what to believe or do": Ennis, 1987, p. 102) is also important. Bensley et al. (2021) assessed the beneficial effects of providing students with a semester-long training in critical thinking which combined an emphasis on thinking errors (e.g., distinguishing between arguments and non-arguments; identifying problems in scientific reasoning) and on misconceptions in psychology. This training produced a 50% improvement in the ability to detect thinking errors and misconceptions in psychology.

There is often a disconnect between the very general statements expressing psychological myths and the reality that most findings in psychology fail to *generalise* across situations and populations. It follows that an effective strategy for detecting myths would involve trying to think of *counterexamples* (e.g., situations in which the statement is disproved). Consider the myth that forgetting is a bad thing (Chapter 3). Counterexamples include forgetting information that is no longer relevant (e.g., where friends of yours used to live; trivial details of events; negative events from the past). What about the myth that the situation overwhelms personality in behaviour? Here are several counterexamples: talking vs. not talking to strangers; deciding whether to go bungee jumping and individual differences in behaviour at a party.

Correcting anti-science and anti-scientist views

We are more likely to agree with others' views on scientific issues if they possess relevant expertise, are trustworthy and are perceived as objective or unbiased (Philipp-Muller et al., 2022). However, individuals differ in their regard for experts. Bensley et al. (2022) devised a Cynicism Scale including items such as "What scientists say cannot be believed because they are biased" (p. 87). Students high in cynicism accepted more psychological myths than low scorers because they were reluctant to accept psychologists' research findings.

Simply increasing individuals' trust in science has mixed effects. While clearly desirable in some ways, it can make them more vulnerable to pseudoscience. O'Brien et al. (2021) found individuals who trust science are more inclined to believe false claims containing scientific references than false claims lacking such references. In addition, reminders of the value of trusting science failed to reduce individuals' belief in false claims. In contrast, reminding people of the value of critical evaluation did reduce their belief in false claims.

Philipp-Muller et al. (2022) identified several other useful strategies to reduce anti-science beliefs. First, it is important to stress that most scientific findings are not clear-cut but rather are a matter of debate and discussion. Second, many people are put off science by the prevalence of scientific jargon. This problem can be alleviated by the provision of lay summaries in coverage of research, and several psychology journals include such summaries as a matter of course. Third, scientists are often perceived as cold and remote, so scientists should emphasise the communal nature of science and express their views with warmth. Fourth, scientists openly admitting that their position has changed as a result of new scientific evidence are perceived as less biased and more persuasive (Wallace et al., 2020).

Members of the public: mistaken extrapolation from limited personal experience

We all spend thousands of hours every year using our basic cognitive processes (e.g., visual perception; face recognition; imagining the future). As a result, it seems reasonable to assume we would have developed a very accurate understanding of the strengths and limitations of those cognitive processes. However, that is often not the case as is indicated by several myths relating to cognition.

The reasons why many people believe several myths about visual perception are discussed at length in Chapter 2. In essence, visual tasks vary in their decision complexity and the involvement of central vs. peripheral vision. Most of the visual tasks we perform in everyday life (e.g., navigating our way around obstacles such as lamp posts and cars) are relatively easy because decision complexity is low and they involve predominantly central vision. As a consequence, we tend to believe that visual perception is almost perfect. In contrast, psychological research often involves tasks high in decision complexity and that require peripheral as well as central vision. We are surprised how limited and error-prone our visual perception is when faced by novel visual tasks that are much more difficult than the ones we face every day.

The myth that forgetting is always a bad thing (Chapter 3) is another example of a misconception depending in part on our limited conscious experience. It can be acutely embarrassing to forget someone's name or forget you have agreed to meet someone, and it can be upsetting to realise when sitting an examination that you have forgotten much of what you thought you knew about a topic. Many instances of forgetting are memorable and lead us to believe that forgetting is always a bad thing.

What about occasions where forgetting has proved useful? Forgetting negative events often makes us happier and forgetting the details of the information we have read in a chapter of a textbook means we remember only the most important information. When we are engaged in decision making when faced by a current problem, it is preferable to forget conflicting memories from the past and instead to remember the gist of how we coped successfully with similar problems in the past. The key point is that we are typically unaware that forgetting has benefited our lives, and this lack of awareness means we underestimate the usefulness of forgetting.

When asked whether happiness is influenced most strongly by what happens to us (Chapter 7), we naturally focus on reasons why we were much happier at certain times of our life than other times. Unsurprisingly, happy times are typically associated with very positive life events (e.g., having a loving relationship; having a great holiday) and unhappy times are associated with negative events (e.g., ending of a relationship; losing one's job).

However, most people accept that individual differences in personality are of importance in explaining why some individuals are consistently happier than others when asked questions specifically focusing on the role of personality in happiness. In other words, we typically use our own limited personal experience to claim that happiness depends mostly on what happens to us and so neglect the role played by personality.

Members of the public: plausible beliefs based on general knowledge (kernel of truth)

One of the main reasons we subscribe to many myths about psychological phenomena is because they contain a kernel of truth. Here I will briefly consider a few examples starting with the myth that the polygraph or lie detector test is very good at detecting lying (Chapter 9). Of key importance is the notion of *face validity*: the subjective impression that a test measures what it is claimed to measure in the absence of any proper evidence. The polygraph test possesses high face validity for many people. The underlying assumptions that guilty individuals asked questions directly relevant to their crime or misdemeanour will become very anxious and that their anxiety can be assessed accurately by measures of physiological activity are plausible.

The main problem with the polygraph test becomes clear when we consider the situation innocent individuals find themselves in. If they are erroneously suspected of being the culprit responsible for a given crime, they are likely to be very anxious while taking the test, especially when asked questions that appear to relate to the crime. If the culprit and an innocent suspect are both anxious, it is very hard to use the polygraph test to identify the actual culprit without there being an unacceptably high probability of deciding that an innocent suspect is guilty.

Most people believe DNA testing provides an almost infallible way of deciding whether a given individual has committed a given crime. The kernels of truth underlying that myth are that everyone has their own unique DNA pattern and that the probability an expert will correctly identify two samples of DNA as coming from the same person is often very high. However, the DNA sample available at crime scenes is often sub-optimal (e.g., it contains DNA from more than one person). Another problem is that DNA analysts typically cannot show *how* or *when* that DNA sample was created.

A final example is the myth that outstanding performance in any given domain can be achieved if we devote 10,000 hours of deliberate practice in that domain (Chapter 4). The kernel of truth is that the major reason why our performance level improves over time is because we devote substantial amounts of time to practice. However, if we lack the necessary innate talent or ability, this will sadly prove totally insufficient to achieve outstanding performance.

What can be done?

It is instructive to consider the following question: "What is the probability you will die on your next summer holiday?" I imagine you would agree the probability is extremely low. However, it would probably seem somewhat higher (and become more accurate) if I asked you, "What is the probability you will die on your next summer holiday from a disease, a car accident, a plane crash, contaminated food or any other cause?" The differences in the subjective probabilities are easily explained by assuming that we often fail to take account of relevant information unless explicitly presented (Tversky & Koehler, 1994).

This example sheds light on why it is that people on average claim that the chances of an experienced examiner mistakenly assuming that DNA samples from two different individuals came from the same person are 1 in 10,000,000 (Koehler, 2017; see Chapter 9). This incredible estimate could only have been produced if those questioned ignored several relevant factors. Suppose they had asked themselves, "What factors could possibly lead experts to mistakenly assume that two DNA samples came from the same individual?" That would probably have led them to consider potential limitations in the quality and quantity of the fingerprint or DNA evidence such as the possibility that two individuals might have very similar fingerprints, possible limited expertise possessed by the examiner, biased decision making by the examiner or an excessively liberal criterion for deciding that two fingerprints matched.

In similar fashion, those individuals agreeing that outstanding performance can be achieved solely by dedicating 10,000 hours to deliberate practice are guilty of neglecting relevant information and factors (Chapter 4). Suppose they focused on counterexamples. Nearly everyone can think of geniuses who achieved fantastic levels of performance at an extremely young age when they must necessarily have spent far fewer hours practising than their older but less successful competitors. Examples include Amadeus Mozart who composed his first symphony at the age of 8 and Magnus Carlsen who first became the No. 1 chess player in the world at the age of 19.

There are other relevant factors that those subscribing to the 10,000-hour myth might have focused on. First, the myth seems to imply that if anyone puts in the hours they could be as successful a tennis player as Serena Williams or Novak Djokovic, as great a playwright as William Shakespeare or as renowned a composer as Mozart. Second, everyone is familiar with the notion that innate talent is a crucial prerequisite for outstanding performance in any domain. The finding that the amount of practice correlates positively with performance in no way rules out the possibility that innate talent is hugely important. Third, ask yourself why very few individuals are willing to devote 10,000 hours to developing outstanding expertise. Is it not probable that only those demonstrating real talent at an early stage of practice are likely to put in the necessary hard work and effort?

Conclusions

There are four very general reasons why tens of millions of people subscribe to numerous psychological myths. First, much of the information on most topics available to members of the public and psychology students is seriously inaccurate. This is a problem of bottom-up processing (i.e., inaccurate input). Second, members of the public have fixed views on most psychological topics. As a result, they may selectively expose themselves to information supporting their views and are loath to change them even when exposed to information contradicting those views. This is a problem of top-down processing.

Of the eight reasons for believing psychological myths discussed earlier in this chapter, five relate to deficient bottom-up processing fuelled by inaccurate or limited information from the media, distorted research, psychology textbooks and personal experience. Two reasons (confirmation bias or wishful thinking and kernel of truth ignoring relevant information) relate directly to inaccurate top-down processing, and only one reason (slipshod thinking about intrinsically improbable beliefs) relates to a mixture of bottom-up and top-down processing. Note, however, that it is possible (and indeed likely) that many psychological myths depend on a mixture of bottom-up and top-down processing.

11 Brave new world

We have seen that most people's beliefs about findings in psychology are frequently well wide of the mark and often reflect their cognitive biases. We have also seen that psychologists are also prone to many cognitive biases. Indeed, they may be especially susceptible to some cognitive biases because of their understandable motivation to obtain support for their favourite theory or theories. What is required is the following: "They [scientists] must prevent their desires and aversions from penetrating their observations of the phenomena that they study and their analyses of these observations" (Cournand, 1977, p. 700).

We saw in Chapter 10 that psychologists are blameworthy with respect to several of the best-known myths in psychology. In this chapter, I will focus more generally on the main errors and biases in experimental research. However, the chapter is entitled, 'Brave new world', because my emphasis is on identifying ways psychological research can be systematically improved and less prone to bias.

Experiments: the gold standard?

How can psychologists make maximal progress in understanding human cognition and behaviour? The most common answer is that they should rely on well-controlled laboratory experiments with such experiments constituting the 'gold standard'. As Diener et al. (2022, p. 1101) pointed out, "It is often claimed that only experiments can support strong causal inferences and therefore they should be privileged in the behavioural sciences". In fact, this claim exaggerates the importance of experiments and the experimental method and underestimates other research strategies.

The hundreds of thousands of experiments carried out by psychologists have been crucially important in the development of psychology. However, many are more limited than generally realised. First, most experiments are relatively narrow in scope because they investigate the effects of only a few independent variables (manipulated environmental factors) on one or a few dependent variables (e.g., aspects of behaviour) over a short time period. In contrast, much of everyday life consists of numerous complex interacting factors having long-term effects on behaviour.

DOI: 10.4324/9781003596677-11

Second, the experimental method is applicable to only a subset of the factors influencing human behaviour (see Chapter 1). Researchers can easily manipulate aspects of the immediate situation (e.g., presentation of visual and/or auditory stimuli). However, our behaviour is also strongly influenced by numerous other factors (e.g., genetics; personality; intelligence; childhood experiences) which cannot be experimentally controlled.

Third, there is paradigm specificity. Paradigm specificity means the findings obtained with a given experimental task are specific to that task or paradigm and fail to generalise to other, apparently similar tasks. In practice, researchers typically use a single task or paradigm and so it is unclear whether the findings obtained with that task/paradigm would generalise to other tasks/paradigms (Yarkoni, 2022).

Fourth, use of the experimental method can often establish that X causes Y in a given experimental context. However, it is often hard (or impossible) to establish precisely *why* X causes Y (i.e., the underlying processes or mechanisms) and experimentation does not demonstrate that X is the *only* cause of Y.

Fifth, as Fiedler et al. (2021, p. 818) pointed out, "No manipulation can be expected to affect only a single theoretical IV [independent variable]". Consider a study on the effects of watching a murder film on participants' behaviour. The researchers may claim this manipulation has served only to increase negative affect. However, the film may also increase participants' physiological arousal, produce thoughts about threatening situations they have experienced, cause them to try to avoid their mood becoming excessively negative and so on.

Sixth, in everyday life our behaviour generally changes our current environment. For example, when chatting with a friend, what they say influences us and what we say influences them. We can contrast this with the typical experimental situation where the participant's behaviour does *not* influence the situation (e.g., the experimenter's behaviour). Wachtel (1973) coined the term 'implacable experimenter' to describe the laboratory situation where participants passively respond to the experimental situation rather than actively altering it. As a consequence, the richness of dynamic interactions between individual and situation is often missing.

This issue is frequently easy to address with non-experimental methods. In personality research, for example, we can ask individuals going about their daily business to describe what they are currently doing. When Wilt and Revelle (2019; see Chapter 6) did this, they discovered extraverts and those high in agreeableness were more likely than introverts or those low in agreeableness to be in a social situation. In addition, individuals high in conscientiousness were more likely than low scorers to be studying.

What can be done?

What is required is to use several different research methods including experiments. Each research method has its own strengths and limitations and so the solution is to combine the findings obtained by each method to obtain a comprehensive database. Diener et al. (2022) described several such methods (e.g., twin studies; longitudinal studies) which are discussed shortly.

Resolving the 'lab dilemma'

Another limitation with laboratory experiments not mentioned so far is the 'lab dilemma': laboratory experiments are well-controlled but the laboratory environment is often very *unrepresentative* of situations encountered in everyday life. In other words, laboratory experiments often lack ecological validity. Here I consider two types of experiments that can have greater ecological validity than most laboratory experiments: virtual reality and natural experiments.

It would be ideal in principle to carry out well-controlled experiments under real-world conditions. However, real-world research is complicated by the presence of various uncontrolled factors. There has been significant progress in this area due to the rapid increase in the use of Virtual Reality (VR; Vallet & van Wassenhove, 2023). VR provides a computer-generated environment within which objects and people appear real. In principle, this solves the lab dilemma by exposing people to a well-controlled but highly realistic environment.

Alternatively, we can conduct natural experiments. According to Grosz et al. (2024, p. 2), "A natural experiment is a 'naturally' occurring event or condition (i.e., an event or condition not created by researchers) that affects some but not all units of a population". For example, we could assess the impact of a major earthquake on people's lives by comparing its after-effects on those directly affected and those only indirectly affected. Comparing these two groups is valid on the reasonable assumption that the group individuals find themselves in is randomly determined. It is also noteworthy that we can investigate individuals' reactions to threats and dangerous events but it would be totally unethical to study in the laboratory.

Here are two examples showing how natural experiments can permit identification of causal factors. First, research indicates longevity and intelligence are predicted to some extent by years of education. However, there are many possible reasons why individuals vary in the years of education they receive, and so we cannot interpret such correlational evidence in causal terms. Davies et al. (2018) carried out an natural experiment taking advantage of the raising of the minimum school-leaving age in the UK from 15 to 16 by comparing those affected or unaffected by this change. The additional year of education reduced mortality several decades later and also modestly increased intelligence.

Second, there is a positive relationship between wealth and psychological well-being but this finding is hard to interpret (see Chapter 7). Wealth may cause enhanced well-being but it is also possible that high well-being facilitates the accumulation of wealth. In addition, wealthier and poorer individuals typically differ in years of education, intelligence, socio-economic status of their family, conscientiousness and so on. In a correlational study, it is not possible to identify factors responsible for the positive relationship between wealth and psychological well-being.

Lindqvist et al. (2020) carried out a natural experiment where they assessed the psychological well-being of individuals who had won varying amounts of money in a lottery. This allowed them to calculate the causal impact of wealth on well-being without the possible confounding effects of the factors discussed earlier. Overall life satisfaction increased progressively as a function of the amount of money that was won and this beneficial effect remained constant for many years afterwards. It is reasonable to conclude that increased wealth caused enhanced life satisfaction, and there were smaller beneficial effects of wealth on happiness and mental health.

In sum, natural experiments possess several advantages. Of most importance, they permit the drawing of causal inferences in numerous real-world conditions. It is thus puzzling that researchers rarely use natural experiments: Grosz et al. (2024) discovered only 0.07% (approximately 1 in 1,400) of published studies in psychology are natural experiments.

Twin studies

Twin studies often provide important insights into the role played by genetic factors in explaining individual differences in behaviour (Chapters 5, 6 and 9). Polderman et al. (2015) analysed data on over 17,000 human traits obtained from over 14 million twin pairs and concluded: "All human traits are heritable: not one trait had a weighted heritability estimate of zero" (p. 708). On average, genetic factors accounted for 49% of individual differences. Bizarrely, Diener et al. (2022) in their discussion of research methods additional to experimentation failed to mention twin studies.

Many findings in psychology have been misinterpreted due to a failure to consider the potential role of genetic factors. For example, it is generally assumed an individual's happiness depends on various environmental factors such as having close friends and/or confidants implying the lack of close friends (i.e., loneliness) causes unhappiness. However, reality is more complex. As discussed in Chapter 7, genetic factors account for 48% of individual differences in loneliness (Boomsma et al., 2005) indicating that loneliness is partially caused by genetic factors rather than simply being an environmental factor causing unhappiness.

Longitudinal studies

Experiments are typically limited because they only assess people's behaviour at a single point in time. It is often important to compare and contrast people's behaviour at different stages of life. This can be done in two ways. First, there are *longitudinal* studies where the same individuals are assessed at several different points of time sometimes spanning a period of many years.

Second, there are *cross-sectional* studies where different groups varying in age are studied in the same time frame.

Psychological findings can differ considerably across groups varying in age. Individual differences in a given trait or behaviour (e.g., personality traits) often depend much more on family or shared environment at the youngest ages than subsequently whereas the influence of genetic factors increases progressively. This pattern occurs because the impact of the immediate environment on children and adults decreases as they become more independent and spend more of their time outside the family home. For example, Hatemi et al. (2009; Chapter 7) investigated individual differences in political attitudes from the age of nine to old age. Genetic factors had no influence on individual differences in political attitudes throughout childhood but accounted for between 40% and 60% of individual differences between the ages of 20 and 75. In contrast, family or shared environmental factors accounted for 26% of individual differences at the age of 9, for 60% at the age of 17, but for only 0% to 20% of individual differences throughout adulthood.

Similar findings have been obtained in twin research on intelligence and personality. Tucker-Drob et al. (2013; Chapter 5) found genetic factors accounted for under 25% of individual differences in intelligence in infancy but for 70% in adolescence. In contrast, family or shared environment accounted for 65% of individual differences in infancy but 0% in adolescence. Knafo and Plomin (2006b) studied prosocial behaviour. Genetic factors accounted for far more individual differences in prosocial behaviour at the age of seven than two (61% vs. 32%), whereas family or shared environment accounted 0% of individual differences at seven but 47% at the age of two.

Conclusions

Several non-experimental methods are extremely useful. However, it is commonly assumed that only experiments permit us to make causal inferences. That assumption is wrong: it is perfectly possible to make causal inferences from natural experiments and twin studies. Another very general point needs to be made. The causal inferences made by researchers always go beyond the observable data and that is as true of experimental research as of non-experimental research (Grosz et al., 2020).

In sum, the notion that causal inferences can be drawn from 100% of research based on the experimental method but by 0% of research not involving the experimental method is a gross oversimplification. In fact, this notion exaggerates the power of the experimental method and minimises the power of non-experimental methods.

Developing new methods

Major advances in science often depend on new theories superseding previous ones. However, developing new methods is also vitally important. Greenwald (2012) reviewed Nobel prizes in physics, chemistry and medicine between 1991 and 2011. Surprisingly, 82% were awarded for contributions to method rather than theory!

The picture is similar in psychology. Between the end of the Second World War and Greenwald's (2012) article, nine Nobel prizes were awarded to scientists working in psychology. Seven were for advances in method and the Nobel prize to Daniel Kahneman was for contributions to method and theory.

In 1981, the Nobel prize for medicine or physiology was divided into two: one prize for Roger Sperry and the other for David Hubel and Torsten Wiesel. Sperry made numerous discoveries about the functional specialisation of the cerebral hemispheres by studying split-brain patients in whom connections between the brain hemispheres had been drastically reduced through surgery. This made it possible to assess cognitive processing in each hemisphere separately. Hubel and Wiesel made numerous discoveries about detailed visual processing in the brain as a result of their invention of an incredibly sensitive technique known as single-unit recording: a micro-electrode 1/10,000th of a millimetre in diameter is inserted into the brain to study activity within single neurons.

Cognitive neuroscience

It is of great importance to cognitive psychology to understand *internal* cognitive processes. Historically, cognitive psychologists relied heavily on behavioural measures (e.g., accuracy; performance speed) to draw *inferences* about internal processes. This approach allowed cognitive psychologists to make considerable progress. However, behavioural measures often provide only limited information making it hard to have confidence in the inferences drawn from them.

In recent decades, cognitive psychology has benefited enormously from the development of several techniques for studying brain activity (Eysenck & Keane, 2020). Some techniques identify with precision where cognitive processes are occurring in the brain (high spatial resolution) whereas others identify the detailed time course of cognitive processes (high temporal resolution).

The most-used technique is functional magnetic resonance imaging (fMRI), which has very good spatial resolution but relatively poor temporal resolution (2 or 3 seconds). An alternative technique is magneto-encephalography (MEG), which has comparable spatial resolution to fMRI but much superior temporal resolution (at the millisecond level). However, MEG is very expensive and this limits its use.

There are also event-related potentials (ERPs) which are based on recordings of electrical brain activity measured at the surface of the scalp. Reliable information about such activity is obtained by presenting the same stimulus (or similar stimuli) repeatedly and then averaging across trials to obtain the ERPs in response to it. This averaging process allows us to distinguish genuine effects of cognitive processing from background or spontaneous brain activity.

Cognitive neuroscience involves combining information from behavioural measures with information obtained from measures of brain activity. In the following sections I consider several examples showing how cognitive neuroscience has clarified our understanding of human cognition beyond what had previously been achieved.

Visual imagery vs. visual perception

There are conflicting theoretical views concerning the relationship between visual imagery and visual perception. Pearson and Kosslyn (2015) argued they are very similar: visual images are depictive representations where "each part of the representation corresponds to a part of the represented object such that the distances among the parts in the representation correspond to the actual distances among the parts" (p. 10089). In contrast, Pylyshyn (2002) argued that performance on imagery tasks depends on stored knowledge of what objects look like but *not* on perception-like processes.

Much behavioural evidence apparently supports Pearson and Kosslyn's (2015) views. Laeng et al. (2014) asked observers to view pictures of animals and to follow each one by forming an image of that animal. There was a striking similarity in the pattern of eye fixations devoted to the various areas of each picture in both conditions. In addition, observers having the greatest similarity in eye-fixation patterns between perception and imagery exhibited the best memory for the size of each animal.

The previous behavioural findings suggest visual perception and imagery involve very similar underlying processes. However, research in cognitive neuroscience has shown that is *not* the case. Such research has established that visual perception proceeds in a bottom-up fashion from early visual areas involved in basic visual processes to higher brain areas associated with memory and expectations (Dijkstra et al., 2017). In contrast, visual imagery is best explained by the reverse hierarchy theory (Dijkstra, 2024), according to which brain activity in imagery proceeds in a top-down fashion from higher brain areas to early visual areas. Evidence that the flow of neural processing during perception is reversed during imagery was reported by Dijkstra et al. (2017, 2020). Strikingly, there is considerable activity within early visual areas during perception compared to little or no activity in those areas during imagery (Spagna et al., 2021).

Dijkstra et al. (2018) used MEG and discovered another important difference between perception and imagery. Visual representations develop over time through a series of processing stages. In contrast, the entire representation was activated simultaneously during imagery, presumably because the relevant information was retrieved all at once from long-term memory.

In sum, visual perception and visual imagery have generally appeared very similar in behavioural studies. However, cognitive neuroscience has indicated that the underlying processes producing this behavioural similarity are very different; indeed, the direction of processing in perception is reversed in imagery.

Anxiety and performance

Trait anxiety is a personality dimension: individuals high in trait anxiety experience anxiety more frequently and intensely than low scorers. It is often assumed anxiety has negative effects on performance. However, many studies have reported comparable performance by individuals high and low in trait anxiety. In one study (Basten et al., 2012), participants were presented with four letters and recalled them in alphabetical order. Trait anxiety had no effect on performance accuracy or response speed. Thus, the behavioural findings suggested task processing was very similar for those high and low in trait anxiety.

Basten et al. (2012) also found that high-anxious individuals had significantly greater activation than low-anxious ones in a region of prefrontal area cortex associated with attentional control. Thus, there was an intriguing *disconnect* between the effects of trait anxiety on behaviour and brain activity.

Similar findings were reported by Barker et al. (2018). Individuals high in trait worry (closely related to trait anxiety) exhibited comparable performance to those low in trait worry with respect to speed and accuracy. However, brain areas associated with attentional control were significantly more activated in high worriers.

How can we explain these findings? According to attentional control theory (Eysenck et al., 2007, 2023), individuals high in trait anxiety are inefficient when performing a cognitive task because they engage in some task-irrelevant processing (e.g., worry). They *compensate* for this inefficiency by strenuous attempts at attentional control. Thus, high-anxious individuals achieve comparable task performance to low-anxious ones by using additional resources to those used by low-anxious individuals: they "pedal faster".

In sum, the behavioural findings from studies such as those of Basten et al. (2012) and Barker et al. (2018) provide no evidence that individuals high in trait anxiety or worry differ from those low in trait anxiety or worry with respect to the processes they use when performing cognitive tasks. It is only when we consider brain activity that it becomes apparent that the comparable performance of the two groups depends on very different underlying processes (Eysenck et al., 2023).

Visual attention: spotlight or zoom lens?

Theorists have likened visual attention to a spotlight or a zoom lens (i.e., the area of focal attention can be increased or decreased like a zoom lens) (Eysenck & Keane, 2020). An alternative notion is that we sometimes exhibit split attention (attention is directed to two or more non-adjacent regions in space). It has proved hard to decide whether split attention is possible based purely on behavioural evidence.

The strongest evidence for split attention comes from research using fMRI. Morawetz et al. (2007) presented stimuli at five locations simultaneously (one in each quadrant of the visual field and one in the centre). In one condition, observers attended to the stimuli in the upper left and bottom right locations and ignored the other stimuli. There were two peaks of brain activation corresponding to the two attended regions but much less activation corresponding to the region in between as predicted on the split-attention notion.

Cognitive neuroscience: interventions

There is convincing evidence for dual-task interference: performance of two tasks (X and Y) is typically impaired when they are performed together rather than singly. However, the precise reasons for dual-task interference are often unclear from behavioural findings. One theory is that dual-task interference occurs because strictly limited processing resources are spread thinly between two tasks in dual-task but not single-task conditions. Another theory is that such interference is due to co-ordination of task demands, which requires use of additional processing resources involving attentional control and general dual-task management to minimise interference in dual-task conditions.

On the resource competition theory, we might expect *under-additive* activation (i.e., reduced activation in brain areas associated with processing of one or both tasks under dual-task conditions). In contrast, on the co-ordination theory, we might expect *over-additive* activation (i.e., increased activation in brain areas such as prefrontal cortex involved in task co-ordination and attentional control). The findings are somewhat variable. However, dual-task performance is often associated with over-additivity due to increased activation within the prefrontal cortex (especially the lateral prefrontal cortex; Strobach et al., 2018).

The previous findings demonstrate an *association* between prefrontal activation and task conditions (dual vs. single). However, they do not show increased prefrontal activation is *required* for dual-task performance. An alternative approach is to assess the involvement of any given brain area in task performance by using interventions designed to increase that area's functioning. One such intervention is transcranial direct current stimulation (tDCS) where a weak electric current is passed through the selected brain area. Anodal tDCS involves stimulation applied via an anode (electrode with a positive charge) which increases cortical excitability and often enhances performance.

If processes associated with prefrontal activation are required for dual-task performance, there should be less dual-task interference if anodal tDCS is applied to the prefrontal cortex. Filmer et al. (2017) discovered that anodal tDCS applied to areas of the prefrontal cortex during training enhanced cognitive control and subsequent dual-task performance. Mahesan et al. (2023)

confirmed those findings and also found anodal tDCS reduced interference between two tasks performed together.

Cognitive neuropsychology

Cognitive neuropsychology focuses on the cognitive performance of brain-damaged patients having a lesion (structural damage to the brain caused by injury or disease). According to cognitive neuropsychologists, studying brain-damaged patients can be very informative about cognition in healthy individuals. That doesn't sound very promising, does it? In fact, however, cognitive neuropsychology has contributed substantially to our understanding of human cognition.

Cognitive neuropsychologists assume the performance of cognitive tasks in healthy individuals typically involves several processes (sometimes called 'processing modules') occurring in a given order. Of central importance is the subtractivity assumption: brain damage impairs one or more processing modules but does not change or add anything. As Shallice (2015) pointed out, these and other assumptions of cognitive neuropsychology are often approximately correct. As a consequence, "A key intellectual strength of cognitive neuropsychology . . . is its ability to provide evidence falsifying plausible cognitive theories" (pp. 387–388).

Earlier we discussed neuroimaging evidence indicating that visual perception depends mostly on bottom-up processes triggered by visual stimuli whereas visual imagery primarily involves top-down processes initiated by accessing relevant stored knowledge. We would thus expect to find some brain-damaged patients with reasonably intact visual perception but severely impaired visual imagery and other patients exhibiting the opposite pattern. Moro et al. (2008) studied two brain-damaged patients who were both very poor at drawing objects from memory (impaired visual imagery) but could copy the same objects when shown a drawing (intact visual perception).

De Gelder et al. (2015) studied a brain-damaged man (T. N.) who was blind as a result of extensive damage to the early visual cortex. In spite of his lack of visual perception, he retained a good ability to engage in visual imagery. Bartolomeo et al. (1997) studied a brain-damaged patient (Madame D). She totally lacked the ability to perceive colours but had an intact ability to imagine all colours vividly.

The previous findings strongly indicate that different processes are involved in visual perception and imagery (confirming the neuroimaging findings). They also disconfirm Pearson and Kosslyn's (2015) theoretical assumption that visual perception and visual imagery involve very similar processes.

Early research and theory on human memory emphasised a distinction between short-term memory and long-term memory (e.g., Atkinson & Shiffrin, 1968). Strong evidence for the validity of the distinction came from the study of the amnesic patient H. M. (Henry Molaison) (see Chapter 3). H. M.'s hippocampus and surrounding areas were removed surgically to treat his epilepsy. His long-term memory for events experienced following surgery was almost non-existent (e.g., he did not know where he lived or who cared for him). However, his short-term memory was essentially intact.

Strong evidence disproving the notion of a single long-term memory system has come from cognitive neuropsychological research. H. M. and other amnesic patients have extremely poor long-term episodic memory (i.e., memory for their personal experiences). However, they exhibit intact (or nearly intact) learning and memory for many motor skills (often referred to as 'procedural memory') (Spiers et al., 2001). Most research in this area has used artificial laboratory tasks. However, Cavaco et al. (2004) used five skill-learning tasks involving real-world skills and discovered that amnesic patients exhibited comparable learning to healthy controls.

Experimenter bias

Problems can occur at any stage of the research process starting with experimental design and finishing with scientific reporting of the findings of any given experiment (Bishop, 2020). Many of these problems are due to experimenter bias, with the experimenter's beliefs, behaviour and expectations distorting experimental designs and other stages of research. There is typically a close relationship between experimenter bias and confirmation bias, which involves an excessive emphasis on obtaining (and reporting) experimental findings supporting the experimenter's hypothesis or hypotheses.

There are many historical examples of experimenter bias influencing scientific findings. For example, Blondlot in 1902 claimed to have discovered a new radiation called N-rays. Even though 40 people subsequently claimed to have observed the effects of N-rays and 100 scientists analysed these effects in 300 research articles, it turned out that N-rays do not actually exist (see Bishop, 2020).

In similar fashion, consider actor-observer bias (we attribute our own actions to the situation but others' actions to their internal dispositions). For example, I fail an examination because the questions were too hard but you fail because you are lazy. At one time, this bias was regarded as a key finding in social psychology and was described as "robust, firmly established, and pervasive" (Malle, 2006, p. 995). However, when Malle reviewed 173 studies on actor-observer bias, the average size of this bias was extremely small.

Experimental design: paradigm specificity

As mentioned earlier, a major problem in experimental psychology is paradigm specificity: the findings obtained from any given task or paradigm often fail to generalise. This is especially likely to occur if experimenters select their task on the basis of dubious assumptions. Consider research on visual search designed to identify how observers detect a target stimulus among several distractors. Treisman and Gelade (1980) introduced a much-used paradigm or task which involved detecting a target (e.g., a green letter T among distractors sharing one feature with it (e.g., a brown letter T or a green letter X; see Chapter 1). Observers apparently searched *randomly* item by item.

We can see how paradigm specificity influenced Treisman and Gelade's (1980) findings by considering visual search in real life. If you were looking for your missing keys, you wouldn't search randomly: you might look in the pockets of your jacket, in drawers or on your desk but you wouldn't search the light socket, the top of the cupboard or under the bed. In other words, your search would be strongly influenced by your *pre-existing knowledge* of where you typically leave keys rather than being random as Treisman and Gelade's (1980) paradigm.

Another example of experimenter bias due to paradigm specificity is Ekman's research on basic facial expressions (see Chapter 10). He attempted to justify his claim that there are only six basic facial expressions of emotion by using highly artificial staged photographs and requiring observers to choose one of three options when deciding which emotion was shown in any given photograph.

What can be done?

All research methods involve assumptions. Experimenters reporting their research should explicit identify and clarify their major assumptions and it is highly desirable that these assumptions are tested (Diener et al., 2022). There should be systematic attempts to replicate the key findings of any experiment using various ways of manipulating the independent variables (aspects of the situation) and the dependent variables (e.g., behavioural measures) to assess their generality. For example, Srinivasan and Martinez (2021) used similar photographs to Ekman's but allowed observers to provide their own chosen description of each one. Their findings differed considerably from those of Ekman because there were large individual differences in the emotions perceived in many of the faces.

Researchers should also consider ecological validity (the extent to which findings can be generalised to real-world situations) when designing their experiments. A failure to do this explains why Treisman and Gelade's (1980) paradigm for studying visual search produces findings very different from those obtained using more naturalistic situations. Similarly, the limitations of Ekman's research on facial expressions arose because the highly artificial experimental designs he used possess very little ecological validity. Cowen and Keltner (2020) used 1,500 naturalistic photographs and obtained evidence for 28 different emotional expressions compared to the six reported by Ekman with his much smaller number of artificial photographs (see Chapter 10).

A potential problem with focusing on ecological validity is that it can lead to a partial loss of experimental control. Earlier in the chapter we discussed virtual reality. The use of virtual reality can often solve this problem by providing ecologically valid situations while at the same time permitting a high level of experimental control (Parsons, 2015).

Experimental design: lurking variables

Joiner (1981) coined the term 'lurking variables' to refer to causal varia-bles of which the researcher is unaware. Here I will broaden its meaning to include causal variables of whose existence the researcher is aware but nev-ertheless omits from their study. For example, the amount of ice cream sold on any given day correlates with the number of people drowning. Obviously, the lurking variable here is temperature: hot weather causes more people to buy ice cream and to go swimming.

The findings from thousands of research studies in psychology have been misinterpreted because of lurking variables excluded from the experimental design. The problem is especially common in studies considering the effects of earlier experiences on subsequent outcomes (Schmidt, 2017). The typical assumption is that causality is *unidirectional*: previous experiences cause sub-sequent outcomes. However, that assumption is often wrong because indi-viduals actively construct and change their environment.

The lurking variable in much research in this area is the role played by genetic factors. As Kendler and Baker (2007) pointed out,

> If the association between individuals and their environment solely takes the form of environment–>person, then genes ought to have no influence on environmental exposures. . . . However, if an individual's own behaviour impacts on the environmental exposures and if the rel-evant aspect of behaviour is itself subject to genetic influences, then these environmental measures ought to be heritable.
>
> (pp. 616–617)

Kendler and Baker (2007) reviewed research on 35 environmental factors associated with mental disorders including divorce, maternal warmth, pater-nal warmth, family cohesion, friend support, confidants and marital quality. On average, genetic factors accounted for 27% of individual differences in each factor.

Vinkhuyzen et al. (2010) extended Kendler and Baker's (2007) research to include leisure activities (e.g., number of years having music lessons; number of years involved in sport; number of years engaged in sport competition). On average, genetic factors accounted for 52% of individual differences in these activities. Aspects of the childhood environment (e.g., being read to; reading books; being bullied; school achievements discussed by parents) were also strongly influenced by genetic factors.

Genetic factors are important even with trivial activities. Kirzinger et al. (2012) discovered 24% of individual differences in days of watching televi-sion per week were due to genetic factors and Hassan (2023) found genetic factors accounted for 25% of individual differences in time playing computer games.

Several psychological myths involve the erroneous assumption that causation necessarily flows only from environmental experiences to behavioural outcomes. For example, it has often been claimed that stressful life events cause increased susceptibility to various mental disorders (Chapter 8). However, causality can also proceed in the opposite direction. We can distinguish between *independent* life events (e.g., miscarriage; death of a romantic partner) outside the individual's control and *dependent* life events (e.g., imprisonment; attempted suicide) under the individual's control. Depressed individuals experience more dependent life events than non-depressed ones indicating that depression increases susceptibility to stressful life events (Boardman et al., 2011).

Rnic et al. (2023) reviewed 95 longitudinal studies on patients with various mental disorders. They discovered clear evidence of a 'vicious cycle': stressful life events increased susceptibility to mental disorders including anxiety, depression and disruptive disorders and having a mental disorder increased susceptibility to dependent stressful life events.

Another myth discussed in this book is the interpretation that the number of hours spent practising expertise in some domain is positively correlated with performance means the former causes the latter (Chapter 4). Of course, this is partially true. However, this interpretation ignores the role played by individual differences in innate talent in determining amount of practice and performance. Another relevant myth is that parenting strongly influences children's adult personality when in fact parental influence depends heavily on genetic factors and scarcely at all on the shared family environment (Chapter 6). Finally, there is the myth that attitudes are predominantly learned even though genetic factors account for 40% of individual differences in attitudes (Chapter 7).

Note also that the effects of genes on behaviour depend on the environment (e.g., the environment can trigger a genetic predisposition). Kendler et al. (1995) found females at high genetic risk of major depressive disorder were much more likely than those at low genetic risk to develop that disorder following a severe life event (15% vs. 6%, respectively). However, the two groups had the same low probability of developing major depressive disorder in the absence of a severe life event.

The environment can also control or inhibit the expression of a genetic predisposition. For example, genetic influences accounted for 40% of individual differences in alcohol use initiation in females not having a religious upbringing but 0% in those receiving a religious upbringing (Koopmans et al., 1999). Dunne et al. (1997) found with respect to age at first sexual intercourse that genetic factors accounted for 49% of individual differences in women and 72% in men born in 1953 or later. For those born in an earlier era (1922–1952) where there were social pressures against premarital sex, genetic factors were much less important (32% for women and 0% for men).

Another major lurking variable is general intelligence or "*g*". General intelligence strongly predicts outcomes such as academic achievement and occupational status and performance (see Chapter 5; Schmidt, 2017). For example, IQ correlates 0.54 with academic achievement (Roth et al., 2015). Liu and Nesbit (2024) assessed the relationship between need for cognition (enjoyment of engaging in effortful cognition) and academic achievement. The two variables correlated 0.20, leading Liu and Nesbit to conclude "students with high need for cognition manifest better academic performance than those with low need for cognition" (p. 173). This is the case because individuals high in need for cognition "seek out, acquire, process, evaluate, and reflect on relevant information for knowledge construction" (p. 173).

Liu and Nesbit (2024, p. 156) chose to ignore the potential role of general intelligence by claiming, "there is only a minor overlap between need for cognition and cognitive ability". In fact, Hill et al. (2013) discovered need for cognition correlated .38 with IQ. The correlation between need for cognition and academic achievement would probably have been non-significant if account had been taken of general intelligence. In other words, any effects of need for cognition on academic achievement are probably due to its overlap with general intelligence.

Here is another example. Numerous studies have established there is a moderate correlation between arithmetic and reading achievement. This correlation has sometimes been explained by assuming that various specific abilities are required when performing arithmetic and reading tasks (e.g., retrieval of words and facts). In fact, however, the correlation mostly depends on the substantial impact of general intelligence on both arithmetic and reading (Ünal et al., 2023).

What can be done?

The central message is that researchers should always at least consider the possibility that genetic factors are of some relevance in explaining their findings. From time to time we have mentioned the comprehensive meta-analysis on twin studies conducted by Polderman et al. (2015), in which they found that individual differences in 17,804 human traits all depended to some extent on genetic factors.

If their findings don't persuade researchers to focus on the potential relevance of genetic factors to their research, nothing will.

Twin studies also provide measures of the impact of shared or family environment and non-shared or unique environment. In addition, twin studies allow us to investigate the complex ways genetic and environmental factors influence each other. Plomin (1990; see Chapter 5) identified three ways this happens with reference to intelligence. Children of high genetic ability spend more years in education than those of low genetic ability (active covariation), their parents provide a more stimulating environment (passive covariation) and their behaviour leads others to discuss more complex issues with them (reactive covariation).

More generally, researchers should ensure they relate their findings to the relevant body of research. If they haven't assessed major relevant factors (e.g., genetic factors; general intelligence), they should at the very least acknowledge that these factors might provide an explanation of their findings. It is also incumbent on other researchers reviewing a research article being considered for publication to require the authors of the article to consider the potential relevance of any lurking variables.

Experimental design: ensuring your therapy is effective

Cuijpers and Cristea (2016) indicated several ways clinical trials of a new form of therapy can be designed so as to maximise the probability that this therapy will appear to be effective (see Chapter 10). Therapeutic effectiveness is typically assessed by means of randomised controlled trials where patients are randomly assigned to receive therapy or not to receive therapy (the control group) and is based on *differences* between the two groups following treatment. Experimenter bias can manifest itself by artificially increasing apparent recovery in the therapy condition or apparent lack of recovery in the control condition. The former can be done by persuading patients to have high expectations of recovery, ignoring those who drop out of treatment (who typically benefit least from therapy) and using numerous outcome measures but only reporting data from those producing favourable findings. The latter can be done by putting control patients in a waiting list condition where they will show little recovery because they are waiting patiently for subsequent treatment.

What can be done?

Harrer et al. (2023) discussed how to make randomised controlled trials as informative and valid as possible. Of primary importance, each randomised controlled trial should be pre-registered. Pre-registration means that all the main features of a proposed randomised control trial (e.g., what will be done with the data from drop outs; identifying the key outcome measures; nature of the control group) should be published *before* any patients are treated. This should prevent researchers from using poor practices such as raising expectations only in the therapy group, switching to whichever outcomes indicate the greatest impact of therapy, deleting the data from patients who drop out of therapy and using only a waiting list control group.

Ideally, pre-registered reports should be published in a scientific journal following peer review ahead of the randomised controlled trial. Pre-registered reports that are deficient (e.g., failure to specify the key outcome measures or how data from drop outs will be analysed) should not be accepted for publication, leading researchers to re-think and subsequently produce a more adequate pre-registered report.

The jingle-jangle fallacies

As we have seen, meta-analyses offer the prospect of developing a cumulative science where current research builds on and extends previous research. Two major obstacles to achieving this goal are the jingle-jangle fallacies. The jingle fallacy occurs when the same word is used to refer to different things. In contrast, the jangle fallacy involves using different words to refer to the same thing. These trivial-sounding fallacies have seriously inhibited progress in several areas of psychology.

The common tendency to ignore the jingle-jangle fallacies helps to explain why there are so many psychological tests. There are upwards of 40,000 tests and measures in psychology (Elson et al., 2023). Of these tests, 43% were used only in a single study and a further 20% were used only in two or three studies. Drastic action is required to slow down the rate at which new tests appear.

Personality

Many allegedly different personality traits are actually very similar, thus exemplifying the jangle fallacy. Two clear-cut examples have been discussed in this book. First, there is research on emotional intelligence as a personality trait or factor (see Chapter 5). Individuals high in emotional intelligence have excellent social skills and empathy and many measures of emotional intelligence as a personality trait have been developed.

A separate body of research has focused on the Big Five personality factors (extraversion, openness, conscientiousness, neuroticism and agreeableness). These factors all correlate with each other which led to the development of a General Factor of Personality (GFP) based on the Big Five. The GDP is a measure of social effectiveness defined by high extraversion, agreeableness, conscientiousness, openness and low neuroticism. van der Linden et al. (2017) discovered that trait emotional intelligence correlates 0.85 with the GFP strongly suggesting the two constructs are essentially identical.

Second, there is research on self-esteem (see Chapter 6). Individuals having high self-esteem are happier and more successful than those with low self-esteem and are also less likely to suffer from anxiety and depression. However, Watson et al. (2002) found self-esteem correlated –0.66 with neuroticism in one study and –0.69 in another. When they considered the various aspects or facets of neuroticism, they discovered self-esteem correlated –0.79 with the depression facet. Thus, high self-esteem and low depression are rather similar constructs.

Watson et al. (2002) also found that self-esteem was positively related to extraversion, conscientiousness, agreeableness and openness. Thus, self-esteem is characterised by the same pattern on the Big Five as trait emotional intelligence. Bibi et al. (2016) found self-esteem correlated 0.82 with trait emotional intelligence indicating the two constructs are very similar and so exemplify the jangle fallacy.

Mental disorders

Major depressive disorder is a very common mental disorder. Numerous measures of depression have been proposed: Santor et al. (2006) identified nearly 300 such measures. Fried (2017) analysed seven of the most popular depression scales in detail. He found convincing evidence of the jingle fallacy. Of the grand total of 52 symptoms of major depression identified in these scales, 40% were included in only one scale and the mean overlap of symptoms across all seven scales was only 36%.

Newson et al. (2021) considered 126 measures of 10 mental disorders types including depression, anxiety, posttraumatic stress disorder, autism and schizophrenia. The similarity of symptoms within any given disorder was relatively modest, ranging from 28% for bipolar disorder to 58% for schizophrenia. Overall, 60% of all symptoms were associated with at least half the disorders and 16% were associated with all (or all but one). Note that the measures varied not only with respect to the symptoms assessed but also whether the focus was on frequency, duration or severity of those symptoms. The heterogeneity and inconsistency across measures are strongly indicative of the jingle fallacy.

What can be done?

Anyone proposing a measure (e.g., of a personality trait) should establish it has both convergent and discriminant validity. Convergent validity is based on the assumption that different measures of the same underlying construct should correlate highly with each other. For example, if someone produces a questionnaire allegedly measuring conscientiousness, then it should correlate highly with previous measures of conscientiousness. Discriminant validity is based on the assumption that two measures of theoretically different underlying constructs should not correlate highly with each other.

The convergent and discriminant validity of numerous measures are unknown even though these forms of validity were identified as important over 60 years ago. Lilienfeld and Strother (2020) found 86% of articles published in the journal *Psychological Assessment* provided no evidence for divergent validity and 65% provided no evidence for convergent or divergent validity.

As mentioned several times in this book, most individual differences in personality can be accounted for by the Big Five factors (Costa & McCrae, 1992). You may well feel there must be several other important personality factors in addition to these five. However, Goldberg (1990; discussed later) provided strong evidence that the Big Five factors are of central importance.

Goldberg (1990) made use of the fundamental lexical hypothesis, according to which language contains adjectives referring to all the most important personality traits. In one study, his participants described themselves across 1,710 adjectives, and Goldberg discovered the findings could best be accounted for by the Big Five personality factors.

We can conceptualise the structure of personality as existing in five-dimensional space with each Big Five factor identified with a different dimension. If someone produces a new test, the odds are high that any personality factor or trait it measures can be related directly to this five-dimensional space. It is only by doing this that our knowledge of personality structure can become cumulative rather than fragmentary.

A central requirement of a psychological test is that it predicts some relevant outcome or outcomes. For example, an intelligence test should predict outcomes such as academic success or job performance. However, a successful new test goes beyond that requirement by exhibiting incremental validity: it predicts outcomes to a greater extent than pre-existing tests. It is obviously more challenging to demonstrate that a new test has incremental validity than simply to show that it predicts relevant outcomes, which helps to explain why numerous researchers have developed new tests without providing evidence of incremental validity.

Demonstrating incremental validity is important because it indicates a test adds something to previous tests. Elson et al. (2023, p. 3) argued that journals should require researchers who have created a new test or other measure to "provide evidence of non-redundancy (with other measures and/or constructs) or incremental validity". This requirement would greatly reduce the number of new tests, adding nothing to previous ones. More generally, Elson et al. argued that reviewers and journal editors should "reject studies that use novel/ad-hoc measures without providing validity evidence from independent data" (p. 3).

The most important reason for focusing on incremental validity is that seriously misleading conclusions have often been drawn when it is not assessed. Consider research on intelligence, which can be conceptualised in hierarchical terms with the general factor (*g*) at the top and several more specific abilities lower down the hierarchy (e.g., spatial ability; verbal ability; see Chapter 4). Numerous studies have found that various specific abilities predict outcomes in training and job performance. For example, spatial ability generally predicts performance in STEM (science, technology, engineering and math) fields which has led many researchers to conclude that this indicates causal effects of spatial ability on performance (Schmidt, 2017).

The previous conclusion is erroneous. General mental ability or *g* is nearly always a strong predictor of numerous work-related outcomes (Salgado & Moscoso, 2019). That means we have to consider its potential role in explaining why there are positive correlations between specific abilities and job performance. This can best be done by demonstrating that specific abilities add incremental validity over and above the validity contributed by general mental ability. In order to do that, researchers must assess general mental ability as well as specific abilities.

Ree and Carretta (2022) reviewed comprehensively the relevant research in the area of job performance. Specific abilities typically possessed little or no incremental validity and nearly all the apparent effects of spatial abilities on job performance were actually due to general mental ability. This is because specific abilities correlate with general mental ability and general mental ability is a cause of an individual's specific abilities.

Granularity problem

The jingle and jangle fallacies both illustrate problems with psychological concepts. There is also the granularity problem: deciding whether to prefer a relatively small number of very broad concepts or categories or a larger number of narrower concepts or categories. For example, one of the most used personality tests (*Revised NEO Personality Inventory* (NEO-PI-R)) has five broad personality factors (openness; neuroticism; agreeableness; extraversion and conscientiousness) plus 30 more specific facets (six facets per factor) (Costa & McCrae, 1992). For example, the neuroticism factor has the following facets: anxiety; depression; angry-hostility; self-consciousness; impulsiveness; and vulnerability.

The diagnosis of mental disorders has exhibited a dramatic increase in granularity. Consider changes in the *Diagnostic and Statistical Manual of Mental Disorders* (DSM), which provides a comprehensive classification of mental disorders and is used extensively in therapy and research. The first edition (DSM-I; 1952) identified 128 mental disorders which increased to 541 in the fifth edition (DSM-5; 2013). There is a granularity problem here: is the substantial increase in the number of mental disorders beneficial or detrimental to progress?

What can be done?

There is no definitive answer to the granularity problem: the appropriate level of granularity depends on the nature of the research questions being addressed. However, psychologists (and non-psychologists) have often believed that high granularity (a high level of detail) is generally preferable to low granularity because it provides richer and more complete information. We can see limitations in that belief by considering the case of the map–territory relation: high-granularity maps are much less useful than less accurate low-granularity maps. Borges (1946/1999) carried this to its logical extreme: he imagined a map that was the same size and contained all the details as the territory being mapped.

How can we resolve the granularity problem with respect to personality? There is strong evidence that the Big Five factors all possess high validity (McCrae, 2020; see Chapter 6). There is also evidence that the 30 facets of personality measured by the NEO-PI-R have some incremental validity. Note, however, that the Big Five personality factors account for 60% of individual differences on the NEO-PI-R which is considerably more than the facets. In addition, Schimmack (2019) found six facets correlated more highly with another Big Five factor than the one they allegedly form part of, and nearly 40% of the facets failed to correlate highly with the 'right' factor.

Other kinds of evidence support the notion that the five factors are more important than their facets. For example, Jang et al. (1996) discovered that genetic factors accounted for more than 40% of individual differences for all of the Big Five factors but for only nine out of 30 facets.

Various kinds of evidence address the granularity problem with respect to the diagnosis of mental disorders. First, there is comorbidity (the simultaneous presence of two or more mental disorders). If the granularity present in DSM-5 is too high, we might expect to find extensive comorbidity. Caspi et al. (2014) discovered 66% of individuals having one mental disorder satisfied the criteria for a second mental disorder, 53% of those having two mental disorders satisfied the criteria for a third mental disorder and 41% of those with three mental disorders satisfied the criteria for a fourth mental disorder.

Second, if the granularity in DSM-5 is appropriate, we might predict that each mental disorder would be influenced by somewhat different genetic factors. However, major anxiety disorders (generalised anxiety disorder; panic disorder; agoraphobia; social anxiety disorder) as well as major depressive disorder are all triggered in part by common genetic factors (Hettema et al., 2006). In addition, several anxiety disorders and major depressive disorder are characterised by high neuroticism, low conscientiousness and low agreeableness (Kotov et al., 2010).

The previous findings have major implications for therapy. Historically, most therapy has been diagnosis-specific (i.e., it varies systematically depending on the specific diagnosis). However, the overlaps among different disorders suggest that transdiagnostic therapy (e.g., the same therapy being given to patients with different anxiety disorders) might be as effective. Barlow et al. (2017) found transdiagnostic cognitive behavioural therapy and disorder-specific cognitive behavioural therapy were comparably successful in reducing the severity of the principal diagnosis immediately following treatment and at 6-month follow-up in patients with anxiety disorders.

The take-home message is that the optimal way to resolve the granularity problem is to assemble as many kinds of relevant evidence as possible. In the case of the number of mental disorders, it is clear that many allegedly separate mental disorders are rather similar. This has led to the development of transdiagnostic therapy which is less expensive than diagnosis-specific therapy in part because patients with different diagnoses can be treated as a group.

Finally, note that the optimal level of granularity often depends on precisely what one is trying to achieve. For example, the facets of the Big Five factors have less general applicability than the personality factors, but combining information from facets and factors provides a fuller account of an individual's personality.

Scientific analysis: meta-analysis

In Chapter 1, there is a discussion of the value of meta-analysis, which involves combining the findings from numerous studies on a given research topic. In principle, meta-analysis can provide more solid and reliable findings than are achievable with individual studies. In view of frequent replication failures, it is highly desirable that any given study should be regarded as contributing towards an evidence base rather than definitively resolving a scientific issue.

There has been a dramatic increase in the number of meta-analyses. According to *Web of Science*, there have been 20,000 meta-analyses in psychology in the past 55 years up to March 2024. However, only three were from the 1970s and 50% date from 2017 onwards.

There is compelling evidence of researcher bias in many meta-analyses. Consider Ebrahim et al.'s (2016) meta-analysis on the effectiveness of anti-depressants. Inspection of the abstracts of 185 meta-analyses indicated that negative statements about the drug being assessed were markedly more common when none of the authors was an employee of the drug's manufacturer (44% vs. 2%).

Unsurprisingly, problems are especially great when the authors of a meta-analysis have a commercial interest in its findings. However, there are major problems with reproducibility of meta-analytic findings even in the absence of commercial interests. Uttal (2012) found the agreement between pairs of meta-analyses designed to identify the brain areas associated with given cognitive function varied between 14% and 51%.

The most serious problems arise because of researcher/experimenter bias which can be present in all meta-analysts' decisions. However, it is probably most damaging with respect to the literature search (i.e., deciding how to identify which studies should be considered for inclusion) and inclusion criteria (i.e., deciding which identified studies will be included in the meta-analysis itself).

With respect to the literature search, a key decision is whether to include unpublished studies (often unpublished because the findings are non-significant). If unpublished studies are to be included, there is then the difficult decision as to the optimal way to track down such studies. With respect to inclusion criteria, it seems desirable to include only high-quality studies. However, numerous conflicting ways of defining high quality have been proposed (Sharpe & Poets, 2020).

What can be done?

As Gurevitch et al. (2016) pointed out,

> Meta-analysis can be a key tool for facilitating rapid progress in science by quantifying what is known and identifying what is not yet known.

Evidence synthesis should become a regular companion to primary scientific research to maximise the effectiveness of scientific inquiry.

(p. 180)

Unfortunately, meta-analyses have too often reflected the biases of the researchers carrying them out rather than making a serious contribution to knowledge.

What can be done? Experimenter/researcher bias can be reduced by focusing on two notions: pre-registration and reproducibility. First, we consider pre-registration, which requires meta-analysts to provide a detailed research protocol *in advance* of their proposed meta-analysis (Lakens et al., 2016). This protocol should include details of the researchers' research questions, the precise way the literature search will be conducted, the inclusion criteria to be adopted, methods of data extraction and how the data will be analysed. It should also include a statement of any conflicts of interest the meta-analysts may have (e.g., they have received funding; they have published a significant proportion of the studies in the area). Ideally, this pre-registered protocol should be submitted to a peer-reviewed journal so experts can assess the extent of any researcher bias before recommending publication.

Second, we consider reproducibility (Lakens et al., 2016). The published report of a meta-analysis should contain all the information required for another researcher to perform the same analyses on the same data and produce the same outcome. Most published meta-analyses fail the reproducibility text. Maggio et al. (2011) found it impossible to reproduce the literature search carried out with respect to 100% of the 34 meta-analyses they examined.

Lakens et al. (2016) found 96% of the meta-analyses they assessed lacked full information and so could not be reproduced. Their study showed "the great difficulty we faced while attempting to reproduce 20 meta-analyses. . . . We believe this is a situation in dire need of improvement" (p. 13).

Meta-analyses on brain mapping

How does the brain function? It used to be assumed that functional specialisation is involved: each brain area or region is specialised for a given function (e.g., colour processing; face processing). That notion was endorsed by early neuroimaging research. For example, neuroimaging research has typically indicated that face processing is associated with activation within an area in ventral temporal cortex known as the 'fusiform face area'. This exemplifies the use of reverse inference: we argue backwards from a pattern of brain activation to the presence of a given cognitive function (e.g., face processing). This approach has unflatteringly been described as 'blobology': a small brain area (a 'blob') is interpreted as being where a given cognitive function occurs.

Reverse inference made sense when only relatively few neuroimaging studies had been carried out. However, it has serious flaws (Eysenck &

Keane, 2020). The so-called 'fusiform face area' is activated in response to many different kinds of objects (Downing et al., 2006) and several other brain areas (e.g., occipital face area; superior temporal sulcus) forming a *network* are also activated during face processing. In sum, the fusiform face area is activated when individuals engage in face processing but it is *not* true that activation of that area necessarily means individuals are processing faces. There is also the issue of paradigm specificity: the finding that a given face-processing task is associated with a particular pattern of brain activation does not guarantee the same pattern would be obtained with a different face-processing task.

The previous problems can largely be eliminated by meta-analysis. Consider the research of Menuet et al. (2022) who investigated relationships among patterns of brain activity (fMRI maps) across numerous cognitive processes (e.g., attention; face perception; semantic processing; emotion; story comprehension; visual word recognition and memory). They identified the mental processes associated with 26,000 fMRI maps and then tested the accuracy of these identifications by attempting to decode the mental processes associated with a further 6,500 fMRI maps. Decoding was successful with respect to over 50 mental processes.

What are the advantages of this meta-analytic approach over previous research focusing on one or a few fMRI studies? First, the identification of a given pattern of brain activation as reflecting, say, semantic processing was based on numerous studies using various different tasks. As a result, it solves the problem of paradigm specificity. Second, it is much more realistic to infer any given cognitive process from a pattern or network of brain activation than from activation of a single small brain region. Third, this approach "enables broad reverse inferences, that is, concluding on mental processes given the observed brain activity" (Menuet et al., 2022, p. 1). That means we could identify the processes used in performing a new cognitive task by assessing the overall pattern of brain activation. Fourth, the approach taken by Menuet et al. represents clear progress in moving towards the goal of understanding the functional organisation of the brain.

Scientific reporting

Scientific analysis of data and reporting of research are frequently biased. This often occurs because of confirmation and other biases possessed by the experimenter. In addition, as Bishop (2020, p. 2) pointed out, "Many editors place emphasis on reporting results in a way that 'tells a good story'".

Psychologists frequently exaggerate the extent to which their findings generalise (e.g., assuming that findings are applicable to other cultures at other times; see Chapter 1). DeJesus et al. (2019) analysed over 1,000 scientific articles for the use of generic statements (i.e., "broad claims about a category as a whole, as distinct from individuals, without reference to frequencies, probabilities, or statistical distributions", p. 18371). Such statements were used to describe findings in 89% of the articles.

The aforementioned findings are surprising because nearly all researchers know the importance of avoiding unwarranted overgeneralisations of their experimental findings. Peters et al. (2022) argued that most researchers exhibit generalisation bias meaning they 'automatically' (i.e., without thinking) tend to overgeneralise their research results. Generalisation bias occurs because our cognitive system often displays "a strong bias to default to the simplest cognitive mechanism" (Stanovich, 2009, p. 64) because of our limited processing resources.

Here is an example of generalisation bias. It is often claimed that "Healthy nutrition increases people's life expectancy" (Peters et al., p. 4). It would be more accurate (but considerably more cognitively demanding) to say instead something like: "Healthy nutrition increases people's life expectancy if they do not have an intolerance for certain foods important to a healthy diet, if they do not face other biological or mental constraints, [and] if they do not eat too much healthy food".

Another key reason why we need to be careful about concluding that healthy nutrition directly increases life expectancy is that the evidence is correlational. Individuals with healthier nutrition have higher socio-economic status on average than those with less healthy nutrition (Pechey & Monsivais, 2016), and so the correlation between nutrition and life expectancy reflects in part the greater financial resources and access to high-quality health care available to those of high socio-economic status.

What can be done?

It is important to raise awareness of the numerous ways researchers overgeneralise their findings given the largely 'automatic' nature of most overgeneralisations and because findings claimed to be generalisable are more likely to be published. Peters et al. (2022) focussed on various ways this can best be achieved. First, journals should require researchers to focus on the generalisability of their findings. Simons et al. (2017) argued that researchers should include "constraints on generality" statements in their articles. These statements should justify researchers' claims to generalisability beyond the specific samples of individuals, situations and stimuli used in the study. This statement should conclude as follows: "We have no reason to believe that the results depend on other characteristics of the participants, materials, or context" (pp. 1125–1126).

Second, researchers should provide sufficient information about their choice of participants, stimuli and experimental design so readers can evaluate for themselves the generalisability of the findings. The information currently provided in most journal articles is deficient in this regard.

More generally, what should be done when reporting scientific research in psychology (or any other science) was encapsulated by the famous physicist Richard Feynman (1985):

> If you're doing an experiment, you should report everything that you think might make it invalid – not only what you think is right about it: other causes that could possibly explain your results . . . if you make a theory . . . then you must also put down all the facts that disagree with it.
>
> (p. 341)

Alas, psychological researchers often fall well short of Feynman's (1985) recommendations. Of special concern, the accumulation of different cognitive biases can lead to seriously misleading conclusions. Consider de Vries et al.'s (2018) analysis of 105 clinical trials on the efficacy of anti-depressants in treating depression, only 50% of which obtained significantly positive outcomes. As a result of publication bias, however, 68% of the published trials had positive outcomes. As a result of outcome reporting bias, 81% of the published trials were reported as having had positive outcomes (e.g., by omitting negative outcomes). As a result of spin (e.g., claiming that non-significant findings were actually significant), 94% of the published trials appeared to have positive outcomes. From the perspective of those reading the published articles, the apparent success rate of anti-depressant trials was 94% rather than the 'true' figure of 50%!

Turner et al. (2022) compared trials of relatively recent anti-depressant drugs against those reported by de Vries et al. (2018). There was significantly less evidence of bias in the more recent trials compared to the older ones, although some bias still remained.

One promising development is that psychology journals increasingly require researchers to include a section devoted to limitations in the research that has been reported. The essence of what is required was described by Clarke et al. (2024) as the 'steel-person principle': "Focus on your most important limitations . . . highlight your biggest and worst limitations. Consider which limitations an exceptional critic would say are the most damning" (p. 3).

Psychology as a cumulative science

The greatest problem facing psychology is the typically fragmentary and narrow nature of psychological experiments. Most experiments test a few hypotheses following from a given theoretical position. As a result, they provide limited information about the impact of a small number of independent variables relevant to the hypotheses on a small number of dependent variables (i.e., behavioural outcomes) using participants selected from a limited population. Unsurprisingly, they cannot be generalised to other situations and populations.

The previous limitations present obstacles to achieving the goal of making psychology a *cumulative science* where findings from numerous experiments are integrated. Another obstacle is the 'toothbrush problem': "Psychologists treat other peoples' theories like toothbrushes – no self-respecting person wants to use anyone else's" (Mischel, 2008). Related to this is the 'silo problem': the tendency for different research teams studying the same topic to ignore the efforts of other research groups.

Yaron et al. (2022) provided clear-cut evidence of the silo problem (and experimenter bias). They analysed hundreds of studies focusing on how consciousness arises from neural activity. There are three main theories in this area (global neuronal workspace; integrated information theory; and recurrent processing theory) differing in the processes and brain areas allegedly involved in consciousness. The researchers' theoretical preference could be predicted 80% of the time solely from the experimental procedures and paradigms they used. This strongly implies that researchers generally use experimental paradigms most likely to support their preferred theory. This interpretation is strengthened by the additional finding that the obtained findings supported the researchers' preferred theory 85% of the time. There was also a general neglect of alternative theories: only 7% of researchers tested the predictions of more than one theory.

What can be done?

The simplest way to avoid the problems associated with narrow and limited research is to carry out larger and more *comprehensive* studies. For example, Spiers et al. (2023) carried out one of the largest studies ever in psychology. They assessed the navigation ability of 3.9 million individuals worldwide who played a video game called *Sea Hero Quest*. Performance on this game predicts real-world navigation performance well, and so it has ecological validity. Across all 63 countries, there was a steady decline in navigation ability from the early 20s onwards. There was a male advantage on the game in all countries, but this advantage was much less in countries with low levels of gender inequality. In sum, the comprehensive nature of this study means that strong generalisations can be made about navigation ability worldwide.

There are other advantages to more comprehensive research. Most research in cognitive psychology involves exploring the effects of two or more variables on performance of a given task. For example, consider two tasks assumed to assess cognitive control (the ability to direct one's attention and actions): the Stroop task and the Simon task. In a study by Erb et al. (2023), the Stroop task consisted of presenting the word 'orange' or 'white' in an orange or white text. Participants responded rapidly on the basis of text colour. There was a congruency effect: speed and accuracy were greater when the word and text colour were the same than when they were different.

The Simon task involved presenting a left- or right-facing arrow at the left or right side of the visual display, with participants responding as rapidly as possible on the basis of arrow direction. There was a congruency effect: speed and accuracy were greater when the arrow direction and location of the arrow were the same than when they were different.

It has typically been assumed that smaller congruency effects on each task indicate superior cognitive control. If that assumption is correct, we would predict that individuals exhibiting good cognitive control on one task should tend to have good cognitive control on the other one. In fact, Erb et al. (2023) discovered there was *no correlation* between congruency effects on the two tasks. This is another example of the jingle fallacy (the same term being used to describe two different things). However, the main take-home message is that it required comprehensive research to discover that the Stroop and Simon tasks do not assess the same underlying cognitive processes.

Megastudies

Another way to escape the limitations of most experimental research is by conducting a megastudy where the effects of numerous independent variables on a given behavioural outcome are assessed. The selection of which independent variables to include in a given megastudy is typically based on suggestions proposed by several research teams. This produces a much broader and more comprehensive approach than is found in traditional research.

Milkman et al. (2022) carried out a megastudy on nearly 700,000 individuals in which they compared the effectiveness of different text nudges designed to increase flu vaccination. A total of 28 research teams suggested text nudges, 22 of which were used in the study. All were effective, but the most effective (increasing flu vaccination by 10%) emphasised that the flu vaccination was "waiting for you". Its effectiveness depended in part on creating a sense of exclusivity.

Milkman et al. (2021) carried out a similar megastudy on the effects of various interventions on increasing weekly gym visits by members of an American fitness chain. Thirty scientists working in small teams generated 54 interventions based on diverse theoretical perspectives. Almost half the interventions significantly increased gym visits, with the most effective intervention (offering small rewards for returning to the gym after a missed workout) increasing gym visits by 27%.

In sum, megastudies offer several advantages (Duckworth & Milkman, 2022). First, they allow several different hypotheses to be tested simultaneously rather than sequentially. Second, they eliminate the 'silo problem' by having researchers with different theoretical perspectives contributing to the experimental design. Third, the fact that all the hypotheses are tested on the same population of participants makes it easier to interpret the findings than when the same hypotheses are tested on different populations in different studies.

Adversarial collaboration

Most researchers advocate a particular theory and then design experiments to support it. As we saw in Yaron et al's. (2022) research, this means other theories are largely ignored. More generally, it has proved difficult to find

> means of constraining researchers' flexibility to cherry-pick how they define their variables and design their empirical tests that make it easier for scholars to support their preferred hypotheses. This freedom . . . enables contradictory conclusions to persist for decades.
>
> (Clark et al., 2022, p. 1)

As the Nobel Laureate Max Planck (1950) pointed out: "A new scientific truth does not triumph by convincing its opponents and making them see the light, but rather because its opponents eventually die" (Planck, p. 33). This is typically a very slow and unsatisfactory way of achieving scientific progress.

How can we reduce the previous obstacles to the development of psychology as a cumulative science? Adversarial collaboration provides an especially promising answer. It involves two or more research groups committed to different theoretical perspectives with respect to a given topic collaborating on devising a common experimental approach, with each research group indicating in advance the predictions following from their preferred theoretical stance. Adversarial collaboration produces broader and more comprehensive research than is the case when advocates of any given theory focus primarily on accumulating narrowly base evidence to support that theory.

We can exemplify the potential advantages of adversarial collaboration by returning to research on major theories of the neural correlates of consciousness. CogitateConsortium (2023) carried out an adversarial collaboration using the most sophisticated techniques currently available to test the adequacy of the global neuronal workspace and integrated information theories.

The findings confirmed the importance to conscious experience of the prefrontal cortex (as claimed by global neuronal workspace theory) and of the posterior cerebral cortex (as claimed by integrated information theory). However, the overall pattern of findings on the content and duration of visual experience was more complex than assumed by either theory. This occurred in part because the two theories have somewhat different goals: integrated information theory focuses on identifying the brain regions sufficient for consciousness whereas global neuronal workspace theory focuses more on the brain regions typically associated with consciousness.

Another example of adversarial collaboration concerns working memory (a limited-capacity system used in the processing and brief holding of information). There is consensus that working memory is of great importance in the performance of numerous cognitive tasks, but there is much divergence in terms of theorising about it. There are currently at least 13 different theoretical perspectives on working memory (Logie et al., 2021b). This diversity led to an adversarial collaboration in which 15 experiments were carried out to test the conflicting predictions of three of the main theories (Logie, 2023).

One reason why the three theories initially made different predictions was that their goals were somewhat different. For example, they differed in terms of whether the central focus was on the overall capacity of working memory or on how that capacity was achieved. By analogy, the speed with which an athlete can run 100 m assesses their overall health and fitness. However, that tells us nothing about the specific processes involving the heart, lungs, muscles and so on that underlie that performance.

All three theories accounted well for only some findings in each experiment. A consequence of the adversarial collaboration was that the three theories moved closer to each other and Logie et al. (2021a) proposed an integrated theory combining concepts from all three theories. This is a clear advance over having 13 separate theories of working memory.

What are the advantages of adversarial collaboration? First, it disrupts the common pattern of several theories in a given domain of research coexisting in near isolation from each other. Adversarial collaboration typically speeds up the process of bad ideas being replaced by better ones. Second, as Clark et al. (2022, p. 7) pointed out, "By holding one another to the same set of high standards, adversaries will design tests that are fairer, more rigorous, and better able to adjudicate between the competing hypotheses".

Third, the scope of experimentation becomes broader. Researcher A may typically focus on independent variables x, y and z in their experimental tests of their preferred theory whereas researcher B may focus on independent variables a, b and c. Adversarial collaboration might well involve experiments in which all six independent variables are included. Researchers' tendency to over-generalise the applicability of their theories is likely to be revealed by such collaborative research.

In view of the various strengths of adversarial collaboration, it has not as yet been used extensively. When Ceci et al (2024) asked 61 psychologists to identify important advances in psychology over recent decades, only two of them nominated adversarial collaboration. One obstacle to the greater use of adversarial collaboration is the expensive nature of most such collaborations. Another obstacle is the reluctance of many researchers to accept the challenge of working with other researchers having very different theoretical perspectives. However, the potential advantages of adversarial collaboration are sufficiently great that these obstacles must be overcome.

Summary

We can draw an analogy between research in psychology and an enormous jigsaw puzzle. Each research study forms one very small piece of the entire jigsaw and a key goal is to work out how all the pieces fit together to complete the puzzle and make psychology a genuinely cumulative science. It is obvious that psychology has so far failed to get anywhere close to achieving that goal. One reason is that no one has even a vague idea of what the finished jigsaw puzzle might look like (and it will probably turn out to be much more complex than the most difficult jigsaw puzzle). Another reason is that most psychologists have made only modest efforts to integrate their research findings with the previous research literature.

Recently, real progress has been made in developing strategies for making psychology a cumulative science rather than an enormous collection of disjointed findings. First, meta-analysis effectively combines the findings from a large number of studies to provide an integrated account provided that strenuous efforts are made to eliminate experimenter bias. Meta-analysis has been especially successful with identifying the brain networks associated with numerous cognitive processes (Menuet et al., 2022).

Second, we need to avoid the jingle-jangle fallacies. If studies are considered in isolation, it is easy to conclude mistakenly that studies using the same word to describe a variable are investigating the same concept when they aren't (jingle fallacy). It is also easy to conclude mistakenly that studies using different words to describe a variable are investigating different concepts when they aren't (jangle fallacy). The solution is to carry out comprehensive studies explicitly designed to decide whether these fallacies are present (Erb et al.'s, 2023, study on cognitive control).

Third, we need to avoid the toothbrush problem where numerous theories in any given research area proceed in splendid isolation from each other. The most promising way of addressing this problem is adversarial collaboration. We have seen examples of how this can produce a more integrative theoretical approach in which competing theories move closer to each other. So far adversarial collaborations have been relatively few in number for various reasons (e.g., the need for researchers to sacrifice some academic freedom; the high costs involved). It must be hoped that the number of adversarial collaborations will increase dramatically in future because the toothbrush problem is a major obstacle to psychology becoming a more cumulative science.

Conclusions

Psychologists (and non-psychologists) trying to enhance their understanding of human cognition and behaviour are confronted by many obstacles. As discussed in Chapter 10, there are several reasons why much of what we read or hear about psychology is seriously distorted. The media distort psychological findings to entertain the public, commercial interests do so to increase their profits, researchers do so to protect and defend their own preferred theories and views on psychology and textbook writers do so to provide simplistic folklore accounts of psychological research.

Sometimes the reasons for distorted interpretations of psychological research lie within ourselves. We choose to believe myths in psychology because they confirm what we would like to believe is the case or what appears to be consistent with our general knowledge and/or personal experience. This is unsurprising given that we live in an era of fake news where it is becoming increasingly difficult to distinguish between what is actually the case and what we are mistakenly told is the case.

How can we prevent ourselves from falling into the trap of believing numerous mythical facts about psychology? As discussed in Chapter 10, the single most important answer is that we should be properly sceptical of psychological findings rather than simply accepting them at face value. For example, we should ask ourselves whether a given psychological finding is invariably the case or whether there are situations where it does not apply. It can be very satisfying to find good reasons for disbelieving conventional wisdom.

Finally, the key take-home message of this book was well expressed by Li and Hartshorne (2024, p. 1): "Don't let perfect be the enemy of better". There is no such thing as 'perfect science' and this is especially the case in psychology because of its unique complexities as a science. However, that doesn't mean that psychologists should be pessimistic. As we have seen, there are numerous ways in which psychologists are increasingly developing better theories and carrying out better research. The top of the mountain may be frustratingly far away, but it is a considerable achievement for psychologists to keep moving slowly but surely upwards towards the summit.

References

Aaronson, S. (2014). My conversation with Eugene Goostman, the chatbot that's all over the news for allegedly passing the Turing test. *Shtetl-Optimised: The Blog of Scott Anderson*. 19th June.

Adair, J. (1972). Demand characteristics or conformity? Suspiciousness of deception and experimenter bias in conformity research. *Canadian Journal of Behavioral Science, 4*, 238–248.

Adams, N.B. (2004). Digital intelligence fostered by technology. *Journal of Technological Studies, 30*, 93–97.

Adiwardana, D., Luong, M.T., So, D.R., Hall, J., Fiedel, N., Kulshreshtha, Y.A., et al. (2020). Towards a human-like open-domain chatbot. *arXiv preprint* arXiv:2001.09977.

Adorno, T.W., Frenkel-Brunswik, E., Levinson, D.J., & Sanford, R.N. (1950). *The authoritarian personality*. New York: John Wiley & Sons.

Ahbel-Rappe, K. (2006). "I no longer believe": Did Freud abandon the seduction theory? *Journal of the American Psychoanalytic Association, 54*, 171–199.

Ahonen, L., Loeber, R., & Brent, D.A. (2019). The association between serious mental health problems and violence: Some common assumptions and misconceptions. *Trauma, Violence, & Abuse, 20*, 613–625.

Airlie, M., Robertson, J., Krosch, M.N., & Brooks, E. (2021). Contemporary issues in forensic science – worldwide survey results. *Forensic Science International, 320*, 110704.

Akhtar, S., Justice, L.V., Knott, L., Kibowski, F., & Conway, M.A. (2018). The 'common sense' memory system and its implications. *International Journal of Evidence & Proof, 22*, 289–304.

Albarracin, D., & Shavitt, S. (2018). Attitudes and attitude change. *Annual Review of Psychology, 69*, 299–327.

Alison, L.J., Smith, M.D., Eastman, O., & Rainbow, L. (2003a). Toulmin's philosophy of argument and its relevance to offender profiling. *Psychology, Crime and Law, 9*, 173–183.

Alison, L.J., Smith, M.D., & Morgan, K. (2003b). Interpreting the accuracy of offender profiles. *Psychology, Crime and Law, 9*, 185–195.

Alkerwi, A., Vernie, R.C., Sauvageot, N., Crichton, G.E., & Elias, M.F. (2015). Demographic and socioeconomic disparity in nutrition: Application of a novel correlated component regression approach. *BMJ Open, 5*, e006814.

Almeida, L.S., Prieto, M D., Ferreira, A.I., Bermejo, M.R., Ferrando, M., & Ferrándiz, C. (2010). Intelligence assessment: Gardner multiple intelligence theory as an alternative. *Learning and Individual Differences, 20*, 225–230.

Altemeyer, B. (1981). *Right-wing authoritarianism*. Winnipeg: University of Ottawa.

Altemeyer, B. (1988). *Enemies of freedom*. San Francisco: Jossey-Bass Publishers.

Altman, W.S., Beers, M.J., Hammer, E.Y., Hardin, E.E., & Troisi, J.D. (2021). Reimagining how we teach introductory psychology: Support for instructors adopting the recommendations of the APA introductory psychology initiative. *Scholarship of Teaching and Learning in Psychology, 7*, 181–191.

Alvarez, C.X., & Brown, S.W. (2002). What people believe about memory despite the research evidence. *The General Psychologist, 37*, 1–6.

Alvarez-Vargas, D., Braithwaite, D., Lortie-Forgas, H., Moore, M., Wan, S.R., et al. (2023). Hedges, mottes, and baileys: Causally ambiguous statistical language can increase perceived study quality and policy relevance. *PLoS One, 18*, e0286403.

Aly, M., & Ranganath, C. (2018). Perspectives on the hippocampus and memory. *Neuroscience Letters, 680*, 1–3.

Amankwaa, A.O., & McCartney, C. (2021). The effectiveness of the current use of forensic DNA in criminal investigations in England and Wales. *Wiley Interdisciplinary Reviews: Forensic Science, 3*(6).

American Psychiatric Association. (1994). *Diagnostic and statistical manual of mental disorders* (4th ed.). Washington, DC: American Psychiatric Association.

American Psychiatric Association. (2013). *Diagnostic and statistical manual of mental disorders* (5th ed). Arlington, VA: American Psychiatric Association.

An, D., & Carr, M. (2017). Learning styles theory fails to explain learning and achievement: Recommendations for alternative approaches. *Personality and Individual Differences, 116*, 410–416.

Andersen, A.M., & Bienvenu, O.J. (2011). Personality and psychopathology. *International Review of Psychiatry, 23*, 234–247.

Anglim, J., Lievens, F., Everton, L., Grant, S.L., & Marty, A. (2018). HEXACO personality predicts counterproductive work behaviour and organisational citizenship behaviour in low-stakes and job applicant contexts. *Journal of Research in Personality, 77*, 11–20.

Areh, I., Verkampt, F., & Allan, A. (2022). Critical review of the use of the Rorschach in European courts. *Psychiatry, Psychology and Law, 29*, 183–205.

Arkoudas, K. (2023). GPT-4 can't reason. *arXiv preprint* arXiv:2308.03762v2 [cs.CL].

Arneson, R. (2013). Egalitarianism. In E.N. Zalta (Ed.), *The Stanford encyclopedia of philosophy* (Summer 2013 ed.). https://plato.stanford.edu/archives/sum2013/entries/egalitarianism/.

Arnett, J. (2008). The neglected 95%: Why American psychology needs to become less American. *American Psychologist, 63*, 602–614.

Asch, S.E. (1951). Effects of group pressure on the modification and distortion of judgements. In H. Guetzkow (Ed.), *Groups, leadership and men*. Pittsburgh, PA: Carnegie.

Asch, S.E. (1956). Studies of independence and conformity: A minority of one against a unanimous majority. *Psychological Monographs, 70*(416).

Asebedo, S.D., Quadria, T.H., Chen, Y., & Montenegro-Montenegro, E. (2022). Individual differences in personality and positive emotion for wealth creation. *Personality and Individual Differences, 199*, 111854.

Ashton, S., Denisova, K., Hurlbert, A., Olkkoven, M., Pierce, B., Rudd, M., et al. (2020). Exploring the determinants of colour perception using #Thedress and its variants: The role of spatio-chromatic context, chromatic illumination, and material–light Interaction. *Perception, 49*, 1235–1251.

Atkinson, R.C., & Shiffrin, R.M. (1968). Human memory: A proposed system and its control processes. In K.W. Spence & J.T. Spence (Eds.), *The psychology of learning and motivation* (Vol. 2). London: Academic Press.

Au, J., Sheehan, E., Tsai, N., Duncan, G.J., Buschkuehl, M., & Jaeggi, S.M. (2015). Improving fluid intelligence with training on working memory: A meta-analysis. *Psychonomic Bulletin and Review, 22*, 366–377.

Avci, G., Sheppard, D.P., Tierney, S.M., Kordovski, V.M., Sullivan, K.L., & Woods, S.P. (2018). A systematic review of prospective memory in HIV disease: From the laboratory to daily life. *The Clinical Neuropsychologist, 32,* 858–890.

Baddeley, A.D., & Hitch, G.J. (1974). Working memory. In G.H. Bower (Ed.), *Recent advances in learning and motivation* (Vol. 8, pp. 47–89). New York: Academic Press.

Baker, M. (2016). Is there a reproducibility crisis? *Nature, 533,* 452–454.

Bandura, A. (1977). *Social learning theory.* Englewood Cliffs, NJ: Prentice Hall.

Bannard, C., Lieven, E., & Tomasello, M. (2009). Modelling children's early grammatical knowledge. *Proceedings of the National Academy of Sciences of the United States of America, 106,* 17284–17289.

Bannert, M.M., & Bartels, A. (2017). Invariance of surface colour representations across illuminant changes in the human cortex. *NeuroImage, 158,* 356–370.

Bargh, R.A., & Ransberger, V.M. (2016). Awareness of the prime versus awareness of its influence: Implications for the real-world scope of unconscious higher mental processes. *Current Opinion in Psychology, 12,* 49–52.

Barker, H., Munro, J., Orlov, N., Morgenroth, E., Moser, J., Eysenck, M.W., et al. (2018). Worry is associated with inefficient functional activity and connectivity in prefrontal and cingulate cortices during emotional interference. *Brain & Behavior, 8,* e01137.

Barlow, D.H., Farchione, T.J., Bullis, J.R., Gallagher, M.W., Murray-Latin, H., Sauer-Zavala, S., et al. (2017). The unified protocol for transdiagnostic treatment of emotional disorders compared with diagnosis-specific protocols for anxiety disorders: A randomised clinical trial. *JAMA Psychiatry, 74,* 875–884.

Baron, R.A., & Ransberger, V.M. (1978). Ambient temperature and the occurrence of collective violence: The "long, hot summer" revisited. *Journal of Personality and Social Psychology, 36,* 351–360.

Barrett, D. (2006). Hypnosis in film and television. *American Journal of Clinical Hypnosis, 49,* 13–30.

Barrett, L.F., Adolphs, R., Marsella, S., Martinez, A.M., & Pollakm, S.D. (2019). Emotional expressions reconsidered: Challenges to inferring emotion from human facial movements. *Psychological Science in the Public Interest, 20,* 1–68.

Bartels, J.M. (2015). Genetics of well-being and its components satisfaction with life, happiness, and quality of life: A review and meta-analysis of heritability studies. *Behavior Genetics, 45,* 137–156.

Bartels, J.M. (2023a). Indoctrination in introduction to psychology. *Psychology Learning & Teaching, 22,* 226–236.

Bartels, J.M. (2023b). Rebuttal to comments of target article: Introductory psychology: Embracing the complexities and controversies. *Psychology Learning & Teaching, 22,* 287–295.

Bartels, J.M., & Peters, D. (2017). Coverage of Rosenhan's "on being sane in insane places" in abnormal psychology textbooks. *Teaching of Psychology, 44,* 169–173.

Bartels, J.M., & Schoenrade, P. (2021). The implicit association test in introductory psychology textbooks: Blind spot for controversy. *Psychology Learning and Teaching, 21,* 113–125.

Barth, M.R., Brand, B.L., & Shae, M. (2023). Distinguishing clinical and simulated dissociative identity disorder using the Miller forensic assessment of symptoms test. *Psychological Trauma: Theory, Research, Practice, and Policy, 15,* 846–852.

Bartlett, F.C. (1932). *Remembering.* Cambridge: Cambridge University Press.

Bartolomeo, P., Bachoud-Levi, A.C., & Denes, G. (1997). Preserved imagery for colours in a patient with cerebral achromatopsia. *Cortex, 33,* 369–378.

Basten, U., Stelzel, C., & Fiebach, C.J. (2012). Trait anxiety and the neural efficiency of manipulation in working memory. *Cognitive, Affective, & Behavioral Neuroscience, 5,* 144–155.

Basterfield, C., Lilienfeld, S.O., Cautin, R.L., & Jordan, D. (2023). Mental illness misconceptions among undergraduates: Prevalence, correlates, and instructional implications. *Scholarship of Teaching and Learning in Psychology, 9,* 115–132.

Bateman, A.L., & Salfati, C.G. (2007). An examination of behavioural consistency using individual behaviours or groups of behaviours in serial homicide. *Behavioral Sciences & the Law, 25,* 527–544.

Baumeister, R.F., Ainsworth, S.E., & Vohs, K.D. (2016). Are groups more or less than the sum of their members? The moderating role of individual identification. *Behavioral and Brain Sciences, 39,* e161.

Baumeister, R.F., Campbell, J.D., Krueger, J.I., & Vohs, K.D. (2003). Does high self-esteem cause better performance, interpersonal success, happiness, or healthier lifestyles? *Psychological Science in the Public Interest, 4,* 1–44.

Baumeister, R.F., & Vohs, K.D. (2018). Revisiting our reappraisal of the (surprisingly few) benefits of high self-esteem. *Perspectives on Psychological Science, 13,* 137–140.

Bavin, E.L., Prior, M., Reilly, S., Bretherton, L., Williams, J, Eadie, P., et al. (2008). The early language in Victoria study: Predicting vocabulary at age one and two years from gesture and object use. *Journal of Child Language, 35,* 687–701.

Baxendale, S. (2004). Memories aren't made of this: Amnesia at the movies. *British Medical Journal, 329,* 1480–1483.

Bayley, P.J., Hopkins, R.O., & Squire, L.R. (2006). The fate of old memories after medial temporal lobe damage. *Journal of Neuroscience, 26,* 13311–13317.

Beaman, A.L., Barnes, P.J., Klentz, B., & McQuirk, B. (1978). Increasing helping rates. *Psychology Bulletin, 4,* 406–411.

Beaty, R.E., Thakral, P.P., Madore, K.P., Benedek, M., & Schacter, D.L. (2018). Core network contributions to remembering the past, imagining the future, and thinking creatively. *Cognitive Neuroscience, 30,* 1939–1951.

Beck, A.T., & Dozois, D.J.A. (2011). Cognitive therapy: Current status and future directions. *Annual Reviews of Medicine, 62,* 397–409.

Beck, E.D., & Jackson, J.J. (2022). A mega-analysis of personality prediction: Robustness and boundary conditions. *Journal of Personality and Social Psychology, 122,* 523–553.

Beck, M.R., Levin, D.T., & Angelone, B. (2007). Change blindness blindness: Beliefs about the roles of intention and scene complexity in change detection. *Consciousness and Cognition, 16,* 131–151.

Benjamin, L.T., Cavell, A., & Shallenberger, W.R. (1984). Staying with initial answers on objective tests: Is it a myth? *Teaching of Psychology, 11,* 133–141.

Benoit, R.G., & Schacter, D. (2015). Specifying the core network supporting episodic simulations and episodic memory by activation likelihood estimation. *Neuropsychologia, 75,* 450–457.

Ben-Shakhar, G. (2012). Current research and potential applications of the concealed information test: An overview. *Frontiers in Psychology, 3,* 342.

Bensley, D.A. (2023). Critical thinking, intelligence, and unsubstantiated beliefs: An integrative review. *Journal of Intelligence, 11,* 207.

Bensley, D.A., & Lilienfeld, S.O. (2015). What is a psychological misconception? Moving towards an empirical answer. *Teaching of Psychology, 42,* 282–292.

Bensley, D.A., Lilienfeld, S.O., Rowan, K.A., Masciocchi, C.M., & Grain, F. (2020). The generality of belief in unsubstantiated claims. *Applied Cognitive Psychology, 34,* 16–28.

Bensley, D.A., Masciocchi, C.M., Krystal, A., & Rowan, K.A. (2021). A comprehensive assessment of explicit critical thinking instruction on recognition of thinking errors and psychological misconceptions. *Scholarship of Teaching and Learning in Psychology, 7,* 107–122.

Bensley, D.A., Watkins, C., Lilienfeld, S.O., Masciocchi, C., Murtaggh, M.P., & Rowan, K. (2022). Scepticism, cynicism, and cognitive style predictors of the generality of unsubstantiated belief. *Applied Cognitive Psychology, 36*, 83–99.

Berezow, A.B. (2012). Why psychology isn't science. *Los Angeles Times.* 13th July. https://www.latimes.com/opinion/la-xpm-2012-jul-13-la-ol-blowbackpscyholog y-science-20120713-story.html.

Berezow, A.B. (2015). *Why psychology and statistics are not science.* RealClearScience. 2nd November.

Berkowitz, L. (1989). Frustration-aggression hypothesis: Examination and reformulation. *Psychological Bulletin, 106*, 59–73.

Berkowitz, S.R., Garrett, B.L., Fenn, L.M., & Loftus, E.F. (2022). Convicting with confidence? Why we should not over-rely on eyewitness confidence. *Memory, 30*, 10–15.

Bernstein, D.A. (2023). The context of indoctrination in introductory psychology. *Psychology Learning & Teaching, 22*, 263–268.

Bernstein, D.A., Cameron, E.L., Khanna, M.M., McGee, J., Smith, E.I., Bihun, J.T., et al. (2023). Misconceptions about psychology after taking introductory psychology. *Scholarship of Teaching and Learning in Psychology.* https://doi.org/10.1037/ stl0000374.

Bibi, S., Saqlain, S., & Mussawar, B. (2016). Relationship between emotional intelligence and self-esteem among Pakistani university students. *Journal of Psychology and Psychotherapy, 6*, 279.

Bichat, X. (1805). *Recherches Physiologiques sur la Vie et la Mort* [Physiological research concerning life and death] (3rd ed.). Paris: Brosson.

Binet, A., & Simon, T. (1905). Méthodes nouvelles pour le diagnostic du niveau intellectuel des anormaux. *Année psychologique, 11*, 191–244.

Bishop, D.V.M. (2020). The psychology of experimental psychologists: Overcoming cognitive constraints to improve research: The 47th Sir Frederic Bartlett Lecture. *Quarterly Journal of Experimental Psychology, 73*, 1–19.

Bisk, Y., Holtzman, A., Thomason, J., Andreas, J., Bengio, Y., Joyce Chai, J., et al. (2020). Experience grounds language. *arXiv preprint* arXiv:2004.10151.

Blanchette Sarrasin, J., Riopel, M., & Masson, S. (2019). Neuromyths and their origin among teachers in Quebec. *Mind, Brain, and Education, 13*, 100–109.

Blank, H., & Launay, C. (2014). How to protect eyewitness memory against the misinformation effect: A meta-analysis of post-warning studies. *Journal of Applied Research in Memory and Cognition, 3*, 77–88.

Bleske-Rechek, A., Morrison, K.M., & Heidtke, L.D. (2015). Causal inference from descriptions of experimental and non-experimental research: Public understanding of correlation-versus-causation. *Journal of General Psychology, 142*, 48–70.

Bleuler, E. (1911/1950). *Dementia Praecox oder Gruppe der Schizophrenien.* Leipzig, Germany: Deuticke [translated by J. Zinkin as *Dementia Praecox or the group of schizophrenias.* New York, NY: International Universities Press].

Block, N. (2011). Perceptual consciousness overflows cognitive access. *Trends in Cognitive Sciences, 15*, 67–75.

Blom, S.S.A.H., Gillebaart, M., De Boer, F., van der Laan, N., & de Ridder, D.T.D. (2021). Under pressure: Nudging increases healthy food choice in a virtual reality supermarket, irrespective of system 1 reasoning. *Appetite, 160*, 105116.

Boardman, J.D., Alexander, K.B., & Stallings, M.C. (2011). Stressful life events and depression among adolescent twin pairs. *Biodemography and Social Biology, 57*, 53–66.

Bohner, G., & Dickel, N. (2011). Attitudes and attitude change. *Annual Review of Psychology, 62*, 391–417.

Booch, G., Fabiano, F., Horesh, L., Kate, L., Lencher, J., Linck, N., et al. (2021). Thinking fast and slow in AI. *Proceedings of the AAAI Conference on Artificial Intelligence, 35*, 15042–15046.

Boomsma, D.I., Willemsen, G., Dolan, C.V., Hawkley, L.C., & Cacioppo, J.T. (2005). Genetic and environmental contributions to loneliness in adults: The Netherlands twin register study. *Behavior Genetics, 35*, 745–752.

Boon, S., Steele, K., & Van der Hart, O. (2011). *Coping with trauma-related dissociation: Skills training for patients and therapists*. New York, NY: Norton.

Boratko, M., Li, X.L., O'Gorman, T., Das, R., Le, D., & McCallum, A. (2020). ProtoQA: A question answering dataset for prototypical common-sense reasoning. *arXiv preprint* arXiv:2005.00771v3.

Borges, J.L. (1946/1999). On exactitude in science. In A. Hurley (Trans.), *Collected fictions* (p. 35). New York: Penguin.

Born, R.T., & Bencomo, G.M. (2021). Illusions, delusions, and your backwards Bayesian brain: A biased visual perspective. *Brain, Behavior and Evolution, 95*, 272–285.

Bosten, J.M. (2022). Do you see what I see? Diversity in human colour perception. *Annual Review of Vision Science, 8*, 101–133.

Bouchard, T.J., Lykken, D.T., McGuem, M., Segal, N.L., & Tellegen, A. (1990). Sources of human psychology differences – the Minnesota study of twins reared apart. *Science, 250*, 223–228.

Bowen, H.J., Kark, S.M., & Kensinger, E.A. (2018). Never forget: Negative emotional valence enhances recapitulation. *Psychonomic Bulletin & Review, 25*, 870–981.

Bower, G.H., Black, J.B., & Turner, T.J. (1979). Scripts in memory for text. *Cognitive Psychology, 11*(2), 177–220.

Bowers, K.S. (1973). Situationism in psychology: An analysis and a critique. *Psychological Review, 80*, 307–336.

Bradley, F.H. (1887). Why do we remember forwards and not backwards? *Mind, 12*, 579–582.

Braffman, W., & Kirsch, I. (1999). Imaginative suggestibility and hypnotisability: An empirical analysis. *Journal of Personality and Social Psychology, 77*, 578–587.

Branden, N. (1994). *The six pillars of self-esteem*. New York: Bantam.

Brewer, W.F., & Treyens, J.C. (1981). Role of schemata in memory for places. *Cognitive Psychology, 13*, 207–230.

Brewin, C.R., Li, H.Y., Ntarantana, V., Unsworth, C., & McNeilis, J. (2019). Is the public understanding of memory prone to widespread "myths"? *Journal of Experimental Psychology: General, 148*, 2245–2257.

Brickman, P., & Campbell, D.T. (1971). Hedonic relativism and planning the good society. In M.H. Appley (Ed.), *Adaptation level theory: A symposium* (pp. 287–302). New York: Academic Press.

Brickman, P., Coates, D., & Janoff-Bulman, R. (1978). Lottery winners and accident victims: Is happiness relative? *Journal of Personality and Social Psychology, 36*, 917–927.

Briñol, P., & Petty, R.E. (2019). The impact of individual differences on attitudes and attitude change. In D. Albarracín & B.T. Johnson (Eds.), *Handbook of attitudes* (2nd ed., Vol. 1, pp. 520–556). New York: Routledge.

Britt, T.W., & Garrity, M.J. (2006). Attributions and personality as predictors of the road rage response. *British Journal of Social Psychology, 45*, 127–147.

Brizidine, L. (2006). *The female brain*. New York: Harmony.

Brown, A.S., Caderao, K.C., Fields, L.M., & Marsh, E.J. (2015). Borrowing personal memories. *Applied Cognitive Psychology, 29*, 471–477.

Brown, G.W., & Harris, T.O. (1978). *Social origins of depression: A study of psychiatric disorder in women*. London: Tavistock.

Brown, R. (2008). American and Japanese beliefs about self-esteem. *Asian Journal of Social Psychology, 11,* 293–299.

Brown, R., & Kulik, J. (1977). Flashbulb memories. *Cognition, 5,* 73–99.

Brown, T.B., Mann, B., Ryder, N., Subbiah, M., Kaplan, J., Dhariwal, P., et al. (2020). Language models are few-shot learners. *Advances in Neural Information Processing Systems, 33,* 1877–1901.

Bruce, V., Henderson, Z., Greenwood, K., Hancock, P.J.B., Burton, A.M., & Miller, P. (1999). Verification of face identities from images captured on video. *Journal of Experimental Psychology: Applied, 5,* 339–360.

Buddhaghosa. (1996). *A treasury of Buddhist stories: From the Dhammapada commentary.* Kandy, Sri Lanka: Buddhist Publication Society.

Buecker, S., Maes, M., Denissen, J.J.A., & Luhmann, M. (2020). Loneliness and the big five personality traits: A meta-analysis. *European Journal of Personality, 34,* 8–28.

Bullmore, E., & Sporns, O. (2012). The economy of brain network organisation. *Nature Reviews Neuroscience, 13,* 336–349.

Burgess, J., Snow, J., Buckner, A., Levi, C., & Grewe, J. (2022). *Psychological misconceptions and the Dunning-Kruger effect.* Utah State University. Unpublished manuscript.

Burt, S.A. (2024). The hypotheses put forward in the nurture assumption inspired much needed research regarding the influence of parenting and peers, but were overstated. *Developmental Review, 71,* 101120.

Burt, S.A., Clark, D.A., Gershoff, E.T., Klump, K.L., & Hyde, L.W. (2021). Twin differences in harsh parenting predict youth's antisocial behaviour. *Psychological Science, 32,* 395–409.

Burton, A.M., Kramer, R.S., Ritchie, K.L., & Jenkins, R. (2016). Identity from variation: Representations of faces derived from multiple instances. *Cognitive Science, 40,* 202–223.

Butler, J.M., Kline, M.C., & Coble, M.D. (2018). NIST inter-laboratory studies involving DNA mixtures (MIX05 and MIX13): Variation observed and lessons learned. *Forensic Science International: Genetics, 37,* 81–94.

Cahalan, S. (2019). *The great pretender: The undercover mission that changed our understanding of madness.* New York, NY: Grand Central.

Calbi, M., Heimann, K., Barratt, D., Siri, F., Umilta, M.A., & Gallese, V. (2017). How context influences our perception of emotional faces: A behavioural study on the Kuleshov effect. *Frontiers in Psychology, 8,* 1684.

Campitelli, G., & Gobet, F. (2011). Deliberate practice: Necessary but not sufficient. *Current Directions in Psychological Science, 20,* 280–285.

Carlsmith, J.M., & Anderson, C.A. (1979). Ambient temperature and the occurrence of collective violence – new analysis. *Journal of Personality and Social Psychology, 37,* 337–344.

Carpenter, J., Sherman, M.T., Kievit, R.A., Seth, A.K., Lau, H., & Fleming, S.M. (2019). Domain-general enhancements of metacognitive ability through adaptive training. *Journal of Experimental Psychology: General, 148,* 51–64.

Carroll, J.B. (1993). *Human cognitive abilities: A survey of factor analytic studies.* New York: Cambridge University Press.

Caspi, A., Houts, R.M., Belsky, D.W., Goldman-Mellor, S.J., Harrington, H., Issrael, S., et al. (2014). The p factor: One general psychopathology factor in the structure of psychiatric disorders? *Clinical Psychological Science, 2,* 119–137.

Cavaco, S., Anderson, S.W., Allen, J.S., Castro-Caldas, A., & Damasio, H. (2004). The scope of procedural memory in amnesia. *Brain, 127,* 1853–1867.

Ceci, S.J., Clark, C.J., Jussim, L., & Williams, W.M. (2024). Adversarial collaboration: An undervalued approach in behavioral science. *American Psychologist.* https://doi.org/10.1037/amp0001391.

Ceci, S.J., & Loftus, E.F. (1994). "Memory work": A royal road to false memories? *Applied Cognitive Psychology, 8,* 351–364.

Centers for Disease Control and Prevention. (2018). *Learn about mental health.* https://web.archive.org/web/20180614105506/https://www.cdc.gov/mentalhe alth/learn/.

Chabris, C.F., Lee, J., Cesarini, D., Benjamin, D., & Laibson, D. (2015). The fourth law of behaviour genetics. *Current Directions in Psychological Science, 24,* 304–312.

Chan, N.A., Zhang, Z., Yin, G.X., Li, Z.M., & Ho, R.C. (2023). Update on hypnotherapy for psychiatrists. *British Journal of Psychiatry, 29,* 361–387.

Chang, H. (2004). *Inventing temperature: Measurement and scientific progress.* Oxford University Press.

Chapman, L.J., & Chapman, J.P. (1969). Illusory correlation as an obstacle to the use of valid psychodiagnostic signs. *Journal of Abnormal Psychology, 74,* 271–280.

Chapman, R.C.G., & Hudson, J.M. (2010). Beliefs about brain injury in Britain. *Brain Injury, 24,* 797–801.

Chater, N., & Loewenstein, G. (2023). The i-frame and the s-frame: How focusing on individual-level solutions has led behavioural public policy astray. *Behavioral and Brain Sciences, 46.* https://doi.org/10.1017/S0140525X22002023.

Chertkoff, J.M., & Kushigian, R.H. (1999). *Don't panic: The psychology of emergency egress and ingress.* Westport, CT: Praeger.

Cheung, C.-K., Cheung, H.Y., & Hue, M.-T. (2015). Emotional intelligence as a basis for self-esteem in young adults. *The Journal of Psychology, 149,* 63–84.

Chomsky, N. (1957). *Knowledge of language; its nature, origin, and use.* New York: Praeger.

Chomsky, N. (1965). *Aspects of the theory of syntax.* Cambridge, MA: MIT Press.

Chomsky, N. (1986). *Knowledge of language: Its nature, origin, and use.* New York: Praeger.

Christensen, K.D., Jayaratne, T., Roberts, J., Kardia, S., & Petty, E. (2010). Understandings of basic genetics in the United States: Results from a national survey of black and white men and women. *Public Health Genomics, 13,* 467–476.

Cicero, M.T. (1840/2009). *De oratore.* New York, NY: General Books.

Clancy, S.A., & McNally, R.J. (2005/2006). Who needs repression? Normal memory processes can explain "forgetting" of childhood sexual abuse. *Scientific Review of Mental Health Practice, 4,* 66–73.

Clark, C.J., Costello, T., Mitchell, G., & Tetlock, P.E. (2022). Keep your enemies close: Adversarial collaborations will improve behavioral science. *Journal of Applied Research in Memory and Cognition, 11,* 1–18.

Clark, D.D., & Sokoloff, L. (1999). Circulation and energy metabolism of the brain. In G.J. Siegel, B.W. Agranoff, R.W. Albers, S.K. Faber, & M.D. Uhler (Eds.), *Basic neurochemisty: Molecular, cellular and medical aspects* (pp. 637–670). Philadelphia, PA: Lippincott.

Clarke, B., Alley, L.J., Ghai, S., Flake, J.K., Rohrer, J.M., Simmons, J.P., et al. (2024). Looking our limitations in the eye: A call for more thorough and honest reporting of study limitations. *Social and Personality Psychology Compass,* e12979. https://doi.org/10.1111/spc3.12979.

Clarke, L. (2002). Panic: Myth or reality? *Contexts, 1,* 21–26.

Claxton, G. (1980). Cognitive psychology: A suitable case for what sort of treatment? In G. Claxton (Ed.), *Cognitive psychology: New directions.* London: Routledge & Kegan Paul.

Clayton, N.S. (2017). Episodic-like memory and mental time travel in animals. In J. Call, G.M. Burghardt, I.M. Pepperberg, C.T. Snowdon, & T. Zentall (Eds.), *APA handbook of comparative psychology: Perception, learning & cognition* (pp. 27–243). Philadelphia, PA: Lippincott, Williams, and Wilkins.

Clayton, N.S., & Wilkins, C. (2018). Seven myths of memory. *Behavioural Processes, 18*, 3–9.

Coffield, F., Moseley, D., Hall, E., & Ecclestone, K. (2004). *Learning styles and pedagogy in post-16 learning. A systematic and critical review.* London: Learning and Skills Research Centre.

CogitateConsortium. (2023). *An adversarial collaboration to critically evaluate theories of consciousness.* https://www.biorxiv.org/content/10.1101/2023.06.23.5462 49v1.full.pdf.

Cohen, J. (1988). *Statistical power analysis for the behavioural sciences* (2nd ed.). Hillsdale, NJ: Erlbaum.

Cohen, M.A., Dennett, D.C., & Kaniwsher, N. (2016). What is the bandwidth of perceptual experience? *Trends in Cognitive Sciences, 20*, 324–335.

Cohen, M.A., Ostrand, C., Frontero, N., & Pham, P.-N. (2021). Characterising a snapshot of perceptual experience. *Journal of Experimental Psychology: General, 150*, 1695–1709.

Cohen, M.A., & Rubenstein, J. (2020). How much colour do we see in the blink of an eye? *Cognition, 200*, 104268.

Cohen, M.A., Sung, S., & Alaoui, Z. (2024). Familiarity alters the bandwidth of perceptual awareness. *Journal of Cognitive Neuroscience, 36*, 1546–1556.

Cohn, A, Fehr, E., & Marechal, M.A. (2014). Business culture and dishonesty in the banking industry. *Nature, 516*, 86–89.

Colodro-Conde, L., Couvy-Duchesne, B., Zhu, G., Coventry, W.L., Byrne, E.M., Gordon, S., et al. (2018). A direct test of the diathesis-stress model for depression. *Molecular Psychiatry, 23*, 1590–2017.

Conway, M.A., Anderson, S.J., Larsen, S.F., Donnelly, C.M., McDaniel, M.A., McClelland, A.G.R., et al. (1994). The formation of flashbulb memories. *Memory & Cognition, 22*, 326–343.

Copeland, B. (2004). *The essential Turing – the ideas that gave birth to the computer age.* Oxford: Clarendon Press.

Corneille, O., & Lush, P. (2023). Sixty years after Orne's American Psychologist article: A conceptual framework for subjective experiences elicited by demand characteristics. *Personality and Social Psychology Review, 27*, 83–101.

Corrigan, P.W., & Rao, D. (2012). On the self-stigma of mental illness: Stages, disclosure, and strategies for change. *Canadian Journal of Psychiatry, 57*, 464–469.

Costa, P.T., & McCrae, R.R. (1980). Influence of extroversion and neuroticism on subjective well-being: Happy and unhappy people. *Journal of Personality and Social Psychology, 38*, 668–678.

Costa, P.T., & McCrae, R.R. (1992). *Revised NEO personality inventory (NEO-PI-R) and NEO five factor inventory (NEO-FFI) professional manual.* Odessa, FL: Psychological Assessment Resources.

Costa, P.T., Terracciano, A., & McCrae, R.R. (2001). Gender differences in personality traits across cultures: Robust and surprising findings. *Journal of Personality and Social Psychology, 81*, 322–331.

Cournand, A. (1977). The code of the scientist and its relationship to ethics. *Science, 198*, 699–705.

Cowen, A.S., & Keltner, D. (2020). What the face displays: Mapping 28 emotions conveyed by naturalistic expression. *American Psychologist, 75*, 349–364.

Craig, H.L., Wilcox, G., Makarenko, E.M., & MacMaster, F.P. (2021). Continued educational neuromyth belief in pre-and in-service teachers: A call for de-implementation action for school psychologists. *Canadian Journal of School Psychology, 36*, 127–141.

Crivelli, C., Jarillo, S., & Fridlund, A.J. (2016). A multidisciplinary approach to research in small-scale societies: Studying emotions and facial expressions in the field. *Frontiers in Psychology, 7*, 1073.

Cuellar, M., Mauro, J., & Luby, A. (2022). A probabilistic formalisation of contextual bias: From forensic analysis to systemic bias in the criminal justice system. *Journal of the Royal Statistical Society Series A: Statistics in Society, 185*, 5620–5643.

Cuijpers, P., & Cristea, I.A. (2016). How to prove that your therapy is effective, even when it is not: A guideline. *Epidemiology and Psychiatric Sciences, 25*, 428–435.

Cuijpers, P., Reijnders, M., & Huibers, M.J.H. (2019). The role of common factors in psychotherapy outcomes. *Annual Review of Clinical Psychology, 15*, 207–231.

Cuijpers, P., van Straten, A., Bohlmeijer, E., Hollon, S.D., & Andersson, G. (2010). The effects of psychotherapy for adult depression are overestimated: A meta-analysis of study quality and effect size. *Psychological Medicine, 40*, 211–223.

Curkovic, M., Kosec, A., & Savic, A. (2019). Re-evaluation of significance and the implications of placebo effect in antidepressant therapy. *Frontiers in Psychiatry, 10*, 143.

Curot, J., Busigny, T., Valton, L., Danuelle, M., Vigard, J.-P., Maillard, L., et al. (2017). Memory scrutinised through electrical brain stimulation: A review of 80 years of experiential phenomena. *Neuroscience and Biobehavioral Reviews, 78*, 161–177.

Curot, J., Roux, F.-E., Sol, J.-C., Valton, L., Pariente, J., & Barbeau, E.J. (2020). Awake craniotomy and memory induction through Electrical Stimulation: Why are Penfield's findings not replicated in the modern era? *Neurosurgery, 87*, E130–E137.

Dahl, A. (2015). The developing social context of infant helping in two U.S. samples. *Child Development, 86*, 1080–1093.

Darley, J.M., & Latané, B. (1968). Bystander intervention in emergencies: Diffusion of responsibility. *Journal of Personality and Social Psychology, 8*, 377–383.

Davies, K., Tonkin, M., Bull, R., & Bond, J.W. (2012). The course of case linkage never did run smooth: A new investigation to tackle the behavioural changes in serial car theft. *Journal of Investigative Psychology and Offender Profiling, 9*, 274–295.

Davies, N.M., Dickson, M., Davey Smith, G., Van Den Berg, G.J., & Windmeijer, F. (2018). The causal effects of education on health outcomes in the UK Biobank. *Nature Human Behaviour, 2*, 117–125.

Dawes, C.T., & Weinschenk, A.C. (2020). On the genetic basis of political orientation. *Current Opinion in Behavioral Sciences, 34*, 173–178.

de Gardelle, V., Sackur, J., & Kouider, S. (2009). Perceptual illusions in brief visual presentations. *Consciousness and Cognition, 18*, 569–577

De Gelder, B., Tamietto, M., Pegna, A.J., & Van den Stock, J. (2015). Visual imagery influences brain responses to visual stimulation in bilateral cortical blindness. *Cortex, 72*, 15–26.

De Pauw, E., Daniels, S., Brijs, T., Hermans, E., & Wets, G. (2011). *The magnitude of the regression to the mean effect in traffic crashes.* 24th ICTCT Workshop, Warsaw, Poland, 27th–28th October.

de Ridder, D., Kroese, F., & van Gestel, L. (2022). Nudgeability: Mapping conditions of susceptibility to nudge influence. *Perspectives on Psychological Science, 17*, 346–359.

De Vries, L.P., Pelt, D.H.M., & Bartels, M. (2024). The stability and change of well-being across the lifespan: A longitudinal twin-sibling study. *Psychological Medicine*, 1–13. https://doi.org/10.1017/S0033291724000692.

De Vries, Y.A., Roest, A.M., de Jonge, P., Cuijpers, P., Munafò, M.R., & Bastiaansen, J.A. (2018). The cumulative effect of reporting and citation biases on the apparent efficacy of treatments: The case of depression. *Psychological Medicine, 48*, 2453–2455.

DeJesus, J.M., Callanan, M.A., Solis, G., & Gelman, S.A. (2019). Generic language in scientific communication. *Proceedings of the National Academy of Sciences, 11637*, 18370–18377.

Del Giudice, M. (2023). Individual and group differences in multivariate domains: What happens when the number of traits increases? *Personality and Individual Differences, 213,* 112282.

Del Giudice, M., Booth, T., & Irwing, P. (2012). The distance between Mars and Venus: Measuring global sex differences in personality. *PLoS One, 7,* e29265.

DellaVigna, S., & Linos, E. (2022). RCTs to scale: Comprehensive evidence from two nudge units. *Econometrica, 90,* 81–116.

Demasi, M., & Gøtzsche, P.C. (2020). Presentation of benefits and harms of anti-depressants on websites: A cross-sectional study. *International Journal of Risk & Safety in Medicine, 31,* 53–65.

DeRubeis, R.J., Hollon, S.D., Amsterdam, J.D., Shelton, R.C., Young, P.R., Salomon, R.M., et al. (2005). Cognitive therapy vs. medications in the treatment of moderate to severe depression. *Archives of General Psychiatry, 62,* 409–416.

Dezecache, G. (2015). Human collective reactions to threat. *Wiley Interdisciplinary Reviews – Cognitive Science, 6,* 209–219.

Dezecache, G., Martin, J.-R., Tessier, C., Safra, L., Pitron, V., Nuss, P., et al. (2021). Nature and determinants of social actions during a mass shooting. *PLoS One, 16,* e0260392.

Diamond, D.M. (2019). When a child dies of heatstroke after a parent or caretaker unknowingly leaves the child in a car: How does it happen and is it a crime? *Medicine, Science and the Law, 59,* 115–126.

Diamond, N.B., Armson, M.J., & Levine, B. (2020). The truth is out there: Accuracy in recall of verifiable real-world events. *Psychological Science, 31,* 1544–1556.

Dickens, W.T., & Flynn, J.R. (2001). Heritability estimates versus large environmental effects: The IQ paradox resolved. *Psychological Review, 108,* 346–369.

Diener, E., Lucas, R.E., & Scollon, C.N. (2006). Beyond the hedonic treadmill: Revising the adaptation theory of well-being. *American Psychologist, 61,* 305–314.

Diener, E., Northcott, R., Zyphur, M., & West, S. (2022). Beyond experiments. *Perspectives on Psychological Science, 17,* 1101–1119.

Dijkstra, N. (2024). Nuancing the heterarchical theory of visual mental imagery. *Physics of Life Reviews, 49,* 10–11.

Dijkstra, N., Ambrogioni, L., Vidaurre, D., & van Gerven, M. (2020). Neural dynamics of perceptual inference and its reversal during imagery. *Elife, 9,* 1–19.

Dijkstra, N., Mostert, P., de Lange, F.P., Bosch, S., & van Gerven, M.A.J. (2018). Differential temporal dynamics during visual imagery and perception. *eLIFE, 7,* Article e33904.

Dijkstra, N., Zeidman, P., Ondobaka, S., van Gerven, M.A.J., & Friston, K. (2017). Distinct top-down and bottom-up brain connectivity during visual perception and imagery. *Scientific Reports, 7,* 5677.

Dillihunt, M.L., & Tyler, K.M. (2006). Examining the effects of multiple intelligence instruction on math performance. *Journal of Urban Learning, Teaching, and Research, 2,* 131–150.

Dismukes, R.K., & Nowinski, J.L. (2006). Prospective memory, concurrent task management, and pilot error. In A. Kramer, D. Wiegmann, & A. Kirlik (Eds.), *Attention: From theory to practice.* Oxford: Oxford University Press.

Dodier, O., Gilet, A., & Colombel, F. (2021). What do people really think of when they claim to believe in repressed memory? Methodological middle ground and applied issues. *Memory, 30,* 744–752.

Dodier, O., Otgaar, H., & Lynn, S.J. (2022). A critical analysis of myths about dissociative identity disorder. *Annales Médico-Psychologiques, 180,* 855–861.

Doğru, Ç. (2022). A meta-analysis of the relationships between emotional intelligence and employee outcomes. *Frontiers in Psychology, 13,* 611348.

Donald, I., & Canter, D. (1992). Intentionality and fatality during the Kings-Cross underground fire. *European Journal of Social Psychology, 22,* 203–218.

Donnellan, M.B., & Lucas, R.E. (2021). *Great myths of personality*. Hoboken, NJ: Wiley-Blackwell.

Donovan, K.M., & Klahm, C.F. (2015). The role of entertainment media in perceptions of police use of force. *Criminal Justice and Behavior, 42*, 1261–1281.

Dowler, K., & Zawilski, V. (2007). Public perceptions of police misconduct and discrimination: Examining the impact of media consumption. *Journal of Criminal Justice, 35*, 193–203.

Downing, P.E., Chan, A.W.Y., Peelen, M.V., Dodds, C.M., & Kanwisher, N. (2006). Domain specificity in visual cortex. *Cerebral Cortex, 16*, 1453–1461.

Draheim, C., Tschukara, J.S., & Engle, R.W. (2024). Replication and extension of the toolbox approach to measuring attention control. *Behavior Research Methods, 56*, 2135–2157.

Dror, I.E. (2020). Cognitive and human factors in expert decision making: Six fallacies and the eight sources of bias. *Analytical Chemistry, 92*, 7998–8004.

Dror, I.E. (2023). The most consistent finding in forensic science is inconsistency. *Journal of Forensic Sciences, 68*, 1851–1855.

Dror, I.E., Charlton, D., & Péron, A.E. (2006). Contextual information renders experts vulnerable to making erroneous identifications. *Forensic Science International, 156*, 74–78.

Dror, I.E., & Hampikian, G. (2011). Subjectivity and bias in forensic DNA mixture interpretation. *Science and Justice, 51*, 204–208.

Dror, I.E., & Langenburg, G. (2019). "Cannot decide": The fine line between appropriate inconclusive determinations versus unjustifiably deciding not to decide. *Journal of Forensic Sciences, 64*. https://doi.org/10.1111/1556-4029.13854.

Drury, J., & Reicher, S.D. (2010). Crowd control. *Scientific American Mind, 21*, 58–65.

du Maurier, G. (1894). *Trilby*. London: Osgood, McIlvane & Co.

Duchaine, B., & Nakayama, K. (2006). Developmental prosopagnosia: A window to context-specific face processing. *Current Opinion in Neurobiology, 16*, 166–178.

Duckworth, A.L., & Milkman, K.L. (2022). A guide to megastudies. *Proceedings of the National Association of Sciences Nexus, 1*, 1–5.

Dudukovic, N.M., Marsh, E.J., & Tversky, B. (2004). Telling a story or telling it straight: The effects of entertaining versus accurate retellings on memory. *Applied Cognitive Psychology, 18*, 125–143.

Duff, M.C., Kurczek, J., Rubin, R., Cohen, N.J., & Tranel, D. (2013). Hippocampal amnesia disrupts creative thinking. *Hippocampus, 23*, 1143–1149.

Dufner, M., Gebauer, J.E., Sedikides, C., & Denissen, J.J.A. (2019). Self-enhancement and psychological adjustment: A meta-analytic review. *Personality and Social Psychology Review, 23*, 48–72.

Dunne, M.P. Martin, N.G., Statham, D.J., Slutske, W.S., Dinwiddie, S.H., Bucholz, K.K., et al. (1997). Genetic and environmental contributions to variance in age at first sexual intercourse. *Psychological Science, 8*, 211–216.

Durisko, Z., Mulsant, B.H., & Andrews, P.W. (2015). An adaptationist perspective on the aetiology of depression. *Journal of Affective Disorders, 172*, 315–323.

Eagly, A.H., & Wood, W. (1999). The origins of sex differences in human behaviour: Evolved dispositions versus social roles. *American Psychologist, 54*, 408–423.

Earl, P.E. (2018). Richard H. Thaler: A Nobel Prize for Behavioural Economics. *Review of Political Economy, 30*, 107–125.

Eaves, L.J., & Eysenck, H.J. (1974). Genetics and the development of social attitudes. *Nature, 249*, 288–289.

Ebrahim, S., Bance, S., Athale, A., Malachowski, C., & Ioannidis, J.R.A. (2016). Meta-analyses with industry involvement are massively published and report no caveats for antidepressants. *Journal of Clinical Epidemiology, 70*, 155–163.

Ehinger, K.A., Hidalgo-Sotelo, B., Rorraibaq, A., & Oliva, A. (2009). Modelling search for people in 900 scenes: A combined source model of eye guidance. *Visual Cognition, 17,* 945–978.

Eichenbaum, H., & Cohen, N.J. (2023). Amnesia: Beyond Scoville and Milner's (1957) research on HM. In M.W. Eysenck & D. Groome (Eds.), *Cognitive psychology: Revisiting the classic studies* (2nd ed., pp. 82–98). London: Sage.

Eisen, M.L., Smith, A.M., Olaguez, A.P., & Skerritt-Perta, A.S. (2017). An examination of show-ups conducted by law enforcement using a field-simulation paradigm. *Psychology, Public Policy, and Law, 23,* 1–22.

Eisner, D.A. (2000). *The death of psychotherapy: From Freud to alien abductions.* Westport, CT: Praeger.

Ekman, P. (2016). What scientists who study emotion agree about. *Perspectives on Psychological Science, 11,* 31–34.

Ekman, P., & Friesen, W.V. (1971). Constants across cultures in the face and emotion. *Journal of Personality and Social Psychology, 17,* 124–129.

Ekman, P., Friesen, W.V., O'Sullivan, M., Chan, A., Diacoyanni-Tarlatzis, I., Heider, K., et al. (1987). Universals and cultural differences in the judgements of facial expressions of emotion. *Journal of Personality and Social Psychology, 53,* 712–717.

Elaad, E., Ginton, A., & Ben-Shakhar, G. (1994). The effects of prior expectations and outcome knowledge on polygraph examiners' decisions. *Journal of Behavioral Decision Making, 7,* 279–292.

Elms, A.C., & Milgram, S. (1966). Personality characteristics associated with obedience and defiance toward authoritative command. *Journal of Experimental Research in Personality, 1,* 282–289.

Elson, M., Hussey, I., Alsalti, T., & Arslan, R.C. (2023). Psychological measures aren't toothbrushes. *Communications Psychology, 1,* 25.

Engelhard, I.M., McNally, R.J., & van Schie, K. (2019). Retrieving and modifying traumatic memories: Recent research relevant to three controversies. *Current Directions in Psychological Science, 28,* 91–96.

Ennis, R.H. (1987). A taxonomy of critical thinking dispositions and abilities. In J. Baron & R. Sternberg (Eds.), *Teaching thinking skills: Theory and practice.* New York: W.H. Freeman.

Epstein, S. (1977). Traits are alive and well. In D. Magnusson & N.S. Endler (Eds.), *Personality at the crossroads: Current issues in interactional psychology.* Hillsdale, NJ: Erlbaum.

Erb, C.D., Germine, L., & Hartshorne, J.K. (2023). Cognitive control across the lifespan: Congruency effects reveal divergent developmental trajectories. *Journal of Experimental Psychology: General, 152,* 3285–3291.

Ericsson, K.A., Krampe, R.T., & Tesch-Römer, C. (1993). The role of deliberate practice in the acquisition of expert performance. *Psychological Review, 100,* 363–406.

Eronen, M.I., & Bringmann, L.F. (2021). The theory crisis in psychology: How to move forward. *Perspectives on Psychological Science, 16,* 779–788.

Evans, J.S.B.T., & Stanovich, K.E. (2013). Dual-process theories of higher cognition: Advancing the debate. *Perspectives on Psychological Science, 8,* 223–241.

Evans, N., & Levinson, S. (2009). The myth of language universals: Language diversity and its importance for cognitive science. *Behavioral and Brain Sciences, 32,* 429–492.

Evett, I.W., & Williams, R.L. (2015). A review of the sixteen points fingerprint standard in England and Wales. *Journal of Forensic Identification, 65,* 557–580.

Exner, J.E. (1974). *The Rorschach: A comprehensive system* (Vol. 1). New York, NY: Wiley.

Exner, J.E. (2003). *The Rorschach: A comprehensive system. Vol. 1: Basic foundations and principles of interpretation* (4th ed.). New York, NY: Wiley.

Eysenck, M.W. (1979). Depth, elaboration, and distinctiveness. In L.S. Cermak & F.I.M. Craik (Eds.), *Levels of processing in human memory*. Hillsdale, NJ: Lawrence Erlbaum Associates Inc.

Eysenck, M.W. (1990). *Happiness: Facts and myths*. Hove, UK: Lawrence Erlbaum.

Eysenck, M.W. (2012). *AS level psychology* (5th ed.). Hove, UK: Psychology Press.

Eysenck, M.W. (2019). The challenge to trait theory: Revisiting Mischel (1968). In P. Corr (Ed.), *Personality and individual differences: Revisiting the classic studies*. London: Sage.

Eysenck, M.W., Derakshan, N., Santos, R., & Calvo, M.G. (2007). Anxiety and cognitive performance: Attentional control theory. *Emotion, 7*, 336–353.

Eysenck, M.W., & Eysenck, C. (2022). *AI vs. humans*. London: Routledge.

Eysenck, M.W., & Groome, D. (Eds.). (2023). *Cognitive psychology: Revisiting the classic studies* (2nd ed.). London: Sage.

Eysenck, M.W., & Keane, M.T. (2020). *Cognitive psychology: A student's handbook* (8th ed.). Abingdon/Oxon: Psychology Press.

Eysenck, M.W., Moser, J.S., Derakshan, N., Hepsomali, P., & Allen, P. (2023). A neurocognitive account of attentional control theory: How does trait anxiety affect the brain's attentional networks? *Cognition and Emotion, 37*, 220–237.

Falk, A., & Hermle, J. (2018). Relationship of gender differences in preferences to economic development and gender equality. *Science, 362*, eaas9899.

Fawcett, J.M., & Hulbert, J.C. (2020). The many faces of forgetting: Toward a constructive view of forgetting in everyday life. *Journal of Applied Research in Memory and Cognition, 9*, 1–18.

Fechner, G.T. (1860/1966). *Elemente der Psychophysik* [Elements of psychophysics] (Vol. 1). Translated by H.E. Adler. New York: Holt, Rinehart and Winston.

Feng, X.R., & Burton, A.M. (2021). Understanding the document bias in face matching. *Quarterly Journal of Experimental Psychology, 74*, 2019–2029, Article 17470218211017902.

Ferguson, C.J., Brown, J.M., & Torres, A.V. (2018). Education or indoctrination? The accuracy of introductory psychology textbooks in covering controversial topics and urban legends about psychology. *Current Psychology, 37*, 574–582.

Ferguson, C.J., & Heene, M. (2012). A vast graveyard of undead theories: Publication bias and psychological science's aversion to the null. *Perspectives on Psychological Science, 7*, 555–561.

Fernbach, P.M., Lightm, N., Scott, S.E., Inbar, Y., & Rozin, P. (2019). Extreme opponents of genetically modified foods know the least but think they know the most. *Nature Human Behaviour, 3*, 251–256.

Ferrero, M., Hardwicke, T.E., Konstantinidis, E., & Vadillo, M.A. (2020). The effectiveness of refutation texts to correct misconceptions among educators. *Journal of Experimental Psychology: Applied, 26*, 411–421.

Ferrero, M., Vadillo, M.A., & León, S.P. (2021). A valid evaluation of the theory of multiple intelligences is not yet possible: Problems of methodological quality for intervention studies. *Intelligence, 88*, 101566.

Feynman, R.P. (1985). *Surely you're joking, Mr. Feynman: Adventures of a curious character*. New York: W.W. Norton.

Fiedler, K., McCaughey, L., & Prager, J. (2021). Quo vadis, methodology: The key role of manipulation checks for validity control and quality of science. *Perspectives on Psychological Science, 16*, 816–826.

Fiedler, K., & Schwarz, N. (2016). Questionable research practices revisited. *Social Psychological and Personality Science, 7*, 45–52.

Fields, R. (1992). Hood must pay in sex-abuse case. *Beacon Journal [Akron, OH]*, C5. 4th August.

Filmer, H.L., Lyons, M., Mattingley, J.B., & Dux, P.E. (2017). Anodal tDCS applied during multitasking training leads to transferable performance gains. *Scientific Reports, 7,* 12988.

Fischer, J., & Whitney, D. (2014). Serial dependence in visual perception. *Nature Neuroscience, 17,* 738–743.

Fischer, P., Krueger, J., Greitemeyer, T., Vogrincic, C., Kastenmüller, A., Frey, D., et al. (2011). The bystander effect: A meta-analytic review on bystander intervention in dangerous and non-dangerous emergencies. *Psychological Bulletin, 137,* 517–537.

Fleeson, W., & Noftle, E.E. (2008). Where does personality have its influence? A supermatrix of consistency concepts. *Journal of Personality, 76,* 1355–1385.

Fleming, N.D., & Baume, D. (2006). Learning styles again: VARKing up the right tree! *Educational Developments, 7,* 4–7.

Fleming, N.D., & Bonwell, C. (2019). *VARK: How do I learn best?* Canterbury, New Zealand: Vark Learn Limited.

Flückiger, C., De Re, A.C., Wampold, B.E., & Horvath, A.O. (2018). The alliance in adult psychotherapy: A meta-analytic synthesis. *Psychotherapy, 55,* 316–340.

Folk, D., & Dunn, E. (2024). How can people become happier? A systematic review of preregistered experiments. *Annual Review of Psychology, 75,* 467–493.

Forensic Research Incorporated. (1997). The validity and reliability of polygraph testing. *Polygraph, 26,* 215–239.

Forer, B.R. (1949). The fallacy of personal validation: A classroom demonstration of gullibility. *Journal of Abnormal and Social Psychology, 44,* 118–123.

Foroughi, C.K., Monforta, S.S., Paczynskia, M., McKnight, P.E., & Greenwood, P.M. (2016). Placebo effects in cognitive training. Proceedings of the National *Academy of Sciences of the United States of America, 113,* 7470–7474.

Foster, D.H., & Reeves, A. (2022). Colour constancy failures expected in colourful environments. *Proceedings of the Royal Society B – Biological Sciences, 289,* 20212483.

Fox, B., & Farrington, D.P. (2018). What have we learned from offender profiling? A systematic review and meta-analysis of 40 years of research. *Psychological Bulletin, 144,* 1247–1274.

Fraley, R.C., & Vazire, S. (2014). The N-pact factor: Evaluating the quality of empirical journals with respect to sample size and statistical power. *PLoS One, 9,* e109019.

Freud, S. (1896). Further remarks on the neuro-psychoses of defence. In *Standard edition* (Vol. 3, pp. 159–188).

Freud, S. (1899). Screen memories. In *Standard edition* (Vol. 3, pp. 301–322). London: Hogarth Press.

Freud, S. (1906). My views on the part played by sexuality in the aetiology of the neuroses. In *Standard edition* (Vol. 7, pp. 271–279).

Freud, S. (1913). *On beginning the treatment (further recommendations on the technique of psycho-analysis). Standard edition.* London, England: Hogarth Press.

Freud, S. (1915/1963). Repression. In J. Strachey (Ed.), *The standard edition of the collected works of Sigmund Freud* (Vol. 14). London: Hogarth.

Freud, S. (1917). Part III: Introductory lectures on psychoanalysis. In J. Strachey (Ed.), *The complete psychological works* (Vol. 2). New York: Norton.

Fried, E.I. (2017). The 52 symptoms of major depression: Lack of content overlap among seven common depression scales. *Journal of Affective Disorders, 208,* 191–197.

Fried, E.I., Mateer, C., Ojemann, G., Wohns, R., & Fedio, P. (1982). Organisation of visuospatial functions in human cortex. *Brain, 105*(Pt. 2), 349–371.

Fugelsang, J.A., Stein, C.B., Green, A.E., & Dunbar, K.N. (2004). Theories and data interactions of the scientific mind: Evidence from the molecular and the cognitive laboratory. *Canadian Journal of Experimental Psychology, 58,* 86–95.

Funder, D.C., & Ozer, D.J. (2019). Evaluating effect size in psychological research: Sense and nonsense. *Advances in Methods and Practices in Psychological Science*, *2*, 156–168.

Furnham, A. (1992). Prospective psychology students' knowledge of psychology. *Psychological Reports*, *70*, 375–382.

Furnham, A., & Cheng, H. (2000). Lay theories of happiness. *Journal of Happiness Studies*, *1*, 227–246.

Furnham, A., & Horne, G. (2021). Myths and misconceptions about intelligence: A study of 35 studies. *Personality and Individual Differences*, *181*, 111014.

Furnham, A., & Hughes, D. (2014). Myths and misconceptions in popular psychology: Comparing psychology students and the general public. *Teaching of Psychology*, *41*, 256–261.

Furnham, A., & Robinson, C. (2022). Myths and misconceptions about personality traits and tests. *Personality and Individual Differences*, *186*, 111381.

Galinsky, A.D., Turek, A., Agarwal, G., Anicich, E.M., Rucker, D.E., Bowles, H.R., et al. (2024). Are many sex/gender differences really power differences? *PNAS Nexus*, *3*, 1–19.

Gandhi, B., & Oakley, D.A. (2005). Does 'hypnosis' by any other name smell as sweet? The efficacy of 'hypnotic' inductions depends on the label 'hypnosis'. *Consciousness and Cognition*, *14*, 304–315.

Gao, A.F., Keith, J.L., Gao, F.-Q., Black, S.E., Moscovitch, M., & Rosenbaum, R.S. (2020). Neuropathology of a remarkable case of memory impairment informs human memory. *Neuropsychologia*, *140*, 107342.

Gardner, D.M. (2011). *Parents' influence on child social self-efficacy and social cognition*. Master's Theses (2009). Paper 116. http://epublications.marquette.edu/theses_open/116.

Gardner, H. (1983). *Frames of mind: The theory of multiple intelligences*. New York: Basic Books.

Gardner, H. (1993). *Creating minds: The theory of creativity as seen through Freud, Einstein, Picasso, Stravinsky, Eliot, Graham, and Gandhi*. New York: Basic Books.

Gardner, H. (2006). *Multiple intelligences: New perspectives*. New York: Basic Books.

Gardner, H. (2013). Multiple intelligences are not 'learning styles'. *Washington Post*. 16th October.

Gardner, H. (2020). *Intelligence reframed: Multiple intelligences for the 21st century*. New York: Basic Books.

Gardner, H., & Hatch, T. (1989). Multiple intelligences go to school: Educational implications of the theory of multiple intelligences. *Educational Researcher*, *18*, 4–9.

Gardner, H., & Krechevsky, M. (1993). The emergence and nurturance of multiple intelligences in early childhood: The Project Spectrum approach. In H. Gardner (Ed.), *Multiple intelligences: The theory in practice* (pp. 86–111). New York: Basic Books.

Gardner, H., Kornhaber, M.L., & Wake, W.K. (1996). Intelligence: Multiple perspectives. Orlando, FL: Harcourt Brace.

Gardner, R.M., & Dalsing, S. (1986). Misconceptions about psychology among college students. *Teaching of Psychology*, *13*, 32–34.

Garrett, B. (2011). *Convicting the innocent: Where criminal prosecutions go wrong*. Cambridge, MA: Harvard University Press.

Gathercole, S.E., Dunning, D.L., Holmes, J., & Norris, D. (2019). Working memory training involves learning new skills. *Journal of Memory and Language*, *105*, 19–42.

Gearhardt, A.N., & DiFeliceantonio, A.G. (2023). Highly processed foods can be considered addictive substances based on established scientific criteria. *Addiction*, *118*, 589–598.

Gegenfurtner, K.R., Weiss, D., & Bloj, M. (2024). Color constancy in real-world settings. *Journal of Vision, 24*(12), 1–22.

Geiselman, R.E., Fisher, R.P., MacKinnon, D.P., & Holland, H.L. (1985). Eyewitness memory enhancement in the police interview – cognitive retrieval mnemonics versus hypnosis. *Journal of Applied Psychology, 70*, 401–412.

Genç, E., Schlüter, C., Fraenz, C., Arning, L., Metzen, D., Nguyen, H.P., et al. (2021). Polygenic scores for cognitive abilities and their association with different aspects of general intelligence – a deep phenotyping approach. *Molecular Neurobiology, 58*, 4145–4156.

Geraerts, E., Schooler, J.W., Merckelbach, H., Jelicic, M., Hunter, B.J.A., & Ambadar, Z. (2007). The reality of recovered memories – corroborating continuous and discontinuous memories of childhood sexual abuse. *Psychological Science, 18*, 564–568.

Gergen, K.J. (1973). Social psychology as history. *Journal of Personality and Social Psychology, 26*, 309–320.

Gerver, C.R., Griffin, J.W., Dennis, N.A., & Beaty, R.E. (2023). Memory and creativity: A metaanalytic examination of the relationship between memory systems and creative cognition. *Psychonomic Bulletin & Review, 30*, 2116–2154.

Geven, L.M., Verschuere, B., Kindt, M., Vakinen, S., & Ben-Shakhar, G. (2022). Countering information leakage in the concealed information test: The effects of item detailedness. *Psychophysiology, 59*, e13957.

Gidziela, A., Ahmadzadeh, Y.I., Michelini, G., Allegrini, A.G., Agnew-Blais, J., Lau, L.Y., et al. (2023). A meta-analysis of genetic effects associated with neurodevelopmental disorders and co-occurring conditions. *Nature Human Behaviour, 7*, 642–656.

Gignac, G.E., & Szodorai, E.T. (2016). Effect size guidelines for individual differences researchers. *Personality and Individual Differences, 102*, 74–78.

Gill, P. (2016). Analysis and implications of the miscarriages of justice of Amanda Knox and Raffaele Sollecito. *Forensic Science International: Genetics, 23*, 9–18.

Gill, P. (2019). DNA evidence and miscarriages of justice. *Forensic Science International, 294*, e1–e3.

Ginton, A. (2023). Calculating the base rate in polygraph populations and the posterior confidence in the obtained results in the comparison question test, built upon the proportion of outcomes: The case of Israel police. *Journal of Police and Criminal Psychology, 38*, 165–171.

Gladwell, M. (2008). *Outliers: The story of success.* New York, NY: Little, Brown.

Gobet, F., & Ereku, M.H. (2014). Checkmate to deliberate practice: The case of Magnus Carlsen. *Frontiers in Psychology, 5*, 878.

Godwin, D., Barry, R.L., & Marois, R. (2015). Breakdown of the brain's functional network modularity with awareness. *Proceedings of the National Academy of Sciences of the United States of America, 112*, 3799–3804.

Goldberg, L.R. (1990). An alternative "description of personality": The big-five factor structure. *Journal of Personality and Social Psychology, 59*, 1216–1229.

Goleman, D. (1995). *Emotional intelligence: Why it can matter more than IQ.* New York: Bantam Books.

Gollwitzer, M., Prager, J., Altenmüller, M.S., & Zein, R.A. (2023). Simplification is not Indoctrination. *Psychology Learning & Teaching, 22*, 245–250.

Gomulicki, B.R. (1956). Recall as an abstractive process. *Acta Psychologica, 12*, 77–94.

Gonthier, C., & Gregoire, J. (2022). Flynn effects are biased by differential item functioning over time: A test using overlapping items in Wechsler scales. *Intelligence, 95*, 101688.

Goodman, G.S., Quas, J.A., Goldfarb, D., Gonzalves, L., & Gonzalez, A. (2019). Trauma and long-term memory for childhood events: Impact matters. *Child Development Perspectives, 13,* 3–9.

Gottesman, I.I. (1991). *Schizophrenia genesis: The origins of madness.* New York: W.H. Freeman/Times Books/Henry Holt & Co.

Gottfredson, L.S. (1997). Why g matters: The complexity of everyday life. *Intelligence, 24,* 79–132.

Götz, F.M., Gosling, S.D., & Rentfrow, P.J. (2022). Small effects: The indispensable foundation for a cumulative psychological science. *Perspectives on Psychological Science, 17,* 205–215.

Grace, K., Salvatier, J., Defoe, A., Zhang, B., & Evans, O. (2018). When will AI exceed human performance? Evidence from experts. *Journal of Artificial Intelligence Research, 62,* 729–754.

Graf, P. (2012). Prospective memory: Faulty brain, flaky person. *Canadian Psychology, 53,* 7–13.

Gray, J. (1992). *Men are from Mars, women are from Venus.* New York: HarperCollins.

Green, J.P., Page, R.A., Rasekhy, R., Johnson, L K., & Bernhardt, S.E. (2006). Cultural views and attitudes about hypnosis: A survey of college students across four countries. *International Journal of Clinical and Experimental Hypnosis, 54,* 263–280.

Greenwald, A.G. (2012). There is nothing so theoretical as a good method. *Perspectives on Psychological Science, 7,* 99–108.

Greenwald, A.G., McGhee, D.E., & Schwartz, J.L.K. (1998). Measuring individual differences in implicit cognition: The implicit association test. *Journal of Personality and Social Psychology, 74,* 1464–1480.

Greenwood, J.D. (1999). Understanding the "cognitive revolution" in psychology. *Journal of the History of the Behavioral Sciences, 35,* 1–22.

Greiwe, T., & Khoshnood, A. (2022). Do we mistake fiction for fact? Investigating whether the consumption of fictional crime-related media may help to explain the criminal profiling illusion. *SAGE Open,* 1–14. April–June.

Griggs, R.A. (2014). Coverage of the Stanford prison experiment in introductory psychology textbooks. *Teaching of Psychology, 41,* 195–203.

Griggs, R.A. (2015). The disappearance of independence in textbook coverage of Asch's social pressure experiments. *Teaching of Psychology, 42,* 137–142.

Griggs, R.A., & Whitehead, G.W. (2014). Coverage of the Stanford prison experiment in introductory social psychology textbooks. *Teaching of Psychology, 41,* 318–324.

Griggs, R.A., & Whitehead, G.W. (2015). Coverage of Milgram's obedience experiments in social psychology textbooks: Where have all the criticisms gone?. *Teaching of Psychology, 42,* 315–322.

Grimm, A., Hulse, L., Preiss, M., & Schmidt, S. (2014). Behavioural, emotional, and cognitive responses in European disasters: Results of survivor interviews. *Disasters, 38,* 62–83.

Groome, D., Eysenck, M.W., & Law, R. (2020). Motivated forgetting: Forgetting what we want to forget. In M.W. Eysenck & D. Groome (Eds.), *Forgetting: Explaining memory failure* (pp. 147–167). London: Sage.

Gross, S.R., & Shaffer, M. (2012). *Exonerations in the United States, 1989–2012: Report by the national registry of exoneration (2012).* http://www.law.umich.edu/special/exoneration/Documents/exonerations_us_1989_2012_full_report.pdf.

Grosz, M.P., Ayaita, A., Arslan, R.C., Buecker, S., Ebert, T., Hünermund, P., et al. (2024). Natural experiments: Missed opportunities for causal inference in psychology. *Advances in Methods and Practices in Psychological Science, 7,* 1–15.

Grosz, M.P., Rohrer, J.M., & Thoemmes, F. (2020). The taboo against explicit causal inference in non-experimental-psychology. *Perspectives on Psychological Science, 15*, 1243–1255.

Growns, B., Towler, A., Dunn, J.D., Salerno, J.M., Schweitzer, N.J., & Dror, I.E. (2022). Statistical feature training improves fingerprint – matching accuracy in novices and professional fingerprint examiners. *Cognitive Research: Principles and Implications, 7*, 60.

Gruetzemacher, R., Paradice, D., & Bok, L.K. (2020). Forecasting extreme labour displacement: A survey of AI practitioners. *Technological Forecasting and Social Change, 161*, 120323.

Guilmette, T.J., & Paglia, M.F. (2004). The public's misconceptions about trauma brain injury a follow up study. *Archives of Clinical Neuropsychology, 19*, 183–189.

Gurevitch, J., Koricheva, J., Nakagawa, S., & Stewart, G. (2016). Meta-analysis and the science of research synthesis. *Nature, 555*, 175–182.

Haghani, M., Cristiani, E., Bode, M.W.F., Boltes, M., & Corbetta, A. (2019). Panic, irrationality, and herding: Three ambiguous terms in crowd dynamics research. *Journal of Advanced Transportation, 2019*(1), 9267643.

Hahn, E., Spinath, F.M., Siedler, T., Wagner, G.G., Schupp, J., & Kandler, C. (2012). The complexity of personality: The advantages of a genetically sensitive multi-group design. *Behavior Genetics, 42*, 221–233.

Haider, Z.F., & von Stumm, S. (2022). Predicting educational and social-emotional outcomes in emerging adulthood from intelligence, personality, and socio-economic status. *Journal of Personality and Social Psychology, 123*, 1386–1406.

Hambrick, D.Z., Macnamara, B.N., & Oswald, F.L. (2020). Is the deliberate practice view defensible? A review of evidence and discussion of issues. *Frontiers in Psychology, 11*, 1134.

Hambrick, D.Z., & Tucker-Drob, E.M. (2015). The genetics of music accomplishment: Evidence for gene-environment correlation and interaction. *Psychonomic Bulletin & Review, 22*, 112–120.

Haney, C., Banks, C., & Zimbardo, P. (1973). Study of prisoners and guards in a simulated prison. *Naval Research Reviews, 26*, 1–17.

Haney, C., & Zimbardo, P.G. (2009). Persistent dispositionalism in interactionist clothing: Fundamental attribution error in explaining prison abuse. *Personality and Social Psychology Bulletin, 35*, 807–814.

Hardt, O., Nader, K., & Nadel, L. (2013). Decay happens: The role of active forgetting in memory. *Trends in Cognitive Sciences, 17*, 111–120.

Harrer, M., Cuijpers, P., Schuurmans, L.K.J., Kaiser, T., Buntrock, C., van Straten, A., et al. (2023). Evaluation of randomised controlled trials: A primer and tutorial for mental health researchers. *Trials, 24*, 562.

Harris, J.R. (1998). *The nurture assumption.* New York: Free Press.

Harris, M.A., & Orth, U. (2020). The link between self-esteem and social relationships: A meta-analysis of longitudinal studies. *Journal of Personality and Social Psychology, 119*, 1459–1477.

Harrower, M. (1976). Rorschach records of the Nazi war criminals: An experimental study after thirty years. *Journal of Personality Assessment, 40*, 341–351.

Hart, C.L., Taylor, M.D., Davey Smith, G., Whalley, L.J., Starr, J.M., Hole, D.J., Wilson, V., & Deary, I.J. (2003). Childhood IQ, social class, deprivation and their relationships with mortality and morbidity risk in later life. *Psychosomatic Medicine, 65*, 877–883.

Hart, W., Albarracin, D., Eagly, A.H., Brechan, I., Lindberg, M.J., & Merrill, L. (2009). Feeling validated versus being correct: A meta-analysis of selective exposure to information. *Psychological Bulletin, 135*, 555–588.

Hassabis, D., Kumaran, D., Vann, S.D., & Maguire, E.A. (2007). Patients with hippocampal amnesia cannot imagine new experiences. *Proceedings of the National Academy of Sciences, USA, 104*, 1726–1731.

Hassan, T. (2023). Genetic and environmental influences on playing video games. *Media Psychology.* https://doi.org/10.1080/15213269.2023.2165504.

Hatemi, P.K., Funk, C., Medland, S., Maes, H., Silberg, J., Martin, N., et al. (2009). Genetic and environmental transmission of political attitudes over the life time. *Journal of Politics, 71*, 1141–1156.

Hatemi, P.K., Hibbing, J., Medland, S., Keller, M., Alford, J., Smith, K., et al. (2010). Not by twins alone: Using extended family design to investigate genetic influence on political beliefs. *American Journal of Political Science, 54*, 798–814.

Hatemi, P.K., Medland, S.E., Klemmensen, R., Oskarsson, S., Littvay, L., Dawes, C.T., et al. (2014). Genetic influences on political ideologies: Twin analyses of 19 measures of political ideologies from five democracies and genome-wide findings from three populations. *Behavior Genetics, 44*, 282–294.

Hatemi, P.K., & Verhulst, B. (2015). Political attitudes develop independently of personality traits. *PLoS One, 10*, e0118106.

Hazell, C.M., Berry, C., Bogen-Johnston, L., & Banerjee, M. (2022). Creating a hierarchy of mental health stigma: Testing the effect of psychiatric diagnosis on stigma. *British Journal of Psychiatry Open, 8*, e174, 1–7.

Heikkinen, H., Patja, K., & Jallinoja, P. (2010). Smokers' accounts on the health risks of smoking: Why is smoking not dangerous for me? *Social Science & Medicine, 71*, 877–883.

Helson, H. (1948). Adaptation-level as a basis for a quantitative theory of frames of reference. *Psychological Review, 55*, 297–313.

Hendrycks, D., Zhao, K., Basart, S., Steinhardt, J., & Song, D. (2021). Natural adversarial examples. *arXiv preprint* arXiv:1907.074v4 [cs.LG].

Hengartner, M.P. (2020). Is there a genuine placebo effect in acute depression treatments? A re-assessment of regression to the mean and spontaneous remission. *BMJ Evidence Based Medicine, 25*, 46–48.

Hengartner, M.P., Ajdacic-Gross, V., Wyss, C., Angst, J., & Rössler, W. (2016). Relationship between personality and psychopathology in a longitudinal community study: A test of the predisposition model. *Psychological Medicine, 46*, 1693–1705.

Hengartner, M.P., Tyrer, P., Ajdacic-Gross, V., Angst, J., & Rössler, W. (2018). Articulation and testing of a personalitycentred model of psychopathology: Evidence from a longitudinal community study over 30 years. *European Archives of Psychiatry and Clinical Neuroscience, 268*, 443–454.

Henningham, J.P. (1996). A 12-item scale of social conservatism. *Personality and Individual Differences, 20*, 517–519.

Henrich, J., Heine, S.J., & Norenzayan, A. (2010). The weirdest people in the world? *Behavioral and Brain Sciences, 33*, 61–83.

Herlitz, A., Hönig, I., Hedebrant, K., & Asperholm, M. (2024). A systematic review and new analyses of the gender-equality paradox. *Perspectives on Psychological Science*, 1–37. https://doi.org/10.1177/17456916231202685.

Herrnstein, R.J., & Murray, C. (1994). *The bell curve: Intelligence and class structure in American life.* New York: Free Press.

Hertwig, R., & Grüne-Yanoff, T. (2017). Nudging and boosting: Steering or empowering good decisions. *Perspectives in Psychological Science, 12*, 973–986.

Hetherington, E.M., & Kelly, J. (2002). *For better or worse: Divorce reconsidered.* New York: W.W. Norton.

Hettema, J.M., Neale, M.C., Myers, J.M., Prescott, C.A., & Kendler, D.S. (2006). A population-based twin study of the relationship between neuroticism and internalising disorders. *American Journal of Psychiatry, 163*, 857–864.

Hicklin, R.A., Ulery, B.T., Ausdemore, M., & Buscaglia, J. (2020). Why do latent fingerprint examiners differ in their conclusions? *Forensic Science International*, *316*, 110542.

Higbee, K.L., & Clay, S.L. (1998). College students' beliefs in the ten-percent myth. *The Journal of Psychology*, *132*, 469–476.

Higgins, E.T., Rossignac-Milon, M., & Echterhoff, G. (2021). Shared reality: From sharing-is-believing to merging minds. *Current Directions in Psychological Science*, *30*, 103–110.

Hilker, R., Helenius, D., Fagerlund, B., Skytthe, A., Christensen, K., Werge, T.M., et al. (2018). Heritability of schizophrenia and schizophrenia spectrum based on the nationwide Danish twin register. *Biological Psychiatry*, *83*, 492–498.

Hill, B.D., Foster, J.D., Elliott, E.M., Shelton, J.T., McCain, J., & Gouvier, W.D. (2013). Need for cognition is related to higher general intelligence, fluid intelligence, *Personality*, *47*, 22–25.

Hirschhorn, R., Biderman, D., Biderman, N., Yaron, I., Bennet, R., & Plotnik, M. (2024). Using virtual reality to induce multitrial inattentional blindness despite trialbytrial measures of awareness. *Behavior Research Methods*, *56*, 3452–3468.

Hirst, W., Phelps, E.A., Meksin, R., Vaidya, C.J., Johnson, M.K., Mitchell, K.J., et al. (2015). A ten-year follow-up of a study of memory for the attack of September 11, 2001: Flashbulb memories and memories for flashbulb events. *Journal of Experimental Psychology: General*, *144*, 604–623.

Hodgins, S., Mednick, S.A., Brennan, P.A., Schulsinger, F., & Engberg, M. (1996). Mental disorder and crime. *Archives of General Psychiatry*, *53*, 489–496.

Hollander, M.W., & Turowetz, J. (2018). Multiple compliant processes: A reply to Haslam and Reicher on the engaged followership explanation of 'obedience' in Milgram's experiments. *British Journal of Social Psychology*, *57*, 301–309.

Hollingworth, A., & Henderson, J.M. (2002). Accurate visual memory for previously attended objects in natural scenes. *Journal of Experimental Psychology: Human Perception & Performance*, *28*, 113–136.

Hollon, S.D. (2020). Is cognitive therapy enduring or antidepressant medications iatrogenic? Depression as an evolved adaptation. *American Psychologist*, *75*, 1207–1218.

Hollon, S.D., Andrews, P.W., & Thomson, J.A. (2021). Cognitive behaviour therapy for depression from an evolutionary perspective. *Frontiers in Psychiatry*, *12*, 667592.

Hollon, S.D., DeRubeis, R.J., Shelton, R.C., Amsterdam, J.D., Salomon, R.M., O'Reardon, J.P., et al. (2005). Prevention of relapse following cognitive therapy vs. medications in moderate to severe depression. *Archives of General Psychiatry*, *62*, 417–422.

Holmes, T.H., & Rahe, R.H. (1967). The Social Readjustment Rating Scale. *Journal of Psychosomatic Research*, *11*, 213–218.

Honts, C.R., Raskin, D.C., & Kircher, J.C. (1987). Effects of physical countermeasures and their electromyographic detection during polygraph tests for deception. *Journal of Psychophysiology*, *1*, 241–247.

Horwitz, T.B., Balbona, J.V., Paulich, K.N., & Keller, M.C. (2023). Evidence of correlations between human partners based on systematic reviews and meta-analyses of 22 traits and UK Biobank analysis of 133 traits. *Nature Human Behaviour*, *7*, 1–16.

Howard, I.P. (1996). Alhazen's neglected discoveries of visual phenomena. *Perception*, *25*, 1203–1217.

Howard-Jones, P.A. (2014). Neuroscience and education: Myths and messages. *Nature Reviews Neuroscience*, *15*, 817–824.

Hsu, N., Badura, K.L., Newman, D.A., & Speach, M.E.P. (2021). Gender, "masculinity," and "femininity": A meta-analytic review of gender differences in agency and communion. *Psychological Bulletin, 147,* 987–1011.

Hughes-Scholes, C., & Powell, M.B. (2008). An examination of the types of leading questions used by investigative interviewers of children. *Policing: An International Journal of Police Strategies and Management, 31,* 210–225.

Hull, C.L. (1943). *Principles of behaviour: An introduction to behaviour theory.* New York: Appleton-Century-Crofts.

Humphreys, G.W. (2016). Feature confirmation in object perception: Feature integration theory 26 years on from the Treisman Bartlett lecture. *Quarterly Journal of Experimental Psychology, 69,* 1910–1940.

Hunter, F.M. (1973). Letters to the editor. *Science, 180,* 361.

Hutchinson, B.T., Pammer, K., Bandara, K., & Jack, B. (2022). A tale of two theories: A meta-analysis of the attention set and load theories of inattentional blindness. *Psychological Bulletin, 148,* 370–396.

Hux, K., Schram, C.D., & Goeken, T. (2006). Misconceptions about brain injury: A survey replication study. *Brain Injury, 20,* 547–553.

Hyde, J.S. (2005). The gender similarities hypothesis. *American Psychologist, 60,* 581–592.

Hyman, I., Boss, S., Wise, B., McKenzie, K., & Caggiano, J. (2009). Did you see the unicycling clown? Inattentional blindness while walking and talking on a cell phone. *Applied Cognitive Psychology, 24,* 597–607.

Hyman, R., & Rosoff, B. (1984). Matching learning and teaching styles: The jug and what's in it. *Theory into Practice, 23,* 35–43.

Iacono, W.G. (2024). Psychology and the lie detector industry: A fifty-year perspective. *Biological Psychology, 190,* 108808.

Iacono, W.G., & Ben-Shakhar, G. (2019). Current status of forensic lie detection with the comparison question technique: An update of the 2003 national academy of sciences report on polygraph testing. *Law and Human Behavior, 43,* 86–98.

Iacono, W.G., & Lykken, D.T. (1997). The validity of the lie detector: Two surveys of scientific opinion. *Journal of Applied Psychology, 82,* 426–433.

Ickes, W., Snyder, M., & Garcia, S. (1997). Personality influences on the choice of situations. In *Handbook of personality psychology* (pp. 165–195). New York: Academic Press.

Ikier, S., Dönerkayalı, C., Halıcı, Ö.S., Gülseren, Z.A.K., Göksal, H., & Akbaş, B. (2024). When is memory more reliable? Scientific findings, theories, and myths. *Applied Neuropsychology: Adult, 31,* 77–94.

Illsley, C. (1987). *Fingerprints and the expert fingerprint witness.* Presentation at the FBI International Sympoium on Latent Prints FBI Academy. 16th July.

Innocence Project. (2021). *Understand the causes: The causes of wrongful conviction.* https://www.innocenceproject.org/eyewitness-identification-reform/.

International Situations Project. (2018). *Worldwide survey of personality and situational experience.* Unpublished raw data.

Irving, D., Clark, R.W.A., Lewandowsky, S., & Allen, P.J. (2018). Correcting statistical misinformation about scientific findings in the media: Causation versus correlation. *Journal of Experimental Psychology: Applied, 28,* 1–9.

Iveson, M.H., Cukic, I., Der, G. Batty, D., & Deary, I.J. (2018). Intelligence and all-cause mortality in the 6-day sample of the Scottish Mental Survey 1947 and their siblings: Testing the contribution of family background. *International Journal of Epidemiology, 47,* 89–96.

Jackson, P.H., & Lorber, J. (1984). Brain and ventricular volume in hydrocephalus. *Zeitschrift für Kinderchirugie, 39,* 91–93.

Jacobs, J. (1887). Experiments on prehension. *Mind, 12,* 75–79.

Jaeggi, S.M., Buschkuehl, M., Jonides, J., & Perrig, W.J. (2008). Improving fluid intelligence with training on working memory. *Proceedings of the National Academy of Sciences of the United States of America, 105,* 6829–6833.

Jaeggi, S.M., Studer-Luethi, B., Buschkuehl, M., Su, Y.F., Jonides, J., & Perrig, W.J. (2010). The relationship between n-back performance and matrix reasoning – implications for training and transfer. *Intelligence, 38,* 625–635.

Jaimes, A., Larose-Hebert, K., & Moreau, N. (2015). Current trends in theoretical orientation of psychologists: The case of Quebec clinicians. *Journal of Clinical Psychology, 71,* 1042–1048.

James, D., & Drakich, J. (1993). Understanding gender differences in amount of talk: Critical review of research. In D. Tannen (Ed.), *Gender and conversational interaction.* Oxford: Oxford University Press.

James, W. (1890). *The principles of psychology.* New York: Holt, Rinehard & Winston.

Jang, K.L., Livesley, W.J., & Vernon, P.A. (1996). Heritability of the big five personality dimensions and their facets: A twin study. *Journal of Personality, 64,* 577–591.

Jardine, B.B., Vannier, S., & Voyer, D. (2022). Emotional intelligence and romantic relationship satisfaction: A systematic review and meta-analysis. *Personality and Individual Differences, 196,* 111713.

Jarrett, C. (2014). *Great myths of the brain.* Chichester: Wiley Blackwell.

Jauhar, S., Cowen, P.J., & Browning, M. (2023). Fifty years on: Serotonin and depression. *Journal of Psychopharmacology, 37,* 237–241.

Jenkins, R., Dowsett, A.J., & Burton, A.M. (2018). How many faces do people know? *Proceedings of the the Royal Society B-Biological Sciences, 285,* 21081319.

Jenkins, R., White, D., Van Montfort, X., & Burton, A.M. (2011). Variability in photos of the same face. *Cognition, 121,* 313–323.

Jensen, A.R. (1980). *Bias in mental testing.* New York: Free Press.

Jensen, A.R. (1989). The relationship between learning and intelligence. *Learning and Individual Differences, 1,* 37–62.

Jensen, J., Bergin, A., & Greaves, D. (1990). The meaning of eclecticism: New survey and analysis of components. *Professional Psychology: Research and Practice, 21,* 124–130.

Jensen, M.S., Yao, R., Street, W.N., & Simons, D.J. (2011). Change blindness and inattentional blindness. *Wiley Interdisciplinary Reviews: Cognitive Science, 2,* 529–546.

Jeong, E.Y., & Jeong, I.-H. (2021). Individual differences in colour perception: The role of low-saturated and complementary colours in ambiguous images. *i-Perception, 12,* 1–19.

Jockin, V., MGue, M., & Lykken, D.T. (1996). Personality and divorce: A genetic analysis. *Journal of Personality and Social Psychology, 71,* 288–299.

John, L.K., Loewenstein, G., & Prelec, D. (2012). Measuring the prevalence of questionable research practices with incentives for truth-telling. *Psychological Science, 23,* 524–532.

Johnson, A.M., Vernon, P.A., & Feiler, A.R. (2008). Behavioural genetic studies of personality: An introduction and review of the results of 50+ years of research. In G.J. Boyle, G. Matthews, & D.H. Saklofske (Eds.), *The Sage handbook of personality theory and assessment* (Vol. 1, pp. 145–173). London: Sage.

Johnson, M.D. (2016). *Great myths of intimate relationships: Dating, sex and marriage.* Chichester: Wiley Blackwell.

Johnson, N.R. (1988). Fire in a crowded theatre: A descriptive investigation of the emergence of panic. *International Journal of Mass Emergencies and Disasters, 6,* 7–26.

Johnson, R.D., & Downing, L.L. (1979). Deindividuation and valence of cues: Effects on prosocial and antisocial behaviour. *Journal of Personality and Social Psychology, 37*, 1532–1538.

Johnson-Laird, P., & Stevenson, R. (1970). Memory for syntax. *Nature, 227*, 412.

Joiner, B.L. (1981). Lurking variables: Some examples. *The American Statistician, 35*, 227–233.

Jonas, E., Schulz-Hardt, S., Frey, D., & Thelen, N. (2001). Confirmation bias in sequential information search after preliminary decisions: An expansion of dissonance theoretical research on selective exposure to information. *Journal of Social and Personality Psychology, 80*, 557–571.

Jones, J.S., Milton, F., Mostazir, M., & Adlam, A.R. (2020). The academic outcomes of working memory and meta-cognitive strategy training in children: A double-blind randomised controlled trial. *Developmental Science, 23*, e12870.

Jones, S.P., Dwyer, D.M., & Lewis, M.B. (2017). The utility of multiple synthesised views in the recognition of unfamiliar faces. *Quarterly Journal of Experimental Psychology, 70*, 906–918.

Judge, T.A., Erez, A., Bono, J.E., & Thoresen, C.J. (2002). Are measures of self-esteem, neuroticism, locus of control, and generalized self-efficacy indicators of a common core construct? *Journal of Personality and Social Psychology, 83*, 693–710.

Judge, T.A., Higgins, C.A., Thoresen, C.J., & Barrick, M.R. (1999). The big five personality traits, general mental ability, and career success across the life span. *Personnel Psychology, 52*, 621–652.

Kagee, A., & Breet, E. (2015). Psychologists' endorsement of empirically unsupported statements in psychology: Noch einmal. *South African Journal of Psychology, 45*, 397–409.

Kahneman, D. (2003). A perspective on judgment and choice: Mapping bounded rationality. *American Psychologist, 58*, 697–720.

Kaiser, T. (2019). Nature and evoked culture: Sex differences in personality are uniquely correlated with ecological stress. *Personality and Individual Differences, 148*, 67–72.

Kaiser, T., Del Giudice, M., & Booth, T. (2020). Global sex differences in personality: Replication with an open online dataset. *Journal of Personality, 88*, 415–429.

Kajonius, P.J., & Johnson, J. (2018). Sex differences in 30 facets of the five-factor model of personality in the large public. *Personality and Individual Differences, 129*, 126–130.

Kalmoe, N.P., & Johnson, M. (2022). Genes, ideology, and sophistication. *Journal of Experimental Political Science, 9*, 255–266.

Karbach, J., & Verhaeghen, P. (2014). Making working memory work: A meta-analysis of executive-control and working memory training in older adults. *Psychological Science, 25*, 2027–2037.

Kassai, R., Futo, J., Demetrovics, Z., & Takacs, Z.K. (2019). A meta-analysis of the experimental evidence on the near- and far-transfer effects among children's executive function skills. *Psychological Bulletin, 145*, 165–188.

Kassin, S.M., & Barndollar, K.A. (1992). The psychology of eyewitness testimony – a comparison of experts and prospective jurors. *Journal of Applied Social Psychology, 22*, 1241–1249.

Kassin, S.M., Bogart, D., & Kerner, J. (2012). Confessions that corrupt: Evidence from the DNA exoneration case files. *Psychological Science, 23*, 41–45.

Kassin, S.M., Dror, I.E., & Kukucka, J. (2013). The forensic confirmation bias: Problems, perspectives, and proposed solutions. *Journal of Applied Research in Memory & Cognition, 2*, 42–52.

Kawasaki, Y., Reid, J.N., Ikeda, K., Liu, M., Bodil, S.A., & Karlsson, B.S.A. (2021). Colour judgements of #The dress and #The jacket in a sample of different cultures. *Perception, 50*, 216–230.

Kaya, N., Girgis, J., Hansma, B., & Birsen Donmezet, B. (2021). Hey, watch where you're going! An onroad study of driver scanning failures towards pedestrians and cyclists. *Accident Analysis and Prevention, 162,* 106380.

Kellman, P.J., Mnookin, J.L., Erlikhman, G., Garrigan, P., Ghose, T., Mettler, E., et al. (2014). Forensic comparison and matching of fingerprints: Using quantitative image measures for estimating error rates through understanding and predicting difficulty. *PLoS One, 9,* e94617.

Kemp, R. (2003). *Homeland security: Best practices for local government.* International City: County Management Association. www.icma.org.

Kenchel, J., Loftus, E.F., & Berkowitz, S.R. (2020). *Eyewitness testimony in actual cases of exoneration.* Poster presented at the annual conference of the American Psychology-Law Society, New Orleans, Louisiana.

Kendler, K.S. (2020). A prehistory of the diathesis-stress model: Predisposing and exciting causes of insanity in the 19th century. *American Journal of Psychiatry, 177,* 576–588.

Kendler, K.S., & Baker, J.H. (2007). Genetic influences on measures of the environment: A systematic review. *Psychological Medicine, 37,* 615–626.

Kendler, K.S., Karkowski, L.M., & Prescott, C.A. (1999). Causal relationship between stressful life events and the onset of major depression. *American Journal of Psychiatry, 156,* 837–841.

Kendler, K.S., Kessler, R.C., Walters, E.E., Mclean, C., Neal, M.C., Heath, A.C., et al. (1995). Stressful life events, genetic liability, and onset of an episode of major depression in women. *American Journal of Psychiatry, 152,* 833–842.

Kendler, K.S., Kuhn, J., & Prescott, C.A. (2004). The inter-relationshp of neuroticism, sex, and stressful life events in the prediction of episodes of major depression. *American Journal of Psychiatry, 161,* 631–636.

Kernis, M.H. (2003). Toward a conceptualization of optimal self-esteem. *Psychological Inquiry, 14,* 1–26.

Kety, S.S. (1974). From rationalisation to reason. *American Journal of Psychiatry, 131,* 957–963.

Keum, T.Y. (2023). Crowds and crowd-pleasing in Plato. *Review of Politics, First View,* 1–19.

Key, K.N., Neushatz, J.S., Gronlund, S.D., Deloach, D., Wetmore, S.A., & McAdoo, R.N. (2023). High eyewitness confidence is always compelling: That's a problem *Psychology, Crime and Law, 29,* 120–147.

Key, W.B. (1973). *Subliminal seduction.* Englewood Cliffs, NJ: Signet.

Kidd, E., & Donnelly, S. (2020). Individual differences in first language acquisition. *Annual Review of Linguistics, 6,* 319–340.

King, J.-R., Sitt, J.D., Faugeras, F., Rohaut, B., El Karoui, I., Cohen, L., et al. (2013). Information sharing in the brain indexes consciousness in non-communicative patients. *Current Biology, 23,* 1914–1919.

Kirby, C.K., Jaimes, P., Lorenz-Reaves, A.R., & Libarkin, J.C. (2019). Development of a measure to evaluate competence perceptions of natural and social science. *PLoS One, 14,* e0209311.

Kirsch, I. (2019). Placebo effect in the treatment of depression and anxiety. *Frontiers of Psychiatry, 10,* 407.

Kirsch, I., Mazzoni, G., Roberts, K., Dienes, Z., Hallquist, M.N., Williams, J., & Lynn, S.J. (2008). Slipping into trance. *Contemporary Hypnosis, 25,* 202–209.

Kirzinger, A.E., Weber, C., & Johnson, M. (2012). Genetic and environmental influences onmedia use and communication behaviours. *Human Communication Research, 38,* 144–171.

Kishi, T., Sakuma, K., Hatano, M., Okuya, M., Matsuda, Y., Jati, M., et al. (2023). Relapse and its modifiers in major depressive disorder after antidepressant discontinuation: Meta-analysis and meta-regression. *Molecular Psychiatry, 28,* 974–976.

Klein, C.T.F., & Helweg-Larsen, M. (2002). Perceived control and the optimistic bias: A meta-analytic review. *Psychology and Health, 17*, 437–444.

Klein, R.A., Vianello, M., Hasselman, F., Adams, B.G., Adams, R.B., Alper, S., et al. (2018). Many Labs 2: Investigating variation in replicability across samples and settings. *Advances in Methods and Practices in Psychological Science, 1*, 443–490.

Knafo, A., & Plomin, R. (2006a). Parental discipline and affection and children's prosocial behaviour. *Journal of Personality and Social Psychology, 90*, 147–164.

Knafo, A., & Plomin, R. (2006b). Prosocial behaviour from early to middle childhood: Genetic and environmental influences on stability and change. *Developmental Psychology, 42*, 771–786.

Knowles, H. (2018). Unchaining the Stanford Prison Experiment: Philip Zimbardo's famous study falls under scrutiny. *The Stanford Daily*. 13th November.

Koch, C., & Tsuchiya, N. (2007). Attention and consciousness: Two distinct brain processes. *Trends in Cognitive Sciences, 11*, 16–22.

Koehler, J.J. (1993). The influence of prior beliefs on scientific judgements of evidence quality. *Organizational Behavior and Human Decision Processes, 56*, 28–55.

Koehler, J.J. (2017). Intuitive error rate estimates for the forensic sciences. *Jurimetrics, 57*, 153–68.

Koehler, J.J., & Liu, S.D. (2021). Fingerprint error rate on close mismatches. *Journal of the Forensic Sciences, 66*, 129–134.

Koivisto, M., & Grassini, S. (2016). Neural processing around 200 ms after stimulus-onset correlates with subjective visual awareness. *Neuropsychologia, 84*, 235–243.

Koopmans, J.R., Slutske, W.S., van Baa, G.C., & Boomsma, D.I. (1999). The influence of religion on alcohol use initiation: Evidence for genotype X environment interaction. *Behavior Genetics, 29*, 445–53.

Kopta, S.M., Lueger, R.J., Saunders, S.M., & Howard, K.J. (1999). Individual psychotherapy outcome and process research: Challenges leading to greater turmoil or a positive transition? *Annual Review of Psychology, 50*, 441–469.

Kotov, R., Gamez, W., Schmidt, F., & Watson, D. (2010). Linking "big" personality traits to anxiety, depressive, and substance use disorders: A meta-analysis. *Psychological Bulletin, 136*, 768–821.

Kovacs, K., & Conway, A.R.A. (2016). Process overlap theory: A unified account of the general factor of intelligence. *Psychological Inquiry, 27*, 151–177.

Kovacs, K., & Conway, A.R.A. (2019). A unified cognitive/differential approach to human intelligence: Implications for IQ testing. *Journal of Applied Research in Memory and Cognition, 8*, 255–272.

Kruger, J., & Dunning, D. (1999). Unskilled and unaware of it: How difficulties in recognising one's own incompetence lead to inflated self-assessments. *Journal of Personality and Social Psychology, 77*, 1121–1134.

Kruger, J., Wirtz, D., & Miller, D.T. (2005). Counterfactual thinking and the first instinct fallacy. *Journal of Personality and Social Psychology, 88*, 725–735.

Kuhn, S., Ihmels, M., & Kutzner, F. (2021). Organic defaults in online-shopping: Immediate effects but no spillover to similar choices. *Journal of Consumer Behavior, 20*, 271–287.

Kukucka, J., Hiley, A., & Kassin, S.M. (2020). Forensic confirmation bias: Do jurors discount examiners who were exposed to task-irrelevant information? *Journal of Forensic Science, 65*, 1978–1990.

Kukucka, J., Kassin, S.M., Zapf, P.A., & Dror, I.E. (2017). Cognitive bias and blindness: A global survey of forensic science examiners. *Journal of Applied Research in Memory and Cognition, 6*, 452–459.

Kurdi, B., Seitchik, A.E., Axt, J., Carroll, T, Karapetyan, A., Kaushik, N., et al. (2018). Relationship between the implicit association test and intergroup behavior: A meta-analysis. *American Psychologist, 74*, 569–586.

Kvavilashvili, L., & Ellis, J. (2004). Ecological validity and twenty years of real-life/laboratory controversy in memory research: A critical (and historical) review. *History and Philosophy of Psychology, 6*, 59–80.

Laeng, B., Bloem, I.M., D'Ascenzo, S., & Tommasi, L. (2014). Scrutinising visual images: The role of gaze in mental imagery and memory. *Cognition, 131*, 263–283.

Lafer-Sousa, R., Hermann, K.L., & Conway, B.R. (2015). Striking individual differences in colour perception uncovered by "the dress" photograph. *Current Biology, 25*, R545–R546.

Lakatos, I. (1976). *Proofs and reputations.* Cambridge, UK: Cambridge University Press.

Lakens, D., Hilgard, J., & Staaks, J. (2016). On the reproducibility of meta-analyses: Six practical recommendations. *BMC Psychology, 4*, 24.

Laland, K., & Seed, A. (2021). Understanding human cognitive uniqueness. *Annual Review of Psychology, 72*, 689–716.

Laposa, J.M., & Rector, N.A. (2014). Effects of videotaped feedback in group cognitive therapy for social anxiety disorder. *International Journal of Cognitive Therapy, 7*, 360–372.

Lassonde, K.A., Kendeou, P., & O'Brien, E.J. (2016). Refutation texts: Overcoming psychological misconceptions that are resistant to change. *Scholarship of Teaching and Learning in Psychology, 2*, 62–74.

Latif, M., & Moulson, M.C. (2022). The importance of internal and external features in recognising faces that vary in familiarity and race. *Perception, 51*, 820–840.

Latorella, K.A. (1998). Effects of modality on interrupted flight deck performance: Implications for data link. *Proceedings of the Human Factors and Ergonomics Society 42nd Annual Meeting, 1–2*, 87–91.

Laurens, S., & Ballot, M. (2021). "We must continue." The strange appearance of "we" instead of "you" in the prods of the Milgram experiment. *Journal of Theoretical Social Psychology, 5*, 556–563.

Le Bon, G. (1895). *Psychologie des foules* [Crowd behaviour]. Paris, France: Alcan.

Le Texier, T. (2019). Debunking the Stanford prison experiment. *American Psychologist, 74*, 823–839.

Levin, D.T., & Angelone, B.L. (2008). The visual metacognition questionnaire: A measure of intuitions about vision. *American Journal of Psychology, 121*, 451–472.

Levin, D.T., Drivdahl, S.B., Momen, N., & Beck, M.R. (2002). False predictions about the detectability of unexpected visual changes: The role of metamemory and beliefs about attention in causing change blindness blindness. *Consciousness and Cognition, 11*, 507–527.

Levin, D.T., Seiffert, A.E., Cho, S.J., & Carter, K.E. (2018). Are failures to look, to represent, or to learn associated with change blindness during screen-capture video learning? *Cognitive Research-Principles and Implications, 3*, 49.

Levin, D.T., & Simons, D.J. (1997). Failure to detect changes to attended objects in motion pictures. *Psychonomic Bulletin and Review, 4*, 501–506.

Lewin, R. (1980). Is your brain really necessary? *Science, 210*, 1232–1234.

Lewis, M., Mathur, M.B., VanderWeele, T.J., & Frank, M.C. (2022). The puzzling relationship between multi-laboratory replications and meta-analyses of the published literature. *Royal Society Open Science, 9*, 211499.

Li, W., & Hartshorne, J.K. (2024). Don't let perfect be the enemy of better: In defence of unparameterised megastudies. *Behavioral and Brain Sciences, 47*, e53.

Lief, H., & Fetkewicz, J. (1995). Retractors of false memories: The evolution of pseudo-memories. *Journal of Psychiatry & Law, 23*, 411–436.

Lilienfeld, S.O., Kirsch, I., Sarbin, T.R., Lynn, S.J., Chaves, J.F., Ganaway, G.K., et al. (1999). Dissociative identity disorder and the socio-cognitive model: Recalling the lessons of the past. *Psychological Bulletin, 125*, 507–523.

Lilienfeld, S.O., Lynn, S.J., Ruscio, J., & Beyerstein, B.L. (2010). *50 Great Myths of popular psychology: Shattering widespread misconceptions about human behaviour*. Chichester: Wiley-Blackwell.

Lilienfeld, S.O., & Strother, A.N. (2020). Psychological measurement and the replication crisis: Four sacred cows. *Canadian Psychology, 61,* 281–288.

Lilienfeld, S.O., Wood, M., & Garb, M.N. (2000). The scientific status of projective techniques. *Psychological Science in the Public Interest, 1,* 27–66.

Lilliengren, P. (2023). A comprehensive overview of randomised controlled trials of psychodynamic psychotherapies. *Psychoanalytic Psychotherapy, 37,* 117–140.

Lindqvist, E., Östling, R., & Cesarini, D. (2020). Long-run effects of lottery wealth on psychological well-being. *Review of Economic Studies, 87,* 2703–2726.

Link, B.G., Phelan, J.C., Bresnahan, M., Stueve, A., & Pescosolido, B.A. (1999). Public conceptions of mental illness: Labels, causes, dangerousness, and social distance. *American Journal of Public Health, 8,* 1328–1333.

Liu, Q., & Nesbit, J.C. (2024). The relation between need for cognition and academic achievement: A meta-analysis. *Review of Educational Research, 94,* 155–192.

Löckenhoff, C.E., Chan, W., McCrae, R.R., De Fruyt, F., Jussim, L., De Bolle, M., et al. (2014). Gender stereotypes of personality: Universal and accurate? *Journal of Cross-Cultural Psychology, 45,* 675–694.

Loeffler, C.E., Hyatt, J., & Ridgeway, G. (2019). Measuring self-reported wrongful convictions among prisoners. *Journal of Quantitative Criminology, 35,* 259–286.

Loehlin, J.C., Horn, J.M., & Willerman, L. (1981). Personality resemblance in adoptive families. *Behavior Genetics, 11,* 309–330.

Loehlin, J.C., Willerman, L., & Horn, J.M. (1987). Personality resemblance in adoptive families: A 10-year follow-up. *Journal of Personality and Social Psychology, 53,* 961–969.

Loewenstein, R.J. (2020). Firebug! Dissociative identity disorder? Malingering? Or . . .? An intensive case study of an arsonist. *Psychological Injury and Law, 13,* 187–224.

Loftus, E.F., & Loftus, G.R. (1980). On the permanence of stored information in the human brain. *American Psychologist, 35,* 409–420.

Loftus, E.F., & Pickrell, J.E. (1995). The formation of false memories. *Psychiatric Annals, 25,* 720–725.

Logie, R.H. (2023). Strategies, debates, and adversarial collaboration in working memory: The 51st Bartlett Lecture. *Quarterly Journal of Experimental Psychology, 76,* 2431–2460.

Logie, R.H., Belletier, C., & Doherty, J.D. (2021a). Integrating theories of working memory. In R.H. Logie, V. Camos, & N. Cowan (Eds.), *Working memory: State of the science* (pp. 389–429). Oxford: Oxford University Press.

Logie, R.H., Camos, V., & Cowan, N. (Eds.). (2021b). *Working memory: State of the science*. Oxford: Oxford University Press.

Lönnqvist, J.-E., Verkasalo, M., Mäkinen, S., & Henriksson, M. (2009). High neuroticism at age 20 predicts history of mental disorders and low self-esteem at age 35. *Journal of Clinical Psychology, 65,* 781–790.

Lorber, J. (1981). Is your brain really necessary? *Nursing Mirror, 152,* 29–30.

Lorber, J. (1983). Is your brain really necessary? In D. Voth (Ed.), *Hydrocephalus im frühen kindesalter: Fortschritte der Grundlagenforschung, Diagnostik und Therapie* (pp. 2–14). Stuttgart: Enke.

Lucas, R.E. (2007). Adaptation and the set-point model of subjective well-being: Does happiness change after major life events? *Current Directions in Psychological Science, 16,* 75–79.

Ludeke, S.G., & Krueger, R.F. (2013). Authoritarianism as a personality trait: Evidence from a longitudinal behaviour genetic study. *Personality and Individual Differences, 55,* 480–484.

Luria, A.R. (1968). *The mind of a mnemonist*. New York: Basic Books.

Lykken, D., & Tellegen, A. (1996). Happiness is a stochastic phenomenon. *Psychological Science*, 7, 186–189.

Lynn, S.J., Boycheva, E., Deming, A., Lilienfeld, S.O., & Hallquist, M.N. (2009). Forensic hypnosis: The state of the science. In J. Skeem, K. Douglas, & S.O. Lilienfeld (Eds.), *Psychological science in the courtroom: Controversies and consensus* (pp. 80–99). New York, NY: Guilford.

Lynn, S.J., Kirsch, I., Terhune, D.B., & Green, J.P. (2020). Myths and misconceptions about hypnosis and suggestion: Separating fact and fiction. *Applied Cognitive Psychology*, 34, 1253–1264.

Lynn, S.J., Maxwell, R., Merckelbach, H., Lilienfeld, S.O., van Heugten-van der Kloet, D., & Miskovica, V. (2019). Dissociation and its disorders: Competing models, future directions, and a way forward. *Clinical Psychology Review*, 73, 101755.

MacCann, C., Jiang, Y.X., Brown, L.E.R., Double, K.S., Bucich, M., & Minbashian, A. (2020). Emotional intelligence predicts academic performance: A meta-analysis. *Psychological Bulletin*, 146, 150–186.

MacCorquodale, K., & Meehl, P.E. (1948). On a distinction between hypothetical constructs and intervening variables. *Psychological Review*, 55, 95–107.

Mack, A., & Rock, I. (1998). *Inattentional blindness*. Cambridge, MA: MIT Press.

Macnamara, B.N., Moreau, D., & Hambrick, D.Z. (2016). The relationship between deliberate practice and performance in sports: A meta-analysis. *Perspectives on Psychological Science*, 11, 333–350.

Madison, P. (1956). Freud's repression concept: A survey and attempted clarification. *International Journal of Psychoanalysis*, 37, 75–81.

Madsen, H.B., & Kim, J.H. (2016). Ontogeny of memory: An update on 40 years of work on infantile amnesia. *Behavioural Brain Research*, 298, 4–14.

Maggio, L.A., Tannery, N.H., & Kanter, S.L. (2011). Reproducibility of literature search reporting in medical education reviews. *Academic Medicine*, 86, 1049–1054.

Magnussen, S., Andersson, J., Cornoldi, C., De Beni, R., Endestad, T., Goodman, G., et al. (2006). What people believe about memory. *Memory*, 14, 595–613.

Mahesan, D., Antonenko, D., Flöel, A., & Fischer, R. (2023). Modulation of the executive control network by anodal tDCS over the left dorsolateral prefrontal cortex improves task shielding in dual tasking. *Scientific Reports*, 13, 6277.

Mahr, J.B., van Bergen, P., Sutton, J., Schacter, D.L., & Heyes, C. (2023). Mnemicity: A cognitive gadget? *Perspectives on Psychological Science*, 18, 1160–1177.

Maier, M., Bartoš, F., Stanley, T.D., Shanks, D.R., Harris, A.J., & Wagenmakers, E.J. (2022). No evidence for nudging after adjusting for publication bias. *Proceedings of the National Academy of Sciences*, 119, e2200300119.

Malle, B.F. (2006). The actor-observer asymmetry in causal attribution: A (surprising) meta-analysis. *Psychological Bulletin*, 132, 895–919.

Malouff, J.M., Schutte, N.S., & Thorsteinsson, E.B. (2014). Trait emotional intelligence and romantic relationship satisfaction: A meta-analysis. *American Journal of Family Therapy*, 42, 53–66.

Mann, L. (1981). The baiting crowd in episodes of threatened suicide. *Journal of Personality and Social Psychology*, 41, 703–709.

Marcus, G. (2020). The next decade in AI: Four steps towards robust artificial intelligence. *arXiv preprint* arXiv:2002.06177.

Marcus, G., & Davis, E. (2020). GPT-3, BloviatorL open language generator has no idea what it's talking about. *MIT Technology Review*, 1–4. 8th August. www.technologyreview.com.

Mark, J. (2011). The menace within. *Stanford Alumni*. July–August.

Marr, D. (1982). *Vision: A computational investigation into the human representation and processing of visual information*. San Francisco, CA: W.H. Freeman.

Marsh, R.J., Dorahy, M.J., Butler, C., Middleton, W., de Jong, P.J., Kemp, S., et al. (2021). Inter-identity amnesia for neutral episodic self-referential and autobiographical memory in dissociative identity disorder: An assessment of recall and recognition. *PLoS One, 16,* e0245849.

Marsh, R.J., Dorahy, M.J., Verschuere, B., Butler, C., Middleton, W., & Huntjens, R.J.C. (2018). Transfer of episodic self-referential memory across amnesic identities in dissociative identity disorder using the autobiographical implicit association test. *Journal of Abnormal Psychology, 127,* 751–757.

Marston, W.M. (1917). Systolic blood pressure symptoms of deception. *Journal Experimental Psychology, 2,* 117–163.

Marston, W.M. (1943). Why 100,000,000 Americans read comics. *The American Scholar, 13,* 35–44.

Martin, R.A. (1989). Techniques for data acquisition and analysis in field investigations of stress. In R.W.J. Neufeld (Ed.), *Advances in the investigation of psychological stress.* New York: Wiley.

Massa, L.J., & Mayer, R.E. (2006). Testing the ATI hypothesis: Should multimedia instruction accommodate verbaliser-visualiser cognitive style? *Learning and Individual Differences, 16,* 321–336.

Matarazzo, J.D. (1972). *Wechsler's measurement and appraisal of adult intelligence* (5th ed.). Baltimore: Williams & Wilkins.

Matt, G.E., & Navarro, A.M. (1997). What meta-analyses have and have not taught us about psychotherapy effects: A review and future directions. *Clinical Psychology Review, 17,* 1–32.

Matteson, L.K., McGue, M., & Iacono, W.G. (2013). Shared environmental influences on personality: A combined twin and adoption approach. *Behavior Genetics, 43,* 491–504.

Maudsley, H. (1867). On some of the causes of insanity. *Journal of Mental Science, 12,* 488–502.

Mayer, J.D., Salovey, P., Caruso, D.R., & Sitarenios, G. (2003). Measuring emotional intelligence with the MSCEIT V2.0. *Emotion, 3,* 97–105.

McCourt, K., Bouchard, T.J., Lykken, D.T., Tellegen, A., & Keyes, M. (1999). Authoritarianism revisited: Genetic and environmental influences examined in twins reared apart and together. *Personality and Individual Differences, 27,* 985–1014.

McCrae, R.R. (2020). The five-factor model of personality: Consensus and controversy. In P.J. Corr & G. Matthews (Eds.), *The Cambridge handbook of personality psychology* (pp. 129–141). Cambridge: Cambridge University Press.

McCrudden, M.T., Barnes, A., McTigue, E.M., Welch, C., & MacDonald, E. (2017). The effect of perspective-taking on reasoning about strong and weak belief-relevant arguments. *Thinking & Reasoning, 23,* 115–133.

McGrew, K.S. (2009). CHC theory and the human cognitive abilities research: Standing on the shoulders of the giants of psychometric intelligence research. *Intelligence, 37,* 1–10.

McGuire, W.J. (1969). The nature of attitudes and attitude change. In G. Lindzey & E. Aronson (Eds.), *The handbook of social psychology* (2nd ed., Vol. 3, pp. 136–314). Reading, MA: Addison-Wesley.

McIntosh, R.D., Moore, A.B., Liu, Y., & Della Sala, S. (2022). Skill and self-knowledge: Empirical refutation of the dual-burden account of the Dunning–Kruger effect. *Royal Society Open Science, 9,* 191727.

McLaughlin, K.A., & Nolen-Hoeksma, S. (2011). Rumination as a transdiagnostic factor in depression and anxiety. *Behaviour Research and Therapy, 49,* 186–197.

McLeod, A. (2001). Therapeutic interventions. In M. Eysenck (Ed.), *Psychology: An integrated approach* (pp. 563–589). Harlow: Addison Wesley Longman.

McMurtrie, J. (2010). Swirls and whorls: Litigating post-conviction claims of finger-print misidentification after the NAS Report. *Utah Law Review, 267–273.*

McNally, R.J. (2003). *Remembering trauma.* Cambridge, MA: Harvard University Press.

McNally, R.J. (2012). Searching for repressed memory. In R.F. Belli (Ed.), *Nebraska symposium on motivation. Vol. 58: True and false recovered memories: Toward a reconciliation of the debate* (pp. 121–147). New York, NY: Springer.

McNally, R.J. (2024). The return of repression? Evidence from cognitive psychology. *Topics in Cognitive Science, 16, 661–674.*

Mehl, M.R., Vazire, S., Ramirez-Esparza, N., Slatcher, R.B., & Pennebaker, J.W. (2007). Are women really more talkative than men? *Science, 317,* 82.

Meijer, E.H., Klein Selle, N., Elber, L., & Ben-Shakhar, G. (2014). Memory detection with the concealed information test: A meta–analysis of skin conductance, respira-tion, heart rate, and P300 data. *Psychophysiology, 51,* 879–904.

Meinz, E.J., Tennison, J.L., & Dominguez, W.A. (2024). Who believes the "50 great myths of psychology"? *Teaching of Psychology, 51,* 30–38.

Melby-Lervåg, M., & Hulme, C. (2016). There is no convincing evidence that work-ing memory training is effective: A reply to Au et al. (2014) and Karbach and Ver-haegh (2014). *Psychonomic Bulletin & Review, 23,* 324–330.

Melnikoff, D.E., & Bargh, J.A. (2018). The mythical number two. *Trends in Cogni-tive Sciences, 22,* 280–293.

Melnikoff, D.E., & Strohminger, M. (2024). Bayesianism and wishful thinking are compatible. *Nature Human Behaviour, 8,* 692–701.

Menuet, R., Meudec, R., Dockès, J., Varoquaux, G., & Thirion, B. (2022). Com-prehensive decoding mental processes from web repositories of functional brain images. *Scientific Reports, 12,* 7050.

Merckelbach, H., & Wessel, I. (1998). Assumptions of students and psychotherapists about memory. *Psychological Reports, 82,* 763–770.

Mertens, S., Herberz, M., Hahnel, U.J., & Brosch, T. (2022). The effectiveness of nudging: A meta-analysis of choice architecture interventions across behavioural domains. *Proceedings of the National Academy of Sciences, 119,* e2107346118.

Meyer, G.J., Finn, S.E., Eyde, L.D., Kay, G.G., Moreland, K.L., Dies, R.R., et al. (2001). Psychological testing and psychological assessment. *American Psycholo-gist, 56,* 128–165.

Michopoulos, I., Furukawa, T.A., Noma, H., Kishimoto, S., Onishi, A., Ostinelli, E.G., et al. (2021). Different control conditions can produce different effect esti-mates in psychotherapy trials for depression. *Journal of Clinical Epidemiology, 132,* 59–70.

Miele, F. (2002). *Intelligence, race, and genetics: Conversations with Arthur J. Jensen.* Boulder, CO: Westview.

Mihura, J.L., Meyer, G.J., Dumitrascu, N., & Bombel, G. (2013). The validity of individual Rorschach variables: Systematic reviews and meta-analyses of the com-prehensive system. *Psychological Bulletin, 139,* 548–605.

Milgram, S. (1959). Note to self. In *Stanley milgram papers (series I, box 23, folder 383).* New Haven, CT: Yale University Archives.

Milgram, S. (1963). Behavioural study of obedience. *Journal of Abnormal and Social Psychology, 67,* 371–378.

Milgram, S. (1965). Some conditions of obedience and disobedience to authority. *Human Relations, 18,* 57–76.

Milgram, S. (1974). *Obedience to authority.* New York: Doubleday.

Milkman, K.L., Gandhi, L., Patel, M.S., Graci, H.N., Gromet, D.M., Hod, H., et al. (2022). A 680,000-person megastudy of nudges to encourage vaccination in phar-macies. *Proceedings of the National Academy of Sciences, 119.*

Milkman, K.L., Gromet, D., Ho, H., Kay, J.S, Lee, T.W., Pandiloski, P., et al. (2021). Megastudies improve the impact of applied behavioural science. *Nature*, 600(7889), 478–483.

Mischel, W. (1968). *Personality and assessment*. London: Wiley.

Mischel, W. (2008). The toothbrush problem. *APS Observer*, 21(11). 1st December. https://www.psychologicalscience.org/observer/the-toothbrush-problem.

Mixon, D. (1971). Further conditions of obedience and disobedience to authority *Dissertation Abstracts International*, 32, 48488. University Microfilms No. 72-6477.

Mixon, D. (1990). *Obedience and civilisation: Authorised crime and the normality of evil*. London: Pluto.

Moncada, A. (2024). When Latin America took the "talking cure". *Americas Quarterly*. 23rd April.

Moncrieff, J., Cooper, R.E., Stockmann, T., Amendola, S., Hengartner, M.P., & Horowitz, M.A. (2023). The serotonin theory of depression: A systematic umbrella review of the evidence. *Molecular Psychiatry*, 28, 3243–3256.

Mondak, J.J., & Halperin, K.D. (2008). A framework for the study of personality and political behaviour. *British Journal of Political Science*, 38, 335–362.

Moravec, H. (1988). *Mind children*. Cambridge, MA: Harvard University Press.

Morawetz, C., Holz, P., Baudewig, J., Treue, S., & Dechent, P. (2007). Split of attentional resources in human visual cortex. *Visual Neuroscience*, 24, 817–826.

Moreno, A. (2021). Molecular mechanisms of forgetting. *European Journal of Neuroscience*, 54, 6912–6932.

Moro, V., Berlucchi, G., Lerch, J., Tomaiuolo, F., & Aglioti, S.M. (2008). Selective deficit of mental visual imagery with intact primary visual cortex and visual perception. *Cortex*, 44, 109–118.

Morris, J., Tattan-Birch, H., Albery, I.P., Heather, N., & Moss, A.C. (2024). Look away now! Defensive processing and unrealistic optimism by level of alcohol consumption. *Psychology & Health*. https://doi.org/10.1080/08870446.2024.2316681.

Moscowitz, A., & Heim, G. (2011). Eugen Bleuler's dementia praecox or the group of schizophrenias (1911): A centenary appreciation and reconsideration. *Schizophrenia Bulletin*, 37, 471–479.

Mosing, M.A., Madison, G., Pedersen, N.L., Kuja-Halkola, R., & Ullén, F. (2014). Practice does not make perfect: No causal effect of music practice on music ability. *Psychological Science*, 25, 1795–1803.

Motta, M., Callaghan, T., & Sylvester, S. (2018). Knowing less but presuming more: Dunning-Kruger effects and the endorsement of anti-vaccine policy attitudes. *Social Science & Medicine*, 211, 274–281.

Mu, W., Luo, J., Rieger, S., Trautwein, U., & Roberts, B.W. (2019). The relationship between self-esteem and depression when controlling for neuroticism. *Collabra Psychology*, 5, 11.

Murphy, G.L. (2011). Models and concepts. In E.M. Pothod & A.J. Wills (Eds.), *Formal approaches in categorisation* (pp. 299–312) Cambridge: Cambridge University Press.

Musek, J. (2007). A general factor of personality: Evidence for the big one in the five-factor model. *Journal of Research in Personality*, 41, 1213–1233.

Musgrave, A., & Pigden, C. (2021). *Imre Lakatos. Stanford encyclopedia of philosophy*. Stanford, CA: Stanford University.

Myers, B., Latter, R., & Abdollahi-Arena, M.K. (2006). The court of public opinion: Lay perceptions of polygraph tests. *Law and Human Behavior*, 30, 509–523.

Nairne, J.S. (2015). The three "Ws" of episodic memory: What, when, and where. *American Journal of Psychology*, 128, 267–279.

Nash, M. (1987). What, if anything, is regressed about hypnotic age regression? A review of the empirical literature. *Psychological Bulletin, 102,* 42–52.

Nathan, D. (2011). *Sybil exposed: The extraordinary story behind the famous multiple personality case.* New York: Free Press.

Nature. (2005). In praise of soft science. *Nature, 435,* 1003.

Nederlof, A.F., Muris, P., & Hovens, J.E. (2013). The epidemiology of violent behaviour in patients with a psychotic disorder: A systematic review of studies since 1980. *Aggressive and Violent Behavior, 18,* 183–189.

Neumann, C., Champod, C., Yoo, M., Genessay, T., & Langenburg, G. (2014). *Improving the understanding and the reliability of the concept of "sufficiency" in friction ridge examination.* Washington, DC: National Institute of Justice – Office of Justice Program.

Newman, D.A., Joseph, D.L., & MacCann, C. (2010). Emotional intelligence and job performance: The importance of emotion regulation and emotional labour context. *Industrial and Organizational Psychology, 3,* 159–164.

Newson, J.J., Pastukh, V., & Thiagarajan, T.C. (2021). Poor separation of clinical symptom profiles by DSM-5 disorder criteria. *Frontiers in Psychiatry, 12,* 775762.

Newton, P.M., & Miah, M. (2017). Evidence-based higher education: Is the learning styles 'myth' important? *Frontiers in Psychology, 8,* 444.

Newton, P.M., & Salvi, A. (2020). How common Is belief in the learning styles neuromyth, and does it matter? A pragmatic systematic review. *Frontiers in Education, 5,* 602451.

Ng, N.F., Schafer, R.J., Simone, C.M., & Osman, A.M. (2020). Perceptions of brain training: Public expectations of cognitive benefits from popular activities. *Frontiers in Human Neuroscience, 14,* 15.

Nguyen, P.L.L., Syed, M., & McGue, M. (2021). Behaviour genetics research on personality: Moving beyond traits to examine characteristic adaptations. *Social and Personality Psychology Compass, 15,* e12628.

Nicholson, I. (2011)."Shocking" masculinity: Stanley Milgram, "obedience to authority," and the "crisis of manhood" in Cold War America. *Isis, 102,* 238–268.

Nielsen, Y.A., Pfattheicher, S., & Thielmann, I. (2024). How much can personality predict prosocial behaviour? *European Journal of Personality,* 1–18. https://doi.org/10.1177/08902070241251516.

Nisbett, R.E., Peng, K., Choi, I., & Norenzayan, A. (2001). Culture and systems of thought: Holistic vs. analytic cognition. *Psychological Review, 108,* 291–310.

Noack, H., Lövdén, M., & Schmiedek, F. (2014). On the validity and generality of transfer effects in cognitive training research. *Psychological Research, 78,* 773–789.

Nørby, S. (2015). Why forget? On the adaptive value of memory loss. *Perspectives on Psychological Science, 10,* 551–578.

Norcross, J.C., & Karpiak, C.P. (2012). Clinical psychologists in the 2010s: 50 years of the APA division of clinical psychology. *Clinical Psychology: Science and Practice, 19,* 1–12.

Norton, A.R., & Abbott, M. (2017). The role of environmental factors in the aetiology of social anxiety disorder: A review of the theoretical and empirical literature. *Behavior Change, 34,* 76–97.

Oberauer, K., & Lewandowsky, S. (2019). Addressing the theory crisis in psychology. *Psychonomic Bulletin & Review, 26,* 1596–1618.

O'Boyle, E.H., Humphrey, R.H., Pollack, J.M., Hawver, T.H., & Story, P.A. (2011). The relation between emotional intelligence and job performance: A meta-analysis. *Journal of Organizational Behavior, 32,* 788–818.

O'Brien, T.C., Palmer, R., & Albarracin, D. (2021). Misplaced trust: When trust in science fosters belief in pseudoscience and the benefits of critical evaluation. *Journal of Experimental Social Psychology, 96,* 104184.

O'Connor, T.G., Caspi, A., DeFries, J.C., & Plomin, R. (2003). Genotype–environment interaction in children's adjustment to parental separation. *Journal of Child Psychology and Psychiatry, 44*, 849–856.

Odegaard, B, Chang, M.Y., Lau, H., & Cheung, S.-H. (2018). Inflation versus filling-in: Why we feel we see more than we actually do in peripheral vision. *Philosophical Transactions of the Royal Society London B Biological Sciences, 373*, 1755.

Ogawa, T., Matsuda, I., Tsuneoka, M., & Verschuere, B. (2015). The concealed information test in the laboratory versus Japanese field practice: Bridging the scientist–practitioner gap. *Archives of Forensic Psychology, 1*, 16–27.

Okubo, L., & Yokosawa, K. (2023). Attentional allocation and the pan-field colour illusion. *Journal of Vision, 23*, 1–13.

Ones, D.S., Viswesvaran, C., & Reiss, A.D. (1996). Role of social desirability in personality testing for personnel selection: The red herring. *Journal of Applied Psychology, 81*, 660–679.

Open Science Collaboration. (2015). Estimating the reproducibility of psychological science. *Science, 349*, aac4716.

Orne, M.T. (1962). On the social psychology of the psychological experiment: With particular reference to demand characteristics and their implications. *American Psychologist, 17*, 776–783.

Orne, M.T. (1979). The use and misuse of hypnosis in court. *International Journal of Clinical and Experimental Hypnosis, 27*, 311–341.

Orth, U., & Robins, R.W. (2022). Is high self-esteem beneficial? Revisiting a classic question. *American Psychologist, 77*, 5–17.

Ost, J. (2017). Adults' retractions of childhood sexual abuse allegations: High-stakes and the (in)validation of recollection. *Memory, 25*, 900–909.

Otgaar, H., Howe, M.L., Dodier, O., Lilienfeld, S.O., Loftus, E.F., Lynn, S.J., et al. (2021). Belief in unconscious repressed memory persists. *Perspectives on Psychological Science, 16*, 454–460.

Otgaar, H., Howe, M.L., & Patihis, L. (2022). What science tells us about false and repressed memories. *Memory, 30*, 16–21.

Otgaar, H., Howe, M.L., Patihis, L., Merckelbach, H., Lynn, S.J., Lilienfeld, S.O., & Loftus, E.F. (2019). The return of the repressed: The persistent and problematic claims of long-forgotten trauma. *Perspectives on Psychological Science, 14*, 1072–1095.

Ottati, V., Bodenhausen, G.V., & Newman, L.S. (2006). Social psychological models of mental illness stigma. In P.W. Corrigan (Ed.), *On the stigma of mental illness: Practical strategies for research and social change* (pp. 99–128). American Psychological Association.

Overgaard, M., Fehl, K., Mouridsen, K., Bergholt, B., & Cleermans, K. (2008). Seeing without seeing? Degraded conscious vision in a blindsight patient. *PLoS One, 3*, e3028.

Overgaard, M., & Sandberg, K. (2021). The perceptual awareness scale – recent controversies and debates. *Neuroscience of Consciousness, 7*, 1–8.

Owen, P.R. (2012). Portrayals of schizophrenia by entertainment media: A content a nalysis of contemporary movies. *Psychiatric Services, 63*, 655–659.

Palfi, B., Parris, B.A., McLatchie, N., Kekecs, Z., & Dienes, Z. (2021). Can unconscious intentions be more effective than conscious intentions? Test of the role of metacognition in hypnotic response. *Cortex, 135*, 219–239.

Papadatou-Pastou, M., Touloumakos, A.K., & Koutouveli, C. (2021). The learning styles neuromyth: When the same term means different things to different teachers. *European Journal of Psychology of Education, 36*, 511–531.

Papatheodorou, S. (2019). Umbrella reviews: What they are and why we need them. *European Journal of Epidemiology, 34*, 543–546.

Papp, B. (2020). Myths and misconceptions about disasters: Do students in the field know better? *Annals of Burns and Fire Disasters, 33,* 253–261.

Parker, A., & Dagnall, N. (2020). Eye-closure and the retrieval of item-specific information in recognition memory. *Consciousness and Cognition, 77,* 102858.

Parker, E.S., Cahill, L., & McGaugh, J.L. (2006). A case of unusual autobiographical remembering. *Neurocase, 12,* 35–49.

Parong, J., Seitz, A.R., Jaeggi, S.M., & Green, C.S. (2022). Expectation effects in working memory training. *Proceedings of the National Academy of Sciences USA, 119,* e2209308119.

Parsons, T.D. (2015). Virtual reality for enhanced ecological validity and experimental control in the clinical, affective and social neurosciences. *Frontiers in Human Neuroscience, 9,* 660.

Pashler, H., McDaniel, M., Rohrer, D., & Bjork, R. (2008). Learning styles: Concepts and evidence. *Psychological Science in the Public Interest, 9,* 105–119.

Patihis, L., Ho, L.Y., Loftus, E.F., & Herrera, M.E. (2021). Memory experts' beliefs about repressed memory. *Memory, 29,* 823–828.

Patihis, L., Ho, L.Y., Tingen, I.W., Lilienfeld, S.O., & Loftus, E.F. (2014). Are the "memory wars" over? A scientist-practitioner gap in beliefs about repressed memory. *Psychological Science, 25,* 519–530.

Patihis, L., & Lynn, S.J. (2017). Psychometric comparison of dissociative experiences scales II and C: A weak trauma-dissociation link. *Applied Cognitive Psychology, 11,* 392–403.

Patihis, L., & Pendergrast, M.H. (2019). Reports of recovered memories of abuse in therapy in a large age-representative U.S. national sample: Therapy type and decade comparisons. *Clinical Psychological Science, 7,* 3–21.

Pearson, J., & Kosslyn, S.M. (2015). The heterogeneity of mental representation: Ending the imagery debate. *Proceedings of the National Association of Sciences, 112*(33), 10089–10092.

Pechey, R., & Monsivais, P. (2016). Socioeconomic inequalities in the healthiness of * food choices: Exploring the contributions of food expenditures. *Preventative Medicine, 88,* 203–209.

Penfield, W. (1958). Some mechanisms of consciousness discovered during electrical stimulation of the brain. *Proceedings of the National Academy of Sciences, 44,* 51–66.

Penfield, W. (1959). The interpretive cortex: The stream of consciousness in the human brain can be electrically reactivated. *Science, 129,* 1719–1725.

Penfield, W. (1969). Consciousness, memory, and, man's conditioned reflexes. In K. Pribram (Ed.), *On the biology of learning.* New York: Harcourt, Brace & World.

Penfield, W., & Perot, P. (1963). The brain's record of auditory and visual experience: A final summary and discussion. *Brain, 86,* 595–696.

Perry, G. (2013). *Behind the shock machine: The untold story of the notorious Milgram psychology experiments.* New York: New Press.

Perry, G., Brannigan, A., Wanner, R.A., & Stam, H. (2020). Credibility and incredulity in Milgram's obedience experiments: A re-analysis of an unpublished test. *Social Psychology Quarterly, 83,* 88–106.

Pescosolido, B.A., Halpern-Manners, A., Luo, L., & Perry, B. (2021). Trends in public stigma of mental illness in the US, 1996–2018. *JAMA Nature Open, 4,* e2140202.

Peters, U., Krauss, A., & Braganza, O. (2022). Generalisation bias in science. *Cognitive Science, 46,* e13188.

Pew Research Center for the People and the Press. (2002). *One year later: New Yorkers more troubled, Washingtonians more on edge.* http://peoplepress.org/reports/display.php3?PageID¼632.

Peyman, H., Sadeghifar, J., Khajavikhan, J., Yasemi, M., Rasool, M., Yaghoubi, Y.M., et al. (2014). Using VARK approach for assessing preferred learning styles of first year medical science students: A survey from Iran. *Journal of Clinical and Diagnostic Research*, *8*, GC01–GC04.

Pezdek, K. (2003). Event memory and autobiographical memory for events of September 11, 2001. *Applied Cognitive Psychology*, *17*, 1033–1045.

Philipp-Muller, A., Leeb, S.W.S., & Petty, R.E. (2022). Why are people antiscience, and what can we do about it? *Proceedings of the National Academy of Sciences*, *119*, 30.

Phillips, I. (2021). Blindsight is a qualitatively degraded conscious vision. *Psychological Review*, *128*, 558–584.

Philpot, R., Liebst, L.S., Levine, Bernasco, W., & Lindegaard, M.R. (2020). Would I be helped? Cross-national CCTV footage shows that intervention is the norm in public conflicts. *American Psychologist*, *75*, 66–75.

Pike, A., McGuire, S., Hetherington, E.M., Reiss, D., & Plomin, R. (1996). Family environment and adolescent depressive symptoms and antisocial behaviour: A multivariate genetic analysis. *Developmental Psychology*, *32*, 590–603.

Pitts, J.F. (1887a). At antietam (part 1). *The Daily Inter Ocean, Section*. 6th June.

Pitts, J.F. (1887b). At antietam (part 2). *The Daily Inter Ocean*. 7th June.

Planck, M. (1950). *Scientific autobiography and other papers*. Philosophical Library.

Plessen, C.Y., Karyotaki, E., Miguel, C, Ciharova, M., & Cuijpers, P. (2023). Exploring the efficacy of psychotherapies for depression: A multiverse meta-analysis. *BMJ Mental Health*, *26*, 1–9.

Plomin, R. (1990). The role of inheritance in behaviour. *Science*, *248*, 183–188.

Plomin, R., & Daniels, D. (2011). Why are children in the same family so different from one another? *International Journal of Epidemiology*, *40*, 563–582.

Plomin, R., & Deary, I.J. (2015). Genetics and intelligence differences: Five special findings. *Molecular Psychiatry*, *20*, 98–108.

Plomin, R., DeFries, J.C., McClearn, G.E., & McGuffin, P. (2001). *Behavioural genetics* (4th ed.). New York: Worth Publishers.

Polderman, T.J., de Leeuw, C.A., Sullivan, P.F., von Bochoven, A., Visscher, P.M., & Posthuma, D. (2015). Meta-analysis of the heritability of human traits based on fifty years of twin studies. *Nature Genetics*, *47*, 702–709.

Pope, H.G., & Hudson, J.L. (1995). Can memories of childhood amnesia be repressed? *Psychological Medicine*, *25*, 121–126.

Pope, H.G., Poliakoff, M.B., Parker, M.P., Boynes, M., & Hudson, J.I. (2007). Is dissociative amnesia a culture-bound syndrome? Findings from a survey of historical literature. *Psychological Medicine*, *37*, 225–233.

Popel, M., Tomkova, M., Tomek, J., Kaiser, L., Uszkoreit, J., Bojar, O., et al. (2020). Transforming machine translation: A deep learning system reaches news translation quality comparable to human professionals. *Nature Communications*, *11*, 4381.

Popper, K.R. (1957). *The poverty of historicism (revised version)*. London: Routledge.

Popper, K.R. (1968). *The logic of scientific discovery*. London: Hutchinson.

Postmes, T., & Spears, R. (1998). Deindividuation and anti-normative behavior: A meta-analysis. *Psychological Bulletin*, *123*, 238–259.

Poulgrain, H.W., Bremner, N.M., Zimmerman, H., Jao, C.-W., Winter, T., Riordan, B.C., et al. (2022). Why so serious? An attempt to mitigate the short-term harmful effects of the film *Joker* on prejudice toward people with mental illness. *Behavioral Sciences*, *12*, 10.

Pratkanis, A.R. (1992). The cargo-cult science of subliminal persuasion. *The Skeptical Inquirer*, 260–272. Spring.

Prince, R.J., & Guastello, S.J. (1990). The Barnum effect in a computerised Rorschach interpretation system. *Journal of Psychology*, *124*, 217–222.

Proulx, G., & Fahy, R.F. (2004). *Account analysis of WTC survivors.* Proceedings of the 3rd International Symposium on Human Behaviour in Fire, Belfast, UK, pp. 1–3.

Pulsifer, M.B., Brandt, J., Salorio, C.F., Vining, E.P.G., Carson, B.S., & Freeman, J.M. (2004). The cognitive outcome of hemispherectomy in 71 children. *Epilepsia, 45,* 243–254.

Pylyshyn, Z.W. (2002). Mental imagery: In search of a theory. *Behavioral and Brain Sciences, 25,* 157–238.

Radelet, M.L., Bedau, H.A., & Putnam, C.E. (1992). *In spite of innocence: Erroneous convictions in capital cases.* Boston: Northeastern University Press.

Ramsøy, T.Z., & Overgaard, M. (2004). Introspection and subliminal perception. *Phenomenological Cognitive Science, 3,* 1–23.

Rapee, R.M., & Lim, L. (1992). Discrepancy between self- and observer ratings of performance in social phobics. *Journal of Abnormal Psychology, 101,* 728–731.

Ray, J.J. (1973). Conservatism, authoritarianism and related variables: A review and empirical study. In G.D. Wilson (Ed.), *The psychology of conservatism.* London: Academic Press.

Ree, M.J., & Carretta, T.R. (2022). Thirty years of research on general and specific abilities: Still not much more than g. *Intelligence, 91,* 101617.

Reicher, S.D., & Haslam, S.A. (2006). Rethinking the psychology of tyranny: The BBC prison study. *British Journal of Social Psychology, 45,* 1–40.

Reicher, S.D., Spears, R., & Postmes, T. (1995). A social identity model of deindividuation phenomena. In W. Stroebe & M. Hewstone (Eds.), *European review of social psychology* (Vol. 6, pp. 161–198). Chichester, UK: Wiley.

Reicher, S.D., Spears, R., Postmes, T., & Kendec, A. (2016). Disputing deindividuation: Why negative group behaviours derive from group norms, not group immersion. *Behavioral and Brain Sciences, 39,* e161.

Reicher, S.D., van Bavel, J.J., & Haslam, S.A. (2020). Debate around leadership in the Stanford Prison Experiment: Reply to Zimbardo and Haney (2020) and Chan et al. (2020). *American Psychologist, 75,* 406–407.

Reinero, D.A., Wills, J.A., Brady, W.J., Mende-Siedlecki, P., Crawford, J.T., & Van Bavel, J.J. (2020). Is the political slant of psychology research related to scientific replicability? *Perspectives on Psychological Science, 15,* 1310–1328.

Reisch, L.A., & Sunstein, C.R. (2016). Do Europeans like nudges? *Judgment and Decision Making, 11,* 310–325.

Repovš, G., & Baddeley, A. (2006). The multi-component model of working memory: Explorations in experimental cognitive psychology. *Neuroscience, 139,* 5–21.

Revelle, W., Dworak, E.M., & Condon, D. (2020). Cognitive ability in everyday life: The utility of open-source measures. *Current Directions in Psychological Science, 29,* 358–363.

Richards, B.A., & Frankland, P.W. (2017). The persistence and transience of memory. *Neuron, 94,* 1071–1084.

Richardson, L., & Lacroix, G. (2021). What do students think when asked about psychology as a science? *Teaching of Psychology, 48,* 80–89.

Richerson, P.J., & Boyd, R. (2005). *Not by genes alone: How culture transformed human evolution.* Chicago, IL: University of Chicago Press.

Ritchie, S.J., & Tucker-Drob, E.M. (2018). How much does education improve intelligence? A meta-analysis. *Psychological Science, 29,* 1358–1369.

Rnic, K., Santee, A.C., Hoffmeister, J.-A., Liu, H., Change, K.K., Chen, R.X., et al. (2023). The vicious cycle of psychopathology and stressful life Events: A meta-analytic review testing the stress generation model. *Psychological Bulletin, 149,* 330–369.

Roberts, B.W., Kuncel, N.R., Shiner, R., Caspi, A., & Goldberg, L.R. (2007). The power of personality: The comparative validity of personality traits, socioeconomic status, and cognitive ability for predicting important life outcomes. *Perspectives on Psychological Science, 2,* 313–345.

Robertson, D.J., Noyes, E., Dowsett, A.J., Jenkins, R., & Burton, A.M. (2016). Face recognition by metropolitan police super-recognisers. *PLoS One, 11,* e0150036.

Robette, N., Génin, E., & Clerget-Darpoux, F. (2022). Heritability: What's the point? What is it not for? A human genetics perspective. *Genetica, 150,* 199–208.

Robin, J., & Moscovitch, M. (2017). Details, gist and schema: Hippocampal-neocortical interactions underlying recent and remote episodic and spatial memory. *Current Opinion in Behavioral Sciences, 17,* 114–123.

Roeckelein, J.E. (1997). Psychology among the sciences: Comparisons of numbers of theories and laws cited in textbooks. *Psychological Reports, 80,* 131–141.

Rogowsky, B.A., Calhoun, B.M., & Tallal, P. (2020). Providing instruction based on students' learning style preferences does not improve learning. *Frontiers of Psychology, 11,* 164. https://doi.org/10.3389/fpsyg.2020.00164.

Rollwage, M., & Fleming, S.M. (2021). Confirmation bias is adaptive when coupled with efficient metacognition. *Philosophical Transactions of the Royal Society B: Biological Sciences, 376,* Article 20200131.

Roozenbeek, J., Maertens, R., Herzog, S.M., Geers, M., Kurvers, R., Sultan, M., et al. (2022). Susceptibility to misinformation is consistent across question framings and response modes and better explained by myside bias and partisanship than analytical thinking. *Judgment and Decision Making, 17,* 547–573.

Rorschach, H. (1921). *Psychodiagnostik* [Psychodiagnostics]. Bern: Huber.

Rosenbaum, M. (1980). The role of the term schizophrenia in the decline of diagnoses of multiple personality. *Archives of General Psychiatry, 37,* 1383–1385.

Rosenhan, D.L. (1973). On being sane in insane places. *Science, 179,* 250–258.

Rosenholtz, R. (2016). Capabilities and limitations of peripheral vision. *Annual Review of Vision Science, 2,* 437–457.

Rosenholtz, R. (2020). Demystifying visual awareness: Peripheral encoding plus limited decision complexity resolve the paradox of rich visual experience and curious perceptual failures. *Attention, Perception, & Psychophysics, 82,* 901–925.

Rosenholtz, R., Sharan, L., & Park, E. (2016). Why don't we see the gorilla? Looking in the wrong places, attending to the wrong stuff, or doing the wrong task? *Journal of Vision, 44,* 82–83.

Rosenthal, R. (1994). Interpersonal expectancy effects: A 30-year perspective. *Current Directions in Psychological Science, 3,* 176–179.

Roth, B., Becker, N., Romeyke, S., Schäfer, S., Domnick, F., & Spinath, F.M. (2015). Intelligence and school grades: A meta-analysis. *Intelligence, 53,* 118–137.

Røysamb, E., Nes, R., Czajkowski, N.O., & Vassend, O. (2018). Genetics, personality and well-being. A twin study of traits, facets and life satisfaction. *Scientific Reports,* 12298.

Rüsch, N., Corrigan, P.W., Waldmann, T., Staiger, T., Bahemann, A., Oexle, N., et al. (2018). Attitudes toward disclosing a mental health problem and re-employment: A longitudinal study. *Journal of Nervous and Mental Disease, 206,* 383–385.

Ruscio, J. (2004). Diagnosis and the behaviours they denote: A critical evaluation of the labelling theory of mental illness. *The Scientific Review of Mental Health Practice, 3,* 5–22.

Rushton, J.P., & Irwing, P. (2008). A general factor of personality (GFP) from two meta-analyses of the big five: Digman (1997) and Mount, Barrick, Scullen, and Rounds (2005). *Personality and Individual Differences, 45,* 679–683.

Russell, P. (1984). *The brain book.* New York: E.P. Dutton.

Sala, G., Aksaylit, N.D., Tatlidil, L.S., Tatsumi, T., Gondo, Y., & Gobet, F. (2019). Near and far transfer in cognitive training: A second-order meta-analysis. *Collabra: Psychology*, *5*, 18.

Salgado, J.F. (2016). A theoretical model of psychometric effects of faking on assessment procedures: Empirical findings and implications for personality at work. *International Journal of Selection and Assessment*, *24*, 209–228.

Salgado, J.F., & Moscoso, S. (2019). Meta-analysis of the validity of general mental ability for five performance criteria: Hunter and Hunter (1984) revisited. *Frontiers in Psychology*, *10*, 2227.

Samhita, L., & Gross, H.J. (2013). The "Clever Hans phenomenon" revisited. *Communicative & Integrative Biology*, *6*, e27122.

Sanbonmatsu, D.M., Cooley, E.H., & Butner, J.E. (2021). The impact of complexity on methods and findings in psychological science. *Frontiers in Psychology*, *11*, 580111.

Sanbonmatsu, D.M., Cooley, E.H., & Posavac, S.S. (2023). The institutional impact of research challenges and constraints on psychology and other social and behavioural sciences. *New Ideas in Psychology*, *70*, 101014.

Sanbonmatsu, D.M., & Johnston, W.A. (2019). Redefining science: The impact of complexity on theory development in social and behavioural research. *Perspectives in Psychological Science*, *14*, 672–690.

Sanbonmatsu, D.M., Posavac, S.S., Behrends, A.A., Moore, S.M., & Uchino, B.N. (2015). Why a confirmation strategy dominates psychological science. *PLoS One*, *10*, e01138197.

Sanchez-Lafuente, C.G., Gonzalez, S.S., & Parra, J.G. (2021). The placebo effect in clinical trials of modern antidepressants: A meta-analysis. *European Neuropsychopharmacology*, *53*, S62–S63.

Santangelo, V., Cavallina, C., Collici, P., Santori, A., Macri, S., McGaugh, J.L., et al. (2018). Enhanced brain activity associated with memory access in highly superior autobiographical memory. *Proceedings of the National Academy of Sciences*, *115*, 7795–7800.

Santor, D.A., Gregus, M., & Welch, A. (2006). Eight decades of measurement in depression. *Measurement: Interdisciplinary Research and Perspectives*, *4*, 135–155.

Sarason, I.G., Smith, R.E., & Diener, E. (1975). Personality research – components of variance attributable to person and situation. *Journal of Personality and Social Psychology*, *32*, 199–204.

Sarraf, L., Lepage, M., & Sauvé, G. (2022). The clinical and psychosocial correlates of self-stigma among people with schizophrenia spectrum disorders across cultures: A systematic review and meta-analysis. *Schizophrenia Research*, *248*, 64–78.

Satici, S.A., Uysal, R., & Deniz, M.E. (2016). Linking social connectedness to loneliness: The mediating role of subjective happiness. *Personality and Individual Differences*, *97*, 306–310.

Sauer, J.D., Palmer, M.A., & Brewer, N. (2019). Pitfalls in using eyewitness confidence to diagnose the accuracy of an individual identification decision. *Psychology, Public Policy, and Law*, *25*, 147–165.

Sauerland, M., Sagana, A., Siegmann, K., Heiligers, D., Merckelbach, H., & Jenkins, R. (2016). These two are different. Yes, they're the same: Choice blindness for facial identity. *Consciousness and Cognition*, *40*, 93–104.

Savage, J.E., Jansen, P.R., Stringer, S., Watanabe, K., Bryois, J., de Leeuw, C.A., et al. (2018). Genome-wide association meta-analysis in 269,867 individuals identifies new genetic and functional links to intelligence. *Nature Genetics*, *50*, 912–919.

Sbarra, D.A., Emery, R.E., Bean, C.R., & Ocker, B.L. (2013). Marital dissolution and major depression in midlife: A propensity score analysis. *Current Psychological Science*, *2*, 249–257.

Schacter, D.L., & Addis, D.R. (2007). The cognitive neuroscience of constructive memory: Remembering the past and imagining the future. *Philosophical Transactions of the Royal Society B: Biological Sciences, 362*, 773–786.

Schacter, D.L., & Madore, K.P. (2016). Remembering the past and imagining the future: Identifying and enhancing the contribution of episodic memory. *Memory Studies, 9*, 245–255.

Scheel, A.M., Schijen, M., & Lakens, D. (2021). An excess of positive results: Comparing the standard psychology literature with registered reports. *Advances in Methods and Practices in Psychological Science, 4*, 1–12.

Scheirer, M.A., & Kraut, R.E. (1979). Increased educational achievement via self-concept change. *Review of Educational Research, 49*, 131–150.

Schellenberg, E.G. (2020). Correlation = causation? Music training, psychology, and neuroscience. *Psychology of Aesthetics, Creativity, and the Arts, 98*, 457–468.

Schimmack, U. (2019). A psychometric replication study of the NEO-PI-R structure. *Replication-Index*, 1–12.

Schmidt, F.L. (2017). Beyond questionable research methods: The role of omitted relevant research in the credibility of research. *Archives of Scientific Psychology, 5*, 32–41.

Schmitt, D.P., Realo, A., Voracek, M., & Allik, J. (2008). Why can't a man be more like a woman? Sex differences in Big Five personality traits across 55 cultures. *Journal of Personality and Social Psychology, 94*, 168–182.

Schreiber, F.R. (1973). *Sybil*. Chicago, IL: Henry Regnery.

Schroder, H.S., Duda, J.M., Christensen, K., Beard, C., & Björgvinsson, T. (2020). Stressors and chemical imbalances: Beliefs about the causes of depression in an acute psychiatric treatment sample. *Journal of Affective Disorders, 276*, 537–545.

Schulz, R., & Decker, S. (1985). Long-term adjustment to physical disability. *Journal of Personality and Social Psychology, 48*, 1162–1172.

Schweingruber, D., & Wohlstein, R.T. (2005). The madding crowd goes to school: Myths about crowds in introductory sociology textbooks. *Teaching Sociology, 33*, 136–153.

Scientific Working Group on DNA Analysis Methods. (2017). *Interpretation guidelines for autosomal STR typing by forensic DNA testing laboratories.* https://www.swgdam.org/files/ugd/43440813b241e8944497e45b16b76bd.pdf.

Scoboria, A., Mazzoni, G., Kirsch, I., & Milling, L.S. (2002). Immediate and persisting effects of misleading questions and hypnosis on memory reports. *Journal of Experimental Psychology: Applied, 8*, 26–32.

Scoboria, A., Wade, K.A., Lindsay, D.S., Azad, T., Strange, D., Ost, J., & Hyman, I.E. (2017). A mega-analysis of memory reports from eight peer-reviewed false memory implantation studies. *Memory, 25*, 146–163.

Scull, A. (2023). Rosenhan revisited: Successful scientific fraud. *History of Psychiatry, 34*, 180–195.

Seifert, C.M., Harrington, M., Michael, A.L., & Shah, P. (2022). Causal theory error in college students' understanding of science studies. *Cognitive Research: Principles and Implications, 7*, 4.

Shadish, W.R., Matt, G.E., Navarro, A.M., Siegle, G., Crits-Christoph, P., Hazlrigg, M.D., et al. (1997). Evidence that therapy works in clinically representative conditions. *Journal of Consulting and Clinical Psychology, 65*, 355–365.

Shallice, T. (2015). Cognitive neuropsychology and its vicissitudes: The fate of Caramazza's axioms. *Cognitive Neuropsychology, 32*, 385–411.

Shanks, D.R. (2017). Regressive research: The pitfalls of post hoc data selection in the study of unconscious mental processes. *Psychonomic Bulletin & Review, 24*, 752–775.

Sharan, L., Park, E., & Rosenholtz, R. (2016). *Difficulty detecting changes in complex scenes depends in part upon the strengths and limitations of peripheral vision.* Cambridge, MA: Massachusetts Institute of Technology. Unpublished manuscript.

Sharpe, D., & Poets, S. (2020). Meta-analysis as a response to the replication crisis. *Canadian Psychology, 61*, 377–387.

Sharpe, D., & Whelton, W.J. (2016). Frightened by an old scarecrow: The remarkable resilience of demand characteristics. *Review of General Psychology, 20*, 349–368.

Shevell, S.K. (2019). Ambiguous chromatic neural representations: Perceptual resolution by grouping. *Current Opinion in Behavioral Sciences, 30*, 194–202.

Shields, C. (2020). Aristotle's psychology. In *The Stanford encyclopedia of philosophy*. Stanford, CA: Stanford University.

Shipstead, Z., Redick, T.S., & Engle, R.W. (2012). Is working memory training effective? *Psychological Bulletin, 138*, 628–654.

Shrivastava, A.K., Karia, S.B., Sonavane, S.S., & De Sousa, A.A. (2017). Child sexual abuse and the development of psychiatric disorders: A neurobiological trajectory of pathogenesis. *Industrial Psychiatry Journal, 26*, 4–12.

Shrout, P.E., & Rodgers, J.L. (2018). Psychology, science, and knowledge construction: Broadening perspectives from the replication crisis. *Annual Review of Psychology, 69*, 487–510.

Sikorski, M. (2022). Is forensic science in crisis? *Synthese, 200*, 188.

Simons, D.J., Boot, W.R., Charness, N., Gathercole, S.E., Chabris, C.F., Hambrick, D.Z., et al. (2016). Do "brain-training" programs work? *Psychological Science in the Public Interest, 17*, 103–186.

Simons, D.J., & Chabris, C.F. (1999). Gorillas in our midst: Sustained inattentional blindness for dynamic events. *Perception, 28*, 1059–1074.

Simons, D.J., & Chabris, C.F. (2011). What people believe about how memory works: A representative survey of the US population. *PLoS One, 6*, e22757.

Simons, D.J., Shoda, Y., & Lindsay, D.S. (2017). Constraints on generality (COG): A proposed addition to all empirical papers. *Perspectives on Psychological Science, 12*, 1123–1128.

Sjöberg, R.L. (2023). Brain stimulation and elicited memories. *Acta Neurochirurgica, 165*, 2737–2745.

Skimina, E., & Cieciuchi, J. (2020). Explaining everyday behaviours and situational context by personality metatraits and higher-order values. *European Journal of Personality, 34*, 29–59.

Smith, C.M., Dzik, P., & Fornicola, E. (2019). Threatened suicide and baiting crowd formation: A replication and extension of Mann (1981). *Social Influence, 14*, 92–103.

Smith, S., & Razzell, P. (1975). *The pools winners*. London: Caliban Books.

Smith-Woolley, E., Ayorech, Z., Dale, P.S., von Stumm, S., & Plomin, R. (2018). The genetics of university success. *Scientific Reports, 8*, 14579.

Snook, B., Cullen, R.M., Bennell, C., Taylor, P.J., & Gendreau, P. (2008). The criminal profiling illusion. *Criminal Justice and Behavior, 35*, 1257–1276.

Snook, B., Eastwood, J., Gendreau, P., Goggin, C., & Cullen, R.M. (2007). Taking stock of criminal profiling: A narrative review and meta-analysis. *Criminal Justice and Behavior, 34*, 437–453.

Sobieszek, A., & Price, T. (2022). Playing games with AIs: The limits of GPT-3 and similar large language models. *Minds and Machines, 32*, 341–364.

Solomon, B.C., & Jackson, J.J. (2014). Why do personality traits predict divorce? Multiple pathways through satisfaction. *Journal of Personality and Social Psychology, 106*, 978–996.

Soto, C.J. (2019). How replicable are links between personality traits and consequential life outcomes? The life outcomes of personality replication project. *Psychological Science, 30*, 711–727.

Spagna, A., Hajhajate, D., Liu, J., & Bartolomeo, P. (2021). Visual mental imagery engages the left fusiform gyrus, but not the early visual cortex: A meta-analysis of neuroimaging evidence. *Neuroscience and Biobehavioral Reviews, 122*, 201–217.

Spengler, M., Damian, R.I., & Roberts, B.W. (2018). How you behave in school predicts life success above and beyond family background, broad traits, and cognitive ability. *Journal of Personality and Social Psychology, 114,* 600–636.

Sperling, G. (1960). The information that is available in brief visual presentations. *Psychological Monographs, 74*(498), 1–29.

Spiers, H.J., Coutrot, A., & Hornberger, M. (2023). Explaining world-wide variation in navigation ability from millions of people: Citizen science project sea hero quest. *Topics in Cognitive Science, 15,* 120–138.

Spiers, H.J., Maguire, E.A., & Burgess, N. (2001). Hippocampal amnesia. *Neurocase, 7,* 357–382.

Sporer, S.L., Penrod, S.D., Read, D., & Cutler, B.L. (1995). Choosing, confidence, and accuracy: A meta-analysis of the confidence-accuracy relation in eyewitness identification studies. *Psychological Bulletin, 118,* 315–327.

Spotts, E.L., Lichtenstein, P., Pedersen, N., Neiderhiser, J.M., Hansson, K., Cederblad, M, et al. (2005). Personality and marital satisfaction: A behavioural genetic analysis. *European Journal of Personality, 19,* 205–227.

Sprengnether, M. (2012). Freud as memorist: A reading of "screen" memories. *American Imago, 69,* 215–240.

Srinivasan, R., & Martinez, A.M. (2021). Cross-cultural and cultural-specific production and perception of facial expressions of emotion in the wild. *IEEE Transactions on Affective Computing, 12,* 707–721.

Stabile, V.J., Baker, K.A., & Mondloch, C.J. (2024). Criterion shifting in an unfamiliar face-matching task: Effects of base rates, payoffs, and perceptual discriminability. *Journal of Applied Research in Memory and Cognition.* https://doi.org/10.1037/mac0000157.

Stanley, T.D., Carter, E.C., & Doucouliagos, H. (2018). What meta-analyses reveal about the replicability of psychological research. *Psychological Bulletin, 144,* 1325–1346.

Stanovich, K.E. (2009). *What intelligence tests miss: The psychology of rational thought.* New Haven, CT: Yale University Press.

Stanovich, K.E., & West, R.F. (2007). Natural myside bias is independent of cognitive ability. *Thinking & Reasoning, 13,* 225–247.

Stanovich, K.E., West, R.F., & Toplak, M.E. (2013). Myside bias, rational thinking, and intelligence. *Current Directions in Psychological Science, 22,* 259–264.

Steadman, H.J., Mulvey, E.P., Monahan, J., Robbins, P.C., Appelbaum, P.S., Grisso, T., et al. (1998). Violence by people discharged from acute psychiatric inpatient facilities and by others in the same neighbourhoods. *Archives of General Psychiatry, 55,* 393–401.

Steblay, N.K., Wells, G.L., & Douglass, A.B. (2014). The eyewitness post identification feedback effect 15 years later: Theoretical and policy implications. *Psychology, Public Policy, and Law, 20,* 1–18.

Stein, M.V., Lynn, S.J., & Terhune, D.B. (2023). Reconciling myths and misconceptions about hypnosis with scientific evidence. *British Journal of Psychiatry Advances, 29,* 391–392.

Steinberg, M., Cicchetti, D., Buchanan, J., Rakfeldt, J., & Rousaville, B. (1994). Distinguishing between multiple personality disorder (dissociative identity disorder) and schizophrenia using the structured clinical interview for DSM-IV dissociative disorders. *Journal of Nervous and Mental Disease, 182,* 495–502.

Steinvorth, S., Levine, B., & Corkin, S. (2005). Medial temporal lobe structures are needed to re-experience remote autobiographical memories: Evidence from H.M. and W.R. *Neuropsychologia, 43,* 479–496.

Stephan, Y., Sutin, A.R., Luchetti, A.R., & Terracciano, A. (2019). Facets of conscientiousness and longevity: Findings from the health and retirement study. *Journal of Psychosomatic Research, 116,* 1–5.

Sternberg, R.J. (1985). *Beyond IQ: A triarchic theory of human intelligence.* Cambridge: Cambridge University Press.

Sternberg, R.J. (2015). Multiple intelligences in the new age of thinking. In S. Goldstein, D. Princiotta, & J.A. Naglieri (Eds.), *Handbook of intelligence: Evolutionary theory, historical perspective, and current concepts* (pp. 229–242). New York: Springer.

Sternberg, R.J., Forsythe, G.B., Hedlund, J., Horvath, J.A., Wagner, R.K., Williams, W.M., Snook, S.A., & Grigorenko, E.L. (2000). *Practical intelligence in everyday life.* New York: Cambridge University Press.

Sternberg, R.J., Ghahremani, M., & Ehsan, H. (2023). Combating myside bias in scientific thinking: A special challenge for the gifted. *Roeper Review, 45,* 178–187.

Stewart, E.E.M., Valsecchi, M., & Schütz, A.C. (2020). A review of interactions between peripheral and foveal vision. *Journal of Vision, 20,* 1–35.

Stewart, R.D., Diaz, A., Hou, X., Liu, X., Vainik, U., Johnson, W., & Mõttus, R. (2024). The ways of the world? Cross-sample replicability of personality trait-life outcome associations. *Journal of Research in Personality, 112,* 104515.

Steyvers, M., & Hemmer, P. (2012). Reconstruction from memory in naturalistic environments. In B.H. Ross (Ed.), *The Psychology of Learning and Motivation, 56,* 126–144.

Stoerig, P., & Barth, E. (2001). Low-level phenomenal vision despite unilateral destruction of primary visual cortex. *Consciousness & Cognition, 10,* 574–587.

Stojanoski, B., Wild, C.J., Battista, M.E., Nichols, E.S., & Owen, A.M. (2020). Brain training habits are not associated with generalized benefits to cognition: An online study of over 1000 "brain trainers". *Journal of Experimental Psychology: General, 150,* 729–738.

Stramaccia, D.F., Meyer, A.K., Rischer, K.M., Fawcett, J.M., & Benoit, R.G. (2021). Memory suppression and its deficiency in psychological disorders: A focused meta-analysis. *Journal of Experimental Psychology: General, 150,* 828–850.

Strayer, D.L., & Drews, F.A. (2007). Cell-phone-induced driver distraction. *Current Directions in Psychological Science, 16,* 128–131.

Strobach, T., Antonenko, D., Abarrin, M., Escher, M., Flöel, A., & Schubert, T. (2018). Modulation of dual-task control with right prefrontal transcranial direct current stimulation. *Experimental Brain Research, 236,* 227–241.

Stronge, S., Cichocka, A., & Sibley, C.G. (2019). The heterogeneity of self-regard: A latent transition analysis of self-esteem and psychological entitlement. *Journal of Research in Personality, 82,* Article No. UNSP 103855.

Strupp, H.H. (1996). The tripartite model and the consumer reports study. *American Psychologist, 51,* 1017–1024.

Stuart, H. (2006). Media portrayal of mental illness and its treatments: What effect does it have on people with mental illness? *CNS Drugs, 20,* 99–106.

Stuart, H., & Arboleda-Flórez, J. (2001). Community attitudes toward people with schizophrenia. *Canadian Journal of Psychiatry, 46,* 245–252.

Suhay, E., & Jayaratne, T.E. (2013). Does biology justify ideology? The politics of genetic attribution. *Public Opinion Quarterly, 77,* 497–521.

Sumner, P., Vivian-Grifths, S., Boivin, J., Williams, A., Venetis, C.A., Davies, A., et al. (2014). The association between exaggeration in health related science news and academic press releases: Retrospective observational study. *British Medical Journal, 349,* g7015.

Synnott, J., Dietzel, D., & Ioannou, M. (2015). A review of the polygraph: History, methodology and current status. *Crime Psychology Review, 1,* 59–83.

Talarico, J.M., & Rubin, D.C. (2003). Confidence, not consistency, characterises flashbulb memories. *Psychological Science, 14,* 455–461.

Taylor, A.K., & Kowalski, P. (2003). *Media influences on the formation of misconceptions about psychology.* Paper presented at the Annual Conference of The American Psychological Association, Toronto, Canada. August.

Taylor, M., Mayne, C., Coutts, L., Kinnane, A., Avent, I., Cho, K., et al. (2024). Kafka's beautiful eyes: Forensic intelligence utilisation of phenotypic information. *Forensic Science International, 361*, 112120.

Tellegen, A., Lykken, D.T., Bouchard, T.J., Wilcox, K.J., Segal, N.L., & Rich, S. (1988). Personality similarity in twins reared apart and together. *Journal of Personality and Social Psychology, 54*, 1031–1039.

Terhune, D.B., & Hedman, L.R. (2017). Metacognition of agency is reduced in high hypnotic suggestibility. *Cognition, 168*, 176–181.

Thakral, P.P., Devitt, A.L., Brashier, N.M., & Schacter, D.L. (2021). Linking creativity and false memory: Common consequences of a flexible memory system. *Cognition, 217*, 104905.

Thakral, P.P., Madore, K.P., Kalinowski, S.E., & Schacter, D.L. (2020). Modulation of hippocampal brain networks produces changes in episodic simulation and divergent thinking. *Proceedings of the National Academy of Sciences of the United States of America, 117*, 12729–12740.

Thaler, R.H., & Sunstein, C.R. (2008). *Nudge: Improving decisions about health, wealth, and happiness.* New Haven, CT: Yale University Press.

Thompson, M.B., Tangen, J.M., & McCarthy, D.J. (2014). Human matching performance of genuine crime scene latent fingerprints. *Law and Human Behavior, 38*, 84–93.

Thompson, W.C. (2009). Painting the target around the matching profile: The Texas sharpshooter fallacy in forensic DNA interpretation. *Law, Probability and Risk, 8*, 257–276.

Thompson, W.C., & Ford, S. (1991). The meaning of a match: Sources of ambiguity in the interpretation of DNA prints. In M. Farley & J. Harrington (Eds.), *Forensic DNA technology* (pp. 93–152). Chelsea, MI: Lewis Publishers.

Thompson, W.C., & Newman, E.J. (2015). Lay understanding of forensic statistics: Evaluation of random match probabilities, likelihood ratios, and verbal equivalents. *Law and Human Behavior, 39*, 332–349.

Thorndike, E.L., & Woodworth, R.S. (1901). The influence of improvement in one mental function upon the efficiency of other functions (I). *Psychological Review, 8*, 247–261.

Thornicroft, G., Brohan, E., Rose, D., Sartorius, N., & Leese, M. (2009). Global pattern of experienced and anticipated discrimination against people with schizophrenia: A cross-sectional survey. *Lancet, 371*, 408–415.

Tomasello, M. (2008). Ontological origins. *Origins of Human Communication*, 109–167.

Tonkin, M. (2012). *Behavioural case linkage: Generalisability, ecological validity, and methodology.* Unpublished doctoral dissertation. Leicester: University of Leicester, UK.

Tooby, J., & Cosmides, L. (1992). The psychological foundations of culture. In J.H. Barkow, L. Cosmides, & J. Tooby (Eds.), *The adapted mind: Evolutionary psychology and the generation of culture.* New York: Oxford University Press.

Torres, A.N., Boccaccini, M.T., & Miller, H.A. (2006). Perceptions of the validity and utility of criminal profiling among forensic psychologists and psychiatrists. *Professional Psychology: Research and Practice, 37*, 51–58.

Trager, J., & Brewster, J. (2001). The effectiveness of psychological profiles. *Journal of Police and Criminal Psychology, 16*, 20–28.

Trahan, L.H., Stuebing, K.K., Fletcher, J.M., & Hiscock, M. (2014). The Flynn effect: A meta-analysis. *Psychological Bulletin, 140*, 1332–1360.

Tran, L.M., Josselyn, S.A., Richards, B.A., & Frankland, P.W. (2019). Forgetting at biologically realistic levels of neurogenesis in a large-scale hippocampal model. *Behavioural Brain Research, 376*, 112180.

Treisman, A.M., & Gelade, G. (1980). A feature-integration theory of attention. *Cognitive Psychology, 12*, 97–136.

Trivedi, M.H., Rush, A.J., Wisniewski, S.R., Nierenberg, A.A., Warden, D., Ritz, L., et al. (2006). Evaluation of outcomes with citalopram for depression using measurement-based care in STAR*D: Implications for clinical practice. *American Journal of Psychiatry, 163*, 28–40.

Troyer, A.K., & Rich, J.B. (2018). *Multifactorial memory questionnaire: Professional manual*. Toronto, Ontario, Canada: Baycrest Centre for Geriatric Care.

Truesdale, K.P., & Stevens, J. (2008). Do the obese know they are obese? *North Carolina Medical Journal, 69*, 188–194.

Trzesniewski, K.H., Donnellan, M.B., Moffitt, T.E., Robins, R.W., Poulton, R., & Caspi, A. (2006). Low self-esteem during adolescence predicts criminal behaviour, and limited economic prospects. *Developmental Psychology, 42*, 381–390.

Tucker-Drob, E.M., Briley, D.A., & Harden, K.P. (2013). Genetic and environmental influences on cognition across development and context. *Current Directions in Psychological Science, 22*, 349–355.

Tulving, E. (1972). Episodic and semantic memory. In E. Tulving & W. Donaldson (Eds.), *Organisation of memory*. London: Academic Press.

Tulving, E. (2002). Episodic memory: From mind to brain. *Annual Review of Psychology, 53*, 1–25.

Tulving, E., & Pearlstone, Z. (1966). Availability versus accessibility of information in memory for words. *Journal of Verbal Learning and Verbal Behavior, 5*, 381–391.

Tulving, E., & Thomson, D.M. (1973). Encoding specificity and retrieval processes in episodic memory. *Psychological Review, 80*, 352–373.

Turing, A.M. (1950). Computing machinery and intelligence. *Mind, 40*, 433–460.

Turner, E.H., Cipriani, A., Furukawa, T.A., Salanti, G., & de Vries, Y.A. (2022). Selective publication of antidepressant trials and its influence on apparent efficacy: Updated comparisons and metaanalyses of newer versus older trials. *PLoS Medicine, 19*, e1003886.

Tversky, A., & Koehler, D.J. (1994). Support theory: A non-extensional representation of subjective probability. *Psychological Review, 101*, 547–567.

Twenge, J.M. (1997). Changes in masculine and feminine traits over time: A meta-analysis. *Sex Roles, 36*, 305–325.

Tyrer, P. (2019). Dissociative identity disorder needs re-examination. *British Journal of Psychiatry Advances, 25*, 294–295.

Uchino, B.N., Thoman, D., & Byerly, S. (2010). Inference patterns in social psychology: Looking back as we move forward. *Social and Personality Psychology Compass, 20*, 417–427.

Ullén, F., Hambrick, D.Z., & Mosing, M.A. (2016). Rethinking expertise: A multi-factorial gene–environment interaction model of expert performance. *Psychological Bulletin, 142*, 427–446.

Ünal, Z.E., Greene, N.R., Lin, X., & Geary, D.C. (2023). What is the source of the correlation between reading and mathematics achievement? Two meta-analytic studies. *Educational Psychology Review, 35*. https://doi.org/10.1007/s10648-023-09717-5.

Uttal, W.R. (2012). *Reliability in cognitive neuroscience: A meta-meta analysis*. Cambridge, MA: MIT Press.

Vallet, W., & van Wassenhove, V. (2023). Can cognitive neuroscience solve the lab-dilemma by going wild? *Neuroscience and Biobehavioral Reviews, 155*, 105463.

van der Linden, D., Pekaar, K.A., Bakker, A.B., Schermer, J.A., Vernon, P.A., Dunkel, C.S., et al. (2017). Overlap between the general factor of personality and emotional intelligence: A meta-analysis. *Psychological Bulletin, 143*, 36–52.

van der Linden, D., Schermer, J.A., de Zeeuw, E., Dunkel, C.S., Pekaar, K.A., Bakker, A.B., et al. (2018). Overlap between the general factor of personality and trait emotional intelligence: A genetic correlation study. *Behavior Genetics*, *48*, 147–154.

van Oorschot, R.A.H., Meakin, G.E., Kokshoorn, B., Goray, M., & Szkuta, B. (2021). DNA transfer in forensic science: Recent progress towards meeting challenges. *Genes*, *12*, 1766. https://doi.org/10.3390/genes12111766.

Vandenbroucke, A.R.E., Fahrenfort, J.J., Meuwese, J.D.I., Scholte, H.S., & Lamme, V.A.F. (2016). Prior knowledge about objects determines neural colour representation in human visual cortex. *Cerebral Cortex*, *26*, 1401–1408.

Vanlancker-Sidtis, D. (2004). When only the right hemisphere is left: Studies in language and communication. *Brain and Language*, *91*, 199–211.

Varnum, M.E.W., Grossmann, I., Kitayama, S., & Nisbett, R.E. (2010). The origin of cultural differences in cognition: Evidence for the social orientation hypothesis. *Current Directions in Psychological Science*, *19*, 9–13.

Vater, C., Wolfe, B., & Rosenholtz, R. (2022). Peripheral vision in real-world tasks: A systematic review. *Psychonomic Bulletin & Review*, *29*, 1531–1557.

Vedejová, D., & Čavojová, V. (2022). Confirmation bias in information search, interpretation, and memory recall: Evidence from reasoning about four controversial topics. *Thinking & Reasoning*, *28*, 1–28.

Vedel, A. (2014). The Big Five and tertiary academic performance: A systematic review and meta-analysis. *Personality and Individual Differences*, *71*, 66–76.

Vinkhuyzen, A.A.E., Van Der Sluis, S., De Geus, E.J.C., Boomsma, D.I., & Posthuma, D. (2010). Genetic influences on 'environmental' factors. *Genes, Brain, and Behavior*, *9*, 276–287.

von Bastian, C.C., Belleville, S., Udale, R.C., Reinhartz, A., Essounni, M., & Strobach, T. (2022). Mechanisms underlying training-induced cognitive change. *Nature Reviews Psychology*, *1*, 30–41.

von Stumm, S., Smith-Woolley, E., Cheesman, R., Pingault, J.-B., Asbury, K., Dale, P.S., et al. (2021). School quality ratings are weak predictors of students' achievement and well-being. *The Journal of Child Psychology and Psychiatry*, *62*, 339–348.

von Wagner, C., Knight, K., Steptoe, A., & Wardle, J. (2007). Functional health literacy and health-promoting behaviour in a national sample of British adults. *Journal of Epidemiology Community Health*, *61*, 1086–1090.

Vredeveldt, A., & de Bruïne, G. (2022). Not universally sinful: Cultural aspects of memory sins. *Journal of Applied Research in Memory and Cognition*, *11*, 465–470.

Wachtel, P.L. (1973). Psychodynamics, behaviour therapy, and the implacable experimenter: An enquiry into the consistency of personality. *Journal of Abnormal Psychology*, *32*, 324–334.

Wagstaff, G.F., Wheatcroft, J.M., Caddick, A.M., Kirby, L.J., & Lamont, E. (2011). Enhancing witness memory with techniques derived from hypnotic investigative interviewing: Focused meditation, eye-closure, and context reinstatement. *International Journal of Clinical and Experimental Hypnosis*, *59*, 146–164.

Wahl, O.F. (1999). *Telling is risky business: Mental health confront stigma*. New Brunswick, NJ: Rutgers University Press.

Wahl, O.F. (2003). News media portrayal of mental illness: Implications for public policy. *American Behavioral Scientist*, *46*, 1594–1600.

Wahl, O.F., Reiss, M., & Thompson, C.A. (2018). Film psychotherapy in the 21st century. *Health Communication*, *33*, 238–245.

Wallace, L.E., Wegener, D.T., & Petty, R.E. (2020). Influences of source bias that differ from source untrustworthiness: When flip-flopping is more and less surprising. *Journal of Personality and Social Psychology*, *118*, 603–616.

Waller, J.C. (2012). Commentary: The birth of the twin study: A commentary on Francis Galton's 'the history of twins'. *International Journal of Epidemiology*, *41*, 913–917.

Wallisch, P. (2017). Illumination assumptions account for individual differences in the perceptual interpretation of a profoundly ambiguous stimulus in the colour domain: "The dress". *Journal of Vision, 17*, 1–14.

Wang, J., & Hoe, M. (2023). Longitudinal causal relationship between depression and self-esteem in Korean older adults. *Asian Social Work and Policy Review, 17*, 78–88.

Wang, R., Wang, Y., Chen, C., Huo, L., & Liu, C. (2024). How do eye cues affect behaviours? Two metaanalyses. *Current Psychology, 43*, 1084–1101.

Warne, R.T. (2020). *In the know: Debunking 35 myths about human intelligence.* Cambridge: Cambridge University Press.

Warne, R.T., & Burton, J.Z. (2020). Beliefs about human intelligence in a sample of teachers and non-teachers. *Journal for the Education of the Gifted, 43*, 143–166.

Waterhouse, L. (2023). Why multiple intelligences theory is a neuromyth. *Frontiers in Psychology, 14*, 1217288.

Watkins, C.E., Campbell, V.L., Nieberding, R., & Hallmark, R. (1995). Contemporary practice of psychological assessment by clinical psychologists. *Professional Psychology: Research and Practice, 26*, 54–60.

Watrin, L., Hülür, G., & Wilhelm, O. (2022). Training working memory for two years – no evidence of transfer to intelligence. *Journal of Experimental Psychology: Learning, Memory, and Cognition, 48*, 717–733.

Watson, D., Hubbard, B., & Wiese, D. (2000). Self-other agreement in personality and affectivity: The role of acquaintanceship, trait visibility, and assumed similarity. *Journal of Personality and Social Psychology, 78*, 546–558.

Watson, D., Suls, J., & Haig, J. (2002). Global self-esteem in relation to structural models of personality and affectivity. *Journal of Personality and Social Psychology, 83*, 185–197.

Watt, C.A., & Kennedy, J.E. (2017). Options for prospective meta-analysis and introduction of registration-based prospective meta-analysis. *Frontiers in Psychology, 7*, 2030.

Weatherford, D.R., Roberson, D., & Erickson, W.B. (2021). When experience does not promote expertise: Security professionals fail to detect low prevalence fake IDs. *Cognitive Research – Principles and Implications, 6*, 25.

Wedding, D., & Niemiec, R.M. (2003). The clinical use of films in psychotherapy. *Journal of Clinical Psychology/In Session, 59*, 207–215.

Weidmann, R., Ledermann, T., & Grob, A. (2017). Big Five traits and relationship satisfaction: The mediating role of self-esteem. *Journal of Research in Personality, 69*, 102–109.

Weinstein, N.D. (1980). Unrealistic optimism about future life events. *Journal of Personality and Social Psychology, 39*, 806–820.

Weiskrantz, L., Warrington, E.K., Sanders, M.D., & Marshall, J. (1974). Visual capacity in the hemianopic field following a restricted occipital ablation. *Brain, 97*, 709–728.

Wells, G.L., & Bradfield, A.L. (1998). "Good, you identified the suspect": Feedback to eyewitnesses distorts their reports of the witnessing experience. *Journal of Applied Psychology, 83*, 360–376.

Wesseldijk, L.W., Bartels, M., Vink, J.M., van Beijsterveldt, C.E.M., Ligthart, L., & Middeldorp, C.M. (2018). Genetic and environmental influences on conduct and antisocial personality problems in childhood, adolescence, and adulthood. *European Journal of Child and Adolescent Psychiatry, 27*, 1123–1132.

Westrick, P.A., Le, H., Robbins, S.B., Radunzel, J.M.R., & Schmidt, F.L. (2015). College performance and retention: A meta-analysis of the predictive validities of ACT scores, high school grades, and SES. *Educational Assessment, 20*, 23–45.

White, A., & O'Hare, P. (2022). In plane sight: Inattentional blindness affects visual detection of external targets in simulated flight. *Applied Ergonomics, 98*, 103578.

White, D., Kemp, R.I., Jenkins, R., Matheson, M., & Burton, A.M. (2014). Passport officers' errors in face matching. *PLoS One, 9,* e103510.

White, D., Wayne, T., & Varela, V.P.L. (2022). Partitioning natural face image variability emphasises between-identity representation for understanding accurate recognition. *Cognition, 219,* 104966.

Whiteford, H.A., Harris, M.G., McKeon, G., Baxter, A., Pennell, C., Barendregt, J.J., et al. (2013). Estimating remission from untreated major depression: A systematic review and meta-analysis. *Psychological Medicine, 43,* 1569–1585.

Willingham, D.T., Hughes, E.M., & Dobolyi, D.G. (2015). The scientific status of learning styles theories. *Teaching Psychology, 42,* 266–271.

Willoughby, E.A., Love, A.C., McGue, M., Iacono, W.G, Quigley, J., & Lee, J.J. (2019). Free will, determinism, and intuitive judgements about the heritability of behaviour. *Behavior Genetics, 49,* 136–153.

Wilmer, J.B. (2017). Individual differences in face recognition: A decade of discovery. *Current Directions in Psychological Science, 26,* 225–230.

Wilmer, J.B., Germine, L., Chabris, C.F., Chatterjee, G., Williams, M., Loken, E., Nakayama, K., & Duchaine, B. (2010). Human face recognition ability is highly heritable. *Proceedings of the National Academy of Sciences USA, 107,* 5238–5241.

Wilmot, M.P., & Ones, D.S. (2022). Agreeableness and its consequences: A quantitative review of meta-analytic findings. *Personality and Social Psychology Review, 26,* 242–280.

Wilmott, J.P., & Michel, M.M. (2021). Transsaccadic integration of visual information is predictive, attention-based, and spatially precise. *Journal of Vision, 21*(14), 1–26.

Wilshire, C.E., Ward, T., & Clack, S. (2021). Symptom descriptions in psychopathology: How well are they working for us? *Clinical Psychological Science, 9,* 323–339.

Wilson, J.P., Hugenberg, K., & Bernstein, M.J. (2013). The cross-race effect and eyewitness identification: How to improve recognition and reduce decision errors in eyewitness situations. *Social Issues and Policy Review, 7,* 83–113.

Wilt, J., & Revelle, W. (2019). The big five, everyday contexts and activities, and affective experience. *Personality and Individual Differences, 136,* 140–147.

Winter, A. (2013). The rise and fall of forensic hypnosis. *Studies in History and Philosophy of Biological and Biomedical Sciences, 44,* 26–35.

Wise, R.A., & Safer, M.A. (2010). A comparison of what U.S. judges and students know and believe about eyewitness testimony. *Journal of Applied Social Psychology, 40,* 1400–1422.

Wise, R.A., Sartori, G., Magnussen, S., & Safer, M.A. (2014). An examination of the causes and solutions to eyewitness error. *Frontiers in Psychiatry, 5,* 102.

Witzel, C., & Toscani, M. (2020). How to make a #theDress. *Journal of the Optical Society of America, 37,* A202–A211.

Wixted, J.T., & Mickes, L. (2022). Eyewitness memory is reliable, but the criminal justice system is not. *Memory, 30,* 37–72.

Wixted, J.T., Mickes, L., Dunn, J.C., Clark, S.E., & Wells, S. (2016). Estimating the reliability of eyewitness identifications from the police line-ups. *Proceedings of the National Academy of Sciences of the USA, 113,* 304–309.

Wixted, J.T., & Wells, G L. (2017). The relationship between eyewitness confidence and identification accuracy: A new synthesis. *Psychological Science in the Public Interest, 18,* 10–65.

Wolfe, J.M., Kosovicheva, A., & Wolfe, B. (2022). Normal blindness: When we Look but fail to see. *Trends in Cognitive Sciences, 26,* 809–818.

Wolfram, T. (2023). (Not just) intelligence stratifies the occupational hierarchy: Ranking 360 professions by IQ and non-cognitive traits. *Intelligence, 98,* 101755.

Wollny, A., Jacobs, I., & Pabel, L. (2020). Trait emotional intelligence and relationship satisfaction: The mediating role of dyadic coping. *Journal of Psychology, 154,* 75–93.

Wood, J.K., Anglim, J., & Horwood, S. (2022). Effect of job applicant faking and cognitive ability on self-other agreement and criterion validity of personality assessments. *International Journal of Selection and Assessment, 30,* 378–391.

Wood, J.M., Garb, H.N., Nezworski, M.T., Lilienfeld, S.O., & Duke, M.C. (2015). A second look at the validity of widely used Rorschach indices: Comment on Mihura, Meyer, Dumitrascu, and Bombel (2013). *Psychological Bulletin, 141,* 236–249.

Wood, J.M., Lilienfeld, S.O., Nezworski, M.T., Garb, H.N., & Wildermuth, J.L. (2010). Validity of Rorschach Inkblot scores for discriminating psychopaths from non-psychopaths in forensic populations: A meta-analysis. *Psychological Assessment, 22,* 336–349.

Wood, J.M., Nezworski, M.T., Garb, H.N., & Lilienfeld, S.O. (2001). The misperception of psychopathology: Problems with the norms of the comprehensive system for the Rorschach. *Clinical Psychology: Science and Practice, 8,* 350–373.

World Health Organisation (WHO). (2018a). *Depression fact sheet.* Updated March 2018. http://www.who.int/en/news-room/fact-sheets/detail/depression.

World Health Organisation (WHO). (2018b). *International classification of diseases, 11th revision (ICD-11).* Geneva: World Health Organisation.

Wright, A.J., & Jackson, J.J. (2023). Do changes in personality predict life outcomes? *Journal of Personality and Social Psychology, 125.* https://doi.org/10.1037/pspp0000472.

Wu, X., Wang, Y., Peng, Z., & Chen, Q. (2018). A questionnaire survey on road rage and anger-provoking situations in China. *Accident Analysis and Prevention, 111,* 210–221.

Wynn, V.E., & Logie, R.H. (1998). The veracity of long-term memories – did Bartlett get it right? *Applied Cognitive Psychology, 12,* 1–20.

Yang, B.W., Stone, A.R., & Marsh, E.J. (2022). Asymmetry in belief revision. *Applied Cognitive Psychology, 36,* 1072–1082.

Yank, V., Rennie, D., & Bero, L.A. (2007). Financial ties and concordance between results and conclusions in meta-analyses: Retrospective cohort study. *British Medical Journal, 335,* 1202–1205.

Yapko, M.D. (1994). Suggestibility and repressed memories of abuse: A survey of psychotherapists' beliefs. *American Journal of Clinical Hypnosis, 36,* 163–171.

Yarkoni, T. (2022). The generalisability crisis. *Behavioral and Brain Sciences, 45,* 1–78.

Yaron, I., Melloni, L., Pitts, M., & Mudrik, L. (2022). The ConTraSt database for analysing and comparing empirical studies of consciousness theories. *Nature Human Behaviour, 6,* 593–604.

Ye, J., Yeung, D.Y., Liu, E.S.C., & Rochelle, T.L. (2019). Sequential mediating effects of provided and received social support on trait emotional intelligence and subjective happiness: A longitudinal examination in Hong Kong Chinese university students. *International Journal of Psychology, 54,* 478–486.

Yesavage, J.A., Fairchild, J.K., Mi, Z., Biswas, K., Davis-Karim, A., Phibbs, C.S., et al. (2018). Effect of repetitive transcranial magnetic stimulation on treatment-resistant major depression in US veterans: A randomised clinical trial. *JAMA Psychiatry, 75,* 884–893.

Yokota, K., Kuraishi, H., Wachi, T., Otsuka, Y., Hirama, K., & Watanabe, K. (2017). Practice of offender profiling in Japan. *International Journal of Police Science and Management, 19,* 187–194.

Young, A.W., & Burton, A.M. (2017). Recognising faces. *Current Directions in Psychological Science, 26,* 212–217.

Young, A.W., & Burton, A.M. (2018). Are we face experts? *Trends in Cognitive Sciences, 22*, 100–110.

Young, S.D., Adelstein, B.D., & Ellis, S.R. (2007). Demand characteristics in assessing motion sickness in a virtual environment: Or does taking a motion sickness questionnaire make you sick? *IEEE Transactions on Visualization and Computer Graphics, 13*, 422–428.

Zeigler-Hill, V. (2006). Discrepancies between implicit and explicit self-esteem: Implications for narcissism and self-esteem instability. *Journal of Personality, 74*, 119–143.

Zell, E., & Johansson, J.S. (2024). The association of self-esteem with health and well-being: A quantitative synthesis of 40 meta-analyses. *Social Psychological and Personality Science*, 1–10. https://doi.org/10.1177/19485506241229308.

Zell, E., Krizan, Z., & Teeter, S.R. (2015). Evaluating gender similarities and differences using meta-synthesis. *American Psychologist, 70*, 10–20.

Zell, E., & Lesick, T.L. (2022). Big five personality traits and performance: A quantitative synthesis of 50+ meta-analyses. *Journal of Personality, 90*, 559–573.

Zell, E., Strickhouser, J.E., Sedikides, C., & Alicke, M.D. (2020). The better-than-average effect in comparative self-evaluation: A comprehensive review and meta-analysis. *Psychological Bulletin, 146*, 118–149.

Zhao, Q., & Gong, L.M. (2019). Cultural differences in attitude toward and effects of self-doubt. *International Journal of Psychology, 54*, 750–758.

Zhou, J.H., Xiaoyu, L., & Huebner, E.S. (2020). Longitudinal association between low self-esteem and depression in early adolescents: The role of rejection sensitivity and loneliness. *Psychology and Psychotherapy: Theory, Research, and Practice, 93*, 54–71.

Zhou, X., & Jenkins, R. (2020). Dunning–Kruger effects in face perception. *Cognition, 203*, 104345.

Zimbardo, P.G. (1969). The human choice: Individuation, reason and order versus deindividuation, impulse, and chaos. *Nebraska Symposium on Motivation, 17*, 237–307.

Zimbardo, P.G. (1983). To control a mind. *Stanford Magazine, 11*, 59–64.

Zimbardo, P.G. (1989). *Quiet rage: The Stanford prison experiment video*. Stanford, CA: Stanford University.

Zou, J.L. (2014). Associations between trait emotional intelligence and loneliness in Chinese undergraduate students: Mediating effects of self-esteem and social support. *Psychological Reports, 114*, 880–890.

Index

For Product Safety Concerns and Information please contact our EU
representative GPSR@taylorandfrancis.com
Taylor & Francis Verlag GmbH, Kaufingerstraße 24, 80331 München, Germany

www.ingramcontent.com/pod-product-compliance
Lightning Source LLC
Chambersburg PA
CBHW071729270326
41928CB00013B/2608